T0110355

Praise for Sönke Neitzel and Harald Welzer's

SOLDIERS

SOLDIERS

German POWs on
Fighting, Killing, and Dying

Sönke Neitzel and Harald Welzer

TRANSLATED FROM THE GERMAN BY
JEFFERSON CHASE

VINTAGE BOOKS
A DIVISION OF RANDOM HOUSE, INC.
NEW YORK

The Library of Congress has cataloged the Knopf edition as follows:
Neitzel, Sönke.
Soldaten / by Sönke Neitzel and Harald Welzer;
translated from the German by Jefferson Chase.
p. cm.
Translation of: Soldaten: Protokolle vom Kämpfen, Töten und Sterben.
Frankfurt am Main : Fischer Verlag, 2011.
Includes bibliographical references.
1. World War, 1939–1945—Military intelligence—Great Britain. 2. World War, 1939–1945—
Prisoners and prisons, British. 3. Prisoners of war—Germany—Attitudes—Sources.
4. Prisoners of war—Great Britain—Attitudes— Sources. 5. World War, 1939–1945—
Anecdotes. 6. Eavesdropping—Great Britain. 7. Soldiers—Germany—Attitudes—Sources.
8. Germany—Armed Forces—History—20th century—Sources. I. Welzer, Harald. II. Title.
D810.S7N37313 2012
940.54'724108931 — dc23
2012005744

Vintage ISBN: 978-0-307-94833-5

Author photographs: Neitzel: © Petra A. Killick; Welzer: © Thomas Langreder

CONTENTS

PROLOGUES

Sönke Neitzel

It was a typical November day in England: a blanket of clouds, misty rain, eight degrees Celsius. As I'd often done before, I'd taken the District Line to Kew Gardens, getting out at the picturesque tube station in South London and hastening to the British national archives to immerse myself in old documents. The rain was even more unpleasant than usual and made me quicken my pace. As always, at the Archives entrance there was an impressive number of security personnel who gave my bag a cursory search. I passed by the small bookshop and went to the coatroom, then proceeded up the stairs to the reading room, where the garish green carpet convinced me that nothing had changed since the last time I'd been here.

In autumn 2001, I was working as a visiting lecturer at the University of Glasgow and was on a short visit to London. A few weeks previously, I had stumbled across Michael Gannon's book about the turning point in the Battle of the Atlantic in May 1943. It contained several pages of minutes of discussions among German U-boat crewmen, and that had made me curious. I was aware of the existence of reports about interrogations of German POWs, but I had never heard anything about reports based on covert surveillance, and I wanted to follow up the lead. I wasn't expecting anything much. What could such reports consist of? A couple of pages of random conversations, recorded by someone somewhere. Countless times before, promising indications of potential new sources had led to dead ends.

But this time it was different. At the desk I'd been assigned, I found a thick bundle of files, perhaps totaling eight hundred pages, held together only by a string. The thin sheets of paper were still immaculately organized. I had to be one of the first people to have ever held them in his hands. I glanced over seemingly endless protocols of German navy men, mostly U-boat crew members, transcribed word for word. If such reports existed for September 1943, I reasoned, there would have been similar ones for October and November 1943 as well. And what about the rest of the war? Indeed, as I discovered, there were thick bundles covering other months as well. Gradually, I realized that this was only the tip of the iceberg. In my excitement, I kept ordering more and more documents and found that not only submarine crews but captured members of the German air force and army had been subjected to covert surveillance as well. I delved into their conversations and was sucked in by the internal world of war that unfolded before me. You could practically hear the soldiers talking, gesticulating, and arguing among themselves. What most surprised me was how openly they talked about fighting, killing, and dying. I flew back to Glasgow with some interesting photocopied passages in my bag. The following day, I bumped into Professor Bernard Wasserstein at the Department of History and told him about my discovery. This was a brand-new source, I related, and would probably make a good topic for a dissertation for someone else. "You want to give it away?" he asked in amazement. The question burned itself into my head. He was right. I myself had to excavate this particular buried treasure.

I kept going back to London and gradually began to comprehend what I had stumbled upon. Over the course of the war, the British intelligence service had systematically subjected thousands of German and hundreds of Italian POWs to covert surveillance, recording passages from conversations they found particularly interesting on wax records and making protocols of them. The protocols had survived the war in their entirety and had been declassified in 1996. But in the years that followed, no one had recognized their value as historical source material. Undiscovered, they were left hibernating on the archive shelves.

In 2003, I published the first excerpts, and two years later a book edition followed containing some two hundred protocols from conversations among German generals. But I had still only made scant progress in evaluating and interpreting this source material. A short time later, I discovered a similar collection of material—some 100,000 pages' worth, twice as extensive as the British files—in the National Archives in Washington, D.C. It was clear that there was no way I could process this seemingly infinite quantity of material on my own.

Harald Welzer

I was speechless when Sönke Neitzel called me and told me about the source material he had found. Previously we had been forced to base our research on perceptions of violence and the willingness to kill on very problematic sources: official investigations, letters from the field, eyewitness reports, and memoirs. The shortcoming of all these statements, reports, and descriptions was that they were consciously composed and addressed to someone specific: a prosecutor, a wife at home, or an audience the authors wanted to win over. When POWs spoke among themselves in the camps, they did so without any such agenda. None of them ever imagined that the stories they told would become a "source," to say nothing of being published. Moreover, with investigations, autobiographies, and interviews with historical witnesses, the people concerned know how a period of history has turned out, and that ex post facto knowledge obscures how they experienced and saw things at the time. In Sönke Neitzel's sources, men were talking live, in real time, about the war and their attitudes toward it. It was a discovery that would give unique, new insight into the mentality of the Wehrmacht and perhaps of the military in general. I was electrified, and we agreed to meet immediately. It was obvious that as a social psychologist without a profound knowledge of the Wehrmacht, I would never be able to interpret the material historically. Conversely, someone with a purely historical perspective would never be able to decode all the communicative and psychological aspects of the protocols. Both Sönke Neitzel and I had worked intensively on the Third Reich, yet we viewed the dialogues among the POWs from very different perspectives. Only by combining our disciplines, social psychology and history, would we be able to do justice to the material as a source for reconstructing a particular mentality and arrive at a revised perspective on soldiers' behavior. We were then able to convince the Gerda Henkel Foundation and the Fritz Thyssen Foundation to support our attempts to start a major new research project. Not long after our initial meeting, we had the financial means to put together a research team to immediately tackle this mind-boggling amount of material.[1] We were able to digitalize all of the British documents and most of the American material and sort through it with the help of content-recognition software. Now, after three years of work, in which we learned a lot that was new and in which we were forced to question a number of truisms our sources failed to bear out, it is time to present the first results of our research.

AUTHORS' NOTE

In the excerpts from the surveillance protocols, British and American intelligence agencies used parentheses to indicate omissions. They also indicated garbled names and places with question marks. Authors' clarifications are indicated with brackets.

SOLDIERS

What the Soldiers Discussed*

"I heard of a case of two fifteen-year-old boys. They were wearing uniform and were firing away with the rest. But they were taken prisoners. A corporal in hospital told me that. They were wearing soldiers' uniform, so what could one do. And I myself have seen that there are twelve-year-old boys in the Russian Army, in the band, for instance, wearing uniform. We once (captured) a Russian military band and they played wonderfully. It was almost too much for you. There was such depth of feeling and yearning in their music; it conjured up pictures of the vastness of RUSSIA. It was terrific, it thrilled me through and through. It was a military band. To get back to the story, the two boys were told to get back westward and to keep on the road. If they tried to run into the woods at the first bend of the road they would get a bullet in them. And they were scarcely out of sight when they slunk off the road, and in a flash they had disappeared. A large detachment was immediately sent to look for them, but they couldn't find them. And then they caught the two boys. Those were the two. (Our people) behaved well and didn't kill them there and then, they took them before the C.C. [concentration camp] again. Now it was clear that they'd done for themselves. They were made to dig their own graves, two pits, and then one of them was shot. He didn't fall into the grave, he fell forwards over it. The other was told to push the first one into the pit before he was shot himself. And he did so, smiling—a boy of fifteen! There's fanaticism and idealism for you"![2]

This story, as told by Staff Sergeant Schmid on June 20, 1942, typifies how the soldiers talk in the protocols. As in all everyday conversations,

---

* Translator's note: The excerpts from surveillance protocols made in British POW camps come from the original British military translations during World War II. Translations of excerpts from American POW camps are my own.

the speaker repeatedly changes the subject, following a chain of associations. In the middle, when Schmid is talking about music, it occurs to him how much he enjoys Russian music, whereupon he briefly describes it before continuing his narrative. Schmid's anecdote begins harmlessly enough, but turns truly horrific at the end with the execution of the two young Russian soldiers. The narrator reports that not only were the two youths murdered, they were made to dig their own graves. The execution runs into a complication, and that leads to the eventual moral of the story. The young soldier about to be killed proves "fanatic" or "idealistic," eliciting the staff sergeant's admiration.

At first glance what we have here is a spectacular combination of topics—war, enemy soldiers, youths, music, Russian expanses, crimes against humanity, and admiration for one's adversary—that don't seem to cohere. Yet they are narrated in a single breath. That is the first thing we need to recognize. The stories we will be examining in this book deviate from what we expect. They were not intended to be well rounded, consistent, or logical. They were told to create excitement, elicit interest, or provide space and opportunity for the interlocutor to add commentary or stories of his own. In this respect, as is true for all everyday conversations, the soldiers' stories tend to jump around in interesting ways. They are full of ruptures and sidebar narratives, and they aim to establish consensus and agreement. People do not converse solely in order to exchange information but to create a relationship with one another, establishing commonalities and assuring themselves that they are experiencing one and the same world. The soldier's world is that of war. That is what makes their conversations seem so extraordinary to readers today. For the soldiers themselves, they were perfectly normal.

The brutality, harshness, and absence of emotion of war are omnipresent, and that is what is so disturbing for us reading the dialogues today, more than sixty years after the fact. Involuntarily, we can only shake our heads in dismay and frequent incomprehension. Yet in order to understand the world of these soldiers, and not just our own world, we need to get beyond such moral reactions. The matter-of-factness with which extreme acts of brutality are related shows that killing and the worst sorts of violence were part of the narrator's and audience's everyday reality. The POWs discussed such topics for hours on end. But they also conversed about airplanes, bombs, radar devices, cities, landscapes, and women:

MÜLLER: When I was at KHARKIV the whole place had been destroyed, except the centre of the town. It was a delightful town, a delightful memory! Everyone spoke a little German—they'd learnt it at school. At TAGANROG, too, there were splendid cinemas and wonderful cafés on the beach. We did a lot of flying near the junction of the Don and the Donetz. . . . It's beautiful country; I travelled everywhere in a lorry. Everywhere we saw women doing compulsory labour service.

FAUST: How frightful!

MÜLLER: They were employed on road-making—extraordinarily lovely girls; we drove past, simply pulled them into the armoured car, raped them and threw them out again. And did they curse![3]

Male conversations are like this. The two soldiers protocolled here, a Luftwaffe lance corporal and a sergeant, at times describe the Russian campaign like tourists, telling of "delightful" towns and memories. Then, suddenly, the story becomes about the spontaneous rape of female forced laborers. The sergeant relates this like a minor, ancillary anecdote, before continuing to describe his "trip." This example illustrates the parameters of what can be said and what is expected in the secretly monitored conversations. None of the violence related goes against his interlocutor's expectations. Stories about shooting, raping, and robbing are commonplace within the war stories. Rarely do they occasion analysis, moral objections, or disagreements. As brutal as they may be, the conversations proceed harmoniously. The soldiers understand one another. They share the same world and swap perspectives on the events that occupy their minds and the things that they've seen and done. They narrate and interpret these things in historically, culturally, and situatively specific frameworks of reference.

Our aim in this book is to reconstruct and describe these frameworks in order to understand what the soldiers' world was like, how they saw themselves and their enemies, what they thought about Adolf Hitler and Nazism, and why they continued fighting, even when the war seemed already lost. We want to examine what was "National Socialist" about these reference frameworks and to determine whether the largely jovial men in the POW camps were indeed "ideological warriors" who set out in a "war of annihilation" to commit racist crimes and stage massacres. To what extent do these men conform to the category, popularized by Daniel Goldhagen in the 1990s, of "willing executioners"? Or, alternatively, do they more greatly resemble the more differentiated, morally ambiguous picture of Wehrmacht soldiers that has emerged from the popular historical exhibits by the Hamburg Institute for Social Research and countless historical examinations? Today's conventional wisdom is that Wehrmacht soldiers were part of a gigantic apparatus of annihilation and thus were participants in, if not executioners of, unparalleled mass murder. There is no doubt that the Wehrmacht was involved in criminal acts, from the killing of civilians to the systematic murder of Jewish men, women, and children. But that tells us nothing about how individual soldiers were involved in such criminality, or about the relationship they themselves had toward their deeds—whether they committed crimes willingly, grudgingly, or not at all. The material here gives detailed information about the relationships between individuals and their actions and challenges our common assumptions about "the Wehrmacht."

One fact needs to be acknowledged. Whatever they may encounter, human beings are never unbiased. Instead, they perceive everything through specific filters. Every culture, historical epoch, or economic system—in short every form of existence—influences the patterns of perception and interpretation and thus steers how individuals perceive and interpret experiences and events. The surveillance protocols reflect, in real time, how German soldiers saw and commonly understood World War II. We will show that their observations and conversations are not what we would usually imagine—in part because they, unlike we today, did not know how the war would end and what would become of the Third Reich and its Führer. The soldiers' future, both real and imaginary, is our past, but for them it was an unfinished book. Most of the soldiers are scarcely interested in ideology, politics, world orders, and anything of that nature. They wage war not out of conviction, but because they are soldiers, and fighting is their job.

Many of them are anti-Semites, but that is not identical with being "Nazis." Nor does anti-Semitism have anything to do with willingness to kill. A substantial number of the soldiers hate "the Jews" but are shocked at the mass executions by firing squads. Some are clear "anti-Nazis" but support the anti-Jewish policies of Hitler's regime. Quite a few are scandalized at hundreds of thousands of Russian POWs being allowed to starve to death, but do not hesitate to shoot POWs themselves if it seems too time-consuming or dangerous to guard or transport them. Some complain that Germans are too "humane" and then tell in the same breath and in great detail how they mowed down entire villages. Many conversations feature a lot of boasting and chest-puffing, but this goes well beyond today's males' bragging about themselves or their cars. Soldiers frequently seek to rack up points with tales of extreme violence, of the women they raped, the planes they shot down, or the merchant ships they sank. On occasion, we were able to determine that such stories were untrue and intended to make an impression, even by relating, for instance, how they sank a ship that was transporting children. That is beyond the pale today, but the parameters of what could be and was said then were different from what obtains today, as are the things which they hoped would elicit admiration and respect. Acts of violence, back then, belonged to that category. Most of the soldiers' stories may initially seem contradictory, but only if we assume that people act in accordance with their "attitudes," and that those attitudes are closely connected with ideologies, theories, and grand convictions.

In reality, people act as they think is expected of them. Such perceived expectations have a lot less to do with abstract "views of the world" than with concrete places, purposes, and functions — and above all with the groups of which individual people are a part.

To understand and explain why German soldiers waged war for five years with a ferocity still unparalleled today, causing an eruption of violence that claimed 50 million lives and decimated an entire continent, we have to see the war, their war, through their eyes. The following chapters will be concerned in detail with the factors that influenced and determined the soldiers' perspective, their frames of reference. Readers who are not interested in Nazi and military frames of reference and are more curious about the soldiers' narratives and discussions about violence, technology, extermination, women, or the Führer should proceed directly to page 44. After we have given a detailed account of the soldiers' views on fighting, killing, and dying, we will compare war as waged by the Wehrmacht with other wars, thereby elucidating what was specifically "National Socialist" about World War II. This much we can reveal in advance: the results of this examination will often be unexpected.

SEEING THE WAR WITH SOLDIERS' EYES:
ANALYZING FRAMES OF REFERENCE

Human beings are not Pavlovian dogs. They don't react with conditioned reflexes to predetermined stimuli. Between stimulus and reaction, something highly specialized happens which epitomizes human consciousness and which distinguishes our species from all other forms of life. Humans interpret what they perceive and on the basis of interpretation draw conclusions, make up their minds, and decide what to do. Belying Marxist theory, human beings never act on the basis of objective conditions; nor do they act, as disciples of rational choice theory long wanted us to believe, solely with an eye toward cost-benefit calculations. Waging war is neither the only logical result of cost-benefit analysis nor a necessary consequence of objective circumstances. A physical body will always fall according to the laws of gravity and never otherwise, but whatever human beings do they could always have done differently. Nor do magic entities such as "mentalities" make people behave a certain way, although psychological structures no doubt influence what human beings do. Mentalities precede but do not determine decisions. Even if people's perceptions and actions are bound up with social, cultural, hierarchical, and biological or anthropological circumstances, human beings always enjoy a certain freedom of interpretation and action. But the ability to interpret and decide presupposes orientation and knowledge of what one is dealing with and what consequences a decision can have. And a frame of reference is what provides orientation.

Frames of reference vary drastically according to historical periods and cultures. Orthodox Muslims, for instance, categorize suitable and unsuitable sexual behavior within a completely different framework from that of secular inhabitants of Western society. Nonetheless, no member of either group is able to interpret what he sees outside references not of his own choice or making. They influence, guide, and even steer his perceptions and interpretations. That is not to say that transgressions of a preexisting frame of reference do not occur in special situations. It is possible to observe or think something new. But this is relatively seldom the case. Frames of reference guarantee economy of action so that most of what happens can be sorted within a familiar matrix. That makes things easier. People called upon to act don't need to start from the very beginning with the question: what is actually going on here? In the vast majority of cases, the answers to this question are preprogrammed and accessible, saved in a corpus of cultural orientation and knowledge. Most everyday tasks are taken care of by routines, habits, and certainties, and that saves individual human beings a colossal amount of work.

Thus when we want to explain human behavior, we first must reconstruct the frame of reference in which given human beings operated, including which factors structured their perception and suggested certain conclusions. Merely analyzing objective circumstances is inadequate. Nor do mentalities explain *why* someone did a specific thing, especially in cases where members of a group whose minds were all formed the same way arrive at entirely different conclusions and decisions. This is the systemic limit upon theories about ideological wars and totalitarian regimes. The question always remains: how are "world views" and "ideologies" translated into individual perceptions and interpretations and how do they affect individual behavior? In order to understand those things, we analyze frames of reference as a way of reconstructing the perceptions and interpretations of people in specific historical situations, here German soldiers during World War II.

When frames of reference are ignored, academic analyses of past actions automatically become normative, since present-day standards are enlisted to allow us to understand what was going on. As a result, past wars and violence often appear bafflingly "horrible," even though horror is a moral and not an analytical concept. Moreover, the behavior of people who exercise violence appears abnormal and psychopathic, despite the fact that when we reconstruct the world from their perspective their rationale for using violence is entirely logical and understandable. Analyzing frames of reference allows us to view the violence of World War II in *nonmoral,* nonnormative fashion. The aim is to understand the preconditions for psychologically normal people to do things they would not otherwise do.

We have to distinguish between different orders of frames of reference:

Frames of the *first order* are the broad sociohistorical backdrop against which people of a given time operate. They are what sociologist Alfred Schütz called "the assumptive world," the things we pre-presume must be the case. They include categories of good and evil and true and false, what is edible and what is not, how much distance we should maintain when speaking to one another, and what is polite or rude. This "world as we feel it to be" has its effects on us less as beings capable of self-reflection than as creatures influenced by the unconscious and our emotions.[4]

Frames of reference of the *second order* are more concrete in a historical, cultural, and often geographical sense. They comprise a sociohistorical space that, in most respects, can be clearly delimited—for instance, the length of a dictatorial regime or the duration of a historical entity like the Third Reich.

Frames of reference of the *third order* are even more specific. They consist of a concrete constellation of sociohistorical events within which people act. They include, for example, a war in which soldiers fight.

Frames of reference of the *fourth order* are the special characteristics, modes of perception, interpretative paradigms, and perceived responsibilities that an individual brings to a specific situation. This is the level of psychology, personal dispositions, and individual decision making.

This book analyzes second- and third-order frames of reference since that is primarily what our source material allows us to best approach.

FUNDAMENTAL ORIENTATIONS: WHAT IS ACTUALLY HAPPENING HERE?

On October 30, 1938, CBS Radio in the United States interrupted its regular programming with a special announcement that there had been a gas explosion on the planet Mars and a cloud of hydrogen was speeding toward the earth. Then, during a radio reporter's interview with an astronomy professor, aimed at clarifying the potential dangers, another announcement was made about a seismic catastrophe of earthquake strength, presumably the result of a meteor hitting our planet. A barrage of news flashes followed. Curiosity seekers at the site of impact reported being attacked by aliens who emerged from the crater. Further objects were said to be striking the earth's surface, and hordes of little green men from Mars were pressing on with their attacks. The military had been deployed, with little success. The aliens were marching on New York. Warplanes took to the air. People began fleeing the danger zone. Panic was breaking out.

At this point a change in frame of reference occurred. Up until the episode about the warplanes, the news reports were simply following the script of a radio play Orson Welles had adapted from H. G. Wells's novel *The War of the Worlds*. But the people fleeing in panic were real. Among the six million Americans who had tuned in to Wells's radio broadcast, two million of them believed every word they heard. Many of them hastily packed their things and ran out into the streets to escape the alleged alien gas attacks. Telephone lines were jammed for hours, and it took hours more until news got around that the whole thing was fictional.[5] This legendary event, which established Orson Welles's fame, vividly illustrated the truth of sociologist William I. Thomas's 1917 theorem: "If men define situations as real, they are real in their consequences." No matter how objectively wrong or irrational people's estimation of reality may be, the conclusions they draw create new realities.

That was the case with the listeners who had not heard the announcement that *The War of the Worlds* was a radio play and who thought the alien invasion was really happening. Nineteen thirties communications technology, of course, did not allow people to quickly check the truth of what they had heard, and those who fled their apartment buildings saw crowds of other people also taking to the streets. What reason did they have to suspect they had been taken in by a hoax? Human beings always seek to confirm their perception and interpretation of reality by observing what other people do, all the more so in unexpected and threatening situations that make people lose their orientation and ask: what is going on here and what should I do?

The War of the Worlds is a spectacular example, but it only illustrates how people behave when they are trying to orient themselves. Modern societies in particular, with their rich variety of functions, roles, and complex situations, demand that their members constantly interpret reality. What is happening here? How can I fulfill expectations of me? Most of these questions remain unconscious because the lion's share of the orientation work happens automatically, steered by routines, habits, prescribed responses, and rules. But in cases where things don't function as they should, when accidents, misperceptions, and mistakes occur, we become explicitly conscious of the need for what we are always implicitly doing: interpreting what is going on in front of our senses.

Naturally, this interpretative work does not happen in a vacuum or start from the very beginning. Interpretation itself is bound to frames, perspectives comprised of many elements that structure and organize experiences as we are in the process of making them. Following the analysis of Gregory Bateson[6] and Alfred Schütz,[7] Erving Goffman described a plethora of such frames and their attendant characteristics. In so doing, he elucidated not only how frames comprehensively organize our everyday perceptions and orientation, but how they yield highly divergent interpretations, depending on contextual knowledge and standpoint of observation. Take the example of fraud. For the swindler, for example, the framework of activity is a "deceptive maneuver," while for his victim it is that which is being deceptively advanced as true.[8] Or, as Polish journalist Kazimierz Sakowicz noted in his diary in the context of World War II and the Holocaust: "For Germans, 300 Jews mean 300 enemies of humanity; for Lithuanians, they mean 300 pairs of shoes and trousers."[9]

CULTURAL TIES

Stanley Milgram once said that he was curious about why people would rather burn to death in a house fire than run outside without trousers. Seen objectively, this is an example of irrational behavior. But subjectively, it shows that standards of decency can become barriers to necessary strategies of survival, and that these barriers can be hard to overcome. In World War II, some Japanese soldiers preferred to take their own lives rather than become prisoners of war. In Saipan, hundreds of civilians jumped to their deaths over cliffs in order to avoid falling into American hands.[10] Even in life-or-death situations, cultural ties and duties often outweigh the instinct for survival. This is why people die in the attempt to rescue a dog from drowning, or decide to become suicide bombers.

Where survival is at stake, cultural baggage weighs heavy and occasionally proves fatal. Or put the matter differently: in all these examples, the main problem is perceived not as a threat to individual survival, but as a danger to established, symbolic, inviolable rules of behavior and status. A danger of this sort can appear so grave to those concerned that no way out is visible. In this sense, people can become victims of their own techniques for survival.

Not Knowing

History itself is not perceived. History happens. Only in retrospect do historians determine which events from a massive inventory of possibilities were "historical," i.e., significant for the eventual way things turned out. Everyday consciousness rarely registers gradual changes of social and physical environment because perception constantly readjusts itself in line with changes in its various environments. Psychologists call this phenomenon "shifting baselines," and examples such as the recent changes in our communicative habits or the radical alteration of normative standards under Nazism show how powerful they can be. In both examples, people were under the impression that everything had basically stayed the same, even though fundamental change had occurred.

Only in retrospect does a slow process, at least one perceived as slow, such as the breakdown of civilization, congeal into an abrupt event. That happens when people realize that a development has had radical consequences. The interpretation of what people perceived within a process that later turned into a catastrophe is a very tricky enterprise—not least because we pose our questions of what people knew with our own hindsight as to how things turned out. Historical actors, of course, possessed no such knowledge. We view history from the end to the beginning and are forced to suspend our own historical knowledge in order to say what people knew at any specific historical juncture. For that reason, Norbert Elias has proposed that reconstructing what people did not or could not have known is one of the most difficult tasks of social science.[11] Or to use the terminology of historian Jürgen Kocka, we could describe this task as the "liquification" of history, the conversion of facts back into possibilities.[12]

Expectations

On August 2, 1914, Franz Kafka in Prague wrote in his diary: "Germany declared war on Russia—afternoon: swimming lessons." This is just one particularly prominent example of events that later observers learn to see as historic not being perceived as such in the real time in which they come together. Indeed, if such events are even registered, it is as a part of everyday life, in which a variety of things are perceived and compete for people's attention. Even an exceptionally intelligent individual like Kafka can find the outbreak of a war no more noteworthy than a swimming lesson later in the day.

From a historical perspective, one can say that the groundwork for a war of annihilation had been laid long before the German army attacked the Soviet Union on June 22, 1941. At the same time, it is doubtful that the soldiers who received their orders that morning truly realized what sort of a war they faced. They expected to make lightning-quick advances, as had been the case in Poland, France, and the Balkans, and not to wage a murderous frontline campaign with previously unprecedented ferocity. Moreover, there was even less reason for them to anticipate that in the course of the war groups of people that had no immediate connection with the hostilities would be systematically eliminated. The frame of reference "war," as it had been previously known, did not presume anything like that.

For the same reason, many Jewish Germans did not recognize the dimensions of the process of exclusion of which they would become the victims. Instead many viewed Nazi rule as a short-term phenomenon that "one will have to get through, or a setback that one could accept, or at the worst a threat that restricted one personally, but that was still more bearable than the arbitrary perils of exile."[13] The bitter irony in the case of Jews was that while past discrimination meant their reference frame did indeed encompass anti-Semitism, persecution, and larceny, it also rendered them unable to see that what was happening in the Third Reich was of a different, absolutely deadly order.

TEMPORALLY SPECIFIC CONTEXTS OF PERCEPTION

On June 2, 2010, in the German town of Göttingen, three bomb squad specialists lost their lives in an attempt to defuse an unexploded bomb from World War II. German media reported extensively on the accident, and it caused a considerable outpouring of sympathy. Yet if the bomb had killed three people in 1944 or 1945, when it was actually dropped, it would have attracted little attention beyond the immediate families of the men killed. During wartime, such deaths were nothing unusual. In January and February 1945, some one hundred residents of Göttingen were killed in bombing raids.[14]

Historically speaking, violence has been enacted and experienced in very different ways. The extraordinary abstinence from violence in modern society, the fact that the public and to a lesser degree the private spheres are relatively free from force, is the result of the civilizing influence of separation of state powers and the state's monopoly on the legitimate use of force. These achievements have allowed for the enormous sense of security that is an integral part of modern societies. In premodern periods, people were far more likely to become the victims of direct physical violence than now.[15] Violence was also far more present in the public sphere, for example, in the form of public punishments and executions.[16] It is therefore reasonable to assume that the frames of reference and the experiences of committing and suffering violence varied throughout history.

ROLE MODELS AND RESPONSIBILITIES

As discussed earlier, roles make up an extensive social arena, especially in modern, functionally differentiated societies, and each type of role brings with it a certain set of responsibilities for those who choose or are forced to play it. Roles represent an intermediate level between cultural ties and responsibilities, and group-specific and individual interpretation and action. Within many roles, we may not even be aware that we are acting according to their standards, although it is obvious that we in fact are. They include all the roles sociologists use to differentiate between societies: roles of gender, age, social origin, and education. The sets of responsibilities and norms they entail are consciously perceived and questioned only in exceptional cases. Nonetheless, such self-evident, everyday roles influence our perception, interpretation, and behavioral options, while they themselves, as is especially the case with gender and age, are subject to normative rules. People expect a different sort of behavior from an elderly lady than from a young male, even though there is no specific catalogue of dos and don'ts, to say nothing of laws. As members of society, all of us "know" such rules implicitly.

The situation is different with explicitly adopted roles, for instance, those we take on in the course of our careers. They bring along new sets of responsibilities to be learned. If a person who has been studying mathematics gets a job at an insurance company, his set of responsibilities changes dramatically, affecting norms of attire, working day, communication, and what that person considers important and insignificant. Other fundamental transitions happen when people become mothers or fathers, or when a pensioner retires from the working world. Furthermore we can observe radical role changes when people enter "total institutions"[17] such as a cloister, a prison, or—as is particularly significant for the present context—the military. Such institutions—say, for instance, the Wehrmacht or the SS—claim total dispensation over the individual. Individuals are given uniforms and special haircuts and thereby lose control over the enactment of their own identities. They no longer do with their time as they see fit but are constantly subjected to external compulsion, drills, harassment, and draconian punishment for violating rules. Total institutions function as hermetically sealed worlds of a special sort, directed toward producing a finished result. Soldiers do not just learn how to use weapons and negotiate various types of terrain. They are taught to obey, to subjugate themselves to hierarchy, and to act on command at a moment's notice. Total institutions establish a specific form of socialization, in which group norms and responsibilities have far more influence on individuals than under normal social conditions. The group to which one belongs may not be freely selected, but it is the only group to which one can relate. One is part of the group because one was assigned to it.[18]

A total institution initially attempts to rob initiates of all forms of self-control. Only after the "initiation" or "apprenticeship" has been completed does a measure of freedom and a spectrum for possible behavior open up. This phenomenon is extreme even in peacetime, and it is the more so during war, when acts of battle are no longer simulation, but everyday reality, and one's own survival may well depend on the smooth functioning of one's unit. At that point, the total institution becomes a total group, allowing only specific spectrums of action precisely defined by rank and command structure.[19] In comparison with civilian roles of every sort, the frame of reference of soldiers at war is characterized by the lack of alternatives. One of the soldiers, whose conversations with a comrade were secretly recorded, put it so: "We're like a machine gun. A weapon for waging war."[20]

In decisions of what, when, and with whom, a soldier's behavior is not subject to his own perception, interpretation, and decision making. The leeway with which a command can be interpreted according to one's own estimation and abilities is extremely small. Depending on the circumstances, the significance of roles within frames of reference varies considerably. Under the pluralistic conditions of civilian life, it can be quite negligible. Under the conditions of war or other extreme situations, though, the significance can be total.

Parts of various civilian roles can also be transferred to the military context, where they become matters of life or death. A harmless action like transferring files can suddenly become murderous, if the context changes. As early as 1962, in his seminal work *The Destruction of the European Jews,* Holocaust historian Raul Hilberg underscored the negative potential of people employing civilian skills for homicidal purposes:

> Every policeman charged with keeping order could become a guard in a ghetto or for a rail transport. Every lawyer at the Main Office for Imperial Security was a candidate for taking over a task force; every finance specialist at the Department of Economic Administration was seen as a natural choice for serving in a concentration camp. In other words, all necessary operations were carried out using the personnel that was available at the time. Wherever one chooses to draw the border with active participation, the machinery of annihilation represented an impressive cross-section of the German populace.[21]

Applied to war, that would mean: every mechanic could repair bombers whose deadly payloads killed thousands of people; every butcher could, as a member of a procurement enterprise, be complicit in the plundering of occupied areas. During World War II, Lufthansa pilots flew long-range sorties in their Fw 200s not to transport passengers, but to sink British merchant ships in the Atlantic. Yet because their activity in and of itself didn't change, those who played these roles rarely saw reason to engage in moral reflection or to refuse to do their jobs. Their basic activity remained the same.

INTERPRETIVE PARADIGM: WAR IS WAR

Specific interpretive paradigms are tightly connected with the sets of demands that accompany every role. Doctors see an illness differently than do patients, just as perpetrators view a crime differently than do victims. The paradigms that direct these interpretations are, in a sense, mini frames of reference. Every interpretive paradigm, of course, includes an entire universe of alternative interpretations and implies nonknowledge. That is disadvantageous in situations so new that previous experience does more to hinder than to help our ability to deal with them.[22] Paradigms are effective in familiar contexts since they remove the need to engage in complex considerations and calculations. One knows what one is dealing with and what the right recipe is for solving a problem. As predetermined, routinized frames for ordering what is happening at a given moment, interpretive paradigms structure our lives to an extraordinarily high degree. They range from stereotypes ("Jews are all . . .") to entire cosmologies ("God will not permit Germany's demise"), and are both historically and culturally very specific. German soldiers in World War II typecast their enemies according to different criteria and characteristics than soldiers in the Vietnam War did, but the procedure and function of the typecasting are identical.

Interpretive paradigms are especially central to how soldiers in World War II experienced others, their own mission, their "race," Hitler, and Jews. Paradigms equip frames of reference with prefabricated interpretations according to which experiences can be sorted. They also include interpretations from different social contexts that are imported into the experience of war. This is especially significant for the notion of "war as a job," which in turn is extremely important for soldiers' interpretations of what they do. This central role can be gleaned from phrases like the "dirty work" or the "fine job" done by the Luftwaffe that recur in the soldiers' conversations. The interpretive paradigm from industrial society for how soldiers experienced and dealt with war also informs philosopher Ernst Jünger's famous description of soldiers as "workers of war." In Jünger's words, war appears as a "rational work process equally far removed from feelings of horror and romanticism" and the use of weapons as "the extension of a customary activity at the workbench."[23]

In fact, commercial work and the work of war are indeed related in a number of respects. Both are subject to division of labor, both depend on technical, specialist qualifications, and both are hierarchically structured. In both cases, the majority of those involved have nothing to do with the finished product and carry out orders without asking questions about whether commands are sensible. Responsibility is either delegated or confined to the particular area on which one directly works. Routine plays a major role. Workers and soldiers carry out recurring physical movements and follow standing instructions. For instance, in a bomber, pilots, bombardiers, and gunners with varying qualifications work together to achieve a finished product: the destruction of a target, whether that target might be a city, a bridge, or a group of soldiers in the open field. Mass executions such as those perpetrated against Eastern European Jews were not carried out only by those who fired the guns, but by the truck drivers, the cooks, the weapons maintenance personnel, and by the "guides" and "carriers," those who brought the victims to their graves and who piled up the corpses. The mass executions were the result of a precise division of labor.

Against this backdrop, it is clear that interpretive paradigms give war a deeper meaning. If I interpret the killing of human beings as work, I do not categorize it as a crime and, thereby, normalize what I am doing. The role played by interpretive paradigms in the reference frame of war emerges clearly from examples like the ones above. Actions that would be considered deviant and in need of explanation and justification in the normal circumstances of everyday civilian life become normal, conformist forms of behavior. The interpretive paradigm, in a sense, automatizes moral self-examination and prevents soldiers from feeling guilt.

Formal Duties

Part of an orienting frame of reference is very simple: it is a universe of regulations and a position within a hierarchy that determines what sort of orders an individual can be told to carry out and which orders he himself can issue to subordinates. Civilian life, too, has a spectrum ranging from total dependence to total freedom, depending on the roles one has to play. A business tycoon may enjoy immense freedom of action and be beyond the command of anything but the law in his business. But the situation might be very different in his family life, where he may be bossed around by a dominant father or an imperious wife.

By contrast, such things are eminently clear in the military. In the army, rank and function unambiguously determine how much leeway individuals have. The lower down one is in the hierarchy, the more dependent one will be on others' commands and decisions. Yet even within total institutions like a military boot camp, a prison, or a closed psychiatric clinic, everyone enjoys at least a small measure of freedom of action. In his book *Asylums,* sociologist Erving Goffman has convincingly described how people can exploit rules in total institutions for their own purposes. According to Goffman, when people in such institutions use jobs in the kitchen or the library to get organized or smuggle desired goods, they are engaged in "secondary adjustments," pretending to follow the rules but actually advancing their own interests. Occupying troops enjoy numerous opportunities for secondary adjustment. In June 1944, for example, a certain Lieutenant Pölert related: "I sent home a tremendous amount of butter and three or four pigs from France. It may have been three to four cwt of butter."[24] Soldiers welcomed such sides of war from which they could personally profit. The leeway afforded by secondary adaptation, however, drastically declines in actual battle and can only be exploited if one enjoys violence. In any case, as the situation grows more confined and drastic, the frame of reference becomes less differentiated.

SOCIAL DUTIES

In cases like total institutions with a limited frame of reference, freedom of choice is minimized while security of orientation grows. At the same time, social duties can intervene in established, unambiguous decision-making structures and make group ties or even chains of command more permeable. For instance, the commandant of the Dautmergen concentration camp, Erwin Dold, disobeyed orders and organized food for "his" inmates, in a unique attempt to improve their chances of survival. He did this in the secure knowledge that his wife supported and even expected such behavior.[25] Another example of the impact of social duties was soldiers who suddenly felt moral scruples when carrying out mass executions, after noticing resemblances between children they murdered and their own kids.[26] Nonetheless, we should be under no illusions about the effect of social duties. We know of a great number of cases in which the real or imaginary presence of a wife actually encouraged soldiers to kill because they felt they were acting in harmony with the wishes and choices of their spouses.

Social duties emerge clearly in the recorded conversations of tank commander Heinrich Eberbach. In October 1944, while interned in the British POW camp Trent Park, he talked about whether he should voluntarily assist Allied propaganda efforts:

> I am fairly well known in tank circles in which I have given many addresses and lectures etc. I am convinced that if I were to make such a proclamation, which would be heard and read by the people—leaflets dropped over the front and so on—it would <u>certainly</u> have a certain effect on the troops. But first I should consider it as an utterly dirty thing to do in every way, it would go against my feelings so much that I could never do it. Then quite apart from that—there are my wife and my children. I wouldn't dream of doing it. I should be ashamed to face my wife if I did. My wife is so patriotic, I could never do it.[27]

The profound influence of social ties results from the fact, contrary to popular assumption, that people behave within social relationships and not for causal reasons or according to rational calculation. Social ties are thus a crucial variable in determining what people decide—all the more so when decisions are made under stress, as in Stanley Milgram's famous simulation. In that experiment, social constellations were decisive in how obediently the subjects behaved toward the authority figure.[28]

Social proximity, perceived or actual, and the duties bound up with it constitute a central element in frames of reference. In the discipline of history, this element rarely comes into focus since, as a rule, sources rarely contain information about a person behaving in a specific way because he felt a sense of duty toward someone else. Further complicating the matter is the fact that social duties are not necessarily conscious. Sometimes they are so deeply internalized that they serve as points of orientation without an individual being aware of them. Psychologists call this phenomenon delegation.

When we pause to consider the one-dimensional reference frame of soldiers faced with military situations and the restriction of soldiers' social environment to their comrades, we begin to see the significance of a sense of social duty. Whereas in civilian life, family, friends, schoolmates, and fellow students or workers represent a pluralistic corpus of diverse figures of reference, soldiers at the front essentially have only their brothers-in-arms. And they are all working within the same reference frame toward the same goal of fulfilling their military tasks while ensuring their own survival. Solidarity and cooperation are decisive factors in battle. Thus, the group always represents the strongest element of the frame of reference. Yet even when they are not engaged in active fighting, individual soldiers are highly dependent on the group. A soldier does not know for how long the war will go on or when he will get his next home leave or transfer, situations in which he will distance himself from the total group and rejoin a pluralistic community. Much has been written about the force of camaraderie. Along with its socializing functions, camaraderie also reveals antisocial elements when it is directed externally. The internal norms of the group determine standards of behavior, while the standards of the nonmilitary world are considered subordinate and insignificant.

In his role as comrade, an individual soldier does not just become a voluntary or involuntary part of a group, forfeiting autonomy in the process. He also receives something in return: security, dependability, support, and recognition. From this perspective, camaraderie entails not only a maximum concentration of social duty, but also the *relief* from duties vis-à-vis all other normally significant aspects of the world. The soldier's frame of reference and, in particular, the soldier's practical everyday existence are highly determined by this give-and-take. In the practical situation of war, camaraderie is no longer a tool of socialization that brings some duties while relieving others. A group of comrades becomes a literal unit of survival, creating binding forces that would never have such power under normal circumstances. This is not a feature unique to National Socialism. In their wide-ranging study of Wehrmacht soldiers, Edward A. Shils and Morris Janowitz also emphasized the central importance of camaraderie as the primary unit of individual orientation and interpretation in wartime.[29] Camaraderie is less about a specific view of the world or ideology, than orientation. Many individuals feel emotionally more at home with their comrades than with family members, who do not share their experience as soldiers and thus cannot understand them. Camaraderie is by no means a romanticized military myth. It is a social environment whose importance outstrips all rival environments.

SITUATIONS

In 1973, scholars at Princeton University carried out a remarkable experiment. A group of theology students were told to compose a short essay on the parable of the Good Samaritan and then take it, upon command, to a specific campus building, where it would be recorded for radio. The students waited around for that specific instruction, but suddenly an authority figure would appear and say: "Are you still here? You should have been over at the building a long time ago. Maybe the assistant is still waiting! You better hurry!" Each of the students duly hastened off to turn in his essay. In front of the entrance to the building in question, they found a seemingly helpless person lying on the ground, coughing and moaning with his eyes closed. There was no way to enter the building without noticing this person, apparently in the greatest of need. How did the theology students react? Only sixteen of forty subjects tried to help; the rest hurried on past the sufferer in order to keep their appointment. Even more confusingly, post-experiment interviews suggested that many of the subjects who had not helped claimed not even to have noticed that a fellow human being was in distress, despite practically stumbling over him.[30]

The experiment shows that people have to perceive before they can act. When we work toward a goal with extreme concentration, we simply shut out things unrelated to that goal. Focus of this sort does not admit moral questioning. It is the product of a necessary and almost always functioning economy of action that seeks to avoid what is nonessential. There is a vast gap between what people believe about their own moral values, convictions, and commitments and their actual behavior. In concrete situations that demand decisions and action, the decisive factors rarely have much to do with ethical considerations and moral tenets. What matters is the achievement of a goal or the fulfillment of a task. The central question is what is the best and most efficient way to get things done. The theology students were not primarily concerned with the ethos of helping out one's fellow man, but with the speed they were supposed to keep up to fulfill a task. The inventors of the Good Samaritan experiment, the psychologists John Darley and C. Daniel Batson, concluded that people who were not in a hurry would likely stop and try to offer assistance. Those in a hurry, on the other hand, would continue to hurry even if the task was to deliver a speech on the parable of the Good Samaritan.[31]

A situation itself seems to have much more influence on what people do than the personal characteristics that get them into a certain situation. That conclusion is supported by the established fact that in the Third Reich, people didn't need to be anti-Semitic to murder Jews or otherwise altruistic to rescue them. In both cases, it was enough for people to find themselves in a social situation in which one or the other course of action seemed called for. Once a given decision has been made, though, subsequent ones follow the path previously trodden. If an individual had taken part in one mass execution, the probability rose that he would participate in a second or third one. The same was true for people who offered assistance.

PERSONAL DISPOSITIONS

Of course, not everything people perceive and do can be reduced to external references. It goes without saying that different individuals bring various tendencies of perception, social interpretive paradigms, age-specific experiences, and special talents, weaknesses, and personal preferences with them into situations that call for interpretation and response. With this in mind, social situations always represent temporary structures that can be used and expanded with various degrees of freedom. A lot depends on the individual. It is certain that the grotesquely simplified relations of power in concentration camps or during the mass executions tended to appeal to violently inclined members of the SS, the reserve police corps, and Wehrmacht soldiers, offering them an opportunity to live out their sadistic desires, while calling forth repulsion in more sensitive, nonviolent people. It makes a big difference what sort of personality structure is confronted with what sort of situation. At the same time, though, we should not overestimate the significance of personal difference. As the Holocaust and the Nazi war of annihilation show, the vast majority of civilians, as well as soldiers, SS men, and police officers, behaved in discriminatory, violent, and inhumane fashion if the situation at hand seemed to encourage and promote such behavior. Only a tiny minority proved capable of humane resistance. According to the standards of the time, humane behavior was deviant, and brutality was conformist. For that reason, the entire collection of events known as the "Third Reich" and the violence it produced can be seen as a gigantic experiment, showing what sane people who see themselves as good are capable of if they consider something to be appropriate, sensible, or correct. The proportion of people who were *psychologically* inclined toward violence, discrimination, and excess totaled, as it does in all other social contexts as well, 5 to 10 percent.

In psychological terms, the inhabitants of the Third Reich were as normal as people in all other societies at all other times. The spectrum of perpetrators was a cross section of normal society. No specific group of people proved immune to the temptation, in Günther Anders's phrase, of "inhumanity with impunity." The real-life experiment that was the Third Reich did not reduce the variables of personality to absolute zero. But it showed them to be of comparatively slight, indeed often negligible, importance.

The Soldiers' World

FRAME OF REFERENCE: THE THIRD REICH

Even as early as 1935, the vast majority of Germans would have been able to identify what was particular about the society of the Third Reich, and they would have contrasted it to the previous Weimar Republic: incipient economic improvement, enhanced feelings of security and orderliness, regained national pride, and an identification with the Führer would have been among those points. Precisely because of the radical distinctions perceived between the Third Reich and the Weimar Republic, often dismissed as an era of overly bureaucratic systems, this second-order reference frame was unusually conscious. Interviews with people from the time are full of statements about a "new" and "better" age dawning, in which the outlook was "pointing up again," things were "moving forward," young people were "getting off the streets," a sense of "community" was becoming palpable. In terms of people's historical experience, the years between 1933 and 1945 were much more clearly contoured than either the preceding Weimar Republic or the post–World War II reconstruction periods in either West or East Germany. That's why it is easier to sketch out a frame of reference for the Third Reich than for comparatively calm periods. The Third Reich was a period with a remarkable density of experiences, full of change and characterized by an eight-year phase of radical euphoria and a four-year period of rapidly increasing fear, violence, loss, and insecurity. The fact that this period etched itself so indelibly into German history is not just due to Nazi crimes against humanity and extreme mass violence. It also has to do with the sense of being involved in something new and momentous, of working on a common National Socialist project. In short, people felt a part of a "great age."

But the history of social mores and mentality during the Third Reich is usually viewed through the prism of the Holocaust—as though the end of a monstrously dynamic social process full of contradictory half developments and "path dependencies" (decisions or outcomes that depend on previous decisions or outcomes) can shed analytic light on the beginning of that process. This is understandable because the horrors inflicted by National Socialism are indelibly etched on our historical understanding of the movement and its campaigns of annihilation. But methodologically, such an approach is pure nonsense. No one would think of writing the biography of an individual from his death to his birth or of reconstructing the history of an institution from the back to the front. Developments are open solely toward the future, not the past. Only in retrospect do developments appear inevitable and compulsory. While they are still developing, social processes contain a rich variety of possibilities, of which only a handful are actually taken up, and they in turn create certain path dependencies and a dynamic of their own.

When we try to reconstruct people's behavior within the reference frame Third Reich, we have to trace how they were "national socialized," how the mélange of ideological desires at play when the Nazis came into power became part of revised social practice in Germany. We also need to look at what stayed the same after Hitler became German chancellor on January 30, 1933. Numerous critics have pointed out that we should not confuse the social reality of the Third Reich with the increasingly perfected images developed by the scriptwriters and directors in Joseph Goebbels's Ministry of Propaganda. The Third Reich did not consist of an endless series of Olympic Summer Games and Nuremberg party rallies, of parades and pathos-laden speeches enrapturing young, blond, pigtailed devotees with tears in their eyes. The Third Reich consisted first and foremost of a multitude of mundane everyday factors that structure people's lives in every imaginable society. Children attended school, and adults went to work or to the unemployment office. They paid their rent, did their shopping, ate breakfast and lunch, met up with friends and family members, read newspapers and books, and talked sports or politics. While all these dimensions of everyday life may have become increasingly tinged with ideology and racism over the twelve years of the Third Reich, they remained habits and routines. Everyday life is characterized by business as usual.

Despite the extreme nature of National Socialism, the citizens of Germany did not wake up in a completely new world on the morning of January 31, 1933. The world was the same—only the news was different. Sebastian Haffner, the well-known German journalist and historian, for instance, described the events of January 30 as a change of government, not a revolution, and the Weimar Republic had seen more than its fair share of changes of government. Haffner's experience of January 30, 1933, consisted of "reading the newspapers, and the feelings they engendered."[32] German newspapers discussed the possible consequences and significance of Hitler's appointment as chancellor, but they did much the same with all other newsworthy stories as well. Haffner recounts conversations he had with his father, discussing what percent of the populace was truly Nazi, how foreign countries were likely to react, and what the working classes would do. In other words, the two men talked about all the things politically interested citizens discuss when confronted with unwelcome events whose ultimate ramifications are unclear. Haffner and his father, in any case, came to the conclusion that the Hitler government had an extremely weak foundation and thus a poor chance of lasting for long. All in all, they found, there was little real reason to worry.

To put the matter in different words: large parts of the existing frame of reference continued to function, and "life carrying on as usual" could be interpreted as a triumph over the Nazis. How could people have hit upon the idea in early 1933 that they needed an entirely new interpretation of reality, that what was happening was not something one could evaluate using customary criteria? Even if someone had sensed that the times were different, where would he have gotten the instruments to decode this new reality?

Social psychologists have clearly defined the phenomenon of "hindsight bias" for the belief, once the end of a social process is determined, to have known from the beginning how things would turn out. In retrospect, one can always find scores of indications for a nascent collapse or disaster. Contemporaries interviewed after the Third Reich all tell of their fathers or grandfathers exclaiming on January 30, 1933: "This means war!"[33] Hindsight bias allows people to position themselves on the side of foresight and knowledge, whereas in reality people who are in the midst of a process of historical transformation never see where that process is headed. To paraphrase Sigmund Freud, people who share an illusion can never recognize it. Only from a great distance can we achieve a perspective from which we can identify the misunderstandings and mistakes of historical actors. Even when one, two, or three levels of functionally differentiated social structure change, countless other ones remain exactly as they were before. In the early Third Reich, there was still bread in the bakeries, and the streetcars still ran. People were still studying toward university degrees and worrying about their sick grandmothers.

The inertia of a society's infrastructure, the way its daily life is experienced, comprises one major part of split consciousness. Another part consists of what is changing and, in particular, of whatever modifies people's frame of reference. That includes the actions of a government that operated with propaganda, restrictions, laws, arrests, violence, and terror as well as opportunities for entertainment and identification. In reaction to those changes, there were changes in the perception and behavior of a populace that, while by no means universally politically engaged, did participate in social affairs and tried to make sense of what was happening. For example, anti-Jewish measures such as the state-encouraged boycott of Jewish businesses in late March and early April 1933 were perceived in contradictory ways within the German populace, as were later anti-Semitic initiatives as well. As paradoxical as it may sound, the capacity for Nazism to engender contradictory responses was an integrating force. National Socialist society still retained enough discrete spaces and parts of the public sphere for people to debate the pros and cons of government measures and actions among like-minded peers.[34]

To believe that a modern dictatorship like National Socialism integrates a populace by homogenizing them is to mistake the way it functions socially. The reverse is the case. Integration proceeds by maintaining difference, so that even those who are against the regime — critics of the Nazis' Jewish policies or committed Social Democrats — have a social arena in which they can exchange their thoughts and find intellectual brethren. This mode of integration extended all the way down to the storm troops and reserve police battalions, which by no means consisted solely of Nazified, unthinking executioners, but included rational people who reached agreement with one another about what they did and whether they did it for good or evil purposes.[35] The mode of social integration in every government office, every company, and every university was difference, not homogeneity. In all those social realms, there were subgroups that differentiated themselves from the rest. This always destroys the cohesion of the social aggregate. Difference lays the foundation for the aggregate.

The Nazi regime ended freedom of the press, censored criticism, and created a highly conformist public sphere with the help of extremely modern, mass media propaganda. This, of course, did not leave individual Germans untouched. Yet it would be a mistake to assume that differences of opinion and discussion were completely eradicated. To quote historian Peter Longerich:

> From more than two decades of research on the social history and changes in mentality of the Nazi dictatorship, we know the populace of the German Empire between 1933 and 1945 did not exist in a condition of totalitarian uniformity. On the contrary, there was a significant amount of dissatisfaction, non-conformist opinion and varied behavior. What is, however, especially characteristic of German society under Nazism was that expressions of such resistance took place above all in the private sphere and at most in a kind of semi-public sphere that included circles of friends and colleagues, people who regularly met in bars and immediate neighbors. Such encounters happened within existing structures in traditional social milieus that had been able to preserve themselves in the face of the Nazi racist community: in church parishes, the relations between neighbors in villages, elite conservative and bourgeois social circles, and those parts of the socialist community that had not been destroyed.[36]

While much of daily life remained the same in Nazi Germany and formed the surface upon which society functioned, there were also drastic political and social changes. The split of society the Nazis brought about in the twelve years from 1933 to 1945 between a majority of members and an excluded minority was not only a goal justified by the Nazis' racist theory and desire for power. It was also a means to realize a particular form of social integration. A number of recent historical works have looked at the history of the Third Reich through the lens of social differentiation. Saul Friedländer has especially focused attention on anti-Jewish practice, repression, and elimination;[37] Michael Wildt has stressed the coercive force used in the early days of the Third Reich as a means of collectivization.[38] Longerich has shown that the social exclusion and then extermination of Jews was by no means an accidental, strangely senseless element of Nazi politics, but their very core. The "de-Jewification" of Germany and broad stretches of Europe was, in Longerich's words, "the instrument for gradually penetrating the various realms of individual existence."[39] This penetration allowed moral standards to be reformatted, bringing about an obvious change in what people considered normal and deviant, good and bad, appropriate and outrageous. Nazi society was by no means amoral. Even the many instances of mass murder cannot be reduced to a collective ethical dissipation. On the contrary, they were the result of the astonishingly quick and deep establishment of a "National Socialist morality" that made the biologically defined *Volk* and the community it entailed the sole criterion for moral behavior and promoted different values and norms than those obtained, for instance, in post–World War II Germany.[40] Included in the Nazi moral canon were the ideas that people were fundamentally unequal, that the worth of the *Volk* outweighed that of the individual, and that what counted was particular and not universal solidarity. To cite just one instance of Nazi morality: it was under Hitler that failure to offer assistance in an emergency became a punishable crime in Germany. Yet that dictate applied only to the Nazi *Volk* community and could not be extended to people's refusal to help Jews.[41] This sort of particular morality was characteristic of the Nazi project in toto. The new European order and, indeed, global domination of which the Nazis dreamed were conceived as a radically inequitable world, in which members of different races would be treated differently under the law.

Nazi social practice enacted the idea that people were radically and irreconcilably unequal. It made the public aware of the "Jewish question" as something negative and the "*Volk* community" as something positive. These topics were then made a permanent focus of action in anti-Jewish measures, regulations, and laws, in instances of disappropriation, deportation, and worse. As a formula for how Nazi society was formed, Friedländer came up with the phrase "repression and innovation." But given that a lot of German society did not change, we need to remember that for most non-Jewish Germans Nazi innovation and repression was but a secondary part of their everyday lives. For them, Nazism was a mix of *continuity,* repression, and innovation.

As a whole, the Nazi project has to be seen as a highly integrative social process beginning in January 1933 and ending with Germany's ultimate defeat in May 1945. "Destiny," as historian Raul Hilberg once dryly remarked, is an "interaction between perpetrators and victims." Psychologically speaking, it is no great wonder that the practical enactment of theories of the master race was a matter of such

consensus. Once the theory was cast in laws and regulations, even the
lowest unskilled laborer could feel superior to a Jewish writer, actor,
or businessman, especially since the ongoing social transformation
entailed Jews' actual social and material decline. The resulting boost
to the self-esteem of members of the *Volk* was reinforced by a reduced
sense of social anxiety. It was a new and unfamiliar feeling to belong,
inalienably and by law, to an exclusive racial elite, of which others,
equally inalienably, could never become part.

As things got worse and worse for some, the others felt better and
better. The National Socialist project did not just promise a gloriously
envisioned future. It also offered concrete advantages in the present
such as better career opportunities in all areas, including the Wehrmacht. The elites at the head of the Nazi Party were extremely young,
and a good many younger members of the *Volk* saw their own heady
personal hopes as connected with the triumph of the "Aryan race."[42]
This backdrop helps us understand the enormous individual and collective energy that was released in Nazi society. "The National Socialist German Workers Party was founded on a doctrine of inequality
between races, but it also promised Germans greater equality among
themselves," writes historian Götz Aly.

> Nazi ideology conceived of racial conflict as an antidote to class
> conflict. By framing its program in this way, the party was propa-
> gating two age-old dreams of the German people: national and
> class unity. That was key to the Nazis' popularity, from which they
> derived the power they needed to pursue their criminal aims. . . .
> In one of his central pronouncements, Hitler promised "the cre-
> ation of a socially just state," a model society that would "con-
> tinue to eradicate all [social] barriers."[43]

If Hitler's ideology had been pure propaganda, the Third Reich
would never have undergone the extremely rapid social change it did.
The central characteristic of the National Socialist project consisted of
the immediate practical realization of its ideological postulates. The
world indeed changed. Propagandistic newspaper articles notwithstanding, the feeling of better days dawning, of living in a "great age"
and "permanently extraordinary situation" established a new frame of
reference. Interviews with people who experienced the Third Reich
reveal even today how psychologically attractive and emotionally

integrative the Nazi initiatives of exclusion and integration were. It is no accident that Germans of that generation tend to describe the Third Reich, up until Germany's military defeat at Stalingrad, as a "great time."[44] Such people were categorically incapable of experiencing the exclusion, persecution, and dispossession of others for what they were. By definition, the others no longer belonged to the community, and thus their inhumane treatment did not conflict with the ethics and social values of the *Volk* community.

In terms of social psychology, the reasons behind support for and trust in the Nazi system are no great mystery. The economic upswing commencing in 1934 may have been financed by state debt and larceny, but as interviews with those who lived at the time reveal, it created a mood of optimism and confidence.[45] In addition, the period saw a number of social innovations with profound implications for individuals' happiness. In 1938, for instance, a third of all German workers enjoyed the benefits of the Nazis' state-subsidized "Strength Through Joy" vacation program—and that at a time when traveling abroad was still considered an exclusive privilege of the wealthy. "It has long been overlooked," writes Hans-Dieter Schäfer, "that upward social mobility during the Third Reich was by no means solely symbolic. . . . People were twice as likely to move up in society in the six peace-time years under Hitler as they had been in the final six years of the Weimar Republic. Nazi state organizations and quasi-private associations absorbed one million people from the working classes."[46] By 1938, Germany no longer suffered from the mass unemployment of the Depression. In 1939, 200,000 foreign workers had to be brought in to cover a shortage of labor.[47] In other words: things were palpably better for members of the *Volk* under National Socialism, and the Nazis' demonstrable success in keeping their social promises engendered a deep faith in the system, especially as it came after the profound economic disappointments of the Weimar Republic.

The material, psychological, and social integration of the majority, together with the simultaneous deintegration of those excluded from the *Volk,* fundamentally changed social values. In 1933, the majority of German citizens would not have been able to conceive that a few years later, with greater or lesser participation by the majority, German Jews would be stripped of their rights and worldly possessions, and then deported to extermination camps. We can sense the enormity of the change in social values, if we imagine what would have happened if the deportations had commenced in February 1933, immediately after Hitler assumed power. The deviation from the accepted norms of the majority would have been too severe to proceed smoothly. Indeed, Nazi ideologues had yet to even formulate the sequence: exclusion—loss of rights—disappropriation—deportation—extermination. In 1933, this sequence may well have been unthinkable. Yet eight years later, such inhuman treatment of others had become part of what ordinary Germans expected, and thus few found it exceptional. People collectively—each in his own individual, more or less committed, skeptical, or disinterested way—produced a common social reality.

Changes in social practice were a major driving force. There were no public protests against the Nazis' anti-Jewish policies, nor was there significant popular complaint at the concrete discrimination suffered by German Jews. This does not mean that most Germans approved of anti-Semitic repression, but Germans' passivity, their toleration of repression, and their restriction of criticism to the private realm of their peers translated politically initiated discrimination into everyday social practice. It would overestimate ideology and play down the practical participation of ordinary community members if we were to reduce the changes in the mentality structure within Nazi society to the propagandistic, legislative, and executive acts of the regime. The active interworking of political initiative, private adaptation, and practical realization was what allowed the National Socialist project to engender such surprisingly rapid consensus. The Third Reich could be called a participatory dictatorship, in which members of the *Volk* community cheerfully did their bit, even if they weren't committed Nazis.

This sketch of the Nazification of German society may suffice to explain Germans' growing sense of satisfaction with the system in the years before 1941. Other sources of popular approval were the Nazis' foreign policy "triumphs" and the "miracle economic recovery," which, though built on sand, made members of the *Volk* feel as though they were living in a society that had a lot to offer. It was within this frame of reference, the Third Reich, that German soldiers heading to war ordered their perceptions, interpretations, and conclusions. This was the backdrop against which they understood the purpose of World War II, categorized their enemies, and evaluated victories and defeats. Those soldiers' experiences of war would go on to modify this frame of reference. As the conflict dragged on, and the prospects of ultimate victory receded, soldiers' faith in what Hans Mommsen called "the realization of the utopian" diminished. But it did not automatically invalidate fundamental ideas about human inequality, the demands of blood, and the superiority of the Aryan race. Even less so did it call into question the third-order military frame of reference. And that will be the topic of the following section.

FRAME OF REFERENCE: WAR

The transformation of the 100,000-man German army of 1933 into the 2.6-million-strong Wehrmacht force that attacked Poland in 1939 was not just an act of material armament. It was accompanied by the consolidation of a frame of reference in which the military acquired positive connotations typical of Germany and the time. The political and military leadership placed great emphasis on anchoring military values within the general populace, making the *Volk* fit for battle, and forming a unified and willing "community of destiny." Working together, these leaders succeeded in militarizing German society to a high degree.[48] Nazi party organizations like the Hitler Youth, the SA, and the SS, along with initiatives like the Imperial Labor Service (*Reichsarbeitsdienst*) and the reintroduction of universal conscription in 1935 increased the fighting capacity of the German people to unprecedented levels. The German populace may not have celebrated the start of World War II in September 1939 with the same euphoria that they had World War I in 1914. In fact, the mood was largely somber. But 17 million German men let themselves be drafted without protest into the Wehrmacht during the course of World War II. Without them Germany would not have been able to fight on until 1945. The success with which German society was militarized was less about getting all German men to support the war than about producing a framework within which they shared or at least did not question military value systems. This cannot be explained only with reference to the massive propaganda efforts of the Nazi and Wehrmacht leadership. On the contrary, the Nazis were able to build upon a radicalization of the military sphere that had taken place in decades before the Third Reich.

The Prussian-led wars from 1864 to 1871 that created the unified German nation had rooted military values deep within German society, and even many of those critical of the state shared them.[49] In

World War I, social models of violence and inequality spread, and the value attributed to qualities like bravery, daring, obedience, and sense of duty increased. Among German military officers, the ideal of the heroic death, epitomized by the soldier willing to defend his position to the last bullet, experienced a new renaissance.[50] This was a general European development, not a particular German phenomenon. The myth of Leonidas at the Battle of Thermopylae and the trope of fighting to the last bullet were also very influential in Britain and France.[51]

During the Weimar Republic, significant parts of German society propagated the idea of national defense and a state willing to take to battle as an alternative to the Treaty of Versailles and the perceived impotence of German democracy.[52] Germany was to mentally prepare for wars to come by encouraging courage, enthusiasm, and willingness for sacrifice.[53] The literary apostles of "soldierly nationalism," men like Ernst Jünger, Edwin Dwinger, or Ernst von Salomon, spread a metaphysical, abstract cult of war among hundreds of thousands of readers, and they were supported in their efforts by a host of right-wing, nationalistic organizations, including the Stahlhelm (Steel Helmet) association. By the end of the 1920s, war memorials that concentrated on representing grief for soldiers killed in battle had given way to monuments creating a mystique of brave fighters on the front lines.[54] Tributes to battles Germany had won during World War I and the wars of German unification became omnipresent. Voices of protest against this romanticizing of the military past and pacifist objectors to the army had increasing difficulty making themselves heard.

The German army, then still known as the Reichswehr, profited from this trend, and their demands could count on a broad echo in society as a whole. By 1933, the groundwork had already been laid for German society to be completely penetrated by the idea of Germany's acute need to defend itself. On May 25, 1934, the president of the German Reich, Paul von Hindenburg, and his war minister, Werner von Blomberg, drew up a list of duties for German soldiers. This document located the roots of the Wehrmacht in a glorious past and defined military honor as an unconditional willingness on the part of soldiers to make sacrifices, including their own lives, for their people and homeland. Fighting courage was identified as the greatest virtue a soldier could possess. The list demanded steely determination, decisiveness, and vigor, while cowardice was dismissed as contemptible, and hesitation unworthy of a soldier. Military leadership entailed an eagerness to make decisions, measured ability, and tireless care for one's charges. Military leaders and troops, the document asserted, had to become an unshakable fighting community of comrades, and in his willingness to carry out his duties the soldier was to serve as a role model of masculine strength for the German people.[55]

This catalogue of duties showed that, while the Wehrmacht of the early 1930s positioned itself as a part of German military tradition, it was adopting new accents. The emphasis on "unconditional willingness to sacrifice" and "steely determination" shows how battle was defined as the central element of soldiers' existence. In keeping with the myths of incredible German courage on the front lines during World War I, living up to the demands of battle was the ultimate litmus test of a soldier's worth, to which all other considerations were subordinate.[56] This catalogue of military virtues did not change substantially during World War II.

Admittedly, a paper published by the highest echelons of the military leadership is not necessarily proof that soldiers adopted a specific military value system into their frame of reference, but personnel files often suggest that was indeed the case. Superiors regularly evaluated every German officer, and the categories the evaluations contained included personality, strength in the face of the enemy, achievements while carrying out duties, and mental and physical abilities. A glance at this nearly endless and often ignored source reveals that the training desired by Germany's military leadership had taken root at least in the reference frame of the corps of officers. In the files, a personality of "high military quality" was defined as being energetic and "strong-willed," "brave and demanding of itself," "physically adroit, tough and with great endurance." Courage, energy, toughness, willingness to act, and decisiveness were needed, if the officers wanted to receive a positive evaluation and position themselves for promotion. It was also important for officers to show that they were "crisis-proof." For instance, a superior wrote of the future lieutenant general Erwin Menny: "He knows no difficulties." Likewise General Heinrich Eberbach was repeatedly praised in the course of his career as a "brisk and prudential tank commander equal to the most difficult situations. . . . He's one of our best." Enumerating his particularly positive traits, a superior characterized Eberbach as "brave, loyal, steadfast."[57]

Negative attributes for soldiers were softness, "lack of energy,"[58] lack of "resilience,"[59] and insufficient "hardness of will and ability to withstand crises."[60] For instance, in 1944 a superior wrote of Major General Albin Nake, the commander of the 158th Reserve Division: "A typically East Prussian commander, who does not possess the severity and decisiveness to lead a division in the most difficult situations."[61] General Otto Elfeldt was criticized for allowing "his sub-commanders too much independence of opinion." [62] A superior wrote of Major General Alexander von Pfuhlstein: "Pfuhlstein is a pessimist. Probably a congenital one. He lacks the conviction of belief in the National Socialist idea. For this reason, he tends to forgive obvious failure in his troops." [63] After this damning report, Pfuhlstein was relieved of his division command. Colonel Walther Korfes, the commander of Grenadier Regiment 726, even became the subject of an investigation as to whether he had been honorably captured or not by British forces. Previously, he had been classified as a "fundamental skeptic and critic."[64]

The evaluations contained within the personnel files of Wehrmacht officers also suggest that the ideological changes brought by National Socialism to the military value system were limited. Significantly the words "sacrifice" and "fanaticism" do not occur in army files. (The ones from the navy were largely destroyed.) Only SS files contain this sort of vocabulary. For instance, an evaluation of SS Lieutenant Colonel Kurt Mayer of April 29, 1943, reports that his "massive success . . . is the result solely of his fanatical willingness to do battle and his circumspect leadership."[65] Willingness to sacrifice and fanaticism were two unquestionable indications of an increasingly ideological system of values. The ideal of the "political soldier," ceaselessly promoted by Nazi propaganda, was not only a courageous but a fanatic fighter, willing to sacrifice himself. These terms repeatedly crop up in conjunction with soldiers who were committed National Socialists. One of the most prominent was Admiral Karl Dönitz. When he assumed command of the German navy on January 30, 1943, he declared that he planned to lead with "ruthless decisiveness, fanatic commitment and the most iron will to victory."[66] In countless commands, he demanded the same commitment from his troops. And Dönitz was hardly alone. Fanaticism became an omnipresent category in the official correspondence of the military leadership in the second half of World War II.

Nonetheless, it is surprising that "National Socialist attitudes," which were introduced as an official category in the fall of 1942, did not play a particularly important role in the evaluation of officers.

In much of the army, common sense seems to have dictated that this political category should not be a decisive criterion. The formulae "National Socialist" and "firmly grounded in National Socialism" were used in inflationary fashion. In June 1943 director of military personnel Lieutenant General Rudolf Schmundt even complained that the terms were thrown about so cavalierly that "they can hardly yield any sort of evaluation."[67] A glance at the files confirms that firm National Socialist beliefs were attributed even to officers with demonstrable skepticism toward the Nazi system. More reliable conclusions about political attitudes could only be made when the evaluations used stronger language, for example, "a solidly rooted National Socialist who orients his duties as a soldier accordingly" (evaluation of Colonel Ludwig Heilmann).[68]

In practice, political orientation never accrued the sort of significance Hitler would have wished for the formation of a "new" Nazi type of soldier. Calls for a fundamental Nazi orientation of troops and the merging of political and military values became a mantra of the Nazi leadership, especially as the war was approaching its end. Nazi propaganda, of course, consistently featured the image of the heroic National Socialist warrior. "Here the deployed German soldier goes beyond his limits," one German newspaper wrote in a report from the front lines on January 16, 1942, "fighting in the way the Führer has commanded: with fanatic commitment and down to the very last man."[69] The longer the war dragged on, the more propagandists called upon the conflation of politics and fighting: "Unlike all preceding generations, the German soldier today unites the military with the political."[70]

Nonetheless, official Wehrmacht reports were written in a different tone. As late as 1944, soldiers' performance was still being described in the terms laid out in 1934. Authors emphasized "especial bravery," "steadfastness," "toughness worthy of emulation," "bold activism," "unshakable fighting spirit," "brash attacks," "gutsy close combat," and "tenacious persistence in almost hopeless situations."[71] Although Hitler's instructions on how to wage war were full of formulations like "fanatic will to victory," "sacred hatred" for the enemy, and "pitiless battle,"[72] Wehrmacht correspondence rarely reflected that language. It appears there were limits to the extent to which the military frame of reference was "national socialized."

The German military canon's orientation around classical martial virtues also clearly emerges in the culture of military medals, which both continued lines of tradition and also broke new ground where commendations for bravery were concerned. In the Third Reich, unlike in Wilhelmine Germany, officers and everyday soldiers were supposed to meld into a single fighting community. This idea was underscored by the fact that all soldiers were eligible for the same medals and commendations, regardless of rank. In World War I, the highest medal in the Prussian military, the Pour le Mérite, was reserved for the officer corps and awarded almost exclusively to high-ranking commanders: among 533 recipients, there were only 11 company chiefs and 2 patrol leaders, among them a young lieutenant named Ernst Jünger.[73] In recommissioning the Iron Cross on September 1, 1939, Hitler consciously followed the tradition of the most important Prussian commendation for bravery, which had been commissioned in the wars of 1813, 1870, and 1914. Soldiers were allowed to wear the medal on their uniforms—Hitler himself wore the Iron Cross he had been given in World War I—and a special clasp was designed for soldiers who had received the distinction in both world wars. But the new Iron Cross was an accolade handed out by the Reich, and not by Prussia. In keeping with tradition, there were Iron Crosses of various classes (Second and First Class, Knight's Cross, Grand Cross), with the intermediate Knight's Cross being introduced as an equivalent to the Prussian Pour le Mérite, which was not recommissioned.[74]

As much as the Nazi regime and parts of the Wehrmacht leadership spoke of fanaticism and willingness to sacrifice in their official correspondence, the way in which medals were awarded rarely conformed to that ideal. In contrast to the highest British military medal, the Victoria Cross,[75] the Knight's Cross was handed out posthumously in approximately 7 percent of cases only. Bearers of the Knight's Cross were not those who had fanatically sacrificed their own lives by throwing themselves in front of tanks. More often, they were soldiers and troop leaders who could boast clearly defined success. The Knight's Cross was a reward for special performance and not a National Socialist encouragement to make the ultimate sacrifice. Hitler only ever involved himself in the awarding of the highest medals. Division and squadron commanders handed out other accolades. Awards commending the political spirit of a soldier remained very rare.

The Third Reich complemented this complexly calibrated system of awards for bravery with a variety of distinctions, unique to Germany, designating function in battle. The navy had badges for U-boats, E-boats (speedboats), destroyers, the High Seas Fleet, armed merchant cruisers, blockade runners, minesweepers, small battle units, and naval artillery. The same was true for the Luftwaffe, which came up with clasps to show how many air raid missions crew members had flown. The German army created a special Infantry Assault, General Assault, Tank Battle, Antiaircraft, and Tank Destruction badges. The most prestigious of these were doubtlessly the Close-Combat Clasp, commissioned in November 1942, which was given "as a visible acknowledgment to those soldiers who had engaged in hand-to-hand combat." Soldiers who had absolved fifty days of such fighting, where one could see "the whites of the enemy's eyes," were given the Gold Close-Combat Clasp. It was considered the highest decoration in the infantry. But the chance of staying alive long enough to receive one was slim. Only 619 awards were recorded, beginning in late summer 1944, an occasion celebrated by Nazi propaganda.[76]

Policies concerning accolades in the Third Reich primarily rewarded frontline soldiers. Historian Christoph Rass has calculated that within the 253rd Infantry Division 96.3 percent of all Iron Crosses were awarded to combat units.[77] Noncombat soldiers were only eligible for the far less prestigious War Merit Cross. The result was a gap in status since men who didn't directly face the enemy had few chances of receiving an accolade, while their comrades on the front line, assuming they could stay alive, could rack up medal upon medal.

Massive numbers, some 2.3 million, of Iron Crosses Second Class, were handed out, but more than 85 percent of members of the Wehrmacht did not receive even the lowest commendation for bravery. Their uniforms remained bare, while the military biographies of seasoned frontline fighters were on display for all the world to see. That brought social prestige and created intentional social pressure. German men knew that they could only prove themselves at the front. As a result, soldiers on home leave often illicitly donned medals to impress their friends and families and to avoid looking like shirkers.[78] Nonetheless, by rewarding the most dangerous wartime deployments, accolades played an important practical role as an incentive in the Third Reich.

The Wehrmacht was careful to protect the prestige of their accolades by clearly defining when they should be awarded and introducing rules to ensure that they reflected true achievement and service.

*First Lieutenant Alfons Bialetzki wearing the Iron Cross First and
Second Class, the Gold Medal for War Wounded, the Parachutist
and Infantry Assault Badge, the Gold Close-Combat Clasp, the
German Cross (Gold Class), and the Knight's Cross. On his upper
right arm he wears two individual antitank identifications and
a Crete armband. (From Florian Berger,* Ritterkreuzträger mit
Nahkampfspange in Gold, *Vienna, 2004)*

With the massive number of Iron Crosses handed out, it was hardly
possible to prevent abuse, yet the transparency of the accolade system
during World War II still made it much more widely accepted than
the system in place in World War I. The Wehrmacht also did its best
to commend soldiers as quickly as possible. Dönitz was not averse
to awarding Knight's Crosses over the radio if a submarine captain
reported achieving a particularly significant victory. Nazi propaganda
constantly featured the bearers of awards for extraordinary bravery,
and Goebbels made a handful of them into full-fledged media stars.[79]
Significantly, in designing such medals, the military downplayed the
swastika symbol. The exception was the German Cross (Gold Class),
which led conservatives, in the words of one commentary, "to feel
less than enthusiastic . . . about the presumptuous National Socialist
emblem."[80]

The symbolism of and policies with which awards were bestowed were designed to create a sense of social acknowledgment, and this anchored military values deep within soldiers' frames of reference. As we will see, the normative models that resulted influenced how German men perceived the world and, in the majority of cases, how they acted as well. But those models didn't necessarily transfer to Nazi ideology; indeed, emphasis on ideology seems to have engendered resistance. As historian Ralph Winkle determined in conjunction with World War I, only in a minority of cases did individual pride at receiving an accolade lead to an acceptance of the political leadership's concurrent and comprehensive expectations concerning individual behavior.[81]

Against the backdrop of a social culture of categorical inequality and a Wehrmacht culture emphasizing the military values of hardness and bravery, we can reconstruct the contours of the typical soldier's frame of reference as he went to war. Significantly, the central values of this orientation remained stable throughout the war, even as soldiers' appraisals of the military leadership and the National Socialist system changed markedly. The military reference frame also obtained across individual differences of politics, "philosophy," and character. In terms of their high estimation of the military values just sketched out, out-and-out National Socialists did not differ from committed anti-Nazis, which is why the two groups didn't behave differently during the war itself. The main differences, as we will discuss later, occurred chiefly between Wehrmacht soldiers and the Waffen SS.

Fighting, Killing, and Dying

"Throwing bombs has become a passion with me. One itches for
it; it is a lovely feeling. It is as lovely as shooting someone down."
A Luftwaffe first lieutenant, July 17, 1940[82]

They say that war brutalizes, that soldiers are turned into beasts by
the experience of violence, by being confronted with mutilated bodies and dead comrades or, in the case of a campaign of annihilation,
with masses of murdered men, women, and children. Even the Wehrmacht and the SS were concerned that constant exposure to extreme
violence, be it as witnesses or perpetrators, would damage soldiers'
"manly discipline" and lead them to engage in unconstrained, unregulated brutality—at the cost of the efficiency needed for both World
War II and mass exterminations.[83] The idea of war brutalizing soldiers
plays a central role in social-psychological research on violence.[84]
Scholars assume that extremely violent experiences change the way
people evaluate their worlds and make them more prone to violent
acts of their own. Autobiographies and war fiction reinforce the
impression that over time, soldiers become brutal as they themselves
are exposed to increasing brutality.

But the words of the Luftwaffe first lieutenant cited above suggest that this notion may be misleading. The brutalization hypothesis
excludes the possibility that violent behavior can be something attractive for which one "itches," and it presumes, with no real proof, that
people need to be somehow pre-trained to commit acts of extreme
violence. Perhaps all that is needed is a weapon or an airplane, some
adrenaline, the feeling of having power in areas where one normally
has none, and a social framework in which killing is permissible, even
desirable.

The hypothesis of successive adjustment to and acceptance of violence may have more to do with self-images that historical actors

would like to maintain and the preconceived ideas of researchers than with the realities of war. The surveillance protocols contain an abundance of material suggesting that soldiers were extremely prone to violence right from the start of World War II. The quote introducing this chapter, for instance, was recorded early on in the war, at a point when the conflict had not become an all-or-nothing struggle for survival. Moreover, the first lieutenant in question had only experienced war from above, from the air. Thus, while many soldiers may recount a process of brutalization when they recall violent events, by their own admission the time in which they are socialized to accept extreme violence often spans no more than a few days.

Let us take the example of a conversation between Lieutenant Meyer,* a Luftwaffe pilot, and Lieutenant Pohl, a Luftwaffe observer, from April 30, 1940:

> POHL: On the second day of the Polish war I had to drop bombs on a station at POSEN. Eight of the 16 bombs fell on the town, among the houses, I did not like that. On the third day I did not care a hoot, and on the fourth day I was enjoying it. It was our before-breakfast amusement to chase single soldiers over the fields with M.G. [machine gun] fire and to leave them lying there with a few bullets in the back.
>
> MEYER: But always against soldiers?
>
> POHL: People (civilians) too. We attacked the columns in the streets. I was in the "Kette" (flight of 3 aircraft). The leader bombed the street, the two supporting machines the ditches, because there are always ditches there. The machines rock, one behind the other, and now we swerved to the left with all machine guns firing like mad. You should have seen the horses stampede!
>
> MEYER: Disgusting, that with the horses . . .
>
> POHL: I was sorry for the horses, but not at all for the people. But I was sorry for the horses up to the last day.[85]

In Pohl's own account it only took him three days to get used to the violence he began exercising as part of the German campaign in Poland.

---

* Asterisks indicate a pseudonym for a POW not explicitly named in the surveillance protocols.

Already on day four of his mission, feelings of desire predominated, as he illustrates with the phrase "before-breakfast amusement." His conversation partner, apparently somewhat taken aback, articulates the hope that those killed were enemy soldiers exclusively, but this hope is quickly dashed. Pohl says he shot at "people," i.e., civilians: in retrospect, the only thing he can't accept is that horses were hit as well. Meyer seems to sympathize with that.

Pohl then continues his narrative by telling how he bombarded an entire city:

> POHL: I was so annoyed when we were shot down; just before the second engine got hot, I suddenly had a Polish town beneath me. I dropped the bombs on to it. I wanted to drop all the 32 bombs on the town. It was no longer possible; but 4 bombs dropped in the town. Down there everything was shot to pieces. On that occasion I was in such a rage . . . one must imagine what it means to drop 32 bombs into an open town. On that occasion I would not have cared a damn. With 32 bombs I would certainly have had 100 human lives on my conscience.
>
> MEYER: Was there plenty of traffic down there?
>
> POHL: Chockablock. I wanted to drop a batch, because the whole place was full of people. I wouldn't have cared. I wanted to drop them at intervals of 20 metres. I wanted to cover 600 metres. It would have been great fun if it had come off.

Pohl seems most concerned about inflicting maximum damage before his plane crashed and indeed, as he himself stresses, taking as many lives as possible. He takes aim where the town is "chockablock," and he's unmistakably irritated at not having achieved the desired results.

Meyer's next question is one of professional curiosity:

> MEYER: How do people react when they are fired at from a plane?
>
> POHL: They go mad. Most of them lay down with their hands up, making the German sign. (Imitating rattle of M.G.): That laid them out. It was really bestial.
>
> On to their faces—they all got the bullets in the back and ran zigzag in all directions like mad. Three rounds of incendiary bullets, when they had that in their backs, hands up—bang—then they lay on their faces. Then I went on firing.

"This is what a Polish city looks like from the nose gunner's position of a warplane." Propaganda photograph from an He 111, September 1939. (Photographer: Roman Stempka; BA 183-S52911)

MEYER: What happens if one lies down at once?

POHL: You get hit all the same. We attacked from 10 metres, and when the idiots ran I had a good target. I had only just to hold my machine-gun. I am sure some of them got a full 22 bullets in them. And then suddenly I scared 50 soldiers and said: "Fire, boys, fire!" and then we just sprinkled them with the M.G.'s. In spite of that I felt the urge, before we were shot down, to shoot a man with my own hand.

In this conversation, one of the parties clearly feels the need to communicate something about himself, while the other tries to analyze whom he's talking to and what the conversation is really about. We don't know how often Meyer spoke with Pohl or whether he knew him well. But he seems somewhat revolted at his cell mate's statement that he'd have liked to have directly shot and killed another human being. He comments:

MEYER: One becomes dreadfully brutal in such undertakings.

POHL: Yes, I've already said that on the first day it seemed ter-

rible to me, but I said to myself: "Hell! orders are orders." On
the second and third days I felt it didn't matter a hoot, and on
the fourth day I enjoyed it. But, as I said, the horses screamed.
I hardly heard the plane, so loud did they scream. One of them
lay there with its hind legs torn off.

At this point in the protocol, there is an interruption, and then Pohl
expounds on the advantages of machine-gun-equipped warplanes.
Because the planes are highly mobile, one can hunt down victims
instead of waiting for them to come into range:

> POHL: A plane with machine-guns is really fine. If you have a
> machine-gun posted anywhere, then you have to wait for the
> people to come along. A 57.
> MEYER: Didn't they defend themselves from the ground? Didn't
> they use A.A. machine guns?
> POHL: They shot down one. With rifles. A whole company fired
> at the word of command. That was the "Do 17." It landed; the
> Germans kept the soldiers at bay with machine guns and set
> fire to the machine.
>   Sometimes I had 228 bombs, including 10 kg bombs. We
> threw them into the midst of the people. And the soldiers. And
> incendiary bombs in addition.

Meyer's questions and comments tend to be technical in nature,
although he does react with emotional dismay on two occasions: when
Pohl tells of killing horses and when he confesses his desire to kill
someone "with his own hands." If Pohl's own account is believed,
he didn't need an adjustment period to get used to violence. He was
apparently able to call up violent impulses almost immediately, with
little prelude. Strikingly, Pohl does not describe having gotten accustomed to violence. Instead, he repeatedly expresses regret for having
perpetrated too *little* violence and a desire for *more* victims.

This conversation was recorded in the summer of 1940; the events
that are its subject happened in September 1939, directly after the
start of World War II. Even if we were to assume that Pohl had had
months of combat experience before his exchange with Meyer, and
that the experience may have brutalized his stories about his first days
of war ex post facto, he was still taken out of the war long before the

drastic escalation of violence that came with Germany's invasion of the Soviet Union. It is beyond doubt that German soldiers committed crimes against humanity in their campaign against Poland, including the murder of civilians and the execution of Jews.[86] But Pohl was in the air force. He hunts down and kills people from the skies, and he does not give the impression of being ideologically motivated when he describes bombarding cities and gunning down people. His victims have no personal attributes by which he selects them. He doesn't care which targets he hits, only *that* he hits targets. He enjoys killing and needs no other motivation. His behavior is not aimed at advancing a larger cause or purpose, but merely at achieving the best results possible. The senseless killing resembles a hunt, a sporting activity in which the only purpose is to be better than others, in this case, by hitting more people with bullets. That's what most angers Pohl about getting shot down. It spoiled the end result of the hunt.

AUTOTELIC VIOLENCE

In the earliest phase of World War II, without having been brutalized himself by previous events, Pohl perpetrated a kind of violence that could hardly have been more brutal. Pohl's individual motivations notwithstanding, such senseless hunting down and killing of people is a perfect example of what German sociologist Jan Philipp Reemtsma called "autotelic violence"—violence committed for its own sake without any larger purpose.[87] Reemtsma distinguished this type of physical violence from attempts to eradicate people because they represent an obstacle to a source of personal gain. Those are practical, instrumental motivations which, moral scruples notwithstanding, are easily comprehensible. Autotelic violence, on the other hand, challenges our powers of comprehension since it radically contradicts the civilized self-image maintained by modern societies and their members. It undermines our faith in the stability of our institutions and rules and, above all, in the state's monopoly on the legitimate exercise of force. "Faith in the modern age," writes Reemtsma, "is unthinkable without the state monopoly on force." The truth of this statement becomes self-evident when we imagine the carnage that would ensue if the protections offered by modern rule of law were suspended even for a single day.

Such faith is the basis for what modern individuals like to believe is their own distance from violence. Violence is considered the exception to the rule, and when it does occur, we seek explanations, even in cases where no instrumental motivations are apparent. By contrast, those who do not assume they will be physically protected constantly reckon with the possibility of violence and are not shocked when it occurs. Faith and violence exist in a precarious equilibrium. In our world, "senseless," "unmotivated," or "raw" violence has to be immediately characterized as "insanity," "rupture," and "barbarism"—i.e., the antithesis of modernity. For this reason, sociological and historical research on violence is accompanied by subjective moralism and often encounters serious difficulties.[88]

From a broader historical perspective, the modern age is the first time in which violence has been considered the antithesis of civilization, something to be suppressed and battled against. Violence, in and of itself, must be contained. Instrumental violence cannot, of course, be entirely prevented, but we can justify or at least explain it. We consider the use of violence to solve problems normal, whereas using violence for its own sake is pathological. Violence is a sign of someone straying from the path of modernity, indeed heading in the opposite direction. Nonetheless, as our most recent wars illustrate,[89] violence is in no danger of extinction. Paradoxically, we can only maintain our faith in modernity if violence is not considered part of the normal daily functioning of modern society. For that reason, we see ourselves as nonviolent, and ostentatiously demonstrate our shock when an act of violence is committed and immediately begin searching for explanations.

The sort of autotelic violence committed by Lieutenant Pohl, however, needs no motivation. It is a reason unto itself. Within a universe of purpose-driven rationality and the universal imperative to justify social behavior, autotelic violence is an erratic exception, unlike everything else in the social realm. But this view may be irrational. Do we feel the need, for instance, to account for the human sex drive? Do we try to explain why human beings eat, drink, and breathe? In all these core areas of human existence, questions may arise as to how people try to satisfy their needs. But we never question the fact that human beings want to eat, drink, breathe, and have sex. Inquiries in those areas focus on mode, not motivation, and perhaps it would be better to do the same when confronting violence. Violence, as German sociologist Heinrich Popitz proposed, is always an option in social behavior, and in phylogenetic terms, this could hardly be otherwise. Ultimately, the human race did not survive thanks to its peaceful demeanor, but because of the violence it committed when hunting or fending off competition for food.

The state's monopoly on the legitimate use of force in Western societies may arguably be the single greatest civilizing innovation in human history, creating previously unknown levels of personal security and freedom. But that doesn't mean that violence has ceased to be a social option. In being transferred to the state, violence changed form, but did not disappear. On the contrary, violence can be converted back to its direct form at any time. Moreover, the state monopolization on force may regulate the central realm of society, namely, all matters of public concern, but by no means does it cause violence to disappear from other segments of society.

In the domestic realm, people continue to use violence against their partners, children, and pets, and violence occurs frequently in relatively isolated social realms like churches and boarding schools. Fistfights and attacks are still common in public spaces like sports arenas, nightclubs, bars, and subways as well as on the street. In addition, there are regular forms of organized public violence beyond the state monopoly, for instance, at boxing or martial arts contests or performances in S&M clubs. One need only to take a drive on an ordinary highway to experience the chronic potential for violence and even homicide among perfectly normal people. It is impossible to imagine television, cinema, or computer games without violence. Indeed, as everyday reality increasingly distances itself from violence, our need for symbolic or compensatory acts of violence may even be growing. And internationally, humankind is far removed indeed from any sort of monopoly on force. States still wage war, no matter how problematic that might be for relatively pacifist societies like contemporary Germany.

In other words, violence has by no means disappeared from societies that consider themselves fundamentally nonviolent. It exists at all times as both a fact and a possibility, and as such plays a major role in human imaginations. That, too, is a kind of presence, even in situations where violence would seem to be absent. If we rewind history seven decades, back to the point when Pohl and Meyer's conversation took place, and consider how much closer to violence people were back then, we will realize that exercising and suffering from violence was something many people experienced on a daily basis. Corporal punishment and severity were the norm in the Wilhelmine educational system of the nineteenth century. Indeed, they were considered not only permissible, but essential to a child's proper upbringing.[90] The educational reforms of the early twentieth century were nothing more than a reflexive response to this phenomenon. Violence continued to feature in German educational institutions of all levels as well as in agricultural labor and trade apprenticeships.

On all levels of society, violence was much more present than it is today. Political violence was common in the Weimar Republic, which saw no shortage of brawls at political meetings, street fights between left- and right-wingers, and political assassinations. Moreover, everyday social interactions—between police and detainees, husbands and wives, teachers and pupils, and parents and children—were permeated with physical violence. After taking power, the Nazis further undermined the state monopoly on legitimate force. Para-state organizations like the SA arose alongside the actual state and operated as a kind of auxiliary police force. They exercised massive violence until the summer of 1934 without ever being called to account by the government. We have already discussed the socializing function of violence and its capacity for differentiating groups within a society, and there is no doubt that the violence perpetrated against Jews and other persecuted groups helped raise the level of violence in Nazi society and in the everyday consciousness of its members.

A pilot and low-level officer named Hagen, for example, described the situation as follows:

> HAGEN: I took part in all that business with the Jews in 1936—these poor Jews! (Laughter.) We smashed the window panes and hauled the people out. They quickly put on some clothes and (we drove them) away. We made short work of them. I hit them on the head with an iron truncheon. It was great fun. I was in the SA at that time. We used to go along the streets at night and haul them out. No time was lost, we packed them off to the station and away they went. They were out of the village and gone in a flash. They had to work in quarries but they would rather be shot than work. There was plenty of shooting, I assure you. As early as 1932, we used to stand outside the windows and shout: "Germany awake!"[91]

In 1940, violence was far more normal, expected, legitimate, and commonplace than it is today. Moreover, if we consider that significant numbers of people were part of an organization whose very purpose was violent, it is perhaps clearer why many, although not all, German soldiers did not need to get accustomed to violence. Violence was part of their frame of reference, and killing part of their duties. Why should they have seen it as something alien to their self-perception, essence, and intellect? That rhetorical question applies all the more in a case like the Luftwaffe, where violence was carried out with fascinating high-tech tools like fighter planes and strafe bombers and experienced as a highly attractive mixture of ability, technological superiority, and thrill.

The initially surprising discovery that not all German soldiers needed a phase of brutalization is supported by the empirically recorded rise in violence against the civilian population directly after Germany's invasion of Poland. Women were raped, Jews harassed, and businesses and private homes plundered, much to the consternation of the German military leadership, which issued a number of largely unsuccessful new regulations on conduct.[92] For example, on October 25, 1939, less than two months after the start of World War II, the commander in chief of the army, General Walter von Brauchitsch, threatened "all those officers who continue to disobey orders and enrich themselves" with dishonorable discharge. "The achievements and success of the Polish campaign," he wrote,

> cannot blind us to the fact that a part of our officer corps lacks a stable internal deportment. There are a considerable number of cases of officers illegally driving people from their homes, confiscating items without permission, enriching themselves by failing to report or stealing goods, mistreating or threatening their inferiors, partly in states of excitement and irresponsible drunkenness, failing to carry out orders with grave consequences for the troops under their command, and committing sexual offenses against married women. The image that results is that of a pack of marauding mercenaries who cannot be reprimanded sharply enough. Whether they are acting consciously or not, these officers are parasites who have no business in our ranks.

Despite this warning, however, Brauchitsch continued to see the need to issue further regulations aimed at maintaining "manly discipline" until the end of 1939.[93]

The same things true of society at large were also true of the army.

People differ, and what for someone like Pohl might have been a source of pleasure could be alien, if not repulsive, to someone like Meyer. Yet because both came from the same institution, the Luft-waffe, and found themselves in the same situation as prisoners of war, their social similarities outweighed their individual differences. Even if Meyer thought his comrade Pohl was a reprehensible swine, Meyer would have likely found Pohl's anecdotes suitable subject matter for later conversations, along the lines of: "I was interned together with this guy who told of how much he enjoyed hunting down human beings . . ."

ADVENTURE

German soldiers rarely used the words "death" and "kill" in their conversation. That may seem surprising since killing is one of soldiers' central duties and the production of dead enemies is a main result to be achieved. But precisely for this reason, death and killing were rarely subjects of discussion. Just as construction workers tend not to discuss bricks and mortar during their breaks, soldiers seldom talked about killing.

Killing others in battle was so commonplace that it hardly merited discussion. Moreover, except in cases like those of solo fighter pilots,[94] battle is a heteronomous undertaking that depends more on factors like group strength, equipment, the tactical situation, and the enemy than on the doings of any one individual soldier. Individual soldiers have little influence over whether they kill anyone and, if so, whom, or whether they themselves get killed. Anecdotes about that possess little amusement value and would have required soldiers to talk about emotions like fear and desperation. It was taboo, within the masculine culture of the military, to admit that one had wet one's pants, vomited in fear, or anything of the kind. Moreover, rehashing things that everyone knows and has experienced for himself (or at least claims to know and have experienced for himself) isn't good conversation. In normal civilian society, one doesn't discuss the minutiae of one's daily work routine or describe the egg one ate for breakfast. A central criterion for a good story, one worth telling and hearing, is something extraordinary, be it especially irritating or welcome, witty, horrible, or heroic.[95] People spend very little time talking about normal everyday life. Why should they? Things that were part of the normal lives of soldiers—including death, killing, and injuries—were background that was taken for granted and *seldom* discussed.

But commonplace routine was only one of the things the soldiers didn't talk about. Another was emotions, especially those of fear or threat, uncertainty, desperation, or sheer concern for one's own survival. Such topics rarely crop up in the surveillance protocols, and previous research has shown that soldiers in general filter them out of their conversations.[96] Soldiers don't like talking about death. It's too real to them. Moreover, just as they only very rarely discuss the all-too-realistic possibility of being killed or wounded themselves, death as a general phenomenon or process seldom occurs in their conversations. In soldier-speak, people are mowed or shot down, drop out of sight, or are simply gone. Obviously, if soldiers were to imagine their own deaths they would have to imagine how they died, and the phenomenon of death, which many of them had experienced often, directly in front of their own eyes, would seem very near. Thus soldiers' conversations about death and killing revolve around violence of all sorts without ever explicitly mentioning death or killing. Navy men, for instance, describe the success of their efforts in numbers of dead or tonnage of ships sunk. But they rarely speak of who or what it was that they sent to a watery grave.

Descriptions of killings like those related by Lieutenant Pohl occur frequently in the protocols with similar frankness and a likewise matter-of-fact tone, although most of them are less detailed. Apparently, soldiers did not fear that their interlocutors would react with confusion, condemnation, or protest when they told of gunning down others. We can likely put that down to the fact that the speakers under surveillance were all men with similar horizons of experience communicating in the same frame of reference. They were all members of the German military and had all waged the same war for the same reason. They didn't need to explain to one another the whys and wherefores of things that readers of the protocols seventy years later might find puzzling. In fact, the character of their conversations is much like the sorts of chats people have at parties or occasions when people with similar experiences happen to come together. They swap stories, asking questions and interjecting remarks of their own. They exaggerate and are keen to show that they all belong to the same group, the same experiential community.

The topics of conversation among soldiers may be different, but the structure of their conversations isn't. Luftwaffe members tend to tell hunting tales, not surprisingly, since many of them were fighter or bomber pilots tasked with destroying specific targets like enemy planes or ground installations. As of 1942, they were also charged with spreading general terror among civilian populations. The tales the men tell are adventure stories that focus on their own flying skill and ability to produce destructive results. Here is one typical example:

> FISCHER: Quite recently I shot down a Boston, I put the rear-gunner out of action first, he had three machine-guns, you could see him firing quite plainly, from the tracers from his machine-guns. I was in a "190" with two machine-guns. I pressed the button for a very short burst. He crumpled up—that's all, not another shot, the barrels were sticking right up. Then I put a short burst into the starboard engine, which caught fire; I then turned my cannons on to the port engine. The pilot very probably got hit at that moment—I kept my thumb on the button the whole time—it went down in flames. There were twenty-five Spitfires after me; they had followed me inland as far as ARRAS.
>
> KOCHON: Where did you land?
>
> FISCHER: On my own aerodrome. They had to turn back, as they couldn't fly so far for lack of fuel. I then returned to ST. OMER. I shot down Bristol Blenheim in a similar manner. I first fired at the side of the tail unit, and the rear-gunner kept firing past us on either side. I swerved to the right and started to fire, and he fired at me like a madman. I swerved right over to the left, and as I was doing so I pressed the button and his cupola flew off, for in pressing the machine-gun button I pressed that of the cannon too. It was knocked to bits, and he was lying dead inside. I kept firing into the tail unit and the tail broke off, with bits of the fin, and the aircraft crashed.[97]

Motorcyclists and extreme-sports enthusiasts tell structurally similar tales. In the soldiers' stories, those killed are mentioned simply by way of providing colorful detail. Victims never have personal attributes. Their role in the anecdotes of German airmen is much the same as that of enemies in video games, particularly of the ego-shooter variety, a half century later. This comparison is hardly anachronistic. In both air combat and video games, the process itself is more important than a clearly defined result. The airman/game player's activity revolves around skill and reflexes, and the results are measured in "counts," the number of various types of targets destroyed. A significant component of the reference frame here is competitive sports, coupled with a typical male fascination with technology. The victim is insignificant either as an individual or part of a collective.

The complete absence of distinguishing details concerning targets makes it apparent that the storytellers aren't concerned with whom they hit. The main thing is *that* they hit their targets, and that the stories they can tell about it afterward are entertaining:

BIEBER*: What kind of targets do you attack in the daytime?

KÜSTER*: It all depends. There are two sorts of war-flight. First of all there are those pirate raids in which factories engaged in war industries and so on are attacked.

BIEBER: But always by single aircraft?

KÜSTER: Yes. And then there are these nuisance raids when it doesn't matter a damn whether you smash up a fishing village or a small town or something else of the sort. You are given some target or other: "You will attack such-and-such a town." And if you don't get it, you just drop your bombs somewhere else.

BIEBER: Do you feel that these pirate raids and nuisance raids are worth while?

KÜSTER: The pirate raids are. We made ours on NORWICH; it was great fun.

BIEBER: Do you mean you simply smashed up a town?

KÜSTER: Yes. Actually we were to have attacked a certain factory, but . . .

BIEBER: Are you told exactly which factories—?

KÜSTER: Yes.

BIEBER: What is there at NORWICH?

KÜSTER: There is an aircraft component parts factory there.

BIEBER: Oh, that was what you were supposed to attack?

KÜSTER: Yes. We had flown over and all at once it began to rain; you could only see about 200 metres. Suddenly we were over the main railway station at NORWICH; it was too late; we should have turned off to the left somewhat sooner. As it was we should have had to bank steeply at an angle of 30° to 95°. There was no point in it, they would have known what we were after. So we flew straight on; the first thing I saw was a funny sort of factory building and I released my bombs. The first bomb fell in that building and the others in the factory. That was in the morning at about 3 o'clock to 8-30.

BIEBER: Why didn't you drop your bombs on the station?

KÜSTER: We saw the station too late. We flew in from the east and the station is right at the approach to the town. We didn't fire on the people at the station; there wouldn't have been any point in it until we had got rid of our bombs. But afterwards we shot up the town; we fired at everything that was there, at cows and horses, it didn't matter what. We fired at the trams and everything; it's great fun. There was no A.A. there.

BIEBER: What happens, are you told about a target like that the day before?

KÜSTER: The actual target is not announced beforehand at all. Everyone plans in advance what he is going to attack; whatever appeals to him. It's left to the crew. And then when the weather is favourable in a given district, each crew is asked: "Have you any particular target?"[98]

The listener in this excerpt from the protocols, Bieber, was a German stool pigeon working for British intelligence. That is why he poses questions, ostensibly out of specialist interest, about the details of German air raids. The storyteller, Lance Corporal Küster, was a gunner on a German bomber. The anecdote is from January 1943.

The anecdote does not touch on a lot of details that might be of interest to civilians. Instead the questions that drive the dialogue between the two airmen are: why wasn't the train station attacked, and when was the target set? The conversation produces entertaining insider-oriented stories structured around three aspects: an action, its execution, and the fun that was had. Questions like why was the mission flown and was it legally and morally justifiable play no role whatsoever. Nor do airmen discuss the dramatically changing strategic and operational framework of air combat.

From the perspective of Luftwaffe fighters, there was no difference between a raid against a military target in the strict sense, an attack intended to terrify civilians, or a bombing mission aimed at a group of partisans:

WINKLER: We had to deal with partisans down there, you can't imagine it . . . suddenly retrained the torpedo pilots to use bombs, dive bombing in the "88." It was wonderful. But it wasn't counted as a warflight.

WUNSCH: Not even as an operational flight?

WINKLER: No it was only a game. We always carried as many 10 kg. fragmentation bombs as possible. The mission lasted 15 minutes and we took off repeatedly throughout the day, from dawn to dusk, we dived—swish—and dropped the bombs. Then we returned, reloaded, took off, dived and dropped our bombs again. It was fun.

WUNSCH: Had they no defenses?

WINKLER: Don't say that, the fellows had AA guns . . . The CO carried 50 kg. bombs. The CO took off first, made a quick survey, "Aha, there's a house with a few motor vehicles." He's a pilot himself, *ssst,* the old "88" dives at an angle of 80 degrees, he presses the little button, banks quickly and makes for home. PWs were brought in the next day by the SS and by a Cossack unit; we had a Cossack unit, and they landed paratroops in there too . . . everywhere swarming with partisans . . . fired every night with tommy guns. They took some prisoners and what do you think the CO had hit? A whole staff with nothing but high officers, including an English General who had been landed there just a few days before.[99]

In this anecdote, violence is clearly experienced as a kind of sport. The "game" Winkler talks about is the dropping of fragmentation bombs on an alleged group of partisans in the Vercors region of the French Alps in July 1944—something he clearly enjoyed. After a series of difficult and deadly missions targeting Allied ships in the Mediterranean, such a relatively easy assignment came as a welcome change. At long last, Winkler had another success story, another tale of a fruitful hunt and what was gunned down. The British staff Winkler hit somewhat haphazardly in the process barely rates a mention.

Conversations of this sort took place in an atmosphere of mutual agreement and tacit consensus. This example is from April 1941:

PETRI*: Have you made daylight raids on ENGLAND?

ANGERMÜLLER*: Yes, on LONDON, on a Sunday and at a height of 30 m. It was fairly stormy weather and the balloons were not

up. I was the only one (who went over). I dropped my bombs
on a railway station—attacked the station three times. Then
I flew off right across ENGLAND and afterwards the papers
reported: "German raider machine guns streets." Of course my
crew enjoyed it, and they fired at everything.

PETRI: At the civil population?

ANGERMÜLLER: Only military objectives!!! (Laughs.)[100]

Angermüller's pride is unmistakable. The attack on London he
describes had a special status because, although it was a solo mission,
he did not just drop bombs, but also flew low to strafe ground targets with machine gun fire. This sort of raid was so uncommon that it
made a British newspaper—at least Angermüller says it did in order to
underscore the impressive nature of his story. Angermüller's answer
to his comrade's question as to whether he shot at civilians is obviously ironic. It was an opportunity for a bit of shared laughter.

THE AESTHETICS OF DESTRUCTION

One of the most central and frequent conversational topics among
soldiers was how their kills were visibly verified. In great detail, they
list the targets they themselves hit as well as those destroyed by their
squadrons and their competitors. This is not surprising when we consider that their superiors handed out awards and promotions on that
basis. (There were also other measures of achievement: Iron Crosses
First Class and Knight's Crosses were bestowed after a certain number of missions or verified kills.) In contrast to infantry soldiers, airmen had immediate concrete evidence of their success. They could
see, with their own eyes, the decapacitated, burning remnants of
enemy machinery or houses, trains, and bridges that went up in flames
or collapsed.

Two aspects of killing from the air made it particularly suitable for
being perceived and experienced as an aesthetic phenomenon. The
destruction was visible, and it could be viewed from a relatively safe
distance:

SIEBERT*: It's grand to be an airman with one's base in GER-
MANY, so far away, and then to attack here.

MERTINS*: One "Stuka" did a great deed. It sank an English warship. It flew over and dropped a 250 kg. bomb into the funnel
and hit the magazine. It destroyed the ship. One saw it, too, in
POLAND. You drop your bombs and know exactly what you
have hit every time.[101]

Just as important as visibility were all the myriad improvements in
bombing accuracy. A first lieutenant related in 1940:

It is as if you threw a 250 Kg. bomb at the side of a ship. That
makes quite a big hole. In case of one ship, at dusk, we were able
to see it ourselves. It struck amidships; it went down with a huge
column of smoke.[102]

Another example came from a major:[103]

I set fire to the tanks at THAMESHAVEN, that was between 15 and
16 hours. I counted 12 myself . . . Yes, a "Gruppe." When I first
started for this target, I thought over whether I should not change
my objective, as I had seen two tankers at PORT VICTORIA which
were just being unloaded at the quayside, and there are a good
many oil tanks there. I got special mention in dispatches for that
undertaking that was the best exploit during the whole battle of
ENGLAND. It is pleasant when your success is immediately recognized; flying over LONDON is no review flight.[104]

Along with detailed discussions of technical questions, the visible aesthetic accompanying individual soldiers' destructive prowess was perhaps the most central theme of German airmen's conversations.
    Interlocutors told stories of attacks and successful kills in the great-
est possible detail and vividness of language:

FISCHER: We were over the THAMES estuary in a "190" and we
fired at every boat we spotted. We hit the mast of one of them
and off it came; it was quite a small ship. When we were flying with bombs we used to bomb factories. Once I was flying
ahead, and the second pair were coming along behind me. It
was near HASTINGS; there was a huge factory right beside the
railway-line almost on the beach. The other man flew towards

the town and dropped his bombs there. I saw the factory and thought how nicely it was smoking; I dropped a bomb, and bang! Up it went.

Once we bombed a station at FOLKESTONE just as a long passenger train was drawing out; down went the bomb right on to the train—oh boy! (Laughter.) Then alongside DEAL station there was a huge shed we bombed that, and I never saw anything like the flame that shot up—there was a terrific explosion. There must have been some highly inflammable stuff in the warehouse. Great bits flew up into the air before us, higher than we were flying ourselves.[105]

This is war as witnessed from above, from the perspective of bomber crews and, in particular, fighter pilots. War looks very different from the ground, where the destruction is actually taking place, where people are running, fleeing, and dying. The German Luftwaffe also suffered significant casualties, more than 1,700 from August 1, 1940, to March 31, 1941,[106] but that contributed to the sporting character of airmen's missions and their aesthetic experience of destruction.

Risk was an essential part of war, and it took particular skill and control over one's machinery if one was to have any hope of surviving:

At HYTHE there's an aerodrome right on the coast but there are no aircraft there. The Oberleutnant said to me one Sunday morning at ten o'clock: "Come along: we're going to do a special job together." We went across, each with the two 250-kilogram bombs underneath, and damn it, we ran into fog. We flew on and came out of the fog, and there was the aerodrome: and suddenly the sun came out and shone brilliantly. We saw the barrack buildings and the soldiers all sitting out on the balcony; we flew up to them, and zoom! Bang! the barracks shot into the air and the soldiers went whirling all over the place. (Laughter.) Adjoining the barracks there was a big hut, and another big house in front of it; so I thought we'd have a crack at those. Everyone was running for their lives, the hens were fluttering about, the hut caught fire—boy, did I laugh! I'll say we gave those guys a packet.[107]

Another conversation explicitly focuses on the fact that air attacks were filmed—a further element in visible destruction. At the latest since the Second Gulf War, we are used to seeing targets being destroyed from the perspective of the person causing the destruction. On the nightly news, we have experienced for ourselves, in real time, how a missile strikes and obliterates a bunker. But the phenomenon began much earlier. World War II also saw, in historian Gerhard Paul's words, "a fusion of camera and weapon."[108]

It began when cameras were mounted on the wings of fighter planes. Later home-movie cameras were integrated into the onboard weaponry so that pilots could document their kills themselves, providing the press with spectacular images. Weekly newsreels showed pictures of targets being destroyed from the perspective of pilots and marksmen, and pictures of dive-bombing attacks proved particularly popular with the viewing public:

> KOCHON: In the bombers there is an automatic camera now under the cannon and the camera turns every time a shot is fired so you get a picture of every shot.
>
> FISCHER: I had an ordinary camera which had been specially built in.
>
> KOCHON: The camera takes a picture when you press the button and so you know whether you scored a hit or not.
>
> FISCHER: We have them now in the wings. We now have three cameras where the cannon used to be. Once I kept my finger on the button for two seconds and the Spitfire fell to pieces. My right wing was covered with oil from the Spitfire.[109]

FUN

> "I can tell you I've killed a lot of people in ENGLAND! In FOLKE-STONE we had definite orders to drop our bombs among the houses. I was called in our Staffel 'the professional sadist.' I went for everything, a bus on the road, a passenger train at FOLKE-STONE. We had orders to drop out bombs right into the towns. I fired at every cyclist."
>
> *Corporal Fischer, pilot of a Messerschmitt 109, May 20, 1942*[110]

The fun to be had from a successful attack played a major role in the Luftwaffe airmen's conversations. The category not only served to mutually confirm the virtuoso skill with which one handled one's air-craft and the superiority one enjoyed over the enemy or others. It also had a considerable communicative significance. Fun was part of what made a story worth telling. It was part of the tension of a well-rounded narrative, comprehensible and with a striking ending, and the mutual laughter it elicited showed that soldiers inhabited one and the same world, a world in which hitting targets and having fun went hand in hand. Victims in the sense of people with whom soldiers could empathize do not appear in their stories. Whether they were talking about ships, planes, or houses, bicyclists, fairground visitors, train and ship passengers, or mothers with children, the victims appear only as targets.

The following anecdotes from Germany's air campaign against England from 1940 to 1944 require no commentary:

ESCHNER: Our KOMMODORE arranged on various occasions a day-time attack for us as a special treat—on shipping and suchlike. He intended this as a special favour for us . . . So we started—myself in front, and I found a ship which was outside a small harbour near LOWESTOFT—there were two ships there with only one guard ship. There was a cloud bank at 5–600m. I could see the ships from a distance of 10 km. I wanted to do a gliding attack and had already got into the gliding angle and attacked; the boat was hit; they opened fire, I opened the throttle and was off. That was great fun.[111]

BUDDE: I've taken part in two intruder patrols attacking houses.
No, only intruder patrols. Whatever we came across; country houses on a hillside made the best targets. You flew up from below, then you aimed—and crash! There was the sound of breaking windowpanes and the roof flew off. But I've only done that with the 190, twice in attacks on villages.
At the Market Place, there were crowds of people and speeches were being made. They ran like hares! That's great fun! It was just before Christmas. We had no losses on that occasion.[112]

BAEUMER: Then in the retreat we played a fine game in the "111." We had a 2-cm cannon built into it in front. Then we flew at low level over the streets, and when any cars came towards us we put on the searchlights and they thought another car was coming towards them. Then we turned the cannon on them. We had plenty of success like that. That was grand, we got a lot of fun out of it. We did it with railway trains, too, and that sort of thing. The nights are comparatively light in RUSSIA anyhow, if the weather doesn't happen to be really bad.[113]

HARRER*: I take my hat off to our mines, when they go off they raze everything to the ground, they knock down 80 houses. I have had friends, who in an emergency—that is they should have dropped their mines in the sea—have dropped them on a small town, and they have seen how the houses were lifted up and fell apart in the air. The mines only have quite a thin wall, a light metal shell. And moreover they have a much better explosive than all our bombs.

When such a thing drops on a block of houses it simply vanishes, just falls to pieces. It was the greatest fun.[114]

V. GREIM: We once made a low-level attack near EASTBOURNE. When we got there, we saw a large mansion where they seemed to be having a ball or something; in any case we saw a lot of women in fancy-dress, and an orchestra. There were two of us doing long distance reconnaissance. [. . .] We turned round and flew towards it. The first time we flew past, and then we approached again and machine-gunned them. It was great fun![115]

HUNTING

A hunt consists of locating, pursuing, felling, and eviscerating game. Hunts come in various forms. The most common ones are the hunt in which a solitary rifle wielder goes after his prey together with a game dog, and the roundup, in which beaters drive the prey into the hunter's sights. Hunting has a sporting aspect. The hunter has to be skillful and alert, smarter than his prey. He has to know how to hide, how to attack without being spotted, and how to shoot well. But hunting also entails special rules. One hunts only at particular times, for instance, and only shoots at individual animals.

Taken together, all these elements correspond to the demands placed upon a fighter pilot. (Indeed, the German for fighter pilot, *Jagdflieger,* contains the word for hunt *Jagd*.) This is why German fighter pilots understood what they did in the context of hunting. It was considered dishonorable, for instance, to fire upon enemy pilots who had ejected from their planes and were parachuting back to ground, even though these men were technically still enemies.[116] Luftwaffe General Adolf Galland supposedly once deemed it "unworthy of a huntsman" to bombard groups of American bombers. The hunt is the source of the "fun" of which Luftwaffe POWs constantly spoke. The only other military men who talked about battle in such sporting terms were U-boat crews.

A good example of this trope is a metaphor used by German navy Lieutenant Wolf-Doetrich Danckworth, the only survivor from the German submarine U-224:

It's still good fun today. When we were after a convoy it was always like a wolf after a flock of sheep, strongly guarded by dogs. Dogs are the corvettes and the sheep are the ships and we were lurking round like wolves until we found a way of slipping in, then we attacked, fired our torpedoes and got out again. The best fun is to hunt.[117]

For soldiers, it made no difference whether the prey consisted of military or civilian targets. In his diary, an enthusiastic Ernst Jünger described how he finally, after two and a half years of war, succeeded in "felling" his first Englishman with a "precise" shot.[118] Soldiers' anecdotes were less concerned with who was killed and why than with the more spectacular results one had achieved. This, too, is an instance of how soldiers saw battle in terms of sports.

The more prominent or important the target, the greater the triumph, and the more interesting the stories that could be told about the kill:

DOCK: I usually took two photos of the same object; the ops. people always kept one. My best pictures were of a Whitley, the first enemy aircraft shot down by the Staffel. How we celebrated our first victory! Until half-past five the next morning; and we had a sortie at seven. We all got into the aircraft as tight as lords! The Whitley was the first our Staffel shot down, then came nothing but four-engined aircraft, Liberators, Hellfires, Stirlings, Sunderlands. Then came Lockheed-Hudsons and so on. We shot down four civil aircraft.

HEIL: Were they armed?

DOCK: No.

HEIL: Why did you shoot them down?

DOCK: Whatever crossed our path was shot down. Once we shot down—there were all sorts of bigwigs in it: seventeen people, a crew of four and fourteen passengers; they came from LONDON. There was a famous English film-star in it too, HOWARD. The English radio announced it in the evening. Those civil aircraft pilots know something about flying! We stood the aircraft on its head, with the fourteen passengers. They must all have hung on the ceiling! (Laughs.) It flew at about 3200 m. Such a silly dog, instead of flying straight ahead when he saw us, he started to take evasive action. Then we got him. Then we let him have it all right! He wanted to get away from us by putting on speed. Then he started to bank. Then first one of us was after him, and then another. All we had to do was to press the button, quietly and calmly. (Laughs.)

HEIL: Did it crash?

DOCK: Of course it did.

HEIL: And did any of them get out?

DOCK: No. They were all dead. Those fools don't try to make a forced landing, even if they can see that it's all up with them.[119]

Dock's anecdote about shooting down the Douglas DC-3 transport airplane carrying the actor Leslie Howard particularly underscores the sporting aspect of the frame of reference of war. His victims are big game. Dock clearly expresses his admiration for the pilot of the Douglas, who tried to avoid being shot down with a spectacular evasive maneuver. But the pilot had no chance against a fighter plane. All Dock and his comrades had to do, as he puts it, was "to press the button, quietly and calmly."[120]

Such anecdotes once again show that most soldiers did not distinguish between military and civilian targets. The point was to sink ships, shoot down planes, and destroy targets—who was killed was simply not very important. Occasionally, POWs even emphasized that their targets were *not* military ones. For example, in January 1945,

The film actor Leslie Howard (1893–1943) played Ashley Wilkes in Gone With the Wind. *He was killed on June 1, 1943, while on board KLM Flight 777 from Lisbon to Bristol, which was shot down over the Bay of Biscay by a Junkers 88 fighter plane. (Photographer unknown; Ullstein Bilderdienst)*

First Lieutenant Hans Harting from the Luftwaffe's Fighter Wing 26 related:

> HARTING: I myself flew to Southern ENGLAND. In 1943 we flew over hourly in "Schwarm" formation, and we were ordered to fire at <u>everything,</u> <u>except</u> military targets. We killed children and women with prams.[121]

A conversation between bomber pilot Wille* and submarine corporal Solm provides an especially drastic example of what conscious attacks on nonmilitary targets meant:

> SOLM: We sank a children's transport.
> WILLE: You or PRIEN?
> SOLM: We did it.
> WILLE: Were they drowned?
> SOLM: Yes, all are dead.
> WILLE: How big was she?
> SOLM: 6,000 (??) tons.

WILLE: How did you know that?

SOLM: Through W/T; the B.D.U. (U-Boat commander) sent through "there is a convoy at such and such a place, so and so many ships with supplies, so and so many ships with this or that cargo, a children's transport, etc., etc. The children's transport is so big, and the other is so big." Whereupon we attacked it. Then came the question "Did you attack the convoy?" We replied "Yes."

WILLE: How did you know that just this ship out of the 50 had the children on board?

SOLM: Because we have a big book. This book contains all the ships of the English and Canadian steamship lines. We look them up in that.

WILLE: That doesn't have the name of the ship, does it?

SOLM: We have that.

WILLE: Are the names of the ships in it?

SOLM: It has them all in by name.

SOLM: Children's transport . . . which gave us great pleasure.[122]

Solm was likely referring to the sinking of the British passenger ship *City of Benares* on September 18, 1940, in which seventy-seven children died.

It is irrelevant in this context that Solm's account deviates from the historic record in a number of respects: German U-boat commanders, for instance, did not know that there were children aboard the *Benares*. What is important is that Solm thinks he can impress his interlocutor with a story about how he sank a ship transporting children.

SINKING SHIPS

Otherwise, the stories told by German navy men and army soldiers starkly differed from those related by Luftwaffe members. For starters, hunting tropes played far less of a role. For purely technical reasons, ships' crews had few opportunities to act individually. Unlike fighter pilots, navy men could not brag about how perfectly they could handle their equipment, since in general they were more dependent on whole crews working as one. The word "fun" hardly occurs in their conversations.

Astonishingly, German infantry soldiers, too, rarely tell of killing others in battle. Franz Kneipp, an SS Untersturmführer in the "Hitler Youth" Division who was captured in Normandy, is one of the few who did. On July 9, 1944, he recalled:

> KNEIPP: One of the radiomen in front of me sprang in the trench. All at once he was hit. Then a dispatch rider came and he also jumped in with me and he took a wound as well. I dressed both of them. Then an American jumped out of the brush with two packs of ammunition in his hand. I took careful aim, and bang, he was gone. Then I shot at windows. I took my scope and saw someone. I took the MG, aimed it at the window and slap, bang, it was over.[123]

German soldiers were most likely to talk about killing when the enemies were defined as partisans or "terrorists" (this trope will be treated in detail in the next section). But both army and navy men were generally reluctant to discuss the topic.

What navy men did enjoy talking about in great detail was the tonnage of the ships they sank. It was irrelevant in terms of medals whether those ships were passenger, merchant, or fishing boats. All sorts of vessels were "knocked over," "shot down," "cracked," or simply "sunk." Navy POWs rarely mention any victims. One exception was this narrative told by an E-boat sailor about an experience in the Baltic Sea:

> We once sank a Russian E-boat, a kind of small anti-aircraft boat with a crew of ten. They are quite small things and run on petrol. We shot one of them into flames. The crew went overboard. Our captain said: "Watch out, we can take those few men on board." We went up to them, there were Russian women among them. The nearest ones started to shoot from the water with pistols. They simply didn't want to be picked up, they were so stupid. Our captain said "We meant to treat them decently. They don't want it so we'll just do the fellows in." We . . . let them have it, they were . . . gone.[124]

If the rescue attempt had gone off without incident, the navy man probably wouldn't have mentioned it. What made the story worth telling was the unusual detail that the Russian women didn't want to be saved, and that they, too, had been killed.

The battles surrounding convoys HX 229 and SC 143 seem to have made a particular impression. Forty-three German submarines attacked the ships, which were on their way from Canada to Great Britain, in March 1943. Over the course of a few days twenty-one Allied merchantmen were drowned.

> People who mutually participated in this witch's cauldron said that not one of the English who had lived through this bombardment would ever sail again. It was such a hell of fire, flames, noise and explosions, dead bodies and screams, that none of all the ships' crews will ever go to sea again. That is definitely one up to us, a clear moral victory, if the enemy's morale should deteriorate to such an extent that he should have no further desire to go to sea. But if they really get short, they will force the crews to sail, exactly as we do.[125]

Evidence that sailors felt pity for the crews of ships they sank were very rare, as were reports about successful rescues. Apparently, the POWs talked very little about whether submarines occasionally rescued and cared for enemies fleeing destroyed vessels. One exception was First Mate Hermann Fox from the submarine U-110:

> Fox: We torpedoed a ship which was bound from SOUTH AMER-ICA, at night, 200 sea-miles off the English coast. We were unable to save the people on board. We found three of them in a boat and gave them food and cigarettes, the poor devils![126]

By contrast, most narratives are simply concerned with how many gross registered tons had been sent to the bottom of the ocean. Victims mainly appear in the anonymous form of masses of killed or dying enemies.

Lieutenant Captain Heinz Scheringer, for instance, told two of his comrades of the final mission of the U-26:

> Scheringer: That would have paid; that would have been a further 20,000 [tons], that would have made 40,000; yes, we should have got something more. It was grand fun when we made the

attack on the whole convoy; everybody picked out their own victim: we'll take this one; no, we'd better take that one, she is bigger still, and then we decided to take the tanker, first. Then, after that, immediately, the one on the left. . . . officers on board, they were "Steuermannsmaate," then we fetched up (mentions a name) again and asked "Which would you take now?" (Laughter.)[127]

Stories concerning ships that were sunk were omnipresent not only among submarine crews, but navy men in general. The strategy of German naval command against Great Britain was one of tonnage: the German navy aimed to sink more ships than Allied dockyards could replace. So the criterion for success was size.[128] That was true as well for the crews of armed German merchant marine vessels. Evidence of this is a dialogue between crew members of the raider MS *Penguin* and its supply ship MS *Atlantis*:

KOPP*: Nobody can beat us. It is too late now. We sank sixteen.
HAHNER*: What do you mean?
KOPP: We can't be beaten for tonnage. She (another raider) had 129 (000) tons or so. We had 136 (000) tons, there were two or three others to be added.
HAHNER: We sank the biggest Egyptian passenger steamer and then two English steamers sailing to AFRICA with aircraft, ammunition and everything.[129]

Games of verbal one-upmanship are common in the surveillance protocols. That's partly because bragging is a frequent element of everyday conversations, in which the person talking tries to outdo his interlocutor with a better story or a superior achievement.

The sailors' stories revolve around the sinking of ships regardless of what type they were. Even navy men taken prisoner early on in World War II think in terms of this paradigm:

BARTZ*: Would it not be better to try to pick off the destroyer first then the ships?
HUTTEL: No, always the tonnage space first; as that will be England's destruction. The "Kommandant" always has to report at the B.D.U. (Befehlshaber der U-Boote—Commander

in Chief U-boats) as soon as we return. We sink everything without previous warning, but they (the English) must not know that.[130]

The excerpt was recorded on February 10, 1940, when the war was only a few months old. As of January 6 of that year, German naval command had allowed U-boat commanders in the North Sea to sink merchant vessels from neutral countries without warning,[131] a move intended to disrupt supplies traveling between Scandinavia and Great Britain. At the same time, submarine crews were to avoid attracting too much attention in order to head off international protests.

Of the six ships sunk by U-55 on its maiden patrol in January 1940, two were Norwegian and one was Swedish. U-boat crews didn't care whom they sent to a watery grave. On the contrary, they spoke enthusiastically about new technological possibilities that would allow them to sink more ships. There was little room in their heads for thoughts about the fates of the crews on enemy ships. Saving enemies was only infrequently an option, and efforts to do so were correspondingly rare:

BARTZ: What do you do with the ships you sink?
HUTTEL: We always allow the crew to drown: what else can you do?[132]

Sinking ships without warning significantly lowered the chances that anyone would survive attacks. On the 5,150 merchant vessels the Allies lost to German submarines in World War II, more than thirty thousand sailors were killed.[133]

German sailors did not need to be socialized in order to kill. No one questioned whether crews of enemy merchant vessels should have to die. Such "collateral casualties" had been an accepted part of naval warfare since 1917. Individual navy men had only limited opportunities to demonstrate their individual skill, bravery, or virtuoso handling of their machinery. If your ship was hit, you sank. If you hit someone else's ship, that person went down. With that in mind, it is not surprising how ostentatiously detached and emotionless German navy POWs were when they told their stories of sinking ships and causing others to drown. The sailors didn't want to let death get too close to them. Torpedoes are fired from a relatively great distance, and in contrast to fighter pilots, submarine crews rarely saw the results of their work. When a submarine launched a surface attack, there were usually only four men on deck, and the captain with his periscope was the only one who saw the target during an underwater attack. At most, the rest of the crew only heard the sounds of a ship sinking—hardly a basis for a great amount of empathy.

War Crimes—Occupiers as Killers

Human beings' understanding of what a war crime is has varied considerably from antiquity to the present day. There is no one standard as to what forms of violence constitute "normal" warfare. In light of the countless people who have lost their lives to war in the course of human history, it's worth asking whether limits set on violence during wartime are the exception and not the rule. Conversely, there has never been a war, or for that matter any form of social behavior, that has been completely without rules. That includes World War II. The frame of reference of that conflict provided soldiers with a clear idea of what forms of violence were and weren't legitimate—although soldiers did occasionally transgress such boundaries.

Nonetheless, the Second World War saw limits on violence, in both a qualitative and quantitative sense, removed to an unprecedented degree. More than any other conflict, World War II approximated the theoretical state of total war.[134] The experience of World War I continued to influence military discussions in the interbellum period, and many people saw the radicalization of war as unavoidable. The experts all agreed that the next war would be a total one.[135] Thus, despite no shortage of initiatives in that direction, there was no way to regulate or restrict the brutalization of armed conflict. The power of the major political ideologies, the general resistance to liberal ideas, the continued development of weaponry such as strategic bombers, and the intensifying plans for mass mobilization doomed all efforts to contain violence.[136] Additionally, the experience of a number of armed conflicts between 1918 and 1939—the Russian Revolution, the suppression of uprisings in Germany, the Spanish Civil War, and the Sino-Japanese War from 1937 to 1939—diametrically opposed attempts to subject wartime violence to accepted rules. The adoption of the Second Geneva Convention on the humane treatment of prisoners of war was not enough to counteract this trend.

Much has been written about the horrible dimensions of unfettered violence in World War II, with many experts trying to explain it as the result of a combination of both situation and intent. Their reasoning draws comparisons with religious and colonial wars, maintaining that the ideologization of war prevented soldiers from recognizing the enemy as a fellow human being. Enemies could thus be killed on a whim. The perspective of the political and military leadership has been well documented, but the question remains: how did ordinary soldiers feel about these issues? What did they regard as war crimes, and which rules of warfare were anchored in their frame of reference?

The POWs in the surveillance protocols never refer to the idea of a war crime, or the Geneva Convention and the Hague Conventions of 1899 and 1907. Their decisive reference point was the customs of war, the things soldiers normally did in combat. From the onset of World War II, both sides engaged in unlimited submarine warfare, and tens of thousands of merchant marines lost their lives, even though they were not, strictly speaking, enemy combatants. Submarine crews generally offered them little assistance, since to do so would have been dangerous, and many navy men were indifferent to others' fate. Nonetheless, it was a general rule not to kill sailors whose ships had been sunk—only a few exceptions are known. Prior to 1942, the German Luftwaffe was officially forbidden from launching "terror attacks" against exclusively civilian targets. But as we have seen, for bomber crews, the distinction between military and civilian targets had long been blurred. Everything was a potential target, even if that idea ran contrary to the official policy of the Luftwaffe high command. The exercise of violence modified the rules of combat and extended the boundaries of what was considered permissible. Tens of thousands of British civilians may have been killed in German air raids, and hundreds of British pilots shredded by German machine gun fire, but it was still taboo to kill a pilot who had ejected from his plane while he was parachuting to the ground. Tank crews who had abandoned their vehicles, on the other hand, were usually gunned down. Different rules applied in the air and on the ground, and though there were occasional violations, those rules retained their force. And since rules and customs of war were interdependent, international laws concerning war crimes were not completely ineffective. They still represented something of a frame of reference.

Rules are least applicable in ground combat. Wherever soldiers take prisoners, secure occupied territories, and battle partisans, particular forms of logic dominate. Often, that logic revolves around troops' security or the satisfaction of material and sexual desires. Individually perpetrated violence, such as rape or killing, becomes more possible and likely. In other words, war opens up a social space that is far more violence-friendly than peacetime. Force becomes expected, accepted, and normal. The conditions under which instrumental violence—the taking of territory, the pilfering of the vanquished, and the rape of women—is allowed to change together with the dynamics of the war itself. The same is true of autotelic violence. The borders between the two types of violence are so permeable that distinctions between legitimate and criminal force in battle become exceedingly tenuous. A lot of what the German POWs relate in the surveillance protocols is typical less of crimes committed by the Wehrmacht specifically than of war crimes in general.

The killing, wounding, and raping of civilians is as much a part of the everyday reality of war as the murder of prisoners, the illegal bombardment of nonmilitary targets, and the strategic terrorization of populaces. The Wehrmacht wasn't the only army to execute prisoners. Both Soviet and U.S. troops did so as well—and not just in World War II. General Bruce Palmer, former acting chief of staff of the U.S. Army, revealed a little bit more than he intended when he wrote: "Americans did indeed commit war crimes in the course of the protracted Vietnam War, but no more in proportion to the number of people involved than have occurred in past wars."[137] Palmer made explicit what is always assumed about military prohibitions of illegal actions. No one believes that they will *not* be violated. Nonetheless, the standards of what constitutes a tolerable level of violations of international law varies from historical period to historical period, and from individual to individual. Within the framework of a total war, soldiers push the limits of legitimacy to the extreme. What distinguishes the Nazi campaigns of extermination from the standard general practice of World War II is the elimination of certain groups who had nothing to do with the war itself, as well as the genocidal treatment meted out to Russian POWs, including the execution of Soviet commissars. Here, racist ideology made itself manifest. It translated the situation of warfare into the most radical practice of destruction and annihilation ever seen in the modern age.

Numerous narrative examples of these tendencies occur in the surveillance protocols, although they are not as frequent as German historiography, which tends to focus on Nazi crimes, leads us to expect. The reason why is simple. The things that emerged, after decades of politicized historical arguing, as the signature characteristics of World War II were by no means anything special in the eyes of German soldiers. The vast majority of them knew of Nazi crimes, and no small number of them were actively involved, but those crimes did not occupy any special place in their frame of reference. Soldiers were most concerned with their own individual survival, their next home leave, the loot they could pilfer, and the fun they could have, and not the suffering of others, especially those considered racially inferior. Soldiers' own fate was always at the center of their perception. Only in rare cases did the fate of enemy troops or occupied peoples seem worthy of note. Everything that threatened one's own survival, spoiled the fun, or created problems could become a target of unlimited violence.

"Taking care" of partisans was rationalized with the idea that they ambushed German soldiers. Revenge was a powerful motivator and functioned regardless of individual soldiers' political attitudes. Thus General Wilhelm von Thoma, who was critical of the Nazi leadership, told the British intelligence officer Lord Aberfeldy:

> THOMA: There was a terrific amount of shooting there on both sides. Or as when they keep on proudly publishing in the French newspaper the monthly balance sheet, so-and-so-many hundreds of trains blown up, so-and-so-many factories burnt down, four hundred and eighty officers and one thousand and twenty men shot. Damn it all—haven't the others got the right to shoot these people if they catch them? Of course they have, but they count it all as war crimes. That's great hypocrisy.[138]

Together with the execution of prisoners, the battle against partisans was the framework in which German soldiers most frequently committed war crimes. The ways in which the German military interpreted international law and the perceptions of individual German soldiers proved a deadly combination. International law did not provide any unambiguous rules for dealing with guerrilla warfare. The 1907 Hague Convention was full of contradictions and open questions concerning the rights and responsibilities of an occupying force. The main problem was not the status of partisans in and of themselves. Insofar as they fulfilled certain conditions, wearing rudimentary uniforms, bearing their arms openly, having a clear command structure, and respecting the laws of warfare, partisans were allowed to assist the armies of their homelands in defensive wars. But the Hague Convention made no mention of what should happen if partisans continued to fight after a state had been forced to capitulate or had been completely occupied. It thus lacked any provision for protecting the rights of resistance movements, even if they wore uniforms.[139]

Rules concerning retaliatory measures were even more problematic and contradictory. Article 50 of the Hague Convention allowed collective punitive measures against a civilian population if a connection between partisans and their general environment could be proven. This rule was open to widely divergent interpretation. In the legal discussion of the interbellum years, no international consensus emerged, and the taking of hostages was deemed legitimate everywhere but in France. Opinions differed on whether they could be killed, with German military lawyers taking the hard-line position that the continued existence of "an arena of battle" justified such measures of retribution. This disagreement appeared one last time in the war crimes trials after World War II. The judges in Nuremberg ruled that the main defendants had acted illegally in ordering the killing of hostages, but in subsequent trials, defendants were deemed to have acted within the scope of the law. Convictions in the latter cases were based solely on the excessive ratios (1 to 100) German occupiers had applied when executing hostages.[140]

Even the pre-Nazi Reichswehr believed that partisans had to be combated with extreme force. A potential wildfire, so the logic ran, needed to be extinguished at the first spark. And although this approach proved ineffective, in some regions the German struggle to put down resistance movements led to an unprecedented spiral of violence. Before long the killing of hostages and innocent victims, and the razing of whole villages, was part of everyday routine. This did not differ dramatically from practices maintained in the Napoleonic Wars or World War I. What was new were the dimensions. The rigor with which German occupiers pursued alleged partisans was one reason that 60 percent of the casualties in World War II, an unprecedented proportion, were civilians. Distinctions between military combatants as legitimate targets of attack and civilian noncombatants, who should have been protected, basically dissolved.

The surveillance protocols offer a number of paradigm examples of how Wehrmacht soldiers viewed the war against partisans, and they show that German military leaders and their troops basically saw eye-to-eye. Drastic measures were justified by psychological deterrence:

> GERICKE: In RUSSIA last year a small German detachment was sent to a village on some job or other. The village was in the area occupied by the Germans. The detachment was ambushed in the village and every man was killed. As a result a strafing party was sent out. There were fifty men in the village; forty-nine of them were shot and the fiftieth was hounded through the neighbourhood so that he should spread abroad what happens to the populations if a German soldier is attacked.[141]

Franz Kneipp and Eberhard Kehrle also related how German occupiers answered attacks with brutal forms of violence. They saw nothing unethical about this. On the contrary, they both felt that partisans deserved to die horrible deaths:

> KNEIPP: There was a lot going on there. Oberst Hoppe . . .
> KEHRLE: Hoppe is well known. He has a Knight's Cross?
> KNEIPP: Yes, he took SCHLÜSSELBERG. He issued the commands. "As you to us, we to you," he said. They were supposed to confess who had hung Germans to death. Just a hint, and everything would be all right. None of them said even that they didn't know anything. Then it was, "All men, exit to the left." They were driven into the woods, and you heard brr, brr.[142]
> KEHRLE: In the Caucasus, with the 1. GD [Mountain Division], when one of us had been killed, no lieutenant needed to give any orders. It was: pistols drawn, and women, children, everything they saw . . .
> KNEIPP: With us, a group of partisans attacked a transport of wounded soldiers and killed them all. A half-an-hour later they were caught, near NOVGOROD. They were thrown in a sandpit, and it started from all sides with MGs and pistols.
> KEHRLE: They should be killed slowly, not shot. The Cossacks were great at fighting partisans. I saw that in the Southern Division.[143]

Interestingly, Kehrle and Kneipp had diametrically opposed attitudes toward the military in general. Kehrle found the primitive life of the army "idiocy" and "absolute shit," while for Kneipp it was a form of "education."[144] Yet despite that, and the inherent differences between a radio operator and an SS infantryman, they completely agreed on the methods needed to deal with partisan warfare.

The practical rules of warfare often established norms deviating from international law. That is why the POWs spoke of war crimes in matter-of-fact terms and rarely showed signs of outrage. What offended them most was the behavior of occupied local populaces. The soldiers thought it was essential to take action against any and every form of noncooperation. Such attitudes prevailed as early as October 1940, as illustrated in this exchange:

> URBICH: But there one sees how the Gestapo takes up every little thing. Especially how it is working in POLAND now.
>
> HARRER*: In NORWAY too. In NORWAY they have had a lot of work recently.
>
> STEINHAUSER: Really?
>
> HARRER: Yes, someone told me . . . (int.)
>
> URBICH: Killed a number of Norwegian officers . . .
>
> HARRER: I'm certain that even when we have actually occupied ENGLAND we shall not be able to walk about (unmolested) as in FRANCE.
>
> STEINHAUSER: I don't think so. There will be the first attempts. But when every tenth man in a town is executed it will soon stop. That is no problem at all, ADOLF will use all means to nip any franc-tireur activity in the bud. Do you know how they work in POLAND? If only one shot is fired there is trouble. Then the procedure is as follows: From whatever town or district of a town shots have been fired all the men are called out. For every shot fired during the following night, in fact during the following period, one man is executed.
>
> HARRER: Splendid![145]

Reflections about the rectitude or proportionality of such forms of extreme violence against civilian populations do not occur in the POWs' conversations. The soldiers do not think to question their behavior. Their task is to take care of the necessities: "work," "extreme measures," and "retribution." They focus on achieving results, not finding reasons.

Stories about war crimes were part of soldiers' everyday communication with one another in the same way that tales of shooting down planes and sinking ships were. In and of themselves, atrocities were nothing unusual. Only unusual actions or individual forms of behavior merited telling. One example focused on the mass executions carried out after SS leader Reinhard Heydrich was assassinated in Poland:

> KAMMBERGER: In Poland the soldiers were excused from duty so they could attend the executions, which were public. After the HEYDRICH affair twenty-five to fifty people were executed daily. They stood on a stool and had to put their heads through a noose, and the one behind had to kick the stool away, with the words: "You don't need that stool, brother."[146]

The appeal of this story for the soldier in question rested not in the killings themselves, but in how they were staged. Soldiers were given time off so they could witness the spectacles, and the executions were accompanied by a ritual of humiliation designed especially for the occasion.

Together with tales revolving around unusual acts of violence, stories concerning individuals who distinguished themselves in some way or another also made for good telling. One example is an anecdote related by Private First Class Müller:

> MÜLLER: In a village in RUSSIA there were partisans, and we obviously had to raze the village to the ground, without considering the losses. We had one man named BROSICKE, who came from BERLIN; if he saw anyone in the village, he took him behind the house and shot him, and with it all the fellow was only nineteen and a half or twenty years old. The order was given that every tenth man in the village was to be shot. "To hell with that! Every tenth man. It is perfectly obvious," said the fellow, "that the whole village must be wiped out." We filled beer bottles with petrol and put them on the table and, as we were going out, we just threw hand grenades behind it. Immediately everything was burning merrily—all roofs were thatched. The women and children and everyone were shot down; only a few of them were partisans. I never took part in the shooting unless I was sure that they were proved to be partisans; but there were a lot of fellows who took a delight in it.[147]

At the end of his story, Müller distances himself from the action by claiming he never fired a shot at innocents. But he still offers a detailed description, in the first-person plural, of how his unit burned down Russian houses. Stories like this illustrate what the soldiers regarded as crimes and what not, and how porous the boundary was between the two. Müller considered executing women and children a crime insofar as it was unclear whether they truly were partisans. Burning down a village, on the other hand, was not.

Müller also conspicuously includes a figure in his story, Brosicke, from whom he can positively distinguish himself. Brosicke's behavior, in Müller's telling, is unambiguously criminal, as is that of those for whom killing was fun. Müller's own behavior, by contrast, is not criminal. This is a typical and significant element in the protocols. By differentiating himself from others, the typical storyteller was able to find a space within a larger criminal endeavor in which he himself could not be accused of behaving immorally. Yet as we have already observed in the various different groups that took part in the mass executions and other anti-Jewish initiatives, individual interpretations of one's own role and duties ultimately helped the killing as a whole to proceed smoothly.[148] Individual attitudes and decisions are not usually overridden by "group pressure" and social influence in the way some sociologists would have us believe. On the contrary, internal differentiation within a group makes it capable of acting as a whole. To adapt a phrase coined by German scholar Herbert Jäger, what we have here is a case of individual action in collective states of emergency.[149]

One good example of this phenomenon occurs in a detailed description by a Private First Class Franz Diekmann about how he combated "terrorists" in France:

> DIEKMANN: I have a lot of terrorists on my conscience, but not so many English soldiers, only one tank commander, a lieutenant or something, whom I shot in his tank when he was opening the cover to have a look out of sheer curiosity. Otherwise, of course, I can't remember what happened in battle, but I went for the terrorists like mad. If I saw one, whom I suspected, I let fly at him immediately. When I saw a comrade of mine bleeding to death, whom they had treacherously shot, I swore to myself: "Just you wait!" At HILAY, on the way back, I was marching gaily along the street, with them, we didn't suspect anything,

when a civilian came along, drew a pistol out of his pocket, fired and my mate collapsed.

HAASE: Did you get him?

DIEKMANN: Not a hope! By the time we realised that things were in such a state in BELGIUM, before the English had even arrived, he had already half bled to death; all I could do was to close his eyes. He just said: "FRANZ, avenge me!" The "Kompanie" came after us and requisitioned lorries. My MG was mounted on one—I had the MG 42—front, right at the top, and we fired into the windows. First of all I gave the order: "Close all windows, everyone must leave the street." We didn't give them time for that. The "Hauptfeldwebel" said: "Wait, don't shoot yet, they're not ready yet!" But he hadn't finished saying this before I pressed the trigger and the MG began rattling away. We covered the windows and anything which showed in the street. I kept on firing across the streets, you know, right into all the side streets. Of course a number of innocent people were killed, but I didn't give a damn for that. Those dirty dogs, to kill an old, married man so treacherously, who had about four or five children at home. You couldn't show any consideration after that, it was out of the question. We would have set all the houses on fire if another shot had been fired.

We fired MGs into the midst of thirty Belgian women. They wanted to raid the German supply dump. But they were chased away in no uncertain manner.

HAASE: They ran away then, did they?

DIEKMANN: No, they were all dead.[150]

One could almost imagine Diekmann as one of the "many pals" from Müller's story, who had "lots of fun" killing, but the two men were describing entirely different situations. What stands out from Diekmann's story is the personal motivation he ascribes to his deeds: the desire to exact revenge for a fallen comrade. Despite the sympathy he shows for the four or five children of that comrade, he doesn't transfer that empathy to his victims, whom he executes completely at random. We do not know which anti-partisan operation Diekmann is referring to here, but it was common for German soldiers to "go wild" and indiscriminately shoot people after a lone incident in which one of them had been killed. On the other hand, the POWs don't always mention motivations and rationale when they tell stories like these. Their common horizon of experience makes that unnecessary. The detail of the fallen comrade could just be a narrative element Diekmann chose to make his story seem more interesting and well rounded.

From June to September 1944, with the Allies on the offensive, Wehrmacht violence against civilians escalated even in France and Belgium. The extent of German war crimes reached a new dimension. So it's hardly surprising that a number of stories which relate atrocities come from these three months:

> BÜSING: We had a lieutenant LANDIG (?), and one of our Oberjäger was shot by the French. How the old boy cursed!
>
> JÄGER*: That was where you were deployed?
>
> BÜSING: It was just a little while ago. We arrived, and the Oberjäger was shot by the partisans. The old boy said nothing, but his jaw was working. Then suddenly he said, "Destroy everything!" So we set out through the entire village. The old boy says: "If you fellows leave a single one of them alive, I'll kill [you] too." We enter the village. Everyone was sleeping in the grey light of dawn. We knocked—nothing. We smashed in doors with the butts of our rifles. There were the women, with short shirts on, nightshirts or pyjamas. "Out, out!" we told them and had them line up in the middle of the street.
>
> JÄGER: Where was that?
>
> BÜSING: In LISIEUX—BAYEUX, up north.
>
> JÄGER: Right at the beginning of the invasion?
>
> BÜSING: Yes, of course. We mowed down everything, everything. We dragged men, women and children from their beds. He knew no mercy.[151]

Jäger was likely a stool pigeon for MI19, but Private First Class Büsing, a paratrooper, seems to have had no idea of this and freely answered his questions. In his own eyes, Büsing's experiences were so commonplace that he doesn't think of holding anything back. As far as he's concerned, his story, brutal as it is, falls clearly within the bounds of what was to be expected. Indeed, German POWs who listened to similar anecdotes were neither shocked nor revolted. The fact that the POWs could remain absolutely unemotional while relating the acts of violence they perpetrated speaks volumes about the violent nature of the world they inhabited. Soldiers were intimately familiar with crimes of all sorts.

Not even stories about killing women and children elicit emotion. A second paratrooper related:

> ENZIEL: Oberjäger MÜLLER from BERLIN was a sniper, he shot the women who went to meet the English soldiers with bunches of flowers, but he ... exactly ... found something like that, he took aim and shot civilians in completely cold blood.
>
> HEUER*: Did you shoot women too?
>
> ENZIEL: Only from a distance. They didn't know where the shot came from.[152]

We have no way of knowing where the difference resided between the "cold-blooded" actions of the sniper Müller and Enziel's long-range gunning down of women, but he apparently thought it was significant. Heuer was another British spy, which is why he tries to tease out information about war crimes with his questions.

Like Enziel and Private First Class Müller, Private First Class Sommer also built a reference person, his first lieutenant, into his narrative:

> SOMMER (re his "Oberleutnant"): In ITALY too, wherever we arrived, he always said: "Let's first bump a few people off!" I know Italian too and always had to carry out the special tasks. He said: "First of all we'll kill twenty men in order to have peace here, to prevent them getting ideas!" (Laughter.) Then we put up a little notice saying: "At the least signs of stubbornness fifty more will be killed!"
>
> BENDER: From what point of view did he pick then, just at random?
>
> SOMMER: Yes, just twenty men like that: "Just come here." They were all taken to the market-place and someone appeared with three MG's—rrrr—and there they lay. That's how it was done. Then he said: "Excellent! The swine!" You can't imagine how he loathed the Italians. There were a few pretty girls in the district where the "Bataillionsstab" was quartered. He didn't touch any civilians <u>there</u>. He never hurt anyone where he lived, on principle.[153]

Their shared laughter indicates that neither Sommer nor Bender saw anything fundamentally immoral about the deeds related in Sommer's story. Bender's reaction was hardly surprising. He was a member of the navy Special Commando 40, a unit whose whole identity was based on a cult of macho toughness.

One interesting detail in this anecdote is the fact that the commanding officer did not want any war crimes committed in the immediate area in which he was quartered. Apparently, he did not want to jeopardize the chance for sexual encounters with local women by behaving brutally toward civilians. Sommer continues his story with an episode that happened in France:

> SOMMER: The Oberleutnant says: "Go get me all the civilians together." It was armored reconnaissance. "The Americans will be here in no time," he said. "It's going to be a circus anyway. So I'm going to organize this thing. Here you make two groups. All the civilians have to be brought here in two groups." Imagine collecting a small city of 5000 to 10,000 inhabitants! It was on the main road to Verdun. So here comes the entire population. They drove them out of their cellars. None of them were partisans or terrorists. The old boy says to me: "Kill the men. Every one, no matter what." There were at least 300 of them. I searched four of them and said "Raise your hands. Anyone who doesn't, gets shot." On two of them, kids around 18 or 19, I found some ammo, packs of it. I say: "Where'd you get that?" "It's a souvenir." "Three packs per man?" I say. I separated them out and—teng, teng, teng—three shots and they dropped to the ground. The others were taken aback. I say: "You've seen that we didn't act unfairly. They had ammunition. What are civilians doing with three packs of ammunition?" Always so that I had cover. They admitted everything. Maybe . . . they said "You swine" and such, but I said: "Thank you. That's the reason people are getting shot now. We have to protect ourselves. If I let them go with ammunition, and they know where more of it is, then they might kill me. Before I let them shoot me, I'll shoot them and have the others searched. It's good that you don't have any ammunition. You can now leave with your women. Go down there three kilometers." They were satisfied and left. I never asked to take part. I've done every kind of shit, but never because I said: "I want to!" Not me.[154]

Sommer's unit, Panzergrenadierregiment 29, had previously been involved in a number of crimes in Italy. The French story refers to atrocities committed in the Robert Espagne region of Lorraine. There, on August 29, 1944, Sommer's unit murdered eighty-six French civilians.[155]

Sommer adopts a position of distance to the events he recounts in two respects. In contrast to his first lieutenant, he tries to find a legitimate reason for the execution of civilians, arriving at the fact that they had ammunition on them. This attempt at legitimation is directed both externally and internally. Apparently, Sommer felt the need to justify what he did, assuring himself that his actions did not amount to mere murder. Moreover, he stresses that he did not act of his own free will. He may have participated in every sort of "shit," but he didn't volunteer to do so. This recalls the sort of differentiation we found in Müller's story. Among those who committed crimes, there were more and less willing executioners, and most of the perpetrators wanted to be seen as part of the latter category.

An anecdote told by Sergeant Gromoll contains an example of legalistic justifications for violence:

> GROMOLL: We once captured four terrorists in FRANCE. They are first taken to an interrogation camp where they are asked where they got their arms from etc., and then they are shot quite indiscriminately. A woman came along who said that terrorists had probably been lying hidden in a house for ten days. We immediately got a troop ready and rushed off there—it was correct, there were four men in the house. They were playing cards and so on. We arrested them because they were presumably terrorists. You can't just shoot them in the middle of a game of cards. Then they looked for arms and they were in the canal, I believe. They had thrown them into the canal.[156]

We can no longer reconstruct the exact details of this incident. But Gromoll's story suggests that German soldiers did not need to find any weapons to conclude that what could have been ordinary card players were terrorists. They could have thrown their weapons in the canal, the logic runs. Legalistic reasoning of this sort suggests that, for some soldiers, it was important to justify killings in terms of a formal structure, a framework that would legitimate their actions, even if those actions really amount to little more than indiscriminate murder.

There was a similar unwritten rule among U.S. troops in Vietnam: "If it's dead and Vietnamese, it's a Vietcong." Private First Class Diekmann tells a story in precisely this mode about a series of executions carried out in France after the Allied invasion of Normandy:

BRUNE (referring to first days after invasion): Why did the terrorists attack your position?

DIEKMANN: They wanted to interfere with our instruments; that was their task. We captured several terrorists alive and killed them on the spot. Those were our orders.

I myself once shot a French Major.

BRUNE: How did you know that he was a Major?

DIEKMANN: He had papers. There was shooting during the night. He came along on a bicycle. Our people were still firing into the houses down in the village with MGs. The whole village was full of them.

BRUNE: Did you stop him?

DIEKMANN: There were two of us, including an "Unteroffizier." He got off his bicycle and we searched his pockets immediately and found some ammunition, which was enough for us. Otherwise I couldn't have done anything to him; you can't simply shoot a man for nothing. The "Unteroffizier" asked him whether he was a terrorist, but he didn't say anything. Then he asked him whether he had any last request — nothing. Then I shot him from behind through the head. He was dead before he knew.

We once shot a woman spy at our position too. She was about twenty-seven years old. She used to work for us in the kitchen.

BRUNE: Was she from the village?

DIEKMANN: Not actually from the village, but she had been living there latterly. The infantry brought her in in the morning, and in the afternoon they stood her up against the Bunker and shot her. She confessed that she was working for the British Secret Service.

BRUNE: Who gave the order, your Chief?

DIEKMANN: Yes, he could do that as CO. I didn't take part in the execution myself; I only watched it.

Once we caught thirty terrorists, there were women and children among them. We put them into a cellar. . . . Stood them against the wall and shot them.[157]

In Diekmann's narrative, the killing of the French major requires a legalistic justification, his carrying ammunition. That identifies the officer as a terrorist. Notably, Diekmann also does not hesitate to include children among the "terrorists" who are placed against a wall and shot.

Fantastic delusions about what sorts of people might belong to the enemy are by no means unique to German soldiers. Similar incidents have been documented among U.S. troops in Vietnam, who sometimes even claimed babies were members of the Vietcong. This is not a sign of insanity. It marks the shifting of a frame of reference so that group membership is more important than all other defining characteristics, including age, in determining who the enemy is. Joanna Bourke, a scholar who has studied soldiers' perceptions of killing in various wars, has argued that such skewed frames of reference do not prove that soldiers personally enjoyed murder. Instead, Bourke suggests, the cold-blooded killing of people categorically defined as belonging to the enemy is part of the normal, everyday practice of warfare.[158]

Paradoxically, though, when such killings are subjected to legal scrutiny, they are treated as exceptions to the rule. The misconception thus arises that, by and large, war adheres to international law, and violations of that law are the deeds of rogue individuals. Autotelic violence, so the logic goes, is not a systematic aspect of war, but a regrettable deviation. But the surveillance protocols show that once the floodgates of violence are opened, *anything* can provide an impetus and justification for soldiers to start shooting.

CRIMES AGAINST POWs

"What shall we do with all these men? We must shoot them, they won't last long anyway."[159]

Ever since antiquity, the mistreatment and murder of prisoners has been an example of extreme wartime violence. But with the mass armies of the modern age, the phenomenon of the POW took on entirely new dimensions. In World War I, there were some 6 to 8 million POWs.[160] In World War II, that number was 30 million.

It was always difficult to feed and house millions of prisoners adequately. Even in World War I, some 472,000 Central Powers soldiers died in Russia.[161] Those numbers increased dramatically in World

War II, and the gravest crime of the Wehrmacht was the mass murder of Soviet POWs. Of the 5.3 to 5.7 million Red Army soldiers captured by the Wehrmacht, some 2.5 to 3.3 million died. The estimates vary, but the percentage of Soviet POWs who died in German custody is somewhere between 45 and 57 percent. Most perished in camps for which the Wehrmacht was responsible: 845,000 in military-administered territory near the front lines, 1.2 million in civilian-administered areas further back from the fighting, 500,000 in the so-called General Gouvernement of Poland, and 360,000 to 400,000 in camps located within the German Reich proper.[162]

The main cause for the horrifying numbers of casualties was the German military leadership's cynical decision to abandon POWs to the fate of starvation, making little to no effort to provide them with adequate nourishment. German military leaders never ceased reminding common soldiers that they were fighting "an enemy race and culture of inferior nature," which one was to encounter with a "healthy feeling of hatred." In this battle, German soldiers were not supposed to show "any bleeding-heart sentiments or mercy."[163]

AT THE FRONT

From the onset of the Third Reich's war with the Soviet Union on June 22, 1941, it was clear that the perennial calls for German soldiers to show steely hardness would have consequences. The Wehrmacht immediately began fighting with unusual brutality. There were numerous reports of "the bodies of countless [Soviet] soldiers lining the roads, without weapons and with their hands raised, showing unmistakable signs of having been shot in the back of the head."[164] One significant factor in the extreme violence was that German predictions about the terrible tactics employed by the Red Army were quickly confirmed. From the first day of the war onward, Soviet forces fought in ways violating international law and foreign to Western European custom.

German anecdotes about Soviet brutality stoked the violence already being perpetrated with the power of imagination. A Lieutenant Leichtfuss reported seeing six German soldiers nailed to a table through their tongues, ten hung up from meat hooks in a slaughterhouse, and twelve to fifteen who were thrown down a well in a small village and then stoned to death. This leads his conversation partner to ask: "Were those soldiers dead who were hanging on the meat hooks?"

> LEICHTFUSS: Yes. The ones with nails through their tongues were dead too. These incidents were taken for a reason for repaying it tenfold, twenty and hundredfold, not in that crude and bestial manner, but simply in the following way. When a small detachment of about ten or fifteen men was captured there, it was too difficult for the soldier or the "Unteroffizier" to transport them back 100 or 120 km. They were locked in a room and three or four hand grenades were flung in through the window.[165]

Reports about Russians mistreating German POWs, mutilating German wounded, and liquidating German soldiers who tried to surrender continued throughout the war and were too frequent and too well documented to be complete fiction. Today, it is estimated that 90 to 95 percent of German POWs captured in 1941 soon died. Most of them were executed directly at the front.[166] The horror stories about German wounded and prisoners being mutilated only encouraged the German Eastern Army's willingness to commit acts of unscrupulous violence.

In early July 1941, General Gotthard Heinrici wrote to his family: "Sometimes there's no mercy at all anymore. The Russian has behaved bestially toward our wounded. And now our people are clubbing and shooting to death anything in a brown uniform. Both sides are driving each other on so that there are enough corpses to fill whole mausoleums."[167] Similar statements can be found through Wehrmacht files. The daily war report of the 61st Infantry Division, for instance, recorded that on October 7, 1941, the bodies of three Wehrmacht soldiers were discovered, whereupon the division commander ordered ninety-three Russian prisoners shot the following day. Many such atrocities were never registered because soldiers lower down in the chain of command, like Lieutenant Schmidt, "took care of things" themselves.

The frontline murder of countless Red Army soldiers was primarily an act of revenge and retribution. The character of the fighting in Russia was completely different from that in Poland, France, or Yugoslavia. The Red Army put up unexpectedly stiff resistance, and many Soviet soldiers preferred to fight to the death rather than surrender.

Embittered hand-to-hand combat led to heavy losses on all sides and further ratcheted up the violence. Consider the following exchange:

SCHMIDT (re Russian PW): What did you do with the fellows?

FALLER: We killed them. Most of them were killed in this battle (?). They didn't surrender either. We often had fellows
whom we wanted to take prisoner and who, when the position was completely hopeless, took the pin out of a hand grenade and held it in front of their stomachs . . . we purposely
refrained from shooting them because we wanted to take them
alive . . . The women fought like wild beasts.

SCHMIDT: What did you do with the women?

FALLER: We shot them too.[168]

Faller's stories show once again that female members of the Red
Army were particularly at risk since women in battle were not part of
German soldiers' frame of reference. Denigrated as "rifle sluts," they
were denied the status of true combatants and thus regarded as on the
same level as partisans. For that reason, they were more likely than
male members of the Red Army to become the victims of excessive
brutality.[169]

Along with the determination of individual soldiers to fight to the
death, what most angered Germans were the tactics used by the Red
Army. Soviet soldiers would often pretend to be wounded or play
dead in order to attack from behind—something Germans regarded
as a massive violation of the customs of warfare. The Hague Conventions did not explicitly prohibit deceptions of this kind, but they
represented a break with the unwritten rules of open warfare. Before
the invasion, manuals written by the German military leadership predicted that the Red Army would use such tricks, and German troops
punished them with extreme brutality. For example, as early as late
June 1941, a regiment of the 299th Infantry Division reported: "Prisoners were not taken because troops were so bitter about the dishon-
est fighting style of the enemy."

Other tactics that were part of conventional warfare were unfamiliar to Germans and thus interpreted as evidence of the Red Army's
refusal to fight fairly. They included opening fire from behind, letting
the enemy advance before unleashing a barrage at short range, and
letting vanguard troops pass by so as to attack them from the rear. A

German soldier named Hölscher, for instance, passed on a description of the Eastern Front he had heard from a friend:

> He said it was incredible the way the Russians fought. They let us approach to within three metres and then mow us down. "Can you imagine," he said, "letting us come right up on top of them. When we capture any of them, we make an end of them at once; we hit them over the head with our rifle-butts." They (the Russians) dig themselves in in the fields and every inch of the grounds has to be fought for. They used not to do that at first, they used to perch up in the trees and shoot down on our men. He said you wouldn't believe how fantastically the devils fought. He said it's appalling what's going on in RUSSIA.[170]

In German soldiers' eyes, there was nothing criminal about their behavior toward the Red Army, even though it, too, clearly violated international law. Soviet misbehavior was justification enough for German troops to execute prisoners, and almost no one, it seems, saw any alternatives.

Thus, within the first weeks of Nazi Germany's campaign against the Soviet Union, new customs of war that flouted international law were established. The exercise of violence was not static, but rather constantly in flux—depending on structural, personal, and situational conditions. In the fall of 1941, for example, the extreme violence of the summer receded. But no sooner had the Eastern Army been compelled to beat a chaotic retreat in the winter of 1941–42, than they once again began regularly executing POWs who could not be transported.[171] Phases of escalation and de-escalation would continue until the end of the war.

The surveillance protocols contain scattered instances in which soldiers describe refusing to commit war crimes against prisoners. An SS Second Lieutenant (Untersturmbahnführer) named Schreiber recounted one such story, including a description of his shock at a prisoner's murder:

> SCHREIBER: We once took a man prisoner and the question arose as to whether we should shoot him from behind. He was 45 years old. He crossed himself and murmured "ra ra" (imitating murmured prayer) as though he knew. I couldn't shoot. I imag-

ined him as a husband with a family and children probably. I said in the office "I won't do it." I went off. I could no longer look at him.[172]

Significantly, the interlocutor here—Navy Lieutenant Bunge—expects a different end to Schreiber's story, one in which the SS man does indeed end up "putting down" the Russian POW. Killings of that sort were common in soldiers' conversations, and it was far more unaccustomed when they did *not* occur. Sergeant Grüchtel had a similar tale to tell:

When I was at RIGA, I needed a few Russian prisoners to clean up the place, I went and got a few—five of them. Then I asked the soldier what I should do with them when I was finished with them and he said: "Shoot them down and leave them there." But I didn't do that, I took them back again to where I'd got them from. You can't do a thing like that.[173]

We have no way of knowing whether stories of this kind are true or not, but they occur very rarely in the protocols. This fact should not be mistaken for evidence that humane treatment of POWs or occupied populations happened any more or less frequently in real life than it did in soldiers' conversations. It merely documents that behavior which today would be considered humane played a very minor communicative role among the POWs. Stories relating what we consider inhumane acts, often told in the first person, were much more frequent than ones describing what would be deemed "good" behavior under contemporary norms.

This might be an indication that describing one's own "good" behavior wasn't bound to increase one's popularity. In situations where killing is regarded as both an everyday practice and a social duty, charitable behavior toward Jews, Russian POWs, and other groups deemed inferior would have represented a violation of the norm. Even after World War II, it took years until stories of that nature elicited greater approval than the sorts of deeds the soldiers usually recounted in the surveillance protocols. Only later did Germans begin to give their recollections other nuances. So the relative infrequency of stories in which German soldiers show pity or empathy with prisoners, or simply treat them decently, might be due to the fact that such behavior was considered antisocial at the time and thus conversationally off-limits. Or perhaps the frame of reference in which others and their behavior were categorized simply did not admit of a category like empathy. In any case, the fact that stories in which soldiers boast of their own inhumanity rarely elicited any criticism suggests that such stories, and not the humane ones, reflected the normal everyday reality of World War II.

IN THE CAMPS

Most Red Army POWs did survive for a few days after being captured. But their martyrdom began as soon as they began making their way to prisoner of war camps:

> GRAF: The infantry said that when they took the Russian P/W back, they had nothing to eat for three or four days and collapsed. Then the guard would just go up to one, hit him over the head and he was dead. The others set on him and cut him up and ate him as he was.[174]

Soviet POWs resorting to cannibalism is a recurring topic in the protocols. A First Lieutenant Klein, for instance, recounts: "When one of them died the Russians often ate him while he was still warm. That's a fact."[175] Lieutenant General Georg Neuffer and Colonel Hans Reimann recalled a POW transport in 1941:

> NEUFFER: That transporting of the Russians to the rear from VYASMA was a ghastly business.
> REIMANN: It was really gruesome. I was present when they were being transported from KOROSTEN to just outside LWOW. They were driven like cattle from the trucks to the drinking troughs and bludgeoned to keep their ranks. There were troughs at the stations; they rushed to them and drank like beasts; after that they were given just a bit of something to eat. Then they were again driven into the wagons; there were sixty or seventy men in one cattle truck! Each time the train halted ten of them were taken out dead: they had suffocated for lack of oxygen. I was in the train with the camp guard and I heard it from the

"Feldwebel," a student, a man with spectacles, an intellectual, whom I asked: "How long has this been going on?"—"Well, I have been doing this for four weeks; I'll not be able to stand it much longer, I must get away; I don't stick it any more!" At the stations the prisoners peered out of the narrow openings and shouted in Russian to the Russians standing there: "Bread! And God will bless you," etc. They threw out their old shirts, their last pairs of stockings and shoes from the trucks and children came up and brought them pumpkins to eat. They threw the pumpkins in, and then all you heard was a terrific din like the rearing of wild animals in the trucks. They were probably killing each other. That <u>finished</u> me. I sat back in a corner and pulled my coat up over my ears. I asked the "Feldwebel": "Haven't you <u>any</u> food <u>at all</u>?" He answered: "Sir, how should we have anything, nothing has been prepared!"

NEUFFER: No, really, all that was incredibly gruesome. Just to see that column of PW after the twin battle of VYASMA—BRIANSK, when the PW were taken to the rear on foot, far beyond SMO-LENSK. I often travelled along that route—the ditches by the side of the roads were full of shot Russians. Cars had driven in to them; it was really ghastly.[176]

The mass starvation of Russian POWs was the result of the absence of adequate measures to feed them. It began in the summer of 1941 and reached its high point that winter, before relenting somewhat in the spring of 1942. By that time some two million Red Army soldiers were dead.

German policies toward POWs changed as the German wartime economy began to suffer from a labor shortage, and the German leadership recognized the instrumental value of people it would have preferred to let starve. Nonetheless, the Wehrmacht brass never fundamentally changed their policy, even if isolated individuals did fight for POWs' lives and protested, however unsuccessfully, against their abysmal treatment.[177]

Reports of the horrible conditions in POW camps occur even more often than recollections of executions in the surveillance protocols. The mass deaths of tens of thousands of people were apparently something remarkable even to hardened veterans of the Eastern Front. A soldier named Freitag recalled:

Soviet prisoners of war en route to a POW camp, July 1942.
Southern section of Eastern Front. (Photographer: Friedrich
Gehrmann; BA 183-B27 116)

There were 50,000 Russian Ps./W in the citadel in TEMPLIN(?). It
was crammed full—they could just stand—they could hardly sit
down, the place was so full. When we arrived at TEMPLIN(?) in
November, there were still 8,000 there, the others were already
under the ground. At that time there was an outbreak of typhus
(Flecktyphus). A sentry said to us: "We've got typhus in the camp,
it'll last another fortnight, and then the Russian prisoners will all
be dead and the Poles too and the Jews." As soon as they noticed
that somebody had typhus, they at once cleared the whole place
out.[178]

Many German soldiers seemed to have been aware of the dimensions of a conflict in which millions of POWs were dying. For example,
Freitag, a Luftwaffe sergeant, remarked in June 1942: "In any case we
had taken 3½ million prisoners, up to Christmas. And then there were
certainly as many, if not more, killed, 'as many more again' said the
communiqué. And if as many as a million of the prisoners survived the
winter, that's a lot."[179] First Lieutenant Verbeek of Artillery Regiment
272 expressed his outrage to a comrade: "Do you know how many

Russian PW died in GERMANY in the winter of 1941/42? Two million actually died, they didn't get anything to eat. Offal was brought from the slaughter-house to the camp for them to eat."[180]

The racist belief in innate German superiority that prevailed among the Eastern Army no doubt encouraged soldiers to liquidate Soviet prisoners, "mow down" enemies in battle, and carry out mass executions in revenge for assassinations. German soldiers' proclivities toward violence were promoted by a mentality that saw the Russians as "an inferior people,"[181] indeed "animals"[182] and "members of a foreign race, Asians."[183] Nonetheless, the tales of mass death in the POW camps were by no means completely free of empathy, be it only as an undertone that the treatment of prisoners was unjust and cruel.

The propagandistic picture of the bestial Red Army soldier incited by Jews and Bolsheviks gradually gave way to a more multifaceted view that included respect for Russian soldiers' military performance. Living in the country probably also altered occupying German soldiers' perspectives on Russian culture and the lifestyles of a populace that had to deal with a relatively rough climate. German soldiers' perceptions of Russians became more differentiated and positive. Moreover, some one million Russians also fought alongside the Wehrmacht as volunteers—a fact that must have revised many Germans' opinions of what "the Russian" was like.[184]

On the other hand, some soldiers in British POW camps felt that Russian prisoners had been treated *too* humanely. Lieutenant General Maximilian Siry, for instance, opined on May 6, 1945:

> SIRY: One mustn't admit it openly, but we were far too soft. All these horrors have landed us in the soup now. But if we'd carried them through to the hilt, made the people disappear completely—no-one would say a thing. These half measures are always wrong.
>
> In the East I suggested once to the "Korps"—thousands of PW were coming back, without anyone guarding them, because there were no people there to do it. It went quite well in FRANCE, because the Frenchman is so degenerate that if you said to him: "You will report to the PW collecting point in the rear" the stupid idiot really did go along there. But in RUSSIA there was a space of 50–80 km., that is to say a 2 to 3 days' march, between the armoured spearheads and the following close formations.

No Russians went to the rear, where they could live all right. So I said: "That's no good, we must simply cut off one of their legs, or break a leg, or the right forearm, so that they won't be able to fight in the next four weeks and so that we can round them up." There was an outcry when I said one must simply smash their legs with a club. At the time, of course, I didn't really condone it either, but now I think it's quite right. We've seen that we cannot conduct a war because we're not <u>hard</u> enough, not barbaric enough. The Russians are that all right.[185]

ANNIHILATION

"The FÜHRER has handed us a great deal abroad by his treatment of the Jewish question. That showed a great lack of tact. You will see that when history comes to be written, the FÜHRER will not get off without blame in spite of his great achievements."

"Yes, but that's inevitable. Every individual makes mistakes."[186]

From 1995 to 1999, an exhibition titled "Crimes of the Wehrmacht" sparked one of the most intense historical debates in postwar German society. Compiled by the Hamburg Institute for Social Research, this collection of documentary material about war crimes committed by the German army and its complicity in the Holocaust toured museums throughout Germany, often to the dismay of older visitors, many of whom had themselves served in the armed forces during the Third Reich. The exhibit is widely regarded as having marked the end of the myth of the "clean" Wehrmacht. One striking thing to emerge from the debates was how vehemently German veterans rejected any suggestion that the armed forces had been involved in the Holocaust. As the surveillance protocols show, this was not a case of either repression or denial. Many of the crimes we today consider part of the Nazi campaigns of annihilation and the Holocaust were seen very differently in the 1940s, for instance, as a battle against partisans. The debates reflected the collision of two frames of reference, today's versus that of the past.

The surveillance protocols reveal that many soldiers were astonishingly well aware of the specific details of the extermination of European Jews. Indeed, on occasion the POWs discuss aspects of the Holocaust

Lieutenant General Maximilian Siry (BA 146–1980–079–67)

that have remained undiscovered by historical research. The soldiers generally do not draw connections between what they know and their own behavior, although it was no secret during World War II that the Wehrmacht had indeed committed a great number of war crimes and was involved in the murder of Jews throughout occupied Europe in a number of ways: as executioners, witnesses, accomplices, support workers, and commentators. On very rare occasions, individual Wehrmacht officers disrupted the mass killings by registering complaints, saving victims, or, in one unusually spectacular instance, threatening the SS with violence in order to hinder the murder of a group of Jews.[187] Naturally, such occasions were exceptions to the rule. Historian Wolfram Wette has estimated that there were only one hundred attempts at rescuing Jews among the 17 million members of the Wehrmacht.[188]

None of the large-scale executions such as Babi Yar, where more than thirty thousand people were shot to death in two days, took place without Wehrmacht involvement. Moreover, the knowledge of the mass executions in Russia and the smaller-scale ones that had preceded them in Poland went far beyond the circles that directly participated in or witnessed those atrocities. The spreading of rumors is an effective means of communication, especially when the subject matter is inhuman, secrecy is supposed to be maintained, and information is restricted. In the surveillance protocols, the topic of crimes against humanity perpetrated upon Jews only occurs explicitly in 0.2 percent of the conversations. But the absolute numbers are of limited relevance, especially since the concept of the war crime played such a minor role in the soldiers' frame of reference. The soldiers' conversations make it clear that practically all German soldiers knew or suspected that Jews were being murdered en masse.

What's surprising for contemporary readers is, above all, the way in which soldiers discussed crimes against humanity:

FELBERT: Have you also known places from which the Jews have been removed?

KITTEL: Yes.

FELBERT: Was that carried out quite systematically?

KITTEL: Yes.

FELBERT: Women and children—everybody?

KITTEL: Everybody. Horrible!

FELBERT: Were they loaded onto trains?

KITTEL: If only they had been loaded onto trains! The things I've experienced! I then sent a man along and said: "I order this to stop. I can't stand it any longer." For instance, in LATVIA, near DVINSK, there were mass executions of Jews carried out by the SS or Security Service.[189] There were about fifteen Security Service men and perhaps sixty Latvians, who are known to be the most brutal, when I kept on hearing two salvoes followed by small arms fire. I got up and went out and asked: "What's all this shooting?" The orderly said to me: "You ought to go over there, sir, you'll see something." I only went fairly near and that was enough for me. 300 men had been driven out of DVINSK; they dug a communal grave and then marched home. The next day along they came again—men, women and children—they were counted off and stripped naked; the executioners first laid all the clothes in one pile. Then twenty women had to take up their position— naked—on the edge of the trench, they were shot and fell down into it.

FELBERT: How was it done?

KITTEL: They faced the trench and then twenty Latvians came up
behind and simply fired once through the back of their heads.
There was a sort of stop in the trench, so that they stood rather
lower than the Latvians, who stood up on the edge and simply
shot them through the head, and they fell down forwards into
the trench. After that came twenty men and they were killed
by a salvo in just the same way. Someone gave the command
and the twenty fell into the trench like ninepins. Then came
the worst thing of all; I went away and said: "I'm going to do
something about this."[190]

Lieutenant General Heinrich Kittel recounted these events on December 28, 1944. In 1941, he was a colonel in a reserve unit of the Army
Group North in Daugavpils, Latvia, where some 14,000 Jews were shot
to death between July and November. His own role in the executions
has never been historically established. He himself spoke from the
perspective of an outraged observer, but as a high-ranking officer he
would have had considerable opportunities to intervene in the course
of events. Unlike ordinary soldiers, Kittel did not have to remain in the
role of the passive spectator. He could have done something.

The narratives in the surveillance protocols are often told from an
observer's perspective, which obscured the fact that the storyteller
may have participated in the events described. The narrators position
themselves in the innocuous role of the reporter—a tendency that historical eyewitnesses frequently maintain even today. The detail Kittel
uses to relate past events is also nothing unusual. Executions made
for good conversation, offering numerous opportunities to weigh up
questions of guilt and responsibility.

Conversation partners rarely pose the sort of intense questions
Felbert does in this excerpt. Much more frequently, the impression is
that, while the details the storyteller recounts may be surprising to his
audience, the overall process of annihilation was something familiar.
Felbert, for instance, is clearly familiar with the fact that Jews were
transported in "cattle cars." The listeners in the protocols rarely react
with astonishment or dismiss what is being said as unbelievable or
unacceptable. The annihilation of European Jews, to put it concisely,
was part of the world the soldiers not only knew, but knew much
better than even the most recent research would lead us to expect.
Undoubtedly, not everyone had knowledge of everything.[191] Nonethe-

less, the surveillance protocols are full of Holocaust specifics, from the asphyxiation of Jews using the exhaust fumes of motorized vehicles to the exhumation and burning of bodies as part of "Action 1005." In it, Jewish concentration camp inmates were forced to dig up the bodies and burn them. Moreover, soldiers traded rumors so furiously that we must assume that nearly all of them knew that massive numbers of Jews were being murdered.

A second surprising aspect of the stories is the unpredictable turns they tend to take from today's perspective. For instance, we would expect Kittel to conclude his narrative by telling how he tried to stop the killings for humanitarian reasons. But that's not the upshot of his story:

> I got into my car and went to this Security Service man and said: "Once and for all, I forbid these executions outside, where people can look on. If you shoot people in the wood or somewhere where no-one can see, that's your own affair. But I absolutely forbid another day's shooting there. We draw our drinking water from deep springs; we're getting nothing but corpse water there." It was the MESCHEFS spa where I was; it lies to the north of DVINSK.[192]

Despite the expressions of horror he occasionally uses, Kittel's objection to the executions is practical and technical. As far as he was concerned, the mass shootings could continue, but not where they were taking place.

What disturbs Kittel is the visibility of the executions and the fact that no one seems to have thought of the risk that the water supply could be infected. Felbert, however, is less interested in those issues than in how the story goes on:

FELBERT: What did they do to the children?

KITTEL (very excited): They seized three-year old children by the hair, held them up and shot them with a pistol and then threw them in. I saw that for myself. One could watch it; the SD [Sicherheitsdienst, the Security Service of the SS] had roped the area off and the people were standing watching from about 300 m. off. The Latvians and the German soldiers were just standing there, looking on.

FELBERT: What kind of SD people are they, then?

KITTEL: Nauseating! I'm convinced that they'll all be shot.

FELBERT: Where were they from, from which formation?

KITTEL: They were Germans and they were wearing the SD uniform with the black flashes on which is written "Sonder-Dienst."

FELBERT: Were all the executioners Latvians?

KITTEL: Yes.

FELBERT: But a German gave the order, did he?

KITTEL: Yes. The Germans directed affairs and the Latvians carried them out. The Latvians searched all the clothes. The SD fellow saw reason and said: "Yes, we will do it somewhere else." They were all Jews who had been brought in from the country districts. Latvians wearing the armband—the Jews were brought in and were then robbed; there was a terrific bitterness against the Jews at DVINSK, and the people simply gave vent to their rage.[193]

At Felbert's insistence, Kittel continues his narrative, and the story takes further surprising turns. His explanation for why the killings are carried out by Latvians, on command from Germans, is the popular anger that allegedly accumulated in Daugavpils. This is one of countless examples in the protocols of obvious contradictions—or even sheer nonsense.[194] In the same breath as Kittel talks about popular resentment as a motivation for the executions, he also says that the Latvians were following *orders* by the German Security Service.

Contradictions crop up all the time in human conversations without disconcerting the participants to any great degree. Transmitting information isn't the only reason people converse. Communication has two discrete functions: passing on information and establishing social relations between participants. To speak in the language of classical communications theory, narratives are as much about relationships as they are about content. The situation in which stories are told is thus often more important than whether what is narrated makes either historical or logical sense. Listeners often forgo questions and requests for explanations because they don't want to disrupt the narrative flow or interrupt the speaker. When captivated by a narrative, they often do not even register whether details can possibly be true or not.

But Felbert in this excerpt is an attentive listener, asking "Against the Jews?"[195] Significantly, another person jumps in to answer that question, perhaps because he has registered a contradiction in Kittel's narrative. He tries to put a positive spin on the story and then invites the general to resume his story:

> SCHAEFER: Yes, because the Russians had dragged off 60,000 Estonians. But, of course, the flames had been fanned. Tell me, what sort of an impression did these people create? Did you ever see any of them shortly before they were shot? Did they weep?
>
> KITTEL: It was terrible. I once saw them being transported but I had no idea they were people who were being driven to their execution.
>
> SCHAEFER: Have the people any idea what is in store for them?
>
> KITTEL: They know perfectly well; they are apathetic. I'm not sensitive myself but such things just turn my stomach; I always said: "One ceases to be a human being; that's got nothing more to do with warfare." I once had the senior chemist for organic chemistry from IG FARBEN as my adjutant and because they had nothing better for him to do he had been called up and sent to the front. He's back here again now, though he got there quite accidentally. The man was done for weeks. He sat in the corner the whole time and wept. He said: "When one considers that it may be like that everywhere!" He was an important scientist and a musician with a highly strung nervous system.[196]

Now it's Felbert's turn to steer the conversation in a different direction:

> FELBERT: That shows why FINLAND deserted us, why ROUMANIA deserted us, why everyone hates us everywhere—not because of that single incident but because of the great number of similar incidents.
>
> KITTEL: If one were to destroy all the Jews of the world simultaneously there wouldn't remain a single accuser. [197]

Kittel assumed the role of the pragmatist in his story. What bothers him about the mass murder of Jews is not the killings per se, but the haphazard methods with which they are carried out. He fails to grasp that Felbert wants to discuss the moral dimensions of mass executions in general and not the specifics of one particular case:

FELBERT (very excited and shouting): It's obvious; it's such a scandal; it doesn't need to be a Jew to accuse us — <u>we ourselves must bring the charge</u>; we must accuse the people who have done it.

KITTEL: Then one must admit that our State system was wrongly built.

FELBERT (shouting): It is, it's obvious that it's wrong, there's no doubt about it. Such a thing is unbelievable.

KITTEL: We are the tools . . .[198]

Felbert explicitly assumes a position diametrically opposed to Kittel's. In outraged tones, he speaks of a "scandal" and the necessity of holding those in charge responsible for it — although he clearly excludes his present company from moral culpability.

Yet the source of even Felbert's outrage is not primarily ethical. It, too, stems from practical, personal considerations: "That will be marked up against us afterwards, as though it had been we who did it." Major General Johannes Bruhn seconds that thought:

BRUHN: If you come along to-day as a German general people think "He knows everything; he knows about that, too," and if we then say: "We had nothing to do with it," the people won't believe us. All the hatred and all the aversion is a result purely and simply of those murders, and I must say that if one believes at all in divine justice, one deserves, if one has five children, as I have, to have one or two killed in this way, one does not deserve victory; one has deserved what has now come to pass.

FELBERT: I don't know at whose instigation that was done — if it came from HIMMLER then he is the arch-criminal. Actually you are the first general who has told us that himself. I've always believed that these articles were all lies.

KITTEL: I keep silent about a great many things; they are too awful.[199]

In these POWs' view, the "state apparatus" should be censured for making Wehrmacht generals into tools of Nazi crimes, for which other groups, most prominently the German Security Service, are actually responsible. Bruhn and Felbert are worried that they will be held culpable for things in which they were not involved. Bruhn's macabre statement that one's children might have to pay with their own blood for the crimes their parents committed shows how far the normative frame of reference he operated in deviated from today's standards. Felbert agrees that the parties truly responsible need to be identified. And Kittel concludes the discussion with what reads almost like a Freudian slip: "I keep silent about a great many things."

The interlocutors then move on to discuss in detail the anti-Jewish measures that preceded the Holocaust. In conclusion, Felbert turns the topic back to the mass executions, posing a somewhat bizarre question:

> FELBERT: What happened to the young, pretty girls? Were they turned into a harem?
> KITTEL: I didn't bother about that. I only found that they did become more reasonable. At least they had concentration camps for the Jews at CRACOW. At any rate, from the moment I had chosen a safe place and I built the concentration camp, things became quite reasonable. They certainly had to work hard. The women question is a very shady chapter.
> FELBERT: If people were killed simply because their carpets and furniture were needed, I can well imagine that if there is a pretty daughter who looks Aryan, she would simply be sent somewhere as a maid-servant.[200]

By 1944, Kittel had been made the defensive commandant of Krakow, and the facility he refers to is the Plaszów concentration camp, where commandant Amon Göth used to shoot inmates from the veranda of his house, and where the industrialist Oskar Schindler negotiated the deals that allowed him to save more than one thousand Jews.[201] Kittel was far less outraged by anti-Jewish repression in Krakow than in Daugavpils because the technical aspects were far better organized. Felbert, on the other hand, remains captivated by the lurid topic of what was done with Jewish women, although the group resists this conversational strand.

The group then returns to the topic of who should truly be held responsible for the Holocaust, chiefly Himmler's Security Service:

> KITTEL: When HIMMLER formed his state within the state, the Security Service was founded like this: they took 50% good

police officials who were not politically tainted, and added to them 50% criminals. That's how the Security Service arose. (Laughter.) There's one man in the criminal department in BERLIN, in that famous "Z" section, whom I frequently used when espionage cases were being held by us in the Ordinance French; and the question then arose of nationality and of whether they had not already got a file, whether the man had not cropped up somewhere before. There is the so-called "Z" section "K." After 1933 he said to me: "We have been sifted through now. The politically tainted officials of the State Police have been got rid of and have either been pensioned off or put into positions where they can no longer do any harm. The sound nucleus of police officials, which every State needs, is now intermingled with people from the underworld of BERLIN, who, however, made themselves prominent in the Movement at the right time. They have now been put to work with the others." He said straight out: "50% of us are decent people and 50% are criminals."

SCHAEFER: I think, if such conditions are permitted in a modern State, one can only say that the sooner this pack of <u>swine</u> disappear, the better.

KITTEL: We fools have just watched all these things going on.[202]

Here the group identifies the guilty parties and offers an explanation in the form of the latter's background. The semi-criminal milieu of the SS Security Service, according to the POWs' logic, is the source of the problems that have emerged, although it remains unclear whether the interlocutors consider the Holocaust or its insufficient organization to be the main problem. It is remarkable how quickly the group switches from outrage to more relaxed and seemingly cheerful topics. The "swine" of which Schaefer speaks are definitely the Security Service, and Kittel is at pains to point out that the Wehrmacht's only failing is that they sat back and watched, instead of intervening.

This excerpt is a perfect example of any number of conversations the POWs had about the Holocaust. One of the interlocutors serves as the expert, while his partner(s) play the role of the inquisitive audience, who themselves possess a degree of background knowledge. Their comments about events are frequently, if not exclusively, negative, but the basis of their criticism is often not what we would expect.

In the end, the speakers usually claim the role of passive onlookers who failed to take sufficient notice that atrocities were occurring.

Another interesting aspect of this discussion is that it was quoted in another conversation. A few weeks later, Major General Bruhn passed on to others what Kittel had reported:

BRUHN: Then they dug their graves and then they picked up the children by their hair and then simply killed them. The SS did that. The soldiers stood there, and besides that the Russian civilian population stood 200 m. away and watched as they were killed there. He [Kittel] proved how vile the whole thing was by the fact that an out-and-out SS man who was employed on his staff later succumbed to a nervous-breakdown and from that day cowards kept saying that he couldn't carry on any longer, it was impossible; he was a doctor. He couldn't get over it. That was his first experience of such things actually being done. A cold shudder ran through SCHAEFER (PW) and me when we heard that, and then we said to KITTEL: "What did you do then? You were lying in bed and heard that, and it was only a few hundred metres away from your house. Then surely you must have reported that to your GOC [general officer commanding]. Surely something was bound to be done about it?" He replied that it was generally known and was quite usual. Then sometimes he also interspersed remarks such as: "There wasn't anything particularly bad about it either," and "they were to blame for everything anyhow," so that I almost assumed at that time, that it hadn't even mattered very much to him personally.[203]

Conversations like this are often like games of Chinese whispers. Researchers in the fields of narrative and memory research have determined that stories necessarily change as they are retold.[204] Details are constantly invented, characters substituted, and settings exchanged according to the needs and wants of the storyteller. Retellers of previously heard stories rarely make these changes consciously. Modifications and embellishments simply seem to be an integral part of the storytelling process, with the content being made to fit the teller's perspective and current situation. For that reason, stories shape and don't just reflect events. Stories also reveal what concerns are most important to both tellers and their audience, as well as what knowledge both groups possess and what historical facts and myths are familiar to them. On the basis of such stories, we can determine the extent to which the events connected with the Holocaust were part of the soldiers' communicative arsenal. This particular story shows how outraged Bruhn was at the coldheartedness of Kittel, who he believes was relatively indifferent to the executions.

It is difficult to say to what degree the Holocaust generally occupied soldiers' thoughts. If we assume that the Allied officers in charge of the surveillance would have been interested in learning about the annihilation of European Jews, conversations about that topic would have been disproportionately recorded. The 0.2 percent of stories that centered on the Holocaust seems surprisingly small, especially considering the fact that the narratives encompass the full spectrum of activities associated with anti-Jewish persecution, from ghettoization to executions and mass murder using gas. The shock felt after the end of the war—and today—at the images from Bergen-Belsen or Buchenwald should not lead us to conclude that all German soldiers necessarily participated in or actively knew about the Holocaust. They knew what they did from scenes they had witnessed or registered, largely passively, and from hearsay. The project of eradicating Europe's Jews was not German soldiers' central task, although they sometimes provided logistical support or collegial assistance, and some soldiers certainly participated in the killings of their own free will. "Jewish actions" were mainly organized by storm trooper units, reserve police battalions, and local groups, and they took place in occupied territories well behind the advancing front lines. Troops actively engaged in battle could thus logically not have had much to do with these acts of mass murder.

Regardless of whether individual soldiers found those acts right or wrong or simply surreal, the Holocaust was not a central part of their world in the way it has been ascribed to them by the German and broader European culture of memory in the past thirty years. Knowledge that mass murders were taking place was widespread. It could hardly have been otherwise. But what did that knowledge have to do with the work of war the soldiers were charged with? In far more innocent eras, a lot of parallel events happen without people taking active notice of all of them. Modern reality is complex. It contains a plethora of "parallel societies." Thus the Holocaust might not have been central even to the consciousness of SS men. To take one notorious example: in his "Posen speech," SS leader Heinrich Himmler openly referred to the destruction of European Jews, but the topic only occupied a few minutes of an address that went on for three hours. This fact often gets overlooked in our sheer horror at some of Himmler's statements, such as "Most of you here know what it means when 100 corpses lie next to each other, when 500 lie there or when 1,000 are lined up."

Our source material has led us to conclude that while soldiers were aware of the Holocaust and knew a fair amount about how it was being carried out, that knowledge did not interest them very much. The percentage of conversations dealing with the Holocaust is very small compared to the endless gabbing about weapons and air raid techniques, military honors, ships sunk, and planes shot down. It was clear to the soldiers that the extermination was happening, and the extermination was integrated into their frame of reference. But it remained quite marginal in terms of what commanded their attention.

On the other hand, relatively rare as they are, soldiers' discussions of the Holocaust are usually very detailed and considerably more precise than the painstaking reconstructions made by postwar prosecutors. The surveillance protocols are both more frank and temporally more proximate to the atrocities. Much of what soldiers discussed had taken place in the very recent past and, even more significantly, had not been subjected to the filters of postwar interpretation. As a result, the protocols are far more direct than postwar testimonies or memoirs, which are typically influenced by the authors' desire to exculpate themselves.

The protocols confirm all the facts about the Holocaust that have thus far been established by historical research, criminal investigations, and survivors' testimony. But here, the ones doing the reconstructing are perpetrators or at least observers of the crimes and members of the perpetrating society:

> BRUNS: Six men with tommy-guns were posted at each pit; the pits were 24 m in length and 3 m in breadth—they had to lie down like sardines in a tin, with their heads in the centre. Above them were six men with tommy guns who gave them the coup de grâce. When I arrived those pits were so full that the living had to lie down on top of the dead; then they were shot and, in order to save room, they had to lie down neatly

in layers. Before this, however, they were stripped of everything at one of the stations—here at the edge of the wood were
the three pits they used that Sunday and here they stood in a
queue 1½ km long which approached step by step—a queuing
up for death. As they drew nearer they saw what was going
on. About here they had to hand over their jewellery and suitcases. All good stuff was put into the suitcases and the remain-
der thrown on a heap. This was to serve as clothing for our
suffering population—and then, a little further on they had
to undress and, 500 m in front of the wood, strip completely;
they were only permitted to keep on a chemise or knickers.
They were all women and small two-year-old children. Then all
those cynical remarks! If only I had seen those tommy-gunners,
who were relieved every hour because of over-exertion, carry
out their task with distaste, but no, nasty remarks like: "Here
comes a Jewish beauty!" I can still see it all in my memory: A
pretty woman in a flame-coloured chemise. Talk about keeping
the race pure: at RIGA they first slept with them and then shot
them to prevent them from talking.[205]

Major General Walter Bruns's description contains a number of astonishing details, including the length of the line of people waiting to be
put to death and the enormous number of individuals this entailed.
Another significant fact concerns those doing the shooting. Together
with the procedure of having the victims line up in rows, this detail
confirms the serial, mechanistic character of the executions.[206] Finally,
we should also take note of the reference to the sexual aspect of the
"Jewish actions."

Bruns describes the mass execution as a highly organized procedure
utilizing division of labor. In the removal of the victims' clothes and
the shifts of the shooters, for example, the perpetrators had clearly
come up with an arrangement that allowed the killings to proceed in
orderly fashion. That had not been the case with the earliest executions. The event Bruns described was the result of a swift profession-
alization of killing. As historian Jürgen Matthäus has summarized,
executions followed a standardized schema: "Jews were first rounded
up in raids and taken in groups of various size to a more-or-less
nearby firing range. Immediately upon their arrival they were made
to dig a mass grave. Then they were forced to disrobe and line up in

front of the pit so that the force of the bullets propelled their bodies into the grave. Those who followed were made to lie down on top of those who had already been killed before they themselves were shot. What the perpetrators like to portray as an 'orderly' execution process was in reality a bloodbath. Near larger cities, although it was officially prohibited, something approaching an 'execution tourism' arose. Various types of Germans, sometimes while on duty and sometimes in their own free time, would visit the firing ranges to watch or take pictures."[207]

Matthäus's summary includes crucial details also found in the protocols: the basic procedure of the "Jewish actions," which was continually being modified; the problems and difficulties encountered when executions were carried out; the modifications and instances of optimization that followed; and the behavior of those involved: the officers, shooters, and victims, as well as the eyewitnesses or, perhaps more accurately, curious audience members.[208] The mass executions, it needs to be reiterated, were the end result of a series of relatively unprofessional experiments about how to kill the greatest number of people in the shortest possible time. Reports from individual death squads were passed on to high-ranking SS and reserve police officers, who then regularly met to debate the most efficient methods.[209] In this fashion, innovations such as having the victims disrobe or choosing the most suitable sort of firearms were quickly incorporated into the job of killing and helped standardize the execution procedure.

The stories told by army, navy, and Luftwaffe soldiers revolve around "Jewish actions" that began in mid-1941 in the occupied territories behind the front lines. In the subsequent four years, some 900,000 Jewish men, women, and children were systematically executed.[210]

GRAF: The infantry say they shot 15,000 Jews on the aerodrome at POROPODITZ. They drove them all together, fired machine guns at them and shot them all. They left about a hundred of them alive. First they all had to dig a hole—a sort of ditch—then they shot them all, except a hundred, whom they left alive. Then these hundred had to put them all in a hole and cover them up, leaving a small opening. Then they shot the hundred and put them in too and closed it. I wouldn't believe it but someone showed me the hole, where they were, all trodden down. Fifteen thousand of them! It's in a clearing in the wood, like this camp here. He says they worked for a fortnight at the hole.[211]

KRATZ: I once saw a big lorry convoy came into NIKOLAJEV, with at least thirty trucks. And what was in them? Nothing but naked bodies—men, women and children all together in one truck. We went over to see where they were going—soldiers: "Come here." I watched; there was a big hole. Formerly they simply made the people stand on the edge, so that they just toppled in. But that meant too much work in throwing the bodies out, because not enough go in when they just fall in anyhow. So men had to get down into the hole—one had to stand up on the edge and the other got down inside. The bodies were laid out on the bottom with others on top—it was nothing but a spongy mass afterwards; they piled one on top of another, like sardines. That sort of thing is not forgotten. I shouldn't like to be an S.S. man. It's not only the Russian commissars who've shot people in the back—others have too. Such things are avenged.[212]

Sergeant Kratz, a mechanic deployed with his unit, Bomber Wing 100, in southern Russia in 1942, focuses on how the executions have been technically optimized. He notes, in a professional tone, that the forms of killing are still not adequate because too few victims fall into the graves.

Kratz's perspective is clinical, as though he were describing just another of the many technical complications one might experience as a soldier, but at the end of his anecdote, he does point out that the execution was something out of the ordinary, something that, in his words, will be "avenged." Descriptions of mass killings often conclude with bits of reflection like this. Many of the speakers seem aware that retribution might follow excesses that went far beyond conventional warfare and the sorts of crimes deemed normal and usual in wartime. Mass executions violated and deviated from wartime expectations to the extent that soldiers assumed that they would bring punitive consequences, if Germany lost the war.

Another dialogue revolving around a "Jewish action" in the Lithuanian capital of Vilnius is worth citing at length because it superbly illustrates the contradictory but clinical ways in which soldiers observed atrocities. The dialogue also shows what details about the Holocaust particularly interested soldiers. The interlocutors were two navy men

Mass executions of Lithuanian Jews in 1942. (Photographer unknown; Preußischer Kulturbesitz Picture Archive)

who were part of a U-boat crew, twenty-three-year-old mechanic Helmut Hartelt and twenty-one-year-old sailor Horst Minnieur, who witnessed the scene he describes while serving with the Reich Labor Service:

> MINNIEUR (re execution of Jews in LITHUANIA, near VILNA while he was a member of the "Arbeitsdienst"): They had to strip to their shirts and the women to their vests and knickers and then they were shot by the "Gestapo." All the Jews there were executed.
>
> HARTELT: In their shirts?
>
> MINNIEUR: Yes.
>
> HARTELT: What was the reason for that?
>
> MINNIEUR: Well, so that they don't take anything into the grave with them. The things were collected up, cleaned and mended.
>
> HARTELT: They used them, did they?
>
> MINNIEUR: Yes, of course.
>
> HARTELT: (Laughs.)
>
> MINNIEUR: Believe me, if you had seen it it would have made you shudder! We watched one of these executions once.
>
> HARTELT: Did they shoot them with machine guns?

Clothing from the victims of the Babi Yar massacre, 1941.
(Hessisches Hauptstaatsarchiv, Wiesbaden)

MINNIEUR: With tommy guns . . . We were actually there when a pretty girl was shot.

HARTELT: What a pity.

MINNIEUR: They were all shot ruthlessly! She knew that she was going to be shot. We were going past on motor cycles and saw a procession; suddenly she called to us and we stopped and asked where they were going. She said they were going to be shot. At first we thought she was making some sort of a joke. She more or less told us the way to where they were going. We rode there and—it was quite true—they were shot.

HARTELT: Did she walk there in her clothes?

MINNIEUR: Yes, she was smartly dressed. She certainly was a marvellous girl.

HARTELT: Surely the one who shot her, shot wide.

MINNIEUR: No one can do anything about it. With . . . like that no one shoots wide. They arrived and the first ones had to line up and were shot. The fellows were standing there with their tommy guns and just sprayed quickly up and down the line, once to the right and once to the left with their tommy guns; there were six men there and a row of—

HARTELT: Then no one knew who had shot the girl?

MINNIEUR: No, they didn't know. They clipped on a magazine, fired to the right and left and that was that! It didn't matter whether they were still alive or not; when they were hit they fell over backwards into a pit. Then the next group came up with ashes and chloride of lime and scattered it over those who were lying down there; then they lined up and so it went on.

HARTELT: Did they have to cover them? Why was that?

MINNIEUR: Because the bodies would rot; they tipped chloride of lime over them so that there should be no smell and all that.

HARTELT: What about the people who were in there who were not properly dead yet?

MINNIEUR: That was bad luck for them; they died down there!

HARTELT: (Laughs.)

MINNIEUR: I can tell you, you heard a terrific screaming and shrieking!

HARTELT: Were the women shot at the same time?

MINNIEUR: Yes.

HARTELT: Were you watching when the pretty Jewess was there?

MINNIEUR: No, we weren't there then. All we know was that she was shot.

HARTELT: Did she say anything beforehand? Had you met her before?

MINNIEUR: Yes, we met her the day before; the next day we wondered why she didn't come. Then we set off on the motor-cycle.

HARTELT: Was she working there too?

MINNIEUR: Yes.

HARTELT: Making roads?

MINNIEUR: No, she cleaned our barracks. The week we were there we went into the barracks to sleep so that we didn't . . . outside —

HARTELT: I bet she let you sleep with her too?

MINNIEUR: Yes, but you had to take care not to be found out. It's nothing now; it was really a scandal, the way they slept with Jewish women.

HARTELT: What did she say, that she — ?

MINNIEUR: Nothing at all. Well, we chatted together and she said she came from down there, from LANDSBERG on the WARTHE, and was at GÖTTINGEN university.

HARTELT: And a girl like that let anyone sleep with her!

MINNIEUR: Yes. You couldn't tell that she was a Jewess; she was quite a nice type, too. It was just her bad luck that she had to die with the others. 75,000 Jews were shot there.[213]

This dialogue brings together a number of things that interested many soldiers about the "Jewish actions" (a term they themselves did not use). One primary interest is in the procedure, which is described in detail. The soldiers also noted that women, too, were executed, even pretty ones. In this case, the teller of the anecdote even appears to have had personal contact with one of the victims, who had done forced labor at his military camp. Hartelt seems to assume that attractive forced laborers were required to service soldiers' sexual desires. Minnieur confirms that this was, of course, the case, but points out that German soldiers had to be careful not to get caught in acts the Nazis considered a defilement of racial purity. Minnieur continues by referring to the practice of Jewish women being shot after sex so that they could not inform on soldiers. Clearly the mass executions opened up an arena for violence in which a variety of acts were permissible. If people were going to be eradicated one way or the other, one was allowed to do otherwise impossible or impermissible things to them before they were murdered. It is striking that these two men, whose use of the formal form of address implies that they did not know one another well, could speak completely frankly about an otherwise delicate topic. Stories of sexual abuse were part of the routine inventory of soldiers' conversations and were not greeted with any sort of moral objections.

The conversation then continues casually. Minnieur reports that the victim went to university in the German city of Göttingen, causing Hartelt to remark that she was sleeping around. Formulations like that exemplify the specific attitudes the soldiers have toward sexual violence. They don't see anything particularly objectionable about rape. They take what they would call a "human" interest in victims who are attractive and feel personally involved in the latter's fate. But in light of the massive number of victims, which Minnieur puts at 75,000, an individual tragedy such as that of a pretty Jewess has no significance.

For the soldiers, murder is destiny, as though some sort of higher power had preordained that select people—whether well educated, attractive, and stylishly dressed or not—*had* to become victims. That demonstrates the frame of reference in which the mass eradication of Jews was interpreted. In this excerpt from the protocols, Hartelt and Minnieur do not just discuss mass murder. They also indirectly communicate that they do not consider mass murder to be unjust, immoral, or indeed negative in any sense. Directly witnessing the killings might, as Minnieur put it, cause a feeling of horror. But murder per se is part of the universe of things that simply happen.

Frame of Reference: Annihilation

"They call us 'German swine.' Look at our great men, such as
WAGNER, LISZT, GOETHE, SCHILLER, and they call us 'German
swine.' I really can't make it out.

"Do you know why that is? It is because the Germans are too
humane and they take advantage of this humaneness and abuse
us."[214]

The strongest indicator that a frame of reference is functioning is the
bewilderment an individual feels at other people seeing things differently than he does. Puzzlement about how members of other nations
could regard Germans as "swine" also tells us a lot about what the
Holocaust meant in ordinary soldiers' lives. The gravity of the atroc-
ity by no means caused Germans to question their self-appointed status as the bearers of high culture. There may have been an undertone
in the protocols suggesting an awareness that limits had been transgressed. But National Socialist moral codes had convinced many soldiers that Jews represented an objective problem that needed to be
solved. This was part of the reference frame in which they interpreted
the events they described to one another. The frame of reference was
why soldiers tended to criticize the way mass murder was taking place,
but not the fact that it was happening.

For example, a W/T (wireless telegraph) operator, who was shot
down in a Junkers 88 bomber over northern Africa in November 1942,
recalled:

AMBERGER: I once spoke to a Feldwebel who said: "This
mass-shooting of Jews absolutely sickens me. This murdering is
no profession! Hooligans can do that."[215]

In the main, soldiers saw the persecution and even annihilation of Jews as sensible while criticizing the means of carrying it out, and that sort of logic also extended to people like Auschwitz commandant Rudolf Höss[216] and Holocaust planner Adolf Eichmann.[217] The participation of people in a variety of functions and at a variety of hierarchical levels was key to the Holocaust—as was the willingness of myriads of others to tolerate what they had witnessed. Marksmen at the shooting grounds where mass executions were carried out[218] or concentration camp doctors[219] charged with selecting who would be killed immediately and who was deemed fit for work were concerned with methods of killing, not with justifying its necessity. The same applies to countless others who were directly or peripherally involved in the Holocaust.

The eradication of European Jews was simply not part of German soldiers' emotional world, even though they sometimes used expressions of horror and even regret when talking about it:

PRIEBE: At CHELM (?)—my father told me about it too, he is in EAST GALICIA, on excavation work. They also employed Jews to begin with. I don't believe anyone could hate or oppose Jews more than my father did, but he also said that the methods they used were horrible. Above all, the works at GALICIA employed Jewish labour only, Jewish engineers and everything imaginable. He says that the people of German blood (Volksdeutsche) in the UKRAINE are completely useless. The Jewish engineers were really damned clever. Then there were various types too. There was a Jewish council in the town which supervised the Jews. My father once spoke to one of his engineers, who said: "Yes, sir, when I look at the Jews en masse, then I can understand why there are anti-Jewish people."

Then came that period of mass arrests and the S.S. commandant simply sent my father a chit saying: "By midday to-day so-and-so many Jews must be named." My father said that it was dreadful for him. They were simply shot. The order came: "So-and-so many shootings are to be reported by such-and-such a date." The S.S. leader, a Sturmbannführer, rounded up the Jews, when there were no more, he sent the Jewish council a . . . "By 1430 hours to-day so-and-so many pounds of meat, fats, spices, etc. must be produced." If it wasn't there by then, one them was shot. But many of the Jews poisoned themselves.

My God, if we ever have those people on top of us again![220]

Lieutenant Priebe may have feared that Jews would avenge themselves someday, but that wasn't the core of his argument. He objected to the treatment of Jews because even a self-proclaimed Jew hater like his father was upset about how he was ordered to deal with them and suffered under what he was allegedly forced to do.

Hannah Arendt pointed out the linguistic tendency under Nazism to speak of those receiving orders as bearing a "burden," implying that those who followed instructions were themselves victims.[221] It was a sign of an intact moral sense to criticize the executions precisely *because* one had always supported the persecution of Jews. In his Posen speech, Himmler himself refers to the "weighty task" of annihilation and the challenge of remaining "morally upright" while killing others. The precondition for a perspective like this was that the *overarching* definition of what was just and unjust had already been turned on its head. Within this frame of reference, killing people could be considered "good" because it benefited the welfare of the racial community. The National Socialist ethics of murder normatively encompassed individual scruples and individual suffering when faced with the task of doing the killing.

Priebe's story continues:

The Jews suffered badly during the Russian advance, when the Russians were in POLAND. A great many of them were shot by the Russians too. An old lawyer said to my father: "I would never have believed that things would come to that in GERMANY." All these things I know from my father, how the S.S. carried out their house to house searches; from the doctors that were there they took everything; all jewellery, they didn't even stop at wedding rings. "What have you got there?" "A wedding ring." "Give it here, you don't need it." Then there's also the damnable fact that the S.S., in their uncontrolled sexual activities, didn't even stop at Jews. EAST GALICIA is now completely free of Jews. There's not a single Jew left in EAST GALICIA. Many Jews arranged to get papers and are still living in POLAND; they've suddenly become Aryan.

When they went to work in the morning—we always had to pass the place on our way to the bombing ground—each morning they came along, old women and men, in separate parties. The women came along, all arm-in-arm; they were forced to sing their Jewish songs. You couldn't help noticing some very well-dressed women among them. There were some really attractive women there. You could really have called them "ladies."

The story went round that they were simply driven into a sort of reservoir. Then water was let in and ran out again at the other end. By then there was nothing left of them at all. The number of young SS fellows who had nervous breakdowns simply because they could carry on with it no longer! There were some real thugs amongst them too. One of them told my father he didn't know what he'd do when all the Jews were dead. He had got so used to it he could no longer exist without it. I couldn't do that either. I simply couldn't. I could kill fellows who had committed crimes, but women and children—and tiny children! The children scream and everything. The only good thing is that they took the SS and not the Armed Forces for that.[222]

The narrator Priebe has no difficulty incorporating even the most contradictory aspects into a single story. The mass destruction of Jews is presented as a ghostly rumor in which Jews simply disappear in a flooded reservoir. In the same breath, Priebe criticizes the SS for stealing Jewish jewelry and "their uncontrolled sexual activities" and assures his listeners that he himself wouldn't have been capable of killing Jews, at least not women and children. The only positive is that the SS and not the military proper is responsible. This view is reminiscent of Major General Kittel, who objected to the location but not the practice of mass killings per se.

Soldiers were only interested in carrying out their tasks, not questioning them. With that in mind, we must acknowledge that there was a certain empiric basis to the following complaint of Himmler's in his Posen speech of October 4, 1943:

It is one of those things that is easily said: "The Jewish people is being exterminated." Every Party member will tell you, "perfectly clear, it's part of our plans, we're eliminating the Jews, exterminating them, a small matter." And then along they all come, all the 80 million upright Germans, and each one has his decent Jew. They say: all the others are swine, but here is a first-class Jew. And none of them has seen it, has endured it.[223]

Himmler's speech is often seen as the height of cynicism and the incarnation of moral corruption. But it can be read more productively as evidence of the moral standards Himmler presumed his high-ranking SS officers would maintain and of what comprised the ethical frame of reference of National Socialism. Aspects of this frame of reference appear throughout the surveillance protocols. They include the rhetorical figure of Germans suffering under the "poor" realization of the "proper" aim of persecuting and even killing Jews, or questions of how one could have better implemented the Holocaust as a central project of National Socialism.

The frame of reference encompassing the mass executions and the extermination camps represents an idiosyncratic amalgamation of anti-Semitism, support for genocide, delegated responsibility, and horror at practical implementation. Excerpts from the protocols show that the soldiers perceived the Holocaust as something unprecedented and even terrible. Their complaints could be summarized in the formula: what must be must be, but not in this form. In Priebe's narrative, that is exactly the perspective of the father as a reference figure: a self-professed Jew hater who objects to how Jews are being treated.

In both the surveillance protocols and postwar testimony about the Holocaust, Germans emphasized the extreme brutality of the native inhabitants of countries Germany occupied, distancing themselves in the process from the crassest examples of "inhumanity." But this, too, only suggests that the criminal nature of the entire endeavor had little to no significance in their frame of reference. In fact, when observed empirically, what historians and sociologists refer to by way of shorthand as annihilation, genocide, or the Holocaust dissolves into an array of countless individual situations and actions. That was how the soldiers perceived events. It was the basis of their interpretation and the source of their answers and solutions to problems. Human beings in general behave according to particular rationales, and it is fundamentally false to imagine that they clearly see universal contexts when acting. For that reason, social processes always produce unintended results, outcomes no one desired but everyone helped to bring about.

Another individual who drew clear distinctions between the historical mission of the Holocaust and its unsatisfactory practice was Colonel Erwin Jösting, commander of the Mainz-Finthen military airfield. In April 1945, he related:

> JÖSTING: A great friend of mine whom I can trust implicitly, an Austrian, still in VIENNA, as far as I know, belonged to "Luftflotte 4," and was down at ODESSA.[224] When he arrived there some "Oberleutnant" or "Hauptmann" said to him: "Would you like to watch? An amusing show is going on down there, umpteen Jews are being killed off." He answered: "Good heavens, no." He had to pass the spot, however, and witnessed the scene. He told me himself that the barn was bunged full of women and children. Petrol was poured over them and they were burnt alive. He saw it himself. He said: "You can't imagine what their screams sound like. Is such a thing right?" I said: "No, it isn't right. You can do whatever you like with them, but not burn them alive or gas them or heaven knows what else! It's not their fault. They should be imprisoned and after the war has been won you can say: 'This people must disappear. Put them in a ship! Sail wherever you wish, we don't care where you land but there is no room for you in GERMANY from now on!' " We have made enemies galore! We killed them everywhere in the East and as a result people hardly believe the real KATYN story any longer, but say we did it ourselves.
>
> No, if I hadn't several proofs of that sort of thing I wouldn't make such a noise about it, but in my opinion it was utterly wrong! What madness was that onslaught on Jewish homes; I happened to be in VIENNA at the time, at BAD VÖSLAU.[225] We were then already short of glass and everything else and then we go and smash all their windows! Those people could easily have been turned out and we could have said: "Well, this business is now taken over by a Christian, Franz MEYER. They'll be compensated, whether well or badly makes no difference." But we were short of everything and still everything was smashed and the houses set ablaze. I quite agree the Jews had to be turned out, that was obvious, but the manner in which it was done was absolutely wrong, and the present hatred is the result. My father-in-law, who certainly couldn't stand Jews, always said: "That will not pass unpunished, say what you like!" I'd

be first to agree to getting rid of the Jews; I'd show them the way—out of GERMANY! But why <u>massacre</u> them? That can be done <u>after</u> the war, when we can say "We have the power, we have the might; we have won the war; we can afford to do it!" But now! Look at the British government—who are they? The Jews. Who governs in AMERICA? The Jews. While Bolshevism is Judaism in excelsis.[226]

To Jösting's eyes, the campaign against Jews as it was being pursued seemed irrational because it squandered badly needed resources and thus worked against the ultimate goal of the final elimination of supposedly pernicious Jewish influence. Jösting feared that "the Jew" was already exacting revenge through the soon-to-be-victorious Allies. Moreover, he worried that Germans would be blamed for crimes they did not commit. He is particularly critical of the timing of actions aimed at exterminating Jews. After the war, he believes, the time would have been far more propitious.

Two other German soldiers saw the situation the same way:

AUE: Perhaps we didn't always do right in killing Jews in masses in the East.

SCHNEIDER: It was undoubtedly a mistake. Well, not so much a mistake as un-diplomatic. We could have done that later.

AUE: After we had finally established ourselves.

SCHNEIDER: We should have put it off until later, because Jews are, and will always remain, influential people, especially in AMERICA.[227]

The surveillance protocols also contain firsthand descriptions of the murder of Jews. In one excerpt, SS Oberscharführer Fritz Swoboda discussed the difficulties of carrying out executions in Czechoslovakia with First Lieutenant Werner Kahrad:

SWOBODA: The executions were like an assembly line. You got a 12 marks bonus, 120 kroner per day for the shooting commandos. We didn't do anything else. Groups of twelve men led in six men and then shot them. I didn't do anything else for maybe 14 days. We got double rations because it puts a lot of strain on your nerves . . . We shot women, too. Women were better than

men. We saw a lot of men, Jews, too, who started crying in their
final moment. If there were weaklings there, two Czech nation-
als came and held them up in the middle . . . The man earned
his double rations and 12 mark bonus, killing 50 women in half
a day. In ROISIN we also carried out executions.

KAHRAD: There was a large airfield there.

SWOBODA: At the barracks, it was a treadmill. They came from
one side, and there was a column of maybe 500 or 600 men.
They came in through the gate and went to the firing range.
There they were killed, picked up and brought away, and then
the next six would come. At first you said, great, better than
doing normal duty, but after a couple days you would have preferred normal duty. It took a toll on your nerves. Then you just
gritted your teeth and at some point you didn't care. There were
some of us who got weak in the knees when shooting women,
and we had selected experienced frontline soldiers. But orders
were orders.[228]

This rare instance of inside access to the Holocaust not only allows us
to hear a mass murderer in his own words. It also highlights the difficulties of organizing mass executions and the rewards and strategies
used to overcome them. The assumption that, because of their experience with violence, all veteran frontline soldiers would be suitable for
executions proved false. If Swoboda is to be believed, some of them
lost their nerve when called upon to kill women. He even admits that
in the beginning he himself had to steel himself, and that there were
special rewards for carrying out this particularly tough form of duty.

Soldiers also mentioned cases in which the corpses of murdered
Jews were exhumed and burnt. The operation took place under the
command of SS Standartenführer Paul Blobel in summer 1942 and
was given the code name "Action 1005." In it, Jewish concentration
camp inmates were forced to dig up the bodies and burn them. In
order to destroy the victims' remains more efficiently, Blobel came up
with special types of bonfires and devices for grinding up bones. The
idea was to destroy evidence of the mass murders, but the secret still
got out:

MÜLLER-RIENZBURG: At LUBLIN the fellows told us they were
in a blue funk that the foreign powers would hit upon their

communal graves, so they dug out the corpses with dredgers.
Near LUBLIN there's another of those large burial grounds.

BASSUS: German burial grounds?

MÜLLER-RIENZBURG: Yes. It reeked of human flesh for weeks.
Once they had to fly over there in an aircraft and they actually
smelt the smell of burning in the air.

BASSUS: Was that near LUBLIN?

MÜLLER-RIENZBURG: At some concentration camp or other in
POLAND.

DETTE: He (IO) said: "Do you know how many Poles have been
shot? Two million." That may be true.[229]

Other soldiers speaking on different occasions also discussed the
details of the extermination of European Jews:

ROTHKIRCH: The gas facilities were all in Poland near LEM-
BERG.[230] There are large gas facilities there. I know that, but
I don't know anything else. Look here, gassing isn't the worst
thing.

RAMCKE: I've only heard of such things here in the POW camp.[231]

ROTHKIRCH: I'm an "Administration General" and the people
here have already interrogated me. It was near LVOV. Actually we washed our hands of it all because these atrocities took
place in a military area. At LVOV in particular I was always
receiving reports of these shootings and they were so bestial
that I wouldn't care to tell you about them.

RAMCKE: What happened?

ROTHKIRCH: To start with the people dug their own graves, then
ten Jews took up their position by them and then the firing
squad arrived with tommy-guns and shot them down, and they
fell into the grave.

Then came the next lot and they, too, were paraded in front of
them and then fell into the grave and the rest waited a bit until
they were shot. Thousands of people were shot. Afterwards
they gave that up and gassed them. Many of them weren't dead
and a layer of earth was shovelled on in between. They had
packers there who packed the bodies in, because they fell in
too soon. The SS did that, they were the people who packed
the corpses in.[232]

Children represented a particular problem at mass executions because they often didn't follow instructions or die quickly enough.[233] The descriptions of the executions of children are among the most grisly events recorded in Holocaust literature and research. It is no wonder, therefore, that Edwin Graf von Rothkirch expresses his disgust.

At a somewhat later point in time, he continues his story with a further episode:

> ROTHKIRCH: Yes; I was at KUTNO,[234] I wanted to take some photographs—that's my only hobby—and I knew an SS-leader there quite well and I was talking to him about this and that when he said: "Would you like to photograph a shooting?" I said: "No, the very idea is repugnant to me." "Well, I mean, it makes no difference to us, they are always shot in the morning, but if you like we still have some and we can shoot them in the afternoon sometime." You can't imagine how these men have become completely brutalised.[235]

This description shows how normal executions seemed to the perpetrators. The SS man's offer to postpone the killings as a favor to a photographer speaks volumes not only about how routine executions had become but also about how openly they were carried out. In this case, no attempt seems to have been made to keep the mass murder secret.

Rothkirch, who talks in dramatic and detailed fashion about the various levels of the extermination process, sees this as a sign of brutalization. But it would again be a mistake to conclude that the speaker himself objects to the extermination of Jews per se:

> ROTHKIRCH: Just think of it some of these Jews got away and will keep talking about it. And the craziest thing of all: how is it possible for pictures to get into the press? For there are pictures in this paper (Welt-woche?). They even filmed it and the films, of course, have got abroad; it always leaks out somehow. At LVOV, just like people catching fish with a net, ten SS men would walk along the street and simply grab any Jews who happened to be walking along. If you happened to look Jewish, you were just added to their catch (laughs). Sometime the world will take revenge for that. If those people, the Jews, come to the helm and take revenge, it will of course be terrible. But

I think it doubtful whether the enemy will permit them to get
there, for most of the foreigners, the English, the French and
the Americans, are also quite clever about the Jews. It won't be
like that. They've allied themselves with the devil in order to
beat us; just as we concluded that alliance with the Bolsheviks
for a time, they are doing the same thing. The important question is: which ideology would gain the upper hand in the world?
And whether they will trust us? One must now work to that
end so that they will trust us and we must steer clear of everything which will arouse them afresh so that we first show them:
"Friends, we want to cooperate in creating a sensible world."[236]

This statement is another bewildering conjunction of seeming contradictions, including Rothkirch's outrage at the way the executions are
carried out, the laconic attitude of the executioner, and the arbitrary
process by which victims are selected. Rothkirch's anti-Semitism is
also unusual. He is one of the few POWs to have spoken of "Jewish
Bolshevism." He is also someone who fears Jewish revenge. The frame
of reference within which he argues, however, admits the possibility
that Germans can regain the international trust they have lost and that
Germans will be allowed to play a part in "creating a sensible world."

We should resist the temptation to shake our heads at these astonishing disparities between perception, interpretation, and argumenta-
tion. What appears hopelessly contradictory today was not necessarily
so six decades ago. People who supported anti-Semitic policies could
criticize how they were put into practice without any inherent contradiction. Indeed, they could even regard anti-Semitic practices as a
mistake that would cause considerable trouble. Hostility toward Jews
did not automatically mean that people wanted to be excluded from
the circle of nations that would shape the world of the future. Rothkirch's belief that anti-Jewish policies were implemented in the wrong
way does not call into question the racist worldview that formed his
frame of reference. Nor did it shake his faith that Germans should be
full-fledged members, worthy of trust and equal in status to others,
in world politics. Rothkirch's views may appear, ex post facto, to be
the products of hubris, naïveté, or sheer stupidity. But they reveal the
contours of the frame of reference within which he acted at the time.

The dilemma is the same one that left many Germans, at least until
the 1970s, unable to comprehend that what they had done or tolerated

in the Third Reich could have been utterly wrong. This resulted from what we today might call an absolute incompatibility of the frame of reference "Third Reich" with the political and normative standards that applied in democratic, post–World War II Germany. This incompatibility is at the root of the frequent, heated debates and scandals surrounding the past in post-Nazi German society.[237]

Incompatibility also occurs in the protocol excerpt cited at the beginning of this section, in which a German POW wonders how others could see Germans collectively as "swine," when they were the people of Liszt or Wagner. In another dialogue, a low-ranking artillery officer and a foot soldier search for an explanation:

HÖLSCHER: It's very strange that they are always against us.
VON BASTIAN: Yes, it's very, very strange.
HÖLSCHER: As ADOLF said, it's possibly all due to the Jews.
VON BASTIAN: Both ENGLAND and AMERICA are under the influence of the Jews.
HÖLSCHER: For instance, he now abuses AMERICA more than he does ENGLAND. He says AMERICA is the arch-enemy.
VON BASTIAN: Yes.
HÖLSCHER: American high finance, Jewish finance. Only after that does he speak about ENGLAND.[238]

Within the frame of reference of the Holocaust, beliefs about the negative traits and enormous influence of Jews are so securely anchored that Jewish treachery can serve as an explanation for practically anything. That explains soldiers' reflexive tendency to cite Jewish stereotypes, even in those anecdotes that begin with someone expressing a modicum of sympathy for the plight of Jews:

QUEISSER: You could only go through the Jewish quarter by tram. A policeman always used to stand on the platform to see that nobody got off. Once the tram stopped and we looked to see what was happening and there was someone lying right across the lines.
WOLF: Dead?
QUEISSER: Yes. They had thrown some fellow down in the road. Oh, I shouldn't like to go through that Jewish quarter again. It was awful. The first time I was there I saw some nice looking

children running about with the Jewish star on them—pretty girls among them. The soldiers did some lively bargaining with the Jews. There were Jews working out by the aerodrome, too, they used to bring us gold goods and we gave them bread in return, only so that they could have something to eat.[239]

Especially significant here is Queisser's use of the phrase "lively bargaining" to describe Jews swapping gold for bread. Even if the narrator found it unpleasant to travel through the "Jewish quarter" (i.e., ghetto), he could not pass up the opportunity to engage in such a lucrative transaction himself. This excerpt provides further evidence of the structure of temporary opportunities that opened themselves up to Wehrmacht soldiers in the course of German persecution and extermination of Jews.

Another story revolves around the role of so-called capos in a forced labor camp. It is one of the few dialogues in which a listener expresses doubt as to what the narrator, in this case a pilot, is telling him:[240]

TAUMBERGER: I myself once saw a column of people in a concentration-camp. I got off somewhere near MUNICH (?) . . . They are constructing something for the secret weapons in the hills there; that's where the new weapons are being produced. These people were employed for that purpose. I once saw them marching by. Those starving creatures in the SOVIET UNION are well fed by comparison. I spoke to someone who was supervising there. They were working inside a chain of sentries, working at a terrific pace, without a break, for twelve hours without stopping—then a twelve hours rest, but there was really no question of rest. They only had about five hours sleep in twenty-four hours. They were prisoners; they wore black caps. They were dashing about among them with clubs this size; they hit them over the head or on the back. They collapsed.

KRUSE: Dry up, old man!

TAUMBERGER: Don't you believe me? I can give you my word of honour that I saw it myself—they were . . . prisoners who beat each other up in that way. The supervisors with black caps got cigarettes. They also received full rations and money, paper money. They never got silver money. They were able to buy some extras with that. In this way they were kept up to the

A streetcar traveling through the Warsaw ghetto in 1941.
(Photographer: Joe J. Heydecker; Deutsches
Historisches Museum, Berlin)

mark; they received bonuses. Each foreman was in charge of about forty or fifty prisoners. They were employed by firms; that's to say they were working for certain firms. The more work that was done, the more piece-work, the more bonuses those Judases got. They therefore beat them up to make them work more. The pipes for the turbine-installations for the reservoir and the hydro-electric plant were fitted there. The supervisor and the bookkeeper had an agreement, stating that three pipes were to be built in daily. For that the supervisor received a certain bonus amount. He received still more money himself if, in two days time, he managed to get one pipe more than was agreed upon built in. I stopped there for about forty-eight hours before continuing my journey, I saw it all on that occasion.[241]

Taumberger's description of the labor camp is basically historically accurate. Kruse's incredulity is apparently directed at the detail that inmates were used as guards, although that is open to interpretation. He could have been expressing doubt at the entire story or the role of the capos, or he might simply have not wanted to hear anything, although Taumberger responds by going into more detail about the capos. Strikingly, he stresses his own moral contempt for people he considers "Judases"—as though they were acting entirely of their own free will.

Postwar family reminiscences do feature occasional instances of Germans who seem to have unambiguously rejected the murder of Jews. An interviewee named Doetsch, for instance, recalled: "In Lvov, I once saw a so-called Jew transport . . . Suddenly there was a lot of movement in the ranks. Up at the front, the SS were beating people up. It was . . . the SS, and they'd gotten drunk. They lined them up in front of anti-tank trenches. The first had to take their place, then machine gun fire, and down they went. The next ones had to push them into the trench before they themselves went down. They weren't even dead. Dirt was shovelled. The next ones . . . can you imagine that? Women and children and old people. I knew exactly what was going on. Someone told me. 'We had orders,' he said, 'but I couldn't watch.' Germans nailed children to the walls. They did *that*."[242]

The protocols do not just contain descriptions of mass executions, but of exterminations using car exhaust fumes. A POW named Rudolf Müller at Fort Hunt in the United States told the following story:

MÜLLER: I was brought up in front of a military tribunal in Russia for refusing to obey orders. I was in charge of the motor pool, but the fellow who was supposed to be in charge had fallen, and I was the second highest ranked person in the garage. I was supposed to adapt a truck by installing rubber inserts. I didn't know what for, so I did it. The truck was sent out and placed at the disposal of the local command. That was the end of the matter for us. When the driver returned, he was pale as a ghost. I asked him what was wrong, and he said he would never forget what we had experienced that day. He said, 'They loaded civilians into the back. Then they stuck a tailpipe back into the truck and sealed up the back. Next to me in the front sat a SS man with a pistol on his lap who ordered me to drive.' He was only 18. What was he supposed to do? He drove off. After a half an hour, they arrived at a pit. The back was full of bodies with some chlorine between them. He reversed and opened the hatch, and they tumbled out. Dead from the exhaust fumes. The next day, I received orders to deliver the truck to the local command. I said the truck wasn't going anywhere. So I was brought up before a military tribunal for disobedience. They intentionally loaded in people and killed them with exhaust fumes.

REIMBOLD: Dear God.

MÜLLER: They forced the driver. There was a fellow with a pistol next to him. And they hauled me up on charges.

REIMBOLD: And that's happening in the name of Germany. No telling what's going to happen to us.[243]

This dialogue is one of the scant bits of direct evidence we have of the gassing of Jews using carbon monoxide fumes. It is also unusual in that the narrator clearly abhors the events he describes—an attitude he was forced to answer for in front of a military hearing. The listener also seems shocked. Apparently, he had previously heard nothing about these kinds of murder.

Let us summarize. German descriptions of all aspects of the Holocaust—from the ghettos to the mass executions to the extermination camps—not only characterized but judged the behavior of those involved. The same was also true for stories about Jewish capos, even though they were not acting of their own free will. The trope of "blaming the victim"[244] is well known from studies on the psychology of prejudice and functions by blotting out the circumstances under which people act, reducing behavior entirely to personality factors. This mechanism is active in all sorts of prejudices against underprivileged or discriminated groups, so it is hardly surprising that it should have played a role in a situation of such completely one-sided violence and extreme social stereotyping. It occurs in descriptions of how women were raped or how those about to be executed behaved. Past experiences are narrated as though the storyteller were describing an experiment on lab animals, without mentioning the conditions under which the experiment was carried out.

This perspective, which completely ignored the conditions one side created in explaining the behavior of their victims, can be related back to a frame of reference in which "the Jews" belonged to a completely different social universe to the tellers of the stories. Auschwitz commandant Rudolf Höss, for instance, was excellently informed about the conditions under which his inmates died—he himself created them. Yet even Höss assumed this perspective in his recollections when he spoke of so-called special commandos—camp inmates forced to bring victims to the gas chambers and take them back out again once they had died:

> Höss: Equally bizarre was the entire behavior of the special commandos. They all definitely knew that, after the action was over, they would suffer the same fate as the thousands of their racial comrades whose extermination they had aided. Yet they diligently participated, much to my amazement. Not only by never telling the victims about what was about to happen, but by offering them help in the removal of clothes or by using violence against those who resisted. Then there was the leading away of those who didn't remain calm and physical restraint during executions. They led the victims in such a way that the latter could not see the soldier standing ready with his weapon, so that the soldier could level it, unnoticed, at the back of their heads. They acted much the same with the ill and the feeble, who could not be brought to the gas chambers. Everything was done as a matter of course, as though they themselves were the executioners.[245]

Voluntary Killers

Let us move on now to two aspects of soldiers' behavior that have thus far been largely ignored by the literature on the Nazi war of annihilation and the Holocaust. Wehrmacht soldiers from various units and of divergent ranks occasionally took part in mass executions, even though they were not ordered to and formally had little to do with "Jewish actions." Daniel Goldhagen, writing about one of the few known cases of this sort, concluded that Germans in general were motivated by a kind of exterminatory anti-Semitism. Goldhagen focused on a Berlin police unit, consisting of musicians and performers, that was sent to the front to entertain troops in mid-November 1942. They asked the commander of a reserve police battalion in the German town of Luckow if they could take a turn shooting Jews at an upcoming execution. Their request was granted, and the entertainers spent the following day amusing themselves by murdering people. Holocaust historian Christopher Browning also mentions this incident.[246] But the question remains: did the Germans in question need anti-Semitic motivation to find killing fellow human beings an entertaining pastime?

Their real motivation was probably a lot more trivial. The police officers in question enjoyed doing things they would never have been allowed to under normal circumstances. They wanted to experience what it felt like to kill without fear of consequences, to exercise total power and do something extraordinary and monstrous, free from the possibility of any negative consequences. This is what sociologist Günther Anders has called the "chance for unpunished inhumanity." For some people, senseless murder was apparently a temptation that could hardly be resisted. Violence of this nature needs neither a motive nor a reason. It is its own motivation.

The surveillance protocols also contain descriptions of how German soldiers took part in mass executions, voluntarily or after having received an invitation to do so.[247] These episodes, mind-boggling as they may be to us today, indicate that Nazi genocide by no means took part in secrecy and was not always viewed with horror and disgust. On the contrary, curious onlookers—local people, Wehrmacht soldiers, and members of the civilian administration—regularly turned up at the execution pits, turning exterminations into a semipublic spectacle with a high amusement value. In fact, in July 1941, Higher SS and Police Leader Erich von dem Bach-Zelewski was forced to ban spectators at mass executions. His order read: "All male Jews between the ages of 17 and 45 who have been found guilty of plundering are to be shot in accordance with military procedure. The executions will be carried out at a distance from cities, villages and roadways. Their graves are to be leveled in such a fashion that they cannot serve as sites of remembrance. I expressly forbid photographs or spectators. Executions and graves are not to be made public."[248] Nonetheless, people continued to flock to executions, taking photographs, probably delighting in the obscene spectacle of helpless, naked women, and offering advice to and cheering on the shooters.[249]

The lure of a good show proved stronger than people's fear of violating rules or disobeying commands. A Major Rösler described "soldiers and civilians . . . pouring in from all directions" to witness one execution: "Police were running around in dirty uniforms. Soldiers, some clad only in bathing trunks, congregated in small groups. And civilians, among them women and children, looked on." At the conclusion of his report, Rösler declares that while he had experienced

*An SS man shoots a civilian in Vinnitsa, Ukraine, in 1942 in front
of an audience. (Photographer unknown; Bildarchiv Preußischer
Kulturbesitz, Berlin)*

no shortage of unpleasantness in his life, he had never seen anything
like this sort of bloodbath carried out in public on what amounted to
an open-air stage. Something of that nature, Rösler complained, ran
contrary to German values and ideals.[250] But no amount of commands
and instructions, it seems, could put an end to the problem of execution tourism. A conference of military administrators on May 8, 1942,
decided that the murder commandos should make "amicable adjustments" and if possible carry out executions at night and not during
daytime. But such measures had little effect.[251]

It is useless to speculate about what may have attracted individual
onlookers to defy the prohibitions and attend executions. Their motivations probably varied. Some probably sought out the thrill of witnessing a spectacular and surreal event that would have never been
allowed to happen in normal life. Others were likely drawn by horror

and disgust, perhaps mixed with a feeling of satisfaction that one was exempt from the fate others were suffering. What is more significant in the present context is the sheer phenomenon of audiences witnessing the mass murders. People being gunned down wholesale didn't elicit the sort of repulsion that made people try to avoid witnessing it. Voyeurism and satisfaction at observing others' misfortune are well-documented psychological phenomena that also occur in contexts other than the Holocaust. This is probably also the explanation for the prominence of descriptions of genocide in the surveillance protocols. If one could not witness an execution oneself, one could at least enjoy the vicarious thrill of a detailed description of what it was like.

A navy mechanic and POW named Kammeyer watched an execution in summer 1941 in Liepaja in today's Latvia, while he was deployed on the Baltic coast:

> KAMMEYER: Nearly all the men there were interned in large camps. I met a fellow one evening and he said, "Some of them are going to be shot tomorrow. Would you like to see it?" A lorry went there every day and he said, "You can come too." The Kommandeur of . . . execution there belonged to the Naval Artillery. The lorry arrived and stopped. In a sort of sandpit there was a trench about twenty metres long. There was a man there . . . they threw him out and he called out in broken German that he wasn't one and so on. I didn't know what was happening until I saw the trench. They all had to get into it and were hurried into it with blows from rifle-butts and lined up face to face; the Feldwebel had a tommy-gun . . . there were five of them, they (shot) them one after the other. Most of them fell like that, with their eyeballs turned up, there was a woman among them. I saw that. It was in LIBAU.[252]

But watching an execution paled in comparison to actually taking part in one. Luftwaffe Lieutenant Colonel von Müller-Rienzburg recalled:

> MÜLLER-RIENZBURG: The SS issued an invitation to go and shoot Jews. All the troops went along with rifles and . . . shot them up. Each man could pick the one he wanted. Those were . . . of the SS, which will, of course, bring down bitter revenge.

BASSUS: You mean to say it was sent out like an invitation to a hunt!

MÜLLER-RIENZBURG: Yes.[253]

It is unclear in this excerpt whether Müller-Rienzburg accepted the invitation or not, although he unambiguously says that others did. Bassus immediately imagines a hunt but does not express any special amazement or surprise at what he's just heard.

A Lieutenant Colonel August von der Heydte also reported—albeit in secondhand fashion— that executions resembled hunts:

HEYDTE: The following is a true story told me by BÖSELAGER (?), who managed to get the "Swords" before being killed. Oberst-leutnant Freiherr von BÖSELAGER (?) was a comrade from my "Regiment." He experienced the following. It must have happened in 1942 or 1941 or whenever it was, sometime at the beginning of the show, I believe in POLAND, when an "SS-Führer" was sent there as a civilian commissar.

GALLER*: Who?

HEYDTE: The "SS-Führer." I believe BÖSELAGER (?) had just been awarded the "Oak-leaves." He was having dinner and after dinner the former said: "Now we'll have a look at a little . . ." They then drove out in a car and—it sounds like a fairytale but it is a fact—shot guns were lying about, ordinary ones, and thirty Polish Jews were standing there. Each guest was given a gun; the Jews were driven past and every one was allowed to have a pot shot at a Jew. Subsequently they were given the coup de grace.[254]

In another conversation, a soldier actually admitted accepting the invitation to take part in an execution. Surprisingly, the story related by Luftwaffe First Lieutenant Fried calls forth unmistakable uneasi-ness in his interlocutor, Infantry First Lieutenant Bentz:

BENTZ: When the Germans asked us if it was true about the atrocities in POLAND, we had to say that it was only a rumour. I am convinced that it's all too true. It's a shameful blot on our history.

FRIED: Yes, the persecution of the Jews.

BENTZ: In principle, I think we've adopted the wrong attitude to the whole of this racial question. It's utter nonsense to say that the Jew has nothing but bad qualities.

FRIED: I once took part in it myself, and it left rather an impression of—towards on [*sic*] me as an officer; that was when I came into contact with the war myself, during the Polish campaign, and I was making transport flights there. I was at RADOM (?) once and had my midday meal with the Waffen S.S. battalion who were stationed there. An S.S. captain or whatever he was said: "Would you like to come along for half-an-hour? Get a tommy-gun and let's go." So I went along. I had an hour to spare and we went to a kind of barracks and slaughtered 1,500 Jews. That was during the war. There were some twenty men there with tommy-guns. It only took a second, and nobody thought anything of it. They had been attacked at night by Jewish partisans and there was a lot of indignation about those damned Poles. I thought about it afterwards—it wasn't very "pleasant."

BENTZ: Were they only Jews?

FRIED: Only Jews and a few partisans.

BENTZ: They were driven past?

FRIED: Yes. When I think about it here—it wasn't very "pleasant."

BENTZ: What—you fired, too?

FRIED: Yes, I did. Some of the people who were inside there said: "Here come the swine," and swore and threw stones and things at them. There were women and children there, too!

BENTZ: They were inside as well?

FRIED: They were there, too—there were whole families, some were screaming terribly and some were just stupid and apathetic.[255]

These two POWs talk past one another somewhat. Their basic outlooks differ considerably, and neither immediately registers that fact. Whereas Bentz rejects the mass murder of Jews and believes that Germany has "the wrong attitude to the whole of this racial question," Fried says he accepted an invitation to execute Jews during Germany's campaign against Poland. At first, Bentz failed to comprehend that Fried was among the executioners. Only when Fried adds that the experience was unpleasant, does Bentz realize whom he's talking to. Fried, though, doesn't let Bentz's obvious dismay disrupt his story.

He continues to relate how he shot not just Jews and partisans, but "women and children" as well. His laconic remark that this was not "pleasant" might have meant that he didn't enjoy killing as much as he thought he would. Or it might simply reflect the fact that he notices his interlocutor is critical of Jewish persecution.

As is the case with the presence of picture-snapping tourists, the phenomenon of soldiers being invited, either alone or in groups, to execute Jews suggests that the people concerned required no period of adjustment before carrying out the most brutal kinds of acts. Fried steps up as a shooter just as immediately as the police entertainers in Goldhagen's and Browning's studies. They killed for entertainment and amusement. They didn't need to be acclimatized.

The openness with which the hosts issued their invitations indicates that they saw nothing unusual about their activities and did not expect them to disconcert or repulse people. We can assume, then, that soldiers participating voluntarily in executions, either by invitation or at their own request, was just as common as spectators attending them for their own amusement. That implies that mass executions did not fall outside the bounds of the soldiers' frame of reference or fundamentally run contrary to the way they viewed the world.

These conclusions are supported by a number of statements in the protocols in which POWs explicitly endorse the annihilation of Jews. One of them is a conversation between two young submarine officers, First Lieutenants Günther Gess and Egon Rudolph:

RUDOLPH: It's dreadful to think of our poor chaps in RUSSIA, with a temperature of 42° below zero (Centigrade).

GESS: Yes, but they know what they're fighting for.

RUDOLPH: Quite—the chains must be burst once and for all.

GESS AND RUDOLPH (singing loudly): "When Jewish blood spurts from the knife, O then twice happy is our life."

GESS: The swine! The low-down dogs!

RUDOLPH: I hope the FÜHRER will grant us prisoners our wish and give each of us a Jew and Englishman to slaughter; to cut into little pieces with a big knife, that will be easy. I'll commit "harakiri" on them. Stick the knife in their belly and twist it round in their entrails.[256]

Outrage

"No honorable soldier wants to have anything to do with it."[257]

Stories about crimes against humanity were nothing new for most of the soldiers. Tales of horror were scattered throughout narratives about other topics: fighting on the front lines, for instance, or being reunited with friends while on leave, although stories about extreme violence were relatively infrequent. They called forth, by today's standards, scant outrage. As we have seen, it was very unusual for soldiers to feel repulsed out of *principle*. Even more rare were instances in which first- or secondhand knowledge of brutality prompted soldiers to reflect on the moral character of the war. Their most common response when confronted with tales of mass murder was to ask, with voyeuristic curiosity, for more details.

It is striking that soldiers never discuss the legal dimension of what was going on. They showed no interest whatsoever in interpretations of the Hague or Geneva Conventions—the documents scarcely crop up in the surveillance protocols. "The whole question of what is allowed or not is finally a question of power," one first lieutenant opined. "If you have the power, everything is permissible." Yet this speaker also distinguished between what forms of violence *could* be carried out and what forms *should*. "In spite of that, our troops should not massacre civilians who do not shoot (at them)," the lieutenant said.[258] It's worth directing our attention now at what acts the POWs did see as evil, awful, or repulsive.

German soldiers considered executing captured partisans as nothing short of a dictate of common sense, beyond question, since partisans did not enjoy the status of combatants. Stories about regular prisoners killed on the front lines were also accepted without commentary since that was everyday practice, particularly on the Eastern Front. Narratives had to depart from standard operating procedure in a massive quantitative or qualitative sense to call forth an intense reaction.

One example is a conversation between Lieutenant Kurt Schröder and a lieutenant named Hurb* from Bomber Wing 100 about the execution of pilots who had been shot down. The discussion was prompted by the news that the Japanese had killed U.S. airmen captured during the first American aerial bombardment of Tokyo:

SCHRÖDER: Yes, well, the Japanese are swine the way they treat their prisoners. They executed that crew which they shot down during the first attack on TOKYO, a week or two later, after a court-martial. That's a dirty business.

HURB: If I come to think of it, that is the only right way, we should have done likewise.

SCHRÖDER: And what of yourself, if you were to be executed here?

HURB: Well, let them go ahead.

SCHRÖDER: That's not a soldier's point of view.

HURB: Of course it is. It was the best thing they could do. If, after the first and second air-raid, we had done it with the Americans and English, at any rate the lives of thousands of women and children would have been spared, because no more crews would have flown on an attack.

SCHRÖDER: Of course they would have continued.

HURB: But not attacking towns. If the airforces had been used only for tactical warfare, that is to say, at the front, and if at the very beginning an example had been made in that request— TOKYO hasn't in fact been attacked again since. Thousands of women and children's lives have been saved by the mere fact of executing twenty men.[259]

Hurb's view that murdering enemy pilots is a legitimate means of preventing attacks on civilian targets is not only naïve. It also reflects the general Wehrmacht belief that brutal measures could be used to dictate the enemy's behavior. Schröder disagrees for both empirical reasons and because such "swinish" behavior runs contrary to what he sees as soldiers' honor. Significantly, he does not argue that such executions violated the Geneva Convention. His views are based on his military ethos.

Similar sorts of arguments, often with the same choice of words, occur in conversations between army men. Colonel Hans Reimann, for instance, thought it was "swinish" that the SS reconnaissance unit "Hitler Youth" executed eighteen Canadian soldiers in Normandy. For him, such behavior was inexcusable. Nonetheless, the topic of what should be allowed rarely led to serious debates among the POWs. Most often, a reference to the excessively brutal SS or the "inhuman" war on the Eastern Front sufficed to establish consensus and allow the conversation to turn to other topics. The discussion between Schröder and Hurb was one of the few that featured two obviously different ethical stances. Most soldiers were simply concerned with establishing points of agreement and avoiding any far-reaching conclusions that could have caused them to question their own actions and views.

German POWs were far more interested in the qualitative and quantitative dimensions of war crimes, and this influenced their perceptions. Reports about Soviet prisoners dying en masse in German POW camps elicited far more outrage than tales of soldiers being executed at the front. What happened in the camps was, in the view of one Luftwaffe sergeant, "a downright disgusting bit of work."[260] Two men named Ernst Quick and Paul Korte agreed that the treatment of Red Army soldiers was "dreadful."[261] Georg Neuffer spoke of "ghastly business,"[262] while a private named Herbert Schulz went even further, saying the war was a point of cultural shame and the greatest crime in human history.[263] As early as September 1940, "terrible things" were being told, for instance of the entire male population of a village being executed after someone fired shots at German occupying troops from a house.[264] A First Sergeant Doebele asked himself: "Why do we do all these things? It's not right."[265]

A translator who was deployed with German troops in occupied Italy was also outraged at how Wehrmacht soldiers had treated the civilian population:

> BLAAS: At BARLETTA they called the population together and told them that they were going to distribute food and then they fired into them with machine guns. Those were the sort of things they did. And they snatched watches and rings off people in the street, like bandits. Our soldiers themselves told us how they carried on. They simply entered a village and if there was anything they didn't like, they just shot down a few people, just like that. They told us about it as though it were quite in order, and as though it were the natural thing to do. One man boasted of how they broke into a church and put on the priest's vestments and committed sacrilege in the church. They behaved like Bolshevists there and then they were surprised when the people turned against them.[266]

The striking thing is that SS Sonderführer Blaas refers to his soldiers not just as bandits but Bolshevists, one of the National Socialists' archenemies. Talking about crimes that had occurred only a few days pre-

viously also reawakened memories of the Eastern Front. "And then
the things they are doing in Russia!" Blaas exclaimed. "They massa-
cred thousands of people, women and children. It was frightful!"[267]
Blaas's experiences in Italy and Russia merged into a kind of orgy
of violence that left him deeply disturbed. Significantly, references to
the SS as the perpetrators, which normally allowed the speakers to
disassociate themselves from the violence depicted in their stories, are
missing here.

The crime that called forth the greatest outrage was the murder of
women and children:

> MEYER: I saw the SS destroy a village in RUSSIA, including the
> women and children, just because the partisans had shot a Ger-
> man soldier. The village was not in any way to blame. They
> burned the village down root and branch, and shot the women
> and children.[268]

This statement by army lieutenant Meyer is unusual insofar as, in the
speaker's eyes, the death of a single German soldier did not justify the
act of retribution. Atrocities committed against women and children
were frequently described as "appalling" or "horrible"[269] deeds that
made one's "blood boil."[270] Soldiers usually quickly distanced themselves from the war crimes they described and then changed the subject. Yet on occasion, stories about the execution of prisoners or the
mass murder of Jews did provide food for moral thought. Germany's
youth had lost all respect for humanity, one POW complained, referring to the relatively young average age of those who perpetrated
crimes against humanity.[271] A soldier named Alfred Drosdowski
called his fellow soldiers "swine" who had given Germany a bad name
for decades to come.[272] A Sergeant Czerwenka even declared: "I have
often felt ashamed of wearing German uniform."[273] After hearing a
cell mate relate details about a mass execution in the town of Luga in
the Leningrad oblast, Franz Reimbold responded: "I tell you. If that's
the way things are, I'll stop being German. I don't want to be German
any more."[274]

When Colonel Ernst Jösting learned from his wife about the conditions under which Jews were deported from Vienna, the two agreed:
"That's bestial, unworthy of a German." Helmut Hanelt came to much
the same conclusion when a comrade named Franz Breitlich described

in detail how thirty thousand Jews had been executed: "It makes you ashamed of being German."[275]

Higher-level ranks were notably more prone to reflect on what conclusions should be drawn from the prevalence of war crimes. For example, Colonel Eberhard Wildermuth opined:

> WILDERMUTH: If only ours were a young and immature people, but they have been infected to the depth of their moral fibre. I must tell you that I have considered this question really seriously; a nation which has accepted such a rule of lies, brute force and crime, in the main without raising any objection, is simply not a people; a people in which the murder of mental defectives was possible and where intelligent people could still say: "That wasn't at all an idea of theirs" should be liquidated. Such bestiality has never been seen in the world before. One might just as well get rid of all consumptives or all suffering from cancer.[276]

Lieutenant General Friedrich von Broich was likewise frank in his assessment:

> BROICH: All we've achieved is that our reputation as soldiers and Germans has been completely besmirched. People say: "You carry out all the orders when people are to be shot, whether it is right or wrong." No one objects to the shooting of spies, but when whole villages, the entire population, including the children, is wiped out, or the people are sent away, as in POLAND or RUSSIA, then, my God, one can say it is pure murder, it is exactly what the Huns of old did. But then of course we are the most civilised people in the world, aren't we?[277]

Broich was also one of the few German officers to object on moral grounds to the *Kommissarbefehl,* Hitler's order that all Soviet political commissars should be immediately executed: "The shooting of the commissars—I have not been able to discover in any war, except in the dimmest past, that orders like that have been issued by the highest authority. I have seen (?) these orders personally. That is a sign that like a God, that man has simply disregarded everybody and all pacts which exist, and exist on both sides—that is megalomania."[278]

Broich's views were exceptional. Most German officers welcomed the *Kommissarbefehl*.[279] Broich's moral reflections were made in the Trent Park officers' POW camp. There, distance from Germany and an abundance of free time led to a number of extraordinary conversations:

> BRUHN: If you were to ask me: "Have we deserved victory or not?" I should say: "No, not after what we've done." After the amount of human blood we've shed knowingly and as a result of our delusions and also partly instigated by the lust of blood and other qualities, I now realize we've deserved defeat; we've deserved our fate, even though I'm accusing myself as well.[280]

We have no way of knowing what personal reasons might have led individual POWs to be critical of Wehrmacht war crimes. Some probably found what German soldiers were ordered to do simply too horrible, while others may have maintained deeply entrenched moral beliefs. Yet significantly, such criticism was constantly advanced from the perspective of the noninvolved observer, powerless to change anything. Rarely did POWs raise the possibility of their own culpability, and the protocols contain almost no evidence of any of them engaging in active resistance. One exception was Colonel Hans Reimann, who told of having approached his superior officer during the Polish campaign in an effort to halt the SS execution of Polish intelligentsia. "He wouldn't think of doing so," Reimann reported his superior saying. "His position and salary meant far more to him."[281]

Breaking the constraints of conformity seemed impossible to most German soldiers, no matter how gruesome the crimes they observed. In this respect, a story told by a Major Arp from the Army Field Command 748 is typical. When Arp was a first lieutenant in Russia, a mother begged him to protect her two children from the Wehrmacht countersabotage secret field police. The next day he saw them shot to death, lying on the ground. He does not tell of an effort on his part to save these people, launching instead into a description of the mass executions in Kaunas, Lithuania. When Arp's interlocutor asks if he had tried to prevent the murders, Arp becomes evasive.[282]

Thus, it is hardly astonishing that the surveillance protocols contain exactly one account of an act of rescue, the truth of which cannot be determined:

> BOCK: In BERLIN I saved Jewish girls, who were to be sent to the concentration camp. I also got a male Jew away, all by train.

LAUTERJUNG: All by the special train?

BOCK: No. I was with the Mitropa. At the back we had some of those steel cupboards where we kept our stock and I put the Jew and the Jewess in there! Afterwards I had the Jew under the carriage in a box. Of course he came out afterwards at BASLE looking like a nigger. He is living in SWITZERLAND and the girl is down in SWITZERLAND too. I took her as far as ZURICH and she went down to CHUR.[283]

RESPECTABILITY

Despite the atrocities they described and their knowledge of the mass murder of Jews and the appalling treatment of Soviet prisoners, the soldiers lived in a moral universe in which they felt like good people—people who, in Himmler's words, had remained "morally upright." The National Socialist ethos of respectability focused on the idea that fighters were not to engage in crimes like murder, rape, and plunder to benefit themselves, but for the sake of a higher cause. This ethos allowed Germans to justify actions that were absolutely evil in terms of Western, Christian morality and to integrate them as unavoidable necessities into their own moral self-image. National Socialist morality contained the idea that the perpetrators of atrocities might themselves suffer from the "dirty work" they did.[284] The trope of sacrifice, too, allowed Germans to kill without feeling guilty. Ideologists of annihilation like Himmler or practitioners like Rudolf Höss continually stressed that destroying human lives was an unpleasant task that ran contrary to their "humane" instincts. But the ability to overcome such scruples was seen as a measure of one's character. It was the coupling of murder and morality—the realization that unpleasant acts were necessary and the will to carry out those acts *in defiance of* feelings of human sympathy—that allowed the perpetrators of genocide to see themselves as "respectable" people, as people whose hearts, in Höss's words, "were not bad."[285]

The autobiographical material left behind by perpetrators—diaries, interviews, and interrogations—has one very conspicuous feature. Even when the people in question showed absolutely no comprehension of the enormity of what they had done, they were very concerned to appear not as "bad people," but as individuals whose moral fiber remained intact despite the extreme nature of the actions. It could be that such statements were shaped by the contexts in which they were made. Autobiographical documents are always self-justifications in which the narrator tries to bring the stories he tells into harmony with the image he has of himself and wants others to have of him. The case of interrogations also features a further legal, complicating component. The perpetrator wants to portray himself as moral *and* avoid incriminating himself.

The situation is different with the surveillance protocols. In them, the speakers do not address their statements to any external moral arena. At the time their conversations were recorded, the POWs did not know how the war was going to turn out or that the "Jewish actions" and other crimes against humanity would attract near universal moral condemnation. In other words, they did not have to define "respectability" or assure one another that they were indeed respectable people.

Only when they refer to foreign countries do the soldiers explicitly talk about "respectability." In those cases, they usually claim to have been more respectable than was actually required:

ELIAS: The German soldier himself, who does not belong to the S.S., has been far too decent.

FRICK: That's true, one is often too decent.

ELIAS: I was down there on my first leave at Christmas, 1939. I was coming out of a restaurant and a Pole came along. He said something or other to me in Polish and bumped into me. I turned round—I knew what was going to happen—and hit him between the eyes with my fist: "You Polish swine." He was thoroughly drunk and lay where he fell. I was cleaning my hand—I was wearing chamois leather gloves, you know—when, suddenly a policeman arrived without his helmet. He said: "What's happening here, my friend?" I replied: "This swine of a Pole just jostled me," "What," he said, "and the swine is still living? There are too many of them about." He looked at him: "Well, brother, we've been waiting for you for a long time. I'll count up to three and if you haven't gone by then, something will happen." He counted "one" and the fellow was up and away. Then he placed himself in front of me: "It would have been better if you'd attacked straight away, if you'd run him through with your bayonet." Well, I walked around the town for a little—it was about four o'clock on a winter's afternoon—when suddenly

I heard a couple of reports. "What's happened?" I wondered. That same evening I heard there had been some slight trouble . . . he had come to blows with the policeman who wanted to arrest him and he tried to escape—he was shot whilst escaping. What had happened was that the policeman, who had said "too many damned people around," also said: "Make-off," and then followed him and killed him, "shot whilst trying to escape."[286]

It wasn't necessary for members of the enemy group—be they partisans, terrorists, or just people who had gotten a bit drunk—to do anything in particular to incur the wrath of German soldiers. The act of "decency" around which this story revolves is simply that the speaker did not immediately kill the "swine of a Pole." The person in question had done nothing more than brush up against the soldier on the street. Nonetheless, it was considered a mark of decency to let the Pole get away with his life, if not for long.

Stories of this sort were by no means restricted to Germany's war in Eastern Europe. A similar situation also took place in Denmark:

DETTE: When were you in DENMARK? Two years ago?

SCHÜRMANN: I was there in January and February of last year.

DETTE: What were the Danes like, friendly?

SCHÜRMANN: No, they beat up many a man. You can't imagine what scum those Danes are, incredibly cowardly, a horrible people altogether. I can remember the following quite well: an Oberleutnant shot a Dane in the tram and he was later court-martialled for it. I can't understand it, the Germans are certainly much too good-natured. It happened like this. The tram started up and a Dane threw him out; he fell flat on his face. He lost his temper—Leutnant SCHMITT always was a hot-tempered man; luckily he just managed to jump on to the second carriage of the tram, then he changed into the first one at the next halt and shot the fellow without turning a hair.[287]

German soldiers, as we have seen throughout this book, cited even the most trivial reasons for putting people to death:

ZOTLÖTERER: I shot a Frenchman from behind. He was riding a bicycle.

WEBER: At close range?

ZOTLÖTERER: Yes.
WEBER: Did he intend capturing you?
ZOTLÖTERER: Certainly not, I just wanted the bicycle.[288]

RUMORS

Fantasies and flights of imagination, difficult as they are to identify empirically, are part of the world in which we feel we exist. It is impossible to deny the enormous destructive force of Germans' mental images of Jews, regardless of whether they were based on quasi-objective sources or merely common stereotypes and biases. Fantasies are not bound to empiric reality. Nonetheless, they can trigger actions that permanently change things in real life, the obvious example being the imaginary universe of Germans in which the Aryan race was superior and thus destined to rule the world. There are too few studies of the opaque area of imagination in the context of the Third Reich. One of them, Charlotte Beradt's compilation of dreams people had during the period, hints at the central role the Führer and other leading Nazis played in the German subconscious.[289] Another source that sheds light on this otherwise obscure aspect of the reference frame of the Third Reich is the love letters written to Hitler. Eight thousand in number, they contain the unrealistic fantasies of women who wanted nothing more than some sort of intimate contact with the Führer.[290]

The surveillance protocols contain little fantasy material. That's likely because the British and American officers in charge of the operation didn't think that conversations of this kind were worth preserving. But the protocols do contain significant information about a topic related to fantasy: rumor. Rumors crop up a lot in the soldiers' tales, especially in the context of the Holocaust, an initiative that was supposed to be kept secret and was felt to be monumentally transgressive. Such rumors sometimes took the form of fantasies about how people were killed or particularly bizarre events.

Sometimes, things the POWs had actually experienced seemed like the products of fantasy. In conjunction with "Action 1005," for instance, Rothkirch related:

ROTHKIRCH: A year ago I was in charge of the guerrilla school where men were being trained in guerrilla warfare; I went on an exercise with them one day and I said: "Direction of march is that hill up there." The directors of the school then said to me: "That's not a very good idea, sir, as they are just burning Jews up there." I said: "What do you mean? Burning Jews? But there aren't any Jews any more." "Yes, that's the place where they were always shot and now they are all being disinterred again, soaked in petrol and burnt so that their bodies shan't be discovered." "That's a dreadful job. There's certain to be a lot of loose talk about it afterwards." "Well, the men who are doing the job will be shot directly afterwards and burnt with them." The whole thing sounds just like a fairy story.[291]

RAMCKE: From the inferno.[292]

Events like the digging up and burning of Jewish corpses challenged the comprehension even of people like Rothkirch who were familiar with the Holocaust. But the Holocaust had path dependencies and consequences of its own, including "Action 1005." In 1941, none of the perpetrators reckoned that the bodies would later have to be disposed of, and the horror this entailed crossed a further boundary of what they could imagine. It's thus no wonder that Rothkirch and Ramcke use imaginary places as points of reference. Things like "Action 1005," they both seem to be saying, cannot be part of their normal reality. They belonged on another nonearthly plane, that of the fairy tale or hell.

Here we see that for the soldiers the Holocaust demarcated a thin, permeable boundary between the real and unreal, the imaginable and unimaginable. The shifting nature of this border opened up space for fantastic rumors:

MEYER: In a city, I think it was TSCHENSTOCHAU, they did the following. The district captain ordered the Jews to be evacuated. They gave them shots of prussic acid. Prussic acid works quickly and then, the end. They took a few final steps and dropped to the ground in front of the hospital. Those are the harmless tricks.[293]

Rumors of this sort floated around freely and could be attached to a variety of events. But they remained uncanny, even as the roles of the actors, in this case Poles, changed.

A low-ranking Luftwaffe officer named Heimer told of Jews being killed by diverting gas into train cars:

> HEIMER: There was a large collecting place, the Jews were always brought out of the houses and then taken to the station. They could take food with them for two or three days, and then they were put in a long distance train with the windows and doors sealed up. And then they were taken right through to POLAND, and just before reaching their destination they pumped in some sort of stuff, some sort of gas, cool gas or nitrogen gas — anyway some odourless gas. That put them all to sleep. It was nice and warm. Then they were pulled out and buried. That's what they did with thousands of Jews! (Laughs.)[294]

Astonishingly, this story was told in late 1942, before the introduction of gas to Auschwitz. It conflates two facts: the deportation of Jews in trains heading eastward and exterminations using exhaust fumes of motor vehicles, which had been taking place in Chelmno, in Riga, and around Poznan since the end of 1941.

The conflation of separate half-understood facts is a typical way in which rumors were started. Heimer's laughter at the end of his anecdote indicates that he regards his story as something unbelievable, and in fact his interlocutor doubted its credibility:

> KASSEL: Surely, you can't do that!
> HEIMER: It's quite simple. Why shouldn't one arrange something like that?
> KASSEL: In the first place it's not possible and secondly you just can't do a thing like that for God's sake!
> HEIMER: All the same it was done.[295]

This is one of the rare instances in the protocols when a listener expressed disbelief and disgust at what he was hearing. But the listener in this case was a British stool pigeon who was trying to elicit further information from Heimer, a W/T [wireless telegraph] operator. That's why he assumes the role of the disbeliever. Thus, even this exception confirms the rule that listeners usually didn't consider even the most horrible of stories to be unlikely or improbable.

One recurring rumor was that the bodies of murdered Jews were dissolved by acid:

TINKES: There were about five goods trains standing ready at the northern railway station and the Jews were fetched out of their beds. Those who could actually prove that they had been French citizens for more than ten to twelve years were allowed to remain, but all the others who had integrated since then, refugees and foreign Jews, were taken away. The French police broke in on them suddenly, pulled them from their beds, packed them into lorries and off the goods trains went — off towards RUSSIA; the lot of them were transported away to the East. Of course there were fantastic scenes; women jumping out of third-floor windows into the street and so on. Nothing was done on our side — it was all the French police, who did that, who carried out the whole business, none of us took part. I was told — I can't know whether it is true or not, anyhow there was some garrison duty (?) man who had worked in a Russian P/W camp for a long time in the general "Gouvernement" — I once had a talk with him out there, we happened to meet in the train and the conversation came round to that subject. "Yes," he said, "the transports arrived at our place. I was beyond WAR-SAW, near DEBLIN, and they arrived there and were de-loused and that was the end of it." I said: "Why de-loused? If a man comes from FRANCE, he doesn't need to be de-loused." "Well," he said, "they are transit camps for soldiers coming from the eastern front, they are de-loused there and then go on leave; and the Jews from the West go to those de-lousing camps too. There are large tanks there, only the Jews get a different de-lousing mixture in their bathing tanks. It takes perhaps a half an hour or an hour, when there are about 200 men in it, and then you can't find anything but a few gold teeth, rings or something, everything else has been dissolved. That is drained off . . . . . camp." That was the way they de-loused the Jew! They put them into these baths, he said and once they were all in, an electric current is passed through the whole thing; that knocks them over and then the acids are added which dissolved the whole damned lot completely. Of course it made my hair stand on end![296]

This story weaves historically accurate details and imaginary elements together into a rumor about how the bodies of victims were completely destroyed. The parts about Jews being deported from France and deceived as to the purpose of the "delousing" are based on fact. Victims heading into the gas chambers were told they were going to be disinfected. The bits about baths with electric currents, into which acids are then poured, were a product of the sort of imagination typical of rumors.

Rumors are an emotional form of communication, spreading a feeling of something monstrous or uncanny. As such, they express an element that rarely occurs in the soldiers' conversations: feelings.

FEELINGS

It was extremely rare for soldiers to talk about negative emotions, at least not those that they themselves had felt. This reluctance is by no means unique to World War II. We find it in all modern wars. Being confronted with extreme violence, be it as a perpetrator, observer, or victim, likely changes individuals in ways that cannot be easily communicated. There may be discursive forms for talking about violence that one has committed oneself: the adventure tales of shooting down planes, "knocking over" civilians, or raping women. But there seem to be no formats for speaking about one's own fears, especially fears of death and dying. The reason for this, psychologically speaking, is probably simple: members of combat units are so close to violence and death that those things are constant, realistic possibilities, and the idea of one's own death is as terrible and unreal for soldiers as it is for civilians. Even in normal social circumstances, people rarely enjoy talking about their own deaths. That reluctance is no doubt all the greater in situations where dying is far more likely, and the likely manner of death will be violent, brutal, painful, and usually lonely and dirty.

One of the few POWs to talk explicitly about his fears, in this case being burned alive in a plane crash, was Luftwaffe Sergeant Rott:

> ROTT: Then I joined our unit. Hauptmann MACHFELD was there then. He was burnt to death at BIZERTA—he was our first Gruppenkommandeur, he had the Knight's Cross. On 26th November he landed in a [Focke-Wulf] "190," and ran off the runway into all those damned bomb craters, the aircraft turned over and caught fire; he screamed like an animal—it was hor-

rible. I was always terrified of being burnt to death, especially in the [Messerschmitt] "109"—I've seen a great many of those aircraft turn over myself. Anyway, his aircraft was blazing, and you would hear his screams, in spite of the fact that there were aircraft warming up their engines. The mechanics themselves couldn't bear to hear it, and they let the aircraft engines run at full speed, so that the screams couldn't be heard. The fire service couldn't do anything— the ammunition was exploding.[297]

Fears about dying also resonated in soldiers' irrational attempts to formulate "rules" about who would be killed:

> BOTT*: In our "Gruppe" there is the superstition that "Oberfeld-webel" are always shot down.
> HÜTZEN*: That's curious. We, too, have the same superstition.[298]

Moreover, certain types of warfare were unpopular because they were particularly dangerous. Nighttime sorties were one example in the Luftwaffe, as two veteran bomber pilots made clear in November 1943:

> HÄRTLING*: I don't like night bombing. When you come over at night you don't really know where you are, and if you crash you don't know what you are falling onto.
> All the people in this camp are lucky devils who have still got away safely. The fighters' bullets must have hit the bombs, as ricochets entered the machine, which could only have come in this way.[299]
> LOREK: I could never sleep after a sortie if I came back about three o'clock. I swear by day-flying only, I detest night-flying. I far prefer day to night. That uncertainty; you may get it on the neck any minute. You can't see the blighter.[300]

Luftwaffe airmen were confronted with different sorts of dangers in the various places and situations in which they were deployed. That emerges clearly from a conversation between two Luftwaffe lance corporals from October 1942. They discuss the toll that the enemy's numerical superiority could take on soldiers' nerves:

Bücher: There are 180 fighters in the Wash alone. Here round London there are at least 260 aircraft. If you came along with twenty aircraft you are sure to have two or three night fighters making for you! I can tell you, you have to twist about like mad. No, it's no joke flying here.

    We had some crews back from Stalingrad with "88's." We came back from Stalingrad, too, to help a bit over England. . . . Night raid on Cambridge. They had nothing more to say when they got back again. Two had been shot down. They didn't say a word. They were glad to get away again.

Weber: In Russia the flying is —

Bücher: Easier, I tell you! We did some flying in Russia! That was fine. But here it's just suicide.[301]

Those remarks echoed the confession of a German airman in October 1940:

Hansel*: During the last six weeks we always had to be in readiness. My nerves are done for. When I was shot down, my nerves were in such a state that I could have howled.[302]

Comrades whose planes had been shot down were one of the recurring topics in Luftwaffe POWs' conversations. But the speakers usually tried to avoid explicitly referring to death. The airman cited above who confessed his fear of being burned alive was the exception to the rule.

Instead, POWs remained abstract when they talked about lost crews, omitting names and causes of death. Why? Talking about death was thought to bring bad luck, as a bomber pilot named Schumann revealed when relating the heavy losses suffered within his crew: "Our morale was . . . low. As we were climbing into the aircraft the W/T operator said: 'Get ready to die.' I've always said it's wrong to talk like that."[303]

When soldiers did discuss the psychological strain that resulted from extreme stress and fears for one's life, they often used comrades as surrogates for expressing what were likely their own emotions:

Fichte*: Six crews have been lost within three months. You can imagine what sort of effect that has on the crews which are left. When they climb into their aircraft they all think: "Are we going to get back?"[304]

These remarks were recorded in March 1943. That same month, a bomber observer named Johann Maschel reported about a comrade whose nerves were completely shot after flying seventy-five missions:

MASCHEL: I have been in the Staffel for a month and a half. We had night crews. From February 15th to March 24th, four crews were lost.

HÖHN: And from January until February 15th you lost only two crews?

MASCHEL: But perhaps they didn't fly so often, only every third day. The weather was only favourable latterly—no fog or anything.

Altogether we had two old and six new crews and of the six new ones three have already crashed . . . and it won't be long before the other new ones do, too—

HÖHN: Surely more new crews are coming along?

MASCHEL: Yes, that's true, but they are all greenhorns, who have only made three or four operational flights. That's the reason why I always used to fly a few times with the old crews, otherwise I should only have made four operational flights, too. And the new ones. . . . We had an N.C.O. crew which hadn't got any aircraft and now . . . have already gone, three crews. Now it's our turn. . . . We've got an old observer in the Staffel, who is still flying, he has been [in] seventy-five operations over POLAND, he's completely finished.

HÖHN: How old is he?

MASCHEL: I believe he is twenty-three or twenty-four and he's lost his hair. He's practically bald, like an old man. He's hollow-cheeked, he looks terrible. He once showed me a picture of himself as a recruit, when he first joined up—he had a face full of character and looked so fresh. When you talk to him he is so nervous, he stutters and can't get a word out.

HÖHN: Why does he still fly operations?

MASCHEL: He has to.

HÖHN: But people must see that he's done for.

MASCHEL: Then they will probably tell him . . . to pull himself

together. The crew he used to have doesn't fly any more. The
pilot was . . . into a sanatorium—then he was allotted to the
other crew.[305]

Maschel, who had ejected from his burning Dornier 217 over Scotland
on March 25, 1943, was a member of Luftwaffe Bomber Wing 2, one
of the few units to continue flying bombing raids against Britain after
the summer of 1941. The wing suffered heavily in their attempt to take
aerial warfare to enemy territory, losing 2,631 men, of whom 507 were
killed in 1943 alone.[306] Statistically, the unit was exhausted, and the
psychological consequences of such heavy losses, as this conversation
shows, were dramatic. The members of the unit were all too aware
that it was only a matter of time until they, too, were shot down. The
Luftwaffe did not have the sort of rotation system used by the British
and American air forces, in which bomber crews were withdrawn from
the front after flying twenty-five sorties.

To numb their growing fear as German prospects deteriorated during
World War II, more and more soldiers turned to alcohol, drinking "like
mad."[307] Staff Sergeant Nitsch of Bomber Wing 100 admitted in September 1943 that they also took stimulants like Pervitin: "We had terrific drinking bouts before each sortie. We had to get up our courage.
However drunk I am, I can always fly. The only thing is, if I get tired.
But then I just took one of those tablets and was then as refreshed and
cheerful as if I'd been drinking champagne. The things really have to
be prescribed by a doctor but we always had some with us."[308]

Surprisingly, though, the protocols do not bear out the idea, postu-
lated by historians, that German fighting morale declined toward the
end of the war.[309] Airmen who were shot down in 1945 do not talk any
more frequently about being afraid to die than those captured earlier.
Instead, they still proudly recount their triumphs and engage in specialist discussions about the technical details of their aircraft.

It was rare for them to reflect on the personal consequences of their
deployment in battle. One of the few exceptions came in June 1942,
before the Luftwaffe had suffered any major defeats:

LESSER: I was a decent boy when I joined the G.A.F., and they've
    made a swine of me. After being on the Eastern Front, I was
    broken in body and soul; at home they had to comfort me.[310]

In many respects, narratives about extreme personal burdens are the mirror image of the tales of adventure, conspicuous in their brutality, that highlighted the sporting side of aerial warfare. The former reveal that war did indeed encompass many emotions, including stress, worry, and fear for one's own life that POWs tended not to talk about, especially to one another. Just as captured soldiers could not bolster their status among their peers by citing attempts at anti-Nazi resistance or expressions of sympathy with the victims of executions or enemy prisoners, there was little to be gained from revealing one's own vulnerability. Stories about "nerves being shot" needed to be told via a surrogate in order to be deemed acceptable. Communicatively, showing any sort of weakness seems to have been perceived as dangerous.

The causes of this communicative block are not solely psychological. The military frame of reference in general, as we can see from statements made by soldiers in the Iraq or Afghanistan wars, does not admit conversations about death, dying, or present-tense fears. Today, we talk about soldiers' suffering from post-traumatic stress disorder, but this diagnosis did not exist during World War II. The military frame of reference left no room for physical weakness—to say nothing of psychological vulnerability. In this respect, no matter how thoroughly they were integrated into the total group of their commando or unit, soldiers were psychologically alone. This helps us understand an otherwise cryptic remark made by a German POW in 1941:

> BARTELS: Those who are dead are better off than we are. We shall have to kick our heels around for God knows how long.[311]

Among the infrequent statements that concern soldiers' own fears were tales about how their aircraft were shot down or their ships sunk. Whereas the hunting tales were characterized by an absolute lack of differentiation vis-à-vis the victims and their suffering, these narratives are extremely detailed. A German sailor, for instance, told of the sinking of the armed merchant cruiser MS *Penguin* in the Indian Ocean in May 1941:

> LEHN*: One (shell) ripped open one side of the deck. At the same instant one hit the bridge. One direct hit was sufficient—steel plates went flying over the ship. A large number of men jumped into the sea. The hatch covers were blown into the sea and afterwards bounced up again. An "Obermaat" jumped in front

of me into the water; when I jumped in myself, he was no longer there—drowned. Many of them were drowned like that.

BLASCHKE*: Did they all have life jackets on?

LEHN: All of them, yes. A good many, who were standing on the
side deck jumped into the sea together, and then flying pieces
of metal fell on them. While the ship was sinking, a shell from
the first forward gun went off, or perhaps it was another hit?
Her (the CORNWALL'S) gunnery was very bad. The shells were
dropping 100 metres over and 100 metres short, but never
scored a hit.[312]

This is what war looked like from the losing perspective—although
even such stories were told by survivors and thus transmitted only
a part of the terror that must have been involved. Dead men, as the
cliché goes, tell no tales.

Soldiers rarely spared any thoughts for those wounded. This is one
of the few exceptions from the protocols:

ABLER: What did they do when the first wounded men arrived
from RUSSIA; what did they do to those who were half crippled
or had been shot in the head; what did they do to them? Do
you know what they did to them in the hospitals? They gave
them something so that by the next day they were put to sleep;
they did that in scores of cases, specially those coming back
from FRANCE or from RUSSIA.

KUCH: They went out as sound men to defend their fatherland,
had bad luck, were shot in the head or something, became completely incapacitated, and (they said) they are eating the bread
out of our mouths, they can't do any more good, they will have
to be looked after all their lives, men like that have no need to
live—so that's the end of them. They died on the quiet—died
of wounds! A thing like that will be avenged; the English don't
need to avenge it, the Supreme Power will take vengeance.[313]

This dialogue not only shows what the soldiers considered to be in
the realm of the possible. It also hints at the fears which they maintained but could only be discussed in stories about the fates of others.
This was apparently one way to express one's feelings without talking
about them directly.

War does not just consist of violence perpetrated and witnessed—the shooting down of planes, the gunning down of enemies, rape, plunder, and mass murder. It also consists of violence suffered. Yet that category carries far less communicative weight among soldiers, and different individuals experience it in different ways. Life during wartime is differentiated and multifaceted. How soldiers experience war depends on factors like place, rank, time, weaponry, and camaraderie. Empirically speaking, what we conceive as the total experience of war can be broken down into a kaleidoscope of diverse, more or less happy or terrible experiences and actions. War is only a total experience insofar as the group, commando, or unit forms the social frame for what soldiers have to endure. That situation does not change in a POW camp. The normal civilian world exists only as the subject of melancholic longing. Or as one soldier put it: "Life is cruel. When I think of my wife—!"[314]

Sex

"I was in an SS quarters . . . [In a] room, there was an SS man lying on the bed, without his tunic but with his pants still on. Next to him, on the edge of the bed, was a very pretty young woman, and I saw her stroke the SS man's chin. I heard her say: "You're not going to shoot me, are you Franz?" The girl was still very young and spoke German without an accent . . . I asked the SS man whether this girl . . . was really going to be taken out and shot. He answered that all Jews were going to be shot. There were no exceptions . . . He also said something to the effect that it was a bitter reality. Sometimes they had the chance to hand over these girls to another execution commando, but mostly there wasn't the time. They had to do it themselves."[315]

This is an excerpt from testimony in a postwar investigation of the crimes of the SS. It depicts how SS men exploited the situation of a war of extermination to commit acts of sexual violence. Wehrmacht soldiers of all stripes were also interested in exploring various sexual opportunities.

Sexual violence is a war crime people like to ascribe to the enemy. The mass rapes of German women by Red Army soldiers at the end of World War II are a standard element of Germans' recollections of that conflict. The same, however, cannot be said of sexual crimes committed by the SS and the Wehrmacht. In this area, the myth of the honorable German fighter remains intact. Sociologist Regina Mühlhäuser has recently investigated the various sexual facets of the German invasion of the Soviet Union.[316] They include not just sexual violations of women as the Wehrmacht occupied towns and villages and in the run-up to mass executions, but also the swapping of sex for favors and the relationships between soldiers and Ukrainian women, some of which resulted in pregnancies or marriages.

It is hardly surprising that sex plays such a major role in war. Sexuality is one of the most important aspects of human existence, especially male human existence. Conversely, it is positively bizarre that sex has so rarely been examined in research on war and violence—be it in the form of rape, "consensual" exploitation of relations of power, prostitution, or homosexuality. This blind spot is by no means the result of lack of good, available sources. It shows how removed from everyday reality sociology and history sometimes can be. Wartime soldiers are by and large youngish men who have been separated from their real or would-be partners and freed from many social restraints. When stationed in occupied areas, they are given the sort of an individual power they would never enjoy in civilian society. Moreover, the sexual opportunities presented by this situation occur within a reference frame of masculine camaraderie, in which bragging about sexual prowess is a normal part of everyday communication.

We should not mistakenly see every form of sexual violence perpetrated by soldiers as an exotic exception, made possible by the unusual situation of war. Everyday life offers no shortage of opportunities for various forms of sexual escapism, provided one can afford them in a financial and social sense. They begin with "boys' nights out" and extend to affairs, visits to prostitutes, and open violence in the form of fights. In other words, like physical violence and all other forms of excess, sexual escapism is anchored in everyday society. It is normally unleashed only within specific formats such as Carnival or niche cultures such as the pornography industry or swinger clubs. The sociological and historical blinders toward this underside of everyday social reality, which manifests itself in millions of ways, is what exoticizes the wartime acts in which soldiers live out their violent and sexual impulses. But strictly speaking, this is nothing more than a shift in the framework that gives the more powerful the opportunity to do things that they already enjoy doing or would like to do.

Mühlhäuser's study is not the only evidence we have of cases in which women were coerced into giving sexual favors with promises that they would not be killed—only to subsequently be taken out and shot. In the British POW camp Latimer House, German sailor Horst Minnieur told his previously cited story about the "pretty Jewess," who became a victim of a mass execution after doing forced labor in a German barracks. What occurs to his listener to say next is the following:

HARTELT: I bet she let you sleep with her too?
MINNIEUR: Yes, but you had to take care not to be found out. It's

nothing new; it was really a scandal, the way they slept with
Jewish women.[317]

It seems to have been common, accepted practice to execute Jewish
women after sex so that soldiers would not have to worry about sanc-
tions following a "racial crime," and Minnieur apparently finds nothing scandalous in admitting that he, too, abused the Jewish victim. In
a study of the German occupation of parts of the Soviet Union, historian Andrej Angrick has determined that officers of SS Einsatzgruppe
Sk 10a habitually raped Jewish women to the point where they fell
unconscious.[318] Historian Bernd Greiner has documented similar
cases in the Vietnam War.[319]

Mass executions alone weren't the only opportunities to perpetrate sexual violence. The same also applied to more everyday situations such as women being forced to strip naked for interrogations at
which multiple male soldiers were present.[320] There were also "theater
groups." These consisted above all, in Angrick's description, of "pretty
Russian women and girls who wanted better food rations . . . After
performances, the girls danced and drank with [SS men], and agree-
ments were eventually reached. Outside of town, the commando leadership would arrange get-togethers of this sort in occupied houses and
named 'custodians' who were to 'watch over' the buildings. There were
also suggestions of other sorts of sexual amusements—love affairs
with the daughters of the local mayor, 'song evenings' with alleged
Russian singers, village festivals and nights of excessive drinking."[321]
Willy Peter Reese wrote:

> [We] became melancholy, shared our romantic longings and
> homesickness and kept on laughing and drinking. We stumbled
> across railroad tracks, danced in rail cars and fired shots into the
> night. We had a female Russian captive perform striptease dances
> and smeared her breasts with shoe polish, getting her as drunk in
> the process as we were ourselves.[322]

Medicinal statistics document the level of sexual activity among soldiers. At a field hospital in Kiev, for example, doctors spent most
of their time treating skin and venereal diseases. After inspecting
the facility, the SS doctor Karl Gebhardt acidly remarked that "the
emphasis no longer lay on clinical and surgical procedure."[323]

The surveillance protocols are full of references to sexually transmitted disease. For example, a navy lieutenant proclaimed:

GEHLEN*: They once made a raid in our area and discovered that
70% of all German soldiers whom they found with girls in the
so-called bunks were suffering from venereal diseases.[324]

That percentage does not seem to have been exceptionally high. In cities like Minsk and Riga, so-called sanitary salons were set up. Soldiers were supposed to visit them after having sex in order to ward off potential infections. An account from Mühlhäuser's study describes them as follows: "The 'sanitization' consisted of being washed with soap and water and cleansed with sublimate solution whereupon a small disinfecting rod was inserted into the urethra. A balm was used to combat potential syphilis. Afterward, the physician would record the treatment in his 'troop sanitization book' and issue the soldier a receipt, proving he had done his duty."[325]

The mere fact that such institutions existed, together with a whole bureaucracy concerning venereal disease, shows how widespread and well known soldiers' sexual activity was. Other than the "racial crime" of having sex with Jewish women, little was kept secret. Some soldiers even boasted about the number of venereal diseases they had contracted.[326] The sanitary services in any case had their hands full trying to prevent infections and keep soldiers fit for battle.

Nonetheless, since neither disciplinary measures nor appeals to soldiers' sense of duty could prevent rampant excess, the Wehrmacht hit upon the idea of running their own brothels. An official announcement from the Security Service in the occupied Soviet Union read: "For the purpose of restricting the spread of sexual diseases, the possibility for enemy agent activity in the everyday interactions between German and Russian persons and the resultant eradication of the necessary distance to persons within the Russian arena, it is being considered whether or not to establish Wehrmacht bordellos in a variety of cities."[327]

The history of how these institutions were set up and how "racially suitable" prostitutes were identified and coerced would demand a chapter of its own. In any case, those details did not concern the POWs in the surveillance protocols. They simply told of their experiences in bordellos:

WALLUS*: In WARSAW our troops formed a queue outside the front door. In RADOM the first room was full, whilst the L.K.W. [*Lastkraftwagen* or truck] people stood outside. Every woman had 14–15 men an hour. They changed the women every two days. We buried a lot of women there.[328]

The administrative framework wasn't always clear, as emerged from a discussion between twenty-four-year-old Captain Wilhelm Dette and Lieutenant Colonel Wilfried von Müller-Rienzburg about the legal consequences of gonorrhea infection:

DETTE: There are the other ranks' brothels. Gonorrhoea is a punishable offence. For quite a long time it wasn't punished. When I had the first case of gonorrhoea in my Staffel I wanted to punish the fellow. They said: "No, no, that won't do, you can't do that." A fortnight before I took off on my last flight, the chief N.O. came and called the whole Staffel together and delivered a short talk saying that there were always about forty-five thousand men in FRANCE suffering from venereal disease.
MÜLLER-RIENZBURG: As far as I know, cases of gonorrhoea were always punished.
DETTE: As a result of that it is now punishable again, with imprisonment: It wasn't merely a military offence; it is because the man doesn't get treated for it.[329]

Leaving aside the disciplinary complications they could have, bordello visits clearly were among the more pleasant aspects of warfare:

CLAUNITZER: In BANAK, that's our most northerly aerodrome, there are still three or four thousand soldiers. As far as any conditions are concerned, they've got the best of everything there.
ULRICH: Variety shows and things like that?
CLAUNITZER: There's something on there, every day. And there are girls there, they've opened a brothel.
ULRICH: German girls?
CLAUNITZER: No, Norwegian girls from OSLO and TRONDHEIM.
ULRICH: There's a brothel car in every town, one for officers and one for other ranks? I know all about it. (Laughter.) Strange goings on.[330]

Wilhelm Dette (right) as a first lieutenant together with the ordnance officer of the "Fliegerführer Atlantik," Lieutenant General Ulrich Kessler (second from left), in June 1943. In the background is an Fw 200. On December 28, 1943, after encountering engine trouble, Dette was forced to crash-land a plane of this type in the Bay of Biscay. He was subsequently taken prisoner by British forces. (KG 40 Archiv, Günther Ott)

Historical research has thus far shed very little light on this everyday fact of warfare. That's hardly surprising since soldiers didn't mention such goings-on in their letters home to their loved ones, and postwar memoirs usually intended to justify the authors' actions rarely include descriptions of whorehouses. Postwar prosecutors' investigations were only concerned with rapes in the context of mass executions. Other forms of potential sexual coercion were legally irrelevant and thus do not crop up in the investigation files.

But without doubt, sex was part of soldiers' everyday existence—with a whole series of consequences for the women involved:

SAUERMANN: The Reichskanzleiführer, I don't know how it was, in any case the Gestapo were involved. We took [funds] from the credit the Reich gave us for the construction of . . . facilities to build a bordello, a whorehouse. We called it a "b barrack." When I left, it was done. All that was missing were women. The guys were running around town hitting up every German girl. That was to be avoided. So they got their Frenchwomen, their Czechs, the entire spectrum of peoples came there, all those women.[331]

Excerpts of this sort contain more information than may be immediately apparent. Sauermann's reference to "their Frenchwomen, their Czechs" implicitly makes it clear that the women in question were not voluntarily prostituting themselves to German soldiers.[332] Conversations about "bordellos" and "girls" are always about forced prostitution and sexual violence, but those concepts are never directly addressed in the protocols. From the soldiers' perspective, it was simply a given that foreign women were at their sexual disposal, especially considering that they weren't allowed to "hit up German girls."

Clearly, sexual violence in war is not always spontaneous and unregulated. Sometimes, as in the example of the "sanitary salons," it was officially administered. In any case, sex was one of the central aspects of soldiers' experience of war—all the more so since it can be safely assumed that the U.S. and British officers who made the protocols had no interest in recording the endless discussions on the topic of women. As neither the British nor the Americans likely thought the subject to be of much use in the war, the surveillance activities tended to concentrate on discussions more relevant to military strategy, conversations about aircraft, bombs, machine guns, and miracle weapons. But it seems entirely plausible that groups of mostly young men would have been just as interested in women as technology, and that the POWs would have talked just as much about sex as about military hardware. One excerpt from the protocols speaks volumes:

18:45 women
19:15 women
19:45 women
20:00 women[333]

Moreover, we can speculate that intervals identified only as "idle talk" would have been partly about women and sex as well. There's no way of verifying this, but the proportion of sex talk that did find its way into the protocols suggests that the subject was very important to the POWs.

Conversations of this nature tended to revolve around where the action was, i.e., where one could find the prettiest girls and the most sexual opportunities. Often the tone is reminiscent of tourists discussing attractions they had seen:

> GÖLLER: I've been to BORDEAUX. The whole of BORDEAUX is one big brothel. There is nothing to beat BORDEAUX. I always said to myself, wait till you get to PARIS; it's supposed to be still worse in PARIS. It can't be worse in any other place, I thought. But the contrary is true. In BORDEAUX the reputation of Frenchwomen is worst of all.
>
> HERMS: In PARIS you only need to sit down in a bar where there's a girl sitting at a table, and you may be quite sure that you can go home with her. The place is appalling, you find girls in thousands. You don't have to take the slightest trouble. It's just the right sort of life for many people.[334]

Ironically, POWs often complained that the so-called blitz girls, *Blitzmädel,* German women assigned to assist the Wehrmacht, were all too willing to engage in a bit of sexual fun. In this area, conventional norms of sexual behavior were maintained in wartime.

What soldiers regarded as the legitimate exploitation of opportunity when foreign women were concerned becomes "repulsive" when practiced by German women—although no small amount of projection may also have been at play:

> SCHÜRMANN: Most "Blitzmädels" say "yes" without much ado. Just think of those "Blitzmädels" in PARIS. They all run around in civvies and one is quite prepared to be accosted by one of them suddenly in German. It's nothing unusual for them to behave promiscuously with the French. They really are some of the worst. They don't give any points to the French whores in any way. The NO we had—I got on very well with him; he was from COLOGNE, and came to us from VILLACOUBLAY—was transferred to a general hospital in PARIS. He said it was nothing unusual to have more women there with V.D. than soldiers. It was an actual fact, he said, that it was not the soldiers who were infecting the girls but the other way round, and that some of the "Blitzmädels" had caught it from the French. He

once had women suffering from V.D. in another institution in
Paris; he said twenty of them had gonorrhoea and more than
ten of them had syphilis, five of them being already incurable.
They then examined all the girls in Paris and sent so-and-so
many home right away; a certain number were infected without being ill themselves, they were carriers and were infect-
ing the soldiers! It must be a scandalous state of affairs in
Paris. I'm inclined to think that the women who volunteer as
"Blitzmädels" do so primarily for that one reason, some of them
anyway.[335]

A twenty-four-year-old U-boat crewman named Günther Schramm
reported on a particularly spectacular example of moral lassitude
among German "girls":

SCHRAMM: The things I saw myself at BORDEAUX were frightful.
Once I had to go to the medical station and there I was taken
through various departments and saw a lot of German girls in
the corridors—it was a shocking sight! They were completely
mad, there were three of them who bore the typical signs of
syphilis in their faces and they were screaming—they were
completely crazy. They made noises and cried: "Only by a nigger!" and so on. They had been associating with negroes. They
behave worse than the French women.[336]

Sometimes, POWs acted like connoisseurs, boasting that they knew
where to get value for money:

DANIELS: I paid 60 francs in a brothel at BREST.
WEDEKIND: Go on with you! At BREST, at GRÜNSTEIN'S, on the
corner there, you don't pay more than 25 francs—that's the
usual charge.[337]

On occasion, soldiers also mildly criticized the behavior of some members of their own units:

NIWIEM*: I must say, sometimes we didn't behave too well in
FRANCE. In PARIS I have seen our soldiers seize girls in the
middle of a restaurant, lay them over the table and . . . ! Married women too![338]

Higher-ranking officers, in particular, were prone to condemn the excesses of men under their command:

> MÖLLER: I, as "Gruppenkommandeur" sometimes have to take action in connection with venereal diseases. On the day I was shot down one of my best pilots reported sick with venereal diseases. This man had just returned to the "Gruppe" from 4 weeks marriage-leave. I said to him "you are a swine"! He'll be glad that I did not return from the flight for I'd certainly have held him responsible.[339]

Complaints of this sort were hardly infrequent. Navy Captain Hans Erdmenger, commodore of the 8th Destroyer Flotilla, remarked bitterly in a 1943 disciplinary report about his unit: "The use of French bordellos has assumed an intensity that violates a healthy development of soldierly personality. Above all, the bordellos are being frequented not just by the younger generation, the 18- to 20-year-olds, but increasingly by lower-level officers. The sense of hygiene, the behavior due toward women and the understanding of the importance of healthy family life for our German people are suffering under this." Erdmenger, a National Socialist true believer, was shocked when the first thing two of his soldiers did after returning from marriage leave was to visit a bordello.[340]

Massive sexual violence caused even greater outrage among many soldiers than visits to the local bordello:

> REIMBOLD: One thing I can tell you directly, there's no rumor about it. In the first officers' quarters where I was held prisoner, there was a very stupid young lieutenant from Frankfurt, a real snot-nose. Eight of us were sitting around a table talking about RUSSIA. And he said: "We got hold of a female spy who was running around in the area. We hit her on the noggin with a stick and then flayed her behind with an unsheathed bayonet. Then we fucked her, threw her out, shot at her and, while she was lying on her back, lobbed grenades. Every time we got one close, she screamed. In the end, she died, and we threw her body away." And imagine this! There were eight German officers sitting at the table with me all laughing their heads off. I couldn't stand it. I got up and said, "Gentlemen, this goes too far."[341]

Reimbold claims to be outraged by a story he attributes to an external person of reference. Events of this sort of brutality are usually narrated secondhand. Some further examples:

> SCHULTKA: The things that are happening today are really beyond the pale. For example, some paratroopers stormed a house in Italy and killed both of the men there. They were both fathers, and one had two daughters. They screwed both of them, really gave them a going over, and then killed them. The house had those wide Italian beds. They tossed the daughters on the bed, stuck the men's dicks in and gave them another real screwing.
>
> CZOSNOWSKI: That's inhuman. But it's common for guys to tell stories about things they never really did. They're colossal braggarts.
>
> SCHULTKA: Then there's the one about the tank trenches in Kiev. There was a guy from the Gestapo, a high-ranking SS leader, who had a Russian, pretty as a picture. He wanted to screw her, but she didn't let him. One day later, she was standing in front of the trench. He mowed her down himself with his MP and then screwed her when she was dead.[342]

Even if some of the sexual horror stories were, as the listener in this excerpt suspected, made up, atrocities of this sort did take place in reality.[343] Reports of rapes rarely elicited surprise, to say nothing of condemnation. Even rapes of German women by the enemy were accepted, as the following story illustrates:

> LANGFELD: Near BABRUYSK, it happened that a bus containing 30 female news agency assistants was attacked by partisans. The bus was driving through the woods, and the partisans shot at it. Tanks arrived but too late. They got the bus, the girls and the partisans. But in the meantime, the girls had all been gone through, given a real good screwing. Some of them were dead. They'd rather spread their legs than get killed, that's understandable. It took three days until they were found.
>
> HELD: They sure had a lot to fuck.[344]

At this point enough has been said about the reports of sexual violence. The stories recorded in the surveillance protocols clearly reveal the omnipresence of sexual desires and sexual violence in the war. The previous two excerpts, from protocols made in the United States, speak volumes about soldiers' view of women as mere means of satisfying sexual desires. Soldiers not only took for granted that sexual opportunities should be used. Talking about it was also nothing unusual or out of the ordinary:

> KOKOSCHKA: There was this disgrace of a private who held a pistol to an Italian girl's head so that she'd fuck him.
> SAEMMER: Yeah, that's what privates are like.[345]

Technology

The technology of war plays only a very minor role in academic discourse, and in this book, too, we are primarily interested in perceptions beyond any sort of technology. Technical topics rarely occur in conversations between army POWs—not surprisingly since the equipment used by infantrymen barely changed in the six years of World War II. German soldiers at the end of the war still used the same standard-issue rifle, the K98, with which they had invaded Poland in September 1939. There were only two types of standard machine guns employed in World War II, and the situation was similar with other infantry and artillery weaponry. Tanks underwent the greatest innovation, but once soldiers had gotten used to new types of armored vehicles, their operation quickly became routine. A Tiger tank was a Tiger tank. The technological framework in the German army changed little. All in all, equipment remained constant, and infantry weaponry in particular consisted of mass-produced items that scarcely merited discussion. On the battlefields of Europe, the technical quality of rifles, tommy guns, and machine guns was quite comparable, with neither side enjoying a decisive advantage.

The situation was completely different in the Luftwaffe, where the quality of technology was far more important than in the army. Aerial warfare was a technological arena, and innovations came fast and furious over the course of the war. Improvements were made in all areas, from aircraft performance to navigation technology to onboard weaponry. The Messerschmitt 109 of 1939 had little to do with the same model plane in 1945.

Nighttime aerial warfare added a new dimension to the conflict. British Bomber Command perfected the technique of aerial bombardment in darkness, forcing the Luftwaffe to constantly develop new strategies for defending against such attacks. One result of this give-and-take was the rise of highly sophisticated radar and navigation technology.

In 1939 a race began to develop the fastest fighter jets, the most precise radar stations, and the most exact navigation procedures. In World

War I, mistakes could be relatively quickly corrected. This was no longer the case in World War II, since the effort needed for development and production was so much greater. Huge amounts of resources—for example, 41 percent of armaments capacity in 1944—were invested in the air industry. By comparison, Germany invested only 6 percent of its resources in tank production in 1944.[346] Nonetheless, in the course of 1942, Britain and the United States gained a decisive advantage over the Luftwaffe, and the German air force was never able to close the gap. With Germany losing ground both quantitatively and qualitatively, the Luftwaffe was deprioritized at the end of 1944. The consequences for the Wehrmacht were devastating and could be felt in every arena of the war.

Technology was a constant, unavoidable element in the lives of pilots, reconnaissance specialists, and aircraft gunners.[347] In aerial warfare, whoever had faster, more maneuverable planes with better weapons survived, while those who fell behind technologically died, regardless of their skill as airmen. Technology thus determined the lives of Luftwaffe troops. It also dominated their perception of the war and the formation of their frame of reference.

The surveillance protocols reflect the importance of technology for each branch of the German armed forces. There is a lot of material of this sort in conversations between Luftwaffe men, somewhat less among German sailors, and only around a tenth as much in discussions between army soldiers. For that reason, this section will be primarily concerned with the Luftwaffe. Especially interesting is what the POWs discussed when they talked about technology, and how technology dominated and changed their perception of the war.

Faster, Further, Bigger

One of the most important topics of discussion among the "artisans" of World War II was the capabilities of their aircraft. Just as automotive fanatics love to converse about the advantages of their cars, Luftwaffe pilots and crewmen constantly boasted about their planes' superiority in three areas: speed, range, and payload. In 1940, a Luftwaffe lieutenant introduced his bunkmate to the Ar 196:

The "Arado" is a single-engined machine with very short wings. It has very good characteristics, and I think it carries two cannon and one gun. It has a range of 270, at most 320 kilometres, and can carry a 250 (?Kg.) bomb. It is a wonderful machine. They are used for guarding U-Boats.[348]

Airplane motors were objects of particular interest:

SCHÖNAUER: The first Gruppe of our Geschwader is getting the "188" now. Aircraft are there already. The "188" has just been fitted with the "801" engine, and is very good and carries quite a lot.

DIEVENKORN: Is it a bomber?

SCHÖNAUER: Yes. It is faster and above all climbs better.[349]

The engine was considered the most important element in a warplane, which is why the first thing Schönauer pointed out was that the Junkers 188 had a new BMW rear engine, making it superior to its predecessor the Ju 88. Luftwaffe POWs spent an enormous amount of time debating the merits of this engine vis-à-vis the Daimler-Benz inline motors DB 603 and 605 and the Junkers Jumo 213. Planes were only as good as the capacity of their engines, and by 1942 the POWs agreed that German motor development was lagging behind the enemy's. They pinned their greatest hopes to the creation of the piston engine Jumo 222, which was supposed to have between 2,000 and 3,000 horsepower. "The Jumo 222," First Lieutenant Fried raved in February 1943, "I have seen it myself, it is terrific . . . 24 cylinders."[350] And First Lieutenant Schönauer was also enthusiastic four months later: "The new Jumo engine—if it is a success, with 2700 hp. at take-off rating—*what an engine!*"[351] But this miracle engine, which Luftwaffe POWs hoped would solve all their problems, never went into mass production.[352]

Amid all the pride German POWs felt for their own equipment, there was grudging admiration for the British and later the Americans. Symptomatic in this regard were the judgments of a first lieutenant and squadron leader of a fighter wing who was shot down over England in September 1940:

At a height of 7000 m. the Spitfire is a shade superior to the "109." Over 7000 m. they are equal. As soon as you understand that, your fear of the Spitfire is banished. The "109" is even superior to the Spitfire if it has a pilot who knows how to fly it well. I would always prefer a "109" to a Spitfire! You always have to fly in long, wide curves, then the Spitfire can't keep up.[353]

The admission that, when battling at lower altitudes, German pilots had a "fear" of the RAF's Spitfire shows the Luftwaffe's great respect for their English counterparts at the high point of the Battle of Britain. Also in September 1940, another pilot even complained:

50% of our old fighter pilots are gone, they know that here, too. These mass attacks are senseless; that is not the way to destroy the English fighters. They'll have to bring over our new fighter a/c, or our fighting branch will look silly! The new "Focke-Wulf" with the radial engine and the air cooling must come over. What will happen if they shoot down one experienced fighter pilot after another?[354]

The POWs agreed that new, technologically improved planes would be needed to turn the tide of the air war, and the complaints about and grudging admiration for the capabilities of enemy aircraft never ceased. "I believe we have bitten off more than we can chew with regard to the G.A.F.," First Lieutenant Henz opined in June 1943. "To be quite honest, we haven't got anything to put up against the four-engined (bombers) at the moment. I have the feeling that we've been asleep for some time."[355] A year later, Sergeant Mäckle seconded that assessment: "The English have much faster air-craft: for instance, none of our aircraft can come up to their Mosquitoes; that's impossible."[356]

Both airmen may have hit the nail on the head in terms of Allied technology, but neither named any reasons why Germany lagged behind. German pilots simply resigned themselves to the fact of the enemy's technological superiority. In November 1944, First Lieutenant Hans Hartigs, an experienced member of Fighter Wing 26, received what was then the Luftwaffe's most modern conventional fighter plane, the Fw 190 D-9. On December 26, he led a formation of fifteen fighters to support German ground troops as part of the Ardennes Offensive or, as it was known to the Allies, the Battle of the Bulge. American Mustangs engaged them in dogfights, and Hartigs was shot down. As a POW, the disappointed pilot remarked: "Even an outstanding pilot can't get away properly from a Mustang by banking in that '190'; it's out of the question. I tried it. *It's out of the question.*"[357]

Germans did not feel technologically inferior only in the second half of the war. Complaints of that nature began as early as 1939, although they became much more frequent as of 1943. All the more eagerly did pilots await the introduction of new planes that would give them the advantage they long craved over the enemy. POWs devoted long and intense discussions to the topic of fantastic new developments that would soon be making themselves felt on the front. In January 1940, a pilot and a radio operator drew some conclusions about where the Luftwaffe stood technologically. They agreed that Germany had "some really smart machines," above all, the "fantastic" Ju 88 bomber.[358] The radio operator said he had heard that his unit was soon to be equipped with the planes. And they expressed confidence that the new version of the Me 110 would shock the British once the planes were finished and came "buzzing like bees."[359] Six months later, two young officers who had been shot down over France discussed the Fw 190, which at the time was still in the test phase:

FIRST LIEUTENANT: The Focke Wulf is said to be really good.
LIEUTENANT: Apparently it is quite marvellous.
FIRST LIEUTENANT: It is said to take off better, although it is heavier, and to be considerably faster.
LIEUTENANT: Very much faster!
FIRST LIEUTENANT: It has a radial engine.
LIEUTENANT: Apparently it is an absolutely marvellous thing![360]

The "marvelous" Fw 190 was at that point in time, June 1940, nothing more than a prototype. Nonetheless, the news had already gotten around that it was easy to start and faster than the Messerschmitt 109 and had the advantage of a rear, or radial, engine. Knowledge about planes still in the developmental phase spread quickly in the Luftwaffe. British surveillance officers, of course, welcomed the Luftwaffe POWs' need to exchange information about the latest planes and exploited this source in masterly fashion. The Royal Air Force knew specifics about each new Luftwaffe plane long before it was actually introduced into combat.

With new and improved planes constantly arriving on the front, airplane crews had a reliable supply of news to discuss. Sometimes the talk was reminiscent of fashion designers debating the merits of a new fall collection. For example, in October 1942, a Sergeant Breit-

An He 177 is loaded with bombs, spring 1944. (Photographer: Linden; BA 1011–668–7164–35A)

scheid told a bunkmate, a bomber aircraft mechanic, that he could not wait to see what the autumn would bring in terms of new planes. The mechanic agreed that there would be much that was new, whereupon Breitscheid exclaimed: "The '190' is not our last fighter."[361]

Promising performances by new aircraft always occasioned a flurry of talk. In August 1942, two bomber pilots discussed the speed of the Luftwaffe's new heavy bomber, the Heinkel He 177:

KAMMEYER: Yes, but the "177" hasn't got a speed of 500 k.p.h.

KNOBEL: What! It does an easy 500 as a reconnaissance aircraft.

KAMMEYER: Opinions vary considerably. In July last year one man stated that it had a speed of 450 and another said it did 400 or 420, whilst a third said it did 380.

KNOBEL: That's quite wrong. Have you seen the aircraft in flight?

KAMMEYER: Yes, I have seen it in the air.[362]

KNOBEL: I am absolutely convinced that it does at least 500 as a reconnaissance aircraft, and I'm also convinced that it can do 500 as a bomber.[363]

This conversation took place six months before the He 177 was commissioned for battle, but German soldiers were already engaged in lively debate about technical details like its top speed. The POWs' naïve enthusiasm for technology sometimes led them to formulate exaggerated expectations for new pieces of military hardware. The English would be "scared to death" of the He 177. It was "the most amazing thing so far produced" with "heavy armament and great speed."[364]

The He 177 was considered a miracle weapon, and rumors abounded as to the feats it had already achieved. Some POWs even claimed it had flown across the Atlantic. Midshipman Knobel had heard in mid-1942 that the plane had flown from the Luftwaffe's test airstrip in Rechlin to Tripoli and Smolensk and back. Asked whether the He 177 had flown over America he replied: "Over CANADA, I think, not over AMERICA."[365] Another POW, a low-level officer, was far more confident when asked whether the He 177 really possessed that sort of range. "Of course," he said. "I was told six months ago by people who know all about the aircraft that '177' had already dropped leaflets over NEW YORK."[366] This story was repeated by a gunner from a Ju 87 dive-bomber in April 1943.[367] The idea of being able to fly to New York and drop leaflets (or better still: bombs) was a bit of wishful thinking, whose appeal was such that the soldiers did not want to let reality disrupt illusion. No such flight ever took place, although rumors that it did survived even the war itself.[368]

Similar stories were told in reference to Japan. Such a flight would have been technically possible, and there were indeed plans of this sort aimed at improving connections between Berlin and Tokyo.[369] The fact that the flight never happened didn't stop soldiers from talking about it. Sergeant Gromoll, for instance, reported that the Me 264 was to be used to shuttle diplomats and dispatches between Japan and Germany, flying across North America with 27,000 liters of fuel on board. A first lieutenant who was shot down over the Algerian coast in November 1942 went into similar detail: "The B.V. 222 flies to JAPAN. It has a cruising speed of 350 k.p.h. They refuel for the last time at PILLAU and fly by night across RUSSIA to JAPAN. The Russians have either no night-fighters or only very few."[370] We have no way of reconstructing how the officer arrived at this fantasy. It's possible that he saw a BV 222 while training on the Baltic Sea and sought to explain the presence of the gigantic amphibious aircraft.

In any case, Luftwaffe POWs were particularly fascinated by large-scale airplanes. The latter were few in number, so any contact with one was something special. Anyone who could claim to have seen a six-engine BV 222 was assured of a rapt audience. The narrators of such stories reveled in details about the size and capabilities of the plane:

> SCHIBORS: The Blohm and Voss 222's, the largest aircraft in the world, brought the reinforcements to LIBYA, taking off from HAMBURG and landing in AFRICA. They each carried 120 men with full equipment. One aircraft was shot down in the MEDITERRANEAN. Apart from that no fighter ever dared approach them. It has eight cannon and seventeen M.G.'s. It is very heavily armed and everyone points his M.G. 15 out of the window. It's a six-engined aircraft, with three engines in each wing. It is three or four times as large as the "52." It carries a few tanks and goodness knows what else — guns and all. It has also flown over bombs for the bomber aircraft. It has a cruising speed of 360 m.p.h. When it's empty it can get away in no time.[371]

Schibors completely exaggerated the BV 222's arsenal and payload capacity. He also substitutes its top speed for its cruising speed as a way of making his story more dramatic. But the plane obviously made a deep impression on him.

The warplane that elicited the greatest hopes was without doubt the Me 262 jet fighter. It began cropping up in POWs' conversations as of December 1942. At first, the information passed on was vague and third-hand.[372] For instance, in April 1943, Sergeant Rott from Bomber Wing 10 said he was convinced that big things were afoot at the Luftwaffe since during a visit, the commodore of another nearby wing had hinted that a new fighter jet was being tested.[373] By late 1943, POWs were offering the first eyewitness reports on the miracle fighting machine.[374] Lieutenant Schürmann can scarcely conceal his enthusiasm when he recounts: "They have a tremendous speed, it is amazing. It can only be estimated. When you see a Focke-Wulf fighter you estimate it is doing about 450 kph, but I estimated that that was doing 700 to 800 kph at least."[375] In spring 1944, speculation grew that the Me 262 would soon be actively deployed. A Lieutenant Fritz recalled a visiting general saying in March 1944 that the Me 262 was about to replace the Ju 88: "He said too that the whole production of those aircraft has been somewhat restricted and preparations were already being made for producing jet-propelled aircraft; that suddenly they would be used in onerous numbers and that we should thereby win back air superiority."[376] Similar rumors were circulated among the general German populace, which was increasingly feeling the hardships of the war. A Private First Class Maletzki reported: "The general morale is not so bad in GERMANY. I have heard people saying: 'When the turbine-fighter comes, then all will be well.' "[377]

None of the POWs seems to have doubted the capabilities of the Me 262 in the slightest. In June 1944, nine days after being shot down, a Ju 88 W/T operator predicted: "After that they'll bring out the turbine-fighters. If they do manage to put large masses of them into operation the English can pack up with their four-engined aircraft. The GAF is on the up-grade again, it will take a little time yet, perhaps six months."[378] A Lieutenant Zink from Fighter Wing 3 entertained similar thoughts: "But the first group will be put into operations in a fortnight's time. 1200 kph. They will suddenly appear over ENGLAND. It rises up to 1200 m in two minutes' time. It climbs at an angle of 44° and at a speed of 800 kph. There is nothing you can do against it. It has eight cannon and can shoot down anything. You could fly about quite comfortably over here, even if a hundred fighters were in the air."[379]

Here Zink conflated the capabilities of the Me 163 rocket interceptor and the Me 262 jet fighter, but even so, this excerpt shows the important role that innovations played in the technological imagination and fantasies of the Luftwaffe POWs. The mass deployment of the aircraft was indeed to remain a fantasy. As of August 1944, the first Me 262s were used in a trial formation, and although pilots were enthusiastic about this "fantastic" new plane,[380] the aircraft had no impact on the outcome of the war. The Me 262 had too many technical bugs that needed ironing out, and the Allied air forces showed that the plane was by no means invulnerable. The approximately two hundred Me 262s deployed during the war shot down some enemy 150 planes, while suffering 100 losses of their own.[381]

When talking technology, the Luftwaffe POWs were right in their element. They were fascinated by the boost pressure of engines, speeds, onboard weaponry, and all the other innovations in new models of warplanes. They did not see these innovations in any sort of broader context. All they were primarily interested in was the next model and the next fantastic aerial battle. They did not ponder questions such as why Germany was no longer capable of producing 2,500-horsepower engines or why the Allies were much quicker to introduce centimeter-wave radar. But that was only to be expected. Just as engineers in car factories don't usually consider global warming when designing automotive parts, and technicians in power plants don't ruminate about the dominance of a few large companies in the energy sector, aerial warfare specialists did not relate their own equipment and expertise to a greater political, strategic, or moral context. Instrumental reason, fascinated by technology, is utterly indifferent to such contexts. This is part and parcel of the basic unsullied faith in technology and progress characteristic of the first half of the twentieth century. Utopian visions of what people could do dominated people's thoughts. So it hardly appeared unlikely to them that a "miracle weapon" would decide the outcome of World War II.

Miracle Weapons

After the German military's defeat at Stalingrad, Nazi propaganda tried to encourage Germans' hopes for ultimate victory in World War II with hints that revenge would soon be at hand.[382] In early 1943, German POWs first began mentioning rumors about a whole new category of weapons. In March of that year, a U-boat W/T operator prophesied:

> There's one thing that only the officers know about, something ghastly. Its use has been forbidden by the FÜHRER. It was invented and was supposed to be released to the U-boats, but the FÜHRER forbade [it], because it was too inhuman. I don't know what it is. . . .
>
> The FÜHRER has said that it's only to be used in the final struggle of the German people, when every ship is important, then they'll use [it]. But so long as we [engage] in honourable warfare it won't be used.[383]

In such excerpts, Hitler played the role of Germany's savior, who would produce a last-minute super-weapon as decisive as it was terrible. For the speaker in this case, it was no doubt comforting to believe his country had a secret weapon up its sleeve. The second in command of the blockade runner MS *Regensburg* reported on April 11, 1943, that the official commentator for the supreme military command (Oberkommando der Wehrmacht) Otto Dietmar had said that "GERMANY would introduce a weapon against which even the strongest enemy troop concentrations would be useless."[384] The POW, navy First Lieutenant Wolf Jeschonnek, didn't know any specifics, but speculated that the weapon in question must be an explosive device or bomb of extraordinary power. Once the bomb was detonated, the POW assured his listeners, everything would be "flattened." Jeschonnek also expressed confidence that when the "new apparatus" was used, "the war will be over." The miracle weapon he claimed had such a range that it would "smash everything up."[385]

Major Walter Burkhardt, a commander of a paratrooper battalion, offered up similar visions. If it were possible to deliver "enormous shells" over a distance of sixty to a hundred kilometers, he promised, "we could set it up in CALAIS and say to the English: Either you make peace tomorrow, or we shall destroy the whole of your ENGLAND. Those things have got a future."[386] Private Honnet of 26th Tank Division was equally confident of Germany's ultimate victory: "If the reckoning comes like that, it will be terrible. They will be able to reduce the whole of ENGLAND to ruins within a few days, not one stone will be left standing."[387]

Within the space of a few short months in 1943, a consensus emerged that the rumored secret weapon had to be a long-distance missile. POWs speculated that it weighed as much 120 tons and carried a 15-ton warhead—ten times the capability of the V2, the missile Nazi Germany did in fact succeed in developing. Sergeant Herbert Cleff promised that it could destroy everything within a ten-kilometer radius of London.[388] (For the British, Cleff proved to be an excellent source of details about the V1 and V2 missiles more than a year before they were deployed.) In March 1944, Hans Ewald, a U-boat W/T operator, said he believed that four such missiles could reduce London to rubble.[389]

Other POWs were more modest in their expectations, predicting a zone of destruction between one and ten square kilometers around the point of impact.[390] But their belief in the effect and imminent deployment of a miracle weapon was so great that many POWs interned near London felt themselves to be at personal risk and hoped they would soon be transferred to a more remote camp—preferably in Canada.[391] The imprisoned soldiers were aware that the general German populace shared their high expectations. "I was in GERMANY in March," Major Heinz Quittnat reported. "I can tell you the following:

the majority of the German people placed their hope in the reprisal weapon. They imagined that when the reprisal weapon was sent into action, the morale of the English people would quickly be broken, and ENGLAND would be ready to come to terms."[392]

The soldiers did not ask themselves why Britain would suddenly capitulate, having weathered ten months of intense aerial bombardment in 1940–41. Notwithstanding technical speculations about the size, payload, and range of the missile, the POWs did not analyze what specific effects such a weapon could have on the war. Instead, they merely voiced their hope that the secret missile would miraculously turn Germany's fate around. An army private first class named Clermont said: "Well, I certainly believe in our reprisals. The English mother-country will be wiped out."[393] Navy Lieutenant Armin Weighardt agreed: "The new weapon is going to win the war! I believe in it!"[394] Likewise, Luftwaffe Lieutenant Hubert Schymczyk told a comrade in April 1944: "I believe absolutely in our reprisals. When it starts here, then it will be all up with poor old ENGLAND."[395]

The belief in a miracle weapon was rampant in all three main branches of the military, which says a lot about the illusions maintained by navy and Luftwaffe officers. Despite possessing technical expertise and despite having directly witnessed Britain's extraordinary military and economic capacities, they never asked themselves how the decisive blow they imagined and hoped for could ever be achieved practically. It seems to have been unthinkable for such men that the war could be lost. For that reason, they *believed* in a utopian technology that would make everything turn out all right. On this topic, as with the POWs' belief in the Führer, the wishes and emotions that soldiers had invested in the National Socialist project and the war were so powerful that they could not be overridden by any countervailing experiences. On the contrary, belief in a miracle weapon grew stronger the more illusory the prospect of German victory and a rosy future became.

In June 1944, shortly after the Allied landing at Normandy, the miracle weapon got its premiere. During the night of June 12–13, the first V1 missiles were hastily fired at London. The first time the weapon was used en masse was four days later, the same day that German propaganda began speaking of retribution. All told, 244 V1 missiles were fired as part of this action. Forty-five crashed immediately, and only 112 reached London.[396]

On June 16, 1944, the Wehrmacht announced: "During the night and this morning, southern England and the London metropolitan area were hit by new explosives of the highest caliber. These areas have been under bombardment, with little interruption, since midnight. Heavy destruction is to be expected."[397] These few dry words seemed to announce the arrival of what tens of thousands of Germans had long been hoping for. The V1—the first of Germany's miracle weapons—was finally being deployed. The newspaper *Das Reich* dubbed the occasion "the day that 80 million Germans have been passionately waiting for." A report from the Security Service in Frankfurt read: "It was moving to hear how simple workers expressed their joy that their unshakable faith in the Führer had been rewarded. One older laborer remarked that the weapon of retribution would now bring victory."[398] It is interesting to note the tight connection between faith in the Führer and belief in a miracle weapon. They are two sides of one coin and manifest both the expectations for salvation Germans projected onto Hitler and the increasing distance of their perceptions from reality. In this case, though, there was no truth to the cliché that faith could move mountains.

By June 29, the Wehrmacht had fired the thousandth V1, causing not inconsiderable damage. The warhead unleashed a wave of pressure upon impact that could level parts of whole streets. And within the month of June, 1,700 British had been killed, and 10,700 wounded. The presence of the weapon of retribution also forced the RAF to maintain a defensive belt, consisting of antiaircraft gunners, barrage balloons, and fighters, south of London. But all of that was of little use to Germany, as the Allies kept bombing German cities, causing a far greater level of destruction and killing far more people. The actual military effect of the miracle weapon was much less than anyone would have thought possible.

The only real value the V weapons had was psychological. While they did not succeed in particularly frightening the enemy, their existence did boost the morale of the German populace and German soldiers. While bad news continued to rain in from the front lines, Nazi propaganda was able to maintain morale at home with euphoric reports about their weapon of retribution. The missile had been consciously named the V1 to encourage hopes that a V2 was on its way. Nonetheless the leadership elite in the Third Reich began to have doubts about the wisdom of stirring up expectations that would prove difficult to meet. In a letter to Hitler, the German armament minister Albert Speer wrote: "Ever since the populace has begun waiting for miracles from new weapons, doubts have arisen as to whether we realize we're in a few-minutes-before-midnight situation and whether we are irresponsibly stockpiling and holding back such weapons. The question thus emerges as to whether this sort of propaganda serves its end."[399] Indeed, as people realized that the V1 was not having the desired effect, disappointment quickly followed.

The surveillance protocols document waves of hope and disappointment concerning the V missiles. For example, First Lieutenant Kostelezky, who was taken prisoner while defending Germany's last foothold on the Cotentin Peninsula in Normandy, complained:

> KOSTELEZKY: When we heard about our reprisal weapon, and the first reports came to us at CHERBOURG about LONDON being a sea of flames, we said to ourselves: "things will be all right after all; let's hold out on our peninsula." Now I realize that all this reprisal business is only fit for a comic paper.[400]

Since Nazi propagandists had no pictures of damage in London at their disposal, no one in Germany had much of an impression of the effect of the V1 missiles. While being transported to POW camps, which were all located near London, captured German soldiers all tried to get a look for themselves at their supposed retribution. Kostelezky is obviously disappointed at having seen so little destruction, and the generals who were interned at Trent Park in July and August 1944 felt the same way.[401]

Still, the belief that the V missiles could change the course of the war took a while to die. Optimistic voices can be heard in the protocols until mid-July 1944,[402] and fresh hopes soon arose concerning the V2. Expressions of soldiers' expectations for that missile were almost word-for-word repetitions of the hopes for its predecessor. Lieutenant Colonel Ocker said in late August of that year: "It's said, we'll say, to have fifty times the effect of the 'V1.' "[403] Midshipman Mischke hoped to get transferred "to Canada. I like life too much. If they use the V-2 and we are still here, then we'll all be killed."[404] Sergeant Kunz of Infantry Regiment 404 was also convinced:

> KUNZ: Where is the V-2 said to be operating? If it is operating, the war will end in our favour . . . When the V-2 is used, then

the war will be over, because wherever the V-2 falls, it destroys all life. Everything is destroyed, whether it be tree, shrub or house, it disintegrates into ashes.[405]

Kunz added that he had witnessed the V2 being tested: "Where the thing has fallen the people were all as though pulverized. It is all as though frozen, that's what it looks like, and if you touch the man, then he falls to pieces." On the basis of his "observations," Kunz concluded that the V2 functioned like a cold bomb that would freeze the enemy. And to back up his wishful thinking about the existence of a German doomsday weapon, Kunz cited a speech by Hitler: "If all should fail, then the most terrible weapon humanity could ever devise will be used. May God forgive me if I use that weapon."[406]

Kunz had been captured on October 22, 1944, in fighting around the encircled western German city of Aachen. The V2 had been in use since September 8, but he seemed unaware of this fact. The hopes Germans placed in the V2 remained unfulfilled, and for that reason, even its propaganda value was scant. The surveillance protocols contain very few mentions of the V2 being used.

Most of the soldiers who spoke of retribution weapons did so under the spell of not just a quasi-religious belief in Hitler but also a comparable faith in technology. They did not doubt for a second that Germany would succeed in developing a super-weapon to turn the tide of the war. Hopes of achieving victory against all odds were directly connected to the conviction that German engineers would make the decisive breakthrough. It was rare for POWs to utter doubts that this would be the case. General Wilhelm von Thoma was one of the few Trent Park inmates who engaged in skeptical reflections: "Let a secret weapon make its appearance; it may destroy a few houses, but that's all—we've got nothing else."[407] A bit later in time, responding to a statement by Göring that retribution was nigh, Thoma was completely dismissive. "A couple of snorters will come across to ENGLAND," he said, and that would be all.[408]

Just as German soldiers failed to link technology with the way the war was actually progressing, they also largely ignored its deadly character. The concrete effects of weaponry were rarely mentioned. With pilots and crew members, the talk was more about shooting down planes and sinking ships, and targeting enemy "material."[409] "I saw myself how my Staffelkapitän, Hauptmann SUHR, brought down a four-engine aircraft with one shot of his 3cm over LINZ," reported Sergeant Gromoll. "He targeted from the front. That's the craziest thing I ever saw."[410] A remark by First Lieutenant Schlösser is nearly identical: "A 3 cm cannon firing an HE shell. If they hit four-engine aircraft they destroy it completely. There's nothing left."[411] The airmen's enthusiasm for new weaponry completely blotted out the fact that ten American soldiers lost their lives in the attack. That was typical of the POWs' general disinterest in the lethal consequences of their actions.

In similar fashion, a bombardier from a Ju 88 proudly described sighting his target through a hole in the clouds over Bristol, England:

> A 500 kg bomb. It went bang inside it. How it blazed away and spread rapidly. We went down specially and had a look to see if it was a dummy fire that they had started—but that was not possible. You could see how the buildings were collapsing, so furious was the conflagration. I hit either a grain elevator or an ammunition dump. We had been out over the sea for some time when we still saw the splinters coming up as from the explosions.[412]

The more destructive the weapon, the more enthusiastically POWs talked about it. Sergeant Willi Zastrau, a radio operator aboard a bomber, for instance, emphasized the advantages of the new explosive used in 1,200-kilogram bombs: "Triolin is the best explosive in the world."[413] Other crew members were likewise enthusiastic about the latest bombs. "I tell you, those are something special," Bomber Gunner Clausz of Bomber Wing 76 raved: "We completely wrecked Bari with them. When they fire into the water just beside a ship, then it goes up, like a fountain, like fireworks! We [destroyed] seventeen ships there, ammunition ships, how they blew up! We were at a height of 2000 m, but I watched it from my under fuselage tunnel, the flames were so high, we passed just over them."[414]

High-tech weapons weren't the only ones that could produce results. Low-tech, dirty weapons also had their effect. A bomber pilot praised the new paths being blazed in bomb development:

> KURT*: (There is) a bomb that is used against troop concentrations and this bomb has a very thin casing and is filled with rusty razor blades, old nails, etc. and has a small explosive charge and is just used for causing casualties.

SCHIRMER*: I don't suppose you would have told him (I.O.) that.

KURT: No, no. It really is filled with rusty old razor blades and old junk; it saves a lot of material. Formerly, for a fragmentation bomb a very large charge was required, and it had to have a thick casing to make it burst properly and produce a lot of fragments. And so material and explosives are saved by having quite a thin casing and filling this up with rubbish .... that has been dropped a lot.[415]

The technology with which Luftwaffe and navy soldiers waged war decided whether and how they could carry out their assigned tasks. For that reason, technology was at the center of their own sense of self and exercised tremendous fascination.

If the technology was efficient, then soldiers had fun carrying out their missions. If equipment wasn't available or was suboptimal, operations not only stood little chance of success, but were far more risky. The soldiers' obsession with technology had dominated their everyday experience of war, and it remained one of their primary topics of conversation as POWs. Yet as incessantly as the men discussed questions of horsepower, cubic capacity, and radio frequencies, all the more rarely did they ask questions about the overall context. Specialists tend to apply their instrumental reasoning to the precise situation and task they have been given. The topic of military technology once again manifested the deep connection between modern industrial labor and the labor of war. World War II was a war of technicians and engineers, pilots, radio operators, and mechanics. The laborers in this war used what they saw as grand and fascinating tools. Technology was an arena men could both talk about and agree on for hours on end.

Faith in Victory

"I never believed that we should lose the war, but I'm convinced
of it now."   *Major Arnold Kuhle, June 16, 1944*[416]

Soldiers' military value systems, their faith in technology, and their
immediate social environment were the main factors forming their
wartime frame of reference. Yet this does not mean they were completely unaffected by daily events in combat. Even when individual
soldiers were not directly involved in them, victories and defeat were
constantly present, be it via newspapers, radio, and tales told by their
comrades, and soldiers paid keen attention to reports of distant battles,
if only because they themselves could always be transferred. Nonetheless, their own direct, personal experiences of war heavily influenced
how they interpreted the pivotal events of the conflict. This section
will examine how soldiers saw the general context of what they were
doing against the backdrop of their frame of reference.

BLITZKRIEG (1939–42)

The militarization of the German people and in particular German
soldiers was one of the most important goals of both the Nazi and
Wehrmacht leaderships and went hand in hand with rearmament. Yet
notwithstanding their considerable success in instilling the idea that
Germany was in dire need of defense from external threats,[417] few
Germans reacted with unrestrained enthusiasm at the start of World
War II in September 1939. It took the quick victories over Poland,
Norway, and especially France, which no one expected to be van-
quished so easily, to unleash true euphoria. The intoxication of vic-
tory was then consolidated by German successes in Africa and the
Balkans.

The mood at this point was especially positive in the Luftwaffe. Conversations between POWs recorded in summer 1940 are dominated

by expectations that German troops would soon land in England and free them from captivity. Nearly everyone was certain that ultimate German victory was imminent: "In a month or 6 weeks the war here will be at an end. I definitely believe that the attack will take place this week, or on Monday next."[418] "I believe the war is already won," said another POW,[419] while a third added, "The chances look very rosy that it won't last long."[420] One Luftwaffe first lieutenant, who'd been shot down early on in the conflict, even started discussing how, after the German conquest of England, he'd like to have some new suits made by fine English tailors.[421]

Even as German losses mounted, the Battle of Britain was lost, and German invasion plans had to be postponed, most captured German pilots remained obsessed by visions of their own country's might. In spring 1941, political and military expectations were still very positive, and Germany's invasion of the Soviet Union did nothing to change the mood. On the contrary, most POWs expected a quick German victory on the Eastern Front, after which a somewhat more intense struggle would bring ultimate victory in the West as well. In 1941–42, very few flying units were transferred back and forth between the two fronts, so the numbers of airmen in British POW camps who had served in the East was very small. The surveillance protocols represent an external view of that theater of war. The Wehrmacht's massive losses in the Soviet Union, German troops' complete exhaustion in fall 1942, and the murderous following winter are hardly reflected in POWs' conversations.[422]

Strategic expectations thus remained constant in 1942, as a statement by Sergeant Willi Zastrau, a W/T operator in Wehrmacht Bomber Wing 2, makes clear:

> ZASTRAU: RUSSIA is done for. They've got nothing to eat now, since we took the UKRAINE. It won't be long before we make peace with RUSSIA; then we can go for ENGLAND and AMERICA.[423]

Only in 1944, when masses of German infantrymen were captured in Italy and France, do the protocols provide valid information about expectations among German army soldiers. A few army troops had been captured as early as 1940, but their numbers were too small to be representative of a specific view of the war. The views that were recorded on tape basically conform to the picture researchers have reconstructed from other sources. Unlike in the Luftwaffe, the euphoria produced in the army by early military triumphs was seriously shaken in 1941–42. Nonetheless, in February 1942, the German military leadership believed that "the dip in troop morale" had been overcome. Examinations of letters sent home had suggested soldiers believed they had "gotten the job done."[424] Surviving the first hardships on the Eastern Front had apparently created a new confidence among "Eastern fighters," who continued to believe in their own innate superiority to their Soviet enemies.[425]

During the Blitzkrieg phase, soldiers conflated larger events in the war with their own personal experiences to produce a rosy vision of the future. A decisive factor here for both Luftwaffe and German army men was their faith in their superiority to enemies on all fronts. Setbacks and even being taken as a POW could not shake this fundamental confidence.

The situation was different for navy men. Their wartime frame of reference was formed by one not insignificant additional point: the knowledge that they were undeniably inferior to the gigantic British Royal Navy, which was six times the size of the German navy at the start of the war. Despite some successes, German sailors had to acknowledge that other branches of the German military, and not the navy, would have to prevail if final victory was to be achieved. The perspective of submarine crews who had been taken prisoner was thus more pessimistic than that of Luftwaffe pilots. For instance, the chief engineer of U-32, First Lieutenant Anton Thimm, already arrived at the conclusion in November 1940: "The English can hold out under existing conditions for years; you only need to look at the shops, and in a large city at that. The U-Boat arm will not accomplish that (break them) nor airmen either. Time is on the side of the English and we cannot afford to give them time."[426] First Lieutenant Hans Jenisch, the U-boat's commander and a bearer of the Knight's Cross, even opined that the U-boat was outmoded as a weapon. That drew protest from another U-boat commander, Wilfried Prelberg, who couldn't believe he was hearing such pessimism from one of his peers. Jenisch's outlook is all the more remarkable because he was a very successful captain whose crew had survived, almost to a man, the sinking of their vessel. And he was not alone in his views. "The U-boat arm is finished," a first mate said with a sigh in June 1941. "Absolutely finished."[427] Others were critical of Germany's strategy for bringing Britain to its knees: "We shall never defeat the English through the blockade."[428] And others still predicted a long war, which "will be very bad for us."[429] Radio operator Willi Dietrich of U-32 was already speculating by November 1940: "Just think of what would happen if we lost the war!"[430]

There was little change in these attitudes over the course of 1942, although naturally there were some optimists who felt victory was at hand in Russia and believed Germany would then launch a successful offensive against Britain. The first officer of the watch of U-32, First Lieutenant Egon Rudolph, painted the following scenario in late 1941:

> RUDOLPH: German soldiers will be everywhere. GIBRALTAR will go up in smoke. Bombs and mines will be exploding everywhere. Our U-boats will lie off LONDON. They'll get such a bellyful! There'll be air-raids day and night! They'll have no rest. Then they can creep away into their rabbit-holes in ENGLAND and eat grass. God punish ENGLAND and her satellite states.[431]

Rudolph was a fanatic Nazi, anti-Semite, and Anglophobe. The vehemence of his language was unusual, and he was in the minority of those who remained optimistic at this juncture in the war. Whereas, when cross-examined, most navy POWs claimed they were counting on German victory, they were much more cautious and skeptical when conversing with one another.[432]

A first mate from U-111, for instance, predicted: "If the war in the east isn't over by the end of this year, we shall probably lose it."[433] And in March 1942, a navy man named Josef Przyklenk confessed to horror when he thought of the future:

> PRZYKLENK: It is obvious that we have retreated in RUSSIA. Even if we retake that strip of territory, about 100 kms, RUSSIA is still there. It is ten times the size of GERMANY. The Russians may have lost their crack troops, but we must reckon that we, too, have lost our crack troops. It doesn't do to think about it. If I am asked whether we shall conquer RUSSIA, I say, "Yes," but when I think it over, then it's a very different matter. In October of last year ADOLF declared that the final battle against the Russians was beginning. That was absolute rubbish.[434]

It's interesting here that Przyklenk admits to telling British interrogators something different from what he actually believes. This is another example of dissonance between what soldiers were supposed to and wanted to think and reality. Przyklenk's response to the dilemma is simply not to think too hard about the situation.

Yet even when German navy men willfully avoided thinking about larger strategic questions, focusing instead on their own concrete experiences of naval warfare, some came to negative conclusions. Karl Wedekind was one of the few survivors when his vessel was sunk during a battle with an Allied convoy. In December 1941, he concluded: "The U-boat warfare is in the cart, the U-boats can do nothing."[435] And even in March 1942, a comparatively good month for German forces, Heinz Weszling expressed unmistakable frustration: "Submarine warfare is a damnable business, U-boat men could tell you some stories! As far as I'm concerned they can scrap the whole lot of U-boats."[436]

FROM STALINGRAD TO NORMANDY (1943–44)

Most army soldiers lost their confidence in final victory after the massive German defeats during the winter of 1942–43.[437] Still, the majority believed that the war would now drag on and end in stalemate. Private Faust concluded: "That was a terrific blow! It's impossible to estimate the proportions of this fiasco."[438] And First Sergeant Schreiber predicted: "If we don't finish the Russians off next year, then we shall be done for. I'm convinced of that. Just think of all the Americans are producing."[439]

In the months that followed, news of victories and defeats caused the mood among POWs to rise and fall, but the general tendency remained the same. Thoughts of defeat began to crop up more often and led to impassioned discussions among the inmates. On March 22, 1943, two bomber pilots, both first lieutenants, debated Germany's prospects in the war:

> FRIED: It's ridiculous to believe in final victory.
> HOLZAPFEL: It's sheer sedition to talk like that.
> FRIED: No, it's not sedition—just look at the U-boats, they're no longer doing so well; and ships are being built for the Allies all over the world.

HOLZAPFEL: I can't think the Government is so stupid as all that.[440]

Holzapfel and Fried had been detained for two weeks together in Latimer House and got along well. Both were experienced pilots who swapped detailed stories about the sorties they had flown over England, and Holzapfel put up with a lot of skeptical remarks from Fried. But Fried crossed the line for him when he cast doubt upon the possibility of ultimate German victory. In Holzapfel's world, that was unthinkable. The consequences of defeat were all too apparent and gruesome to contemplate.

Aside from some hopeless optimists, who still talked about Germany invading England in summer 1943,[441] most of the soldiers simply considered total defeat impossible. German euphoria at early Blitzkrieg successes and conviction in their own innate superiority blocked acknowledgment of the course the war was actually taking. Expectations and reality were diverging ever more from one another, creating cognitive dissonance. For that reason, soldiers' estimations of the situation were increasingly colored by wishful thinking, for example, the hope that the German "leadership" would put things right.

One day, when a Sergeant Kratz, a bomber aircraft mechanic from a Do 217, was flipping through an English newspaper, he was taken aback by a map showing troop movement on the Eastern Front. "So far I've always believed that the retreat was a tactical one," he said. His bunkmate Lelewel answered: "The best thing is not to worry. It doesn't help at all."[442] Lelewel's response was telling. What good was the insight that the war was being lost? The POWs themselves were part of this war. They had invested their energy, imagination, and hopes in it, had risked their own lives, and, in most cases, lost comrades for it. What option did they have other than to pursue it to the bitter end? It is rare for people to retrospectively question decisions and experiences that are made under situations of duress and hardship. Moreover, people tend to justify things done with ambivalent feelings so as to preserve their own self-image. Therefore, subjectively, it often seems more sensible to repeat an action than to question it by pursuing a corrective. Once a person has overcome his doubts and scruples, the rule of "path dependency" dictates that he will overcome them again a second, third, and fourth time in similar situations. For this reason, it seemed anything but helpful to soldiers to reflect on the senselessness of their own endeavors.

The enthusiasm of men who had been engaged for years in a fruit-less battle against English air defenses emerged strikingly in a con-versation between three pilots who had been shot down in one of Germany's last bombing raids on London, the so-called Baby Blitz. Lieutenant Hubertus Schymczyk recalled how the offensive was announced, and in so doing, everything suddenly seemed as it was in the good old days:

> SCHYMCZYK: I still remember Major ENGEL[443] coming in during briefing on 1st January and saying: "Heil, comrades," he always said that, "today is a special event for us people of KG 2. It is the first time for two and a half years that we are not the only ones to fly over LONDON, but about four or five hundred of our comrades from the GAF will accompany us!" Whereupon there was wild cheering. You can't imagine the tremendous enthusiasm that caused.[444]

Most Luftwaffe pilots were mentally incapable of forming a halfway objective picture of the war. It is astonishing that the heavy losses they suffered in their battle with the RAF, be it in France or the Mediter-ranean, did not make a more negative impression—although those who engaged in some reflection and were prepared to draw conclu-sions from the information at their disposal sometimes did see things with crystal clarity. One of them was Wilfried von Müller-Rienzburg, a thirty-eight-year-old Viennese Luftwaffe officer, who declared: "We can't win the war unless a miracle happens. Only a few complete idi-ots still believe we can. It is only a question of a few months before we come to grief. In the spring we shall be fighting on four fronts and then, of course, we haven't got a hope. We've lost *this* war."[445]

Navy POWs were even more pessimistic than their army or navy comrades in the period between Stalingrad and the Allied landing at Normandy. In their immediate social environment, there had been practically no success stories since spring 1943, and the tide turned irrevocably in the Battle of the North Atlantic in May 1943. The Ger-man navy had become almost insignificant militarily, and crews' views of the future were correspondingly bleak. "It's a dog's life nowadays," twenty-one-year-old sailor Horst Minnieur complained on Novem-ber 27, 1943. "It would be best to sink the boat in harbour. Going to sea in a U-boat is nothing but suicide."[446] Another comrade seconded that thought. "It's a horrible business, going to sea nowadays."[447] And nineteen-year-old Fritz Schwenninger added, "What the U-boat has to go through today is only comparable with STALINGRAD."[448]

Two sailors who had been lucky enough to escape the sinking of the battleship *Scharnhorst* questioned whether it was worth carrying on given the disastrous course of the war:

> WALLEK: The chances of victory are 100 to 1 against us. We are fighting against the three mightiest peoples of the earth.
>
> SCHAFFRATH: It was madness to start the war, and I simply can't understand how they think they are going to win now; but we have a lot of people who can't think for themselves and can't see that. The invasion will certainly come this year and then they will march straight into GERMANY.[449]

Navy Commander in Chief Karl Dönitz tried with all the means at his disposal to combat such pessimism and skepticism. In an ordinance prohibiting "compulsive criticism and complaint" in September 1943, he called for an end to the doomsaying. From now on, the grand admiral commanded, there would only be "fighting, working and keeping silent."[450] Joseph Goebbels was impressed by this emphasis on morale. In his diary, he noted that, thanks to his "iron hardness," Dönitz appeared to be succeeding in turning around the naval campaign and ending the crisis. Dönitz, Goebbels wrote, was cleaning out the old, worn-out officer corps, overcoming the "provocative resignation in the face of wartime developments," and offering new ideas for continuing the submarine campaign. But macho appeals and motivational speeches by the leadership made little headway against the far more persuasive force of navy men's own experience. More and more sailors believed Germany would lose the war—45 percent, according to a British survey of POWs carried out in fall 1943.[451]

Historian Rafael Zagovec has pointed out that similar results emerged from a survey of German army soldiers in Tunisia in April 1943. The Allies were indeed startled that German soldiers seemed to have lost most of their confidence in final victory and belief in their own cause. That survey found that a majority were "sick and tired" and disinterested in broader questions.[452] At the time, American military experts could hardly explain why their enemies continued to fight.

Of course, not all German soldiers looked toward the future with such desperation. With the reentrenchment of the fronts in late 1943, morale and confidence rose, and the Nazi and Wehrmacht leadership did their best to bolster the revival. The measures included the creation of the National Socialist Leading Officers, Nazi officials charged with political propaganda, on December 22, 1943. These "brave leaders of national defense," in Hitler's words, were charged with getting soldiers to believe in final victory, even if they did not know how it was going to be achieved.[453] It isn't possible to reconstruct whether this initiative had any success, but if so, it probably wasn't all that great. While references to propaganda slogans do occur regularly in the surveillance protocols, and some POWs seem to have internalized them, there was no change in the general downward spiral of morale.

THE FINAL YEAR OF WAR

"The commencement of the invasion is generally received as a release from unbearable tension and oppressive uncertainty. . . . In the past, news of the beginning of the invasion was greeted with great enthusiasm."

Security Service report from June 8, 1944[454]

World War II was long decided in June 1944, when the Allies deployed a huge armada to land their troops on the beaches of Normandy. Today we know that the only thing that could have scuttled the operation was bad weather. But in 1944, the situation was far less clear. The Allies may have no longer doubted their ability to win the war, but they were uncertain as to whether the leap to the continent would succeed. Eisenhower even prepared a radio speech for the eventuality that the mission failed. And on the German side, many people believed that the landing of troops represented a chance for Germany to achieve a stalemate or even win the conflict.[455]

The surveillance protocols confirm the impression that the majority of soldiers by no means thought the battle had been lost. On the contrary, for many of them, the Allied invasion represented an opportunity for the Wehrmacht to alter the course of the war. A conversation between Colonel Hauck and Colonel Annacker—two commanders of the 362nd Infantry Division, who had been captured in Italy—is typical of the expectations soldiers typically had on the day after the Normandy landing:

HAUCK: We must succeed in halting this invasion.

ANNACKER: Yes, that's what I keep on saying. It's all over if we don't succeed.

HAUCK: That would be the end.

ANNACKER: If we were to succeed in halting this invasion, GERMANY would have a basis for negotiation.[456]

A Captain Gundlach, who had defended his bunker in the small coastal town of Ouistreham to the very last, shared similar hopes:

GUNDLACH: It is presumed that our leadership could never be so careless, or supposing our FÜHRER was not convinced—that's to say, if the prospect of still winning the war by some means did not exist—then it is known that he would be honest enough to say: "Here people, condemn me!" If he was not still convinced of having something up his sleeve which could still prove the deciding factor of the war, he would put a bullet through his head, in order not to experience what could no longer be carried out rather than plunge his people into an abyss.[457]

In this statement, we can observe the convergence of faith in final victory and faith in the Führer.

Yet no matter how much energy the Nazi leadership or German soldiers themselves put into mobilizing their last reserves of confidence, the massive material advantage of Allied troops, and especially their aerial and artillery dominance, crushed any remaining hopes. Soldiers no longer talked about setbacks on the front or battles that had been lost; their entire world collapsed like a house of cards. The path was freed for the sort of fundamental criticism that had previously been lacking—a Private First Class Hirst even opined, "I'll do anything I can to end the war and see that Germany is completely defeated"[458]— and not just among foot soldiers, but officers as well.

Typical in this regard was a conversation between Majors Arnold Kuhle and Sylvester von Saldern, both of whom had fought on the front lines as infantry commanders and had been taken prisoner in June 1944 on the Cotentin Peninsula:

V. SALDERN: When you see the troops against which we are supposed to fight—

KUHLE: The Americans above all, what splendid people!

V. SALDERN: Things look bad for us at home now. We have thirteen million foreigners in the REICH. That will lead to a lot of trouble.

Now they have cheated us. But I still can't believe it yet. I'm still convinced that it will turn out differently. I still can't think they can drive a people to destruction in such a short time.

KUHLE: What do you think is still there to help us and save us?

V. SALDERN: I can't know! It's damnable about the reprisal weapon too, because that wasn't ready either.

KUHLE: I once said the FÜHRER had said that if the invasion came he would send the whole GAF into action at the place of the invasion, even if it meant having all forces in all the other theatres of war without air cover. That story was over as far as I was concerned. After I had seen one single German reconnaissance aircraft in the air between the 6th and the 16th, and apart from that, complete mastery of the air by the Americans. We can bring out whole armies, and they'll smash them up completely with their air force within a week. Above all we have no petrol at all left. We can no longer move any numbers of troops by means requiring petrol; only by rail or marching on foot.

V. SALDERN: Well, once you're convinced that it's all up, that's to say that the collapse will come sooner or later, you can only say that the sooner it happens, the better.

KUHLE: We haven't one "General" who stands up for himself. The only one who does that is SIMON, otherwise not one. We have no other who risks anything. All those who risked anything have gone. Our conduct of the war suffers from the fact that none of them have any sense of responsibility any longer, and nobody wants to take any responsibility.

Do you think that anyone can prevent it? The few naval coastal batteries can be put out of action by a small "bedside-rug" of bombs, not even a carpet. They have such superiority of materials, they smash everything up! Do you know how they landed in FRANCE?

V. SALDERN: I saw it. Like a peace-time tomorrow.

KUHLE: There's no longer any trace of leadership at all. Who's actually running the show? RUNDSTADT or ROMMEL!

V. SALDERN: The moment the first paratroops landed, the damned business started. They split everything up and put in one odd "Bataillon" here, and a "Kompanie" there. I had not more than twenty men left in my "Regiment" afterwards. All the others I had were transport people, clerks, and depot "Bataillons" — what can you do with them! The NCOs are no good, and the officers are no good. It's all damnable.

KUHLE: I have always been an optimist. I never believed that we should lose the war, but I'm convinced of it now. It's only a matter of weeks.

If the front collapses, things will collapse at home too. They can do whatever they like at home, and nothing will be any help. The Americans will straighten things out nicely for themselves!

BORNHARD asked me this afternoon whether I had heard the rumour that General POPPE had been shot for treason.[459]

Kuhle and Saldern both reached the sobering conclusion that Germany had no chance against an overpowering enemy. Hitler had not been able to keep his promises, and weapons of retaliation were tactically useless. The two men's faith in the Führer and their trust in the German military leadership collapsed simultaneously. With that, Kuhle and Saldern see no way to continue nurturing hopes for a happy ending. The facts are the facts: the war is lost, and Germany's collapse is only a question of a few weeks. Two days later Saldern opined: "Let's hope a German general turns up, who says, as you do: 'We have lost the war, so the sooner we make an end the better.' "[460]

Most of the POWs brought to England from the battlefields of Normandy drew such broad conclusions. A Major Hasso Viebig was of the opinion that "a responsible German government would now try to bring the war to an end." Major Rudolf Becker responded: "Well, of course they know perfectly well that the war is lost, and that this is the end of National Socialism etc. The only question is: are they fighting for the fatherland or for their self preservation?"[461] Becker recalled a speech made in April 1944 in which General Heinz Guderian urged German troops to turn back the invasion as a means of giving the Führer a chance at concluding a halfway honorable peace. Becker therefore wondered why Guderian, who had seen things so clearly, had not taken action, allowing himself instead to be named army chief of staff.[462]

Normally officers feel less pressure the higher they rank, but many generals who had experienced the battles of attrition in Normandy thought the same way Kuhle or Becker did. Even the supreme commander of Army Group B, Field Marshal Erwin Rommel, was convinced by June 1944 that the war was lost and corresponding political consequences should follow.[463] On the other hand, some soldiers still vacillated in their interpretation of the situation. Major Heinz Quittnat, for example, ventured: "My personal opinion is that if we are going to lose the war, it is a crime to continue fighting a day longer. If we have a chance of winning the war, of course, we should continue. But I can't decide that."[464] Quittnat's words came shortly after he himself had experienced American troops taking Cherbourg. Previously, he had spent years on the Eastern Front. How could such a person, we are tempted to ask today, feel unable to decide whether or not the war could still be won? In this case, Quittnat was probably trying to shield himself from the logical consequences of what he knew. As though having been caught thinking illicit thoughts, he quickly qualified his statement: "As a good German of course I hope that we shall win the war." But doubts were equally quick to reemerge: "On the other hand if we win the war 100%, that would be pretty bad too, with our present regime. I would not remain a regular army officer then, at any rate."[465]

An analysis of the standardized questionnaires handed out to all German POWs in the U.S. camp of Fort Hunt yields an even more precise picture of the end of German hopes for winning the war. In June 1944, half of the 112 German POWs questioned believed Germany would emerge victorious. By August, it was only 27 of 148, and by September, only 5 of 67.[466] Admittedly, the sample size was too small to be representative. But the answers still reveal that the main change of heart came in August 1944, as the Allies broke through German lines in Normandy and surrounded German troops in Falaise, taking most of them prisoner.

Those who dreamed of a German counteroffensive leading to a victorious comeback had shrunk to a tiny minority.[467] A Captain Barthel still declared on August 19, 1944: "It still won't be fatal for us if FRANCE falls."[468] Such inveterate optimists were usually young officers and, quite often, navy men. Sailors were more likely to be optimistic since they experienced a different and, to a certain extent, "cleaner" war than their army counterparts. They did not have to endure weeks of shelling, witness tens of thousands of their comrades dying, or suffer through months of privations in a fight for survival. As horrible as naval warfare may have been for many sailors, it could not be compared with the battles of attrition that took place on land.[469]

After Stalingrad, the successful Allied landing at Normandy, the battles of attrition in the hedgerow country of the Bocage, and the Wehrmacht's pell-mell retreat from France represented the second major psychological caesura in German soldiers' perception of the war. Never before had so many people been killed in one place in such a short time as in these twelve weeks of 1944. It was the quantitative equivalent of a second Battle of Stalingrad. Moreover, the symbolic import was undeniable. Germany's victory over France in 1940 had made the Wehrmacht feel like the lords of Europe. Losing France sealed Germany's total defeat in most soldiers' eyes.

To a certain extent, the Wehrmacht recovered some of its morale in fall 1944 after fleeing in panic across the German border.[470] There, they had at least been able to regroup and form a coherent front, and no longer were tens of thousands of soldiers being taken prisoner. But there was a major difference between a willingness to fight on and faith in victory. Members of the German armed forces still functioned fairly well as soldiers, but the surveillance protocols make it clear that the stabilization of the front on Germany's borders did little to improve German soldiers' expectations for the future. The Ardennes Offensive also raised only a flicker of hope—and solely among the soldiers who participated in it.[471]

By August 1944, a qualitative shift in evaluations of the war had taken place. One good example is the reflections of Colonel Gerhard Wilck, fortress commander in the German city of Aachen, after being taken prisoner in October 1944:

> WILCK: The people are so war weary and so minded to make an end at any cost that I fear that that feeling will spread all over GERMANY. Hopelessness is spreading strongly everywhere—I mean hopelessness in that <u>no one</u> believes that a turn of the tide can come. You catch the feeling yourself. Even <u>if</u> we have something in that background, a V-2 or something of the sort, it cannot possibly ever be decisive now.[472]

Wilck talked here of "the people," but what he meant more specifically was himself, together with his men and the population of Aachen.

Wilck was the first commander ordered by Hitler to defend a German city. But having been beaten down in a hopeless fight, Wilck no longer saw any way out.

In early 1945, there was a further decline in morale, as can be traced in the American surveillance protocols.[473] And official army reports described units openly talking about being "sick and tired" of the war.[474] The reluctant insight that the war was in fact lost also affected German soldiers' behavior, particularly in the West, where many tried to get captured.

However, indications of a general decline in morale should not obscure the fact that there was a small group who believed in final victory right up until the very end. They tended to be higher officers or members of special units, for example, veteran fighter pilots. On March 18, 1945, First Lieutenant Hans Hartigs, who had already been imprisoned for two and a half months, asked newly arrived POW Lieutenant Antonius Wöffen from Luftwaffe Fighter Wing 27:

HARTIGS: What was the morale of the officers and men like?
WÖFFEN: On the whole, our morale is still quite good. It's obvi-
    ous that the present situation is lousy but there still exists the
    great hope that things still won't turn out as bad as they look.
    On the other hand, one can't speak of belief any more.[475]

German soldiers' interpretations of how the war was going generally followed the major milestones: the Blitzkrieg victories, the Battle of Stalingrad in 1942–43, and the Allied landing at Normandy in 1944. Yet interestingly, different branches of the military arrived at different interpretations. Put in simple terms: the Luftwaffe was more optimistic than the navy, while the army was, at least by 1944, the most pessimistic.

Luftwaffe pilots were a relatively small group of elite fighters who went to battle convinced of their superiority over the enemy. Despite all the difficulties of their mission, they led a pretty good life. Particularly in France, pilots enjoyed amenities foot soldiers could only dream of. Moreover, even if the qualitative and quantitative advantages of the Allies began to show as of 1943, Luftwaffe pilots could still celebrate individual triumphs in 1944–45. Fighter pilots still shot down enemy aircraft, and crews aboard bombers still dropped their deadly payloads on cities, ships, and troops. Navy men necessarily viewed the war more skeptically because they had been fighting a far stronger enemy ever since September 1939.

The army soldiers who experienced the fighting at Normandy and the collapse of the front in France are the most disillusioned group in the protocols. Examples of individual successes, such as enemy soldiers killed or tanks destroyed, play hardly any role in their conversations. Instead their discussions are full of everyday experiences of powerlessness at facing a materially far better equipped foe. The overarching mood of futility is impossible to ignore.

Today, it may seem surprising that soldiers only dared to believe in the downfall of the Third Reich as of mid-1944. Why did it take them so long to arrive at this conclusion when, from a military perspective, the war had likely been decided by the end of 1941 at the latest? A particular form of perception is part of the explanation. Someone with a high-paying job rarely thinks about the structural problems of the global economy, and even when he does, he does so calmly. People who have a certain task in a war behave similarly. As long as the war continues, the task remains. For that reason, people only saw that Germany was headed for defeat when they experienced it personally. Ahead of the disastrous summer of 1944, many German soldiers still had reason to hope. At that juncture, Germany still occupied half of Europe, and Allied aerial bombardment was restricted to German cities. Thus, German troops in Italy could maintain, with a certain justification, that they would stand their ground against the Allies. The same was true, incidentally, for soldiers in Army Group Center on the Eastern Front.

Without doubt, it would have been possible for German soldiers to view their own experiences and the war in general more critically. They could have asked themselves: what did it say about the war effort when Germany had to postpone the ground invasion of England, when the Wehrmacht failed to end the Russian campaign as promised in fall 1941, when the United States with its huge economic potential entered the fray, or when German troops retreated ever closer to the homeland? Anyone who read newspapers, listened to the radio, watched the weekly newsreels, or simply discussed the situation with comrades, friends, and family, could have realized where things were headed without overtaxing his brain. Yet like most other people in most other situations, German soldiers were strictly bound to the necessities of their immediate social environment. As long as major historical events do not have direct personal consequences, they do not fundamentally change perceptions, interpretations, and decisions. Human beings think in concrete, not in abstract, terms. What in retrospect may seem to be an increasingly obvious reality remains irrelevant for an individual acting in real time, as long as he himself is not directly caught up in the looming disaster. There are notable exceptions,[476] but most people only notice the coming of a flood when the first story of their house is already submerged. And even then, hopes persist that the water level will recede.

Germans lost hope in increments during World War II. If Germany was not able to achieve final victory, they told themselves, at least it could force an honorable peace settlement. Giving up every last bit of hope would have invalidated all the effort and emotions they had invested in the war with one fell swoop. People typically cling to hopes and instances of wishful thinking that, with the benefit of hindsight, appear completely irrational. Why do workers fight to save a company that has no realistic chance of surviving on the market? Because they have invested all their energy, dreams, hopes, time, and opportunities in it. And this characteristic is by no means restricted to "everyday people." The higher their status, the less people are able to acknowledge failure. General Ludwig Crüwell put it this way. In November 1942, shortly after receiving word that the 6th Army was surrounded at Stalingrad, he retorted: "Are hundreds of thousands of men to be killed in this way again for nothing? That's unthinkable."[477]

Faith in the Führer

Shortly before the end of World War II, Colonel Martin Vetter, the commander of Paratrooper Regiment 17, and fighter pilot Anton Wöffen from Luftwaffe Fighter Wing 27 had a discussion about National Socialism. Both men had been captured a few days earlier in two separate towns in Germany. For them, the war was over, and it was time for a general evaluation:

> VETTER: Whatever you think of National Socialism, Adolf Hitler is the leader and he has given the German people a very great deal up till now. At last we were able once more to be proud of our nation. One should never forget that.

WÖFFEN: Nothing can ever take that away.

VETTER: Despite the fact that I'm convinced he will become the
grave-digger of the German REICH.

WÖFFEN: Yes, her grave-digger.

VETTER: He's that all right. Undoubtedly.[478]

This excerpt is an extraordinary document. Adolf Hitler—or the
"leader," as he is termed throughout the surveillance protocols—is
simultaneously deemed Germany's great benefactor and its grave-
digger.

How could these two contradictory positions coexist? Were the
POWs schizophrenic? Most certainly not. On the contrary, this short
dialogue illustrates the diverse aspects of Germans' faith in the Führer. Wöffen and Vetter's conversation took place in March 1945, when
it was obvious Germany was crashing to defeat. Doubts about Hitler's
military acumen had been growing since 1943. Nonetheless, despite
Germans' dissolving confidence in final victory, their belief in their
Führer and the cult of personality surrounding Hitler remained intact
for an astonishingly long time. Not even the imminent demise of the
Third Reich could shake this quasi-religious faith. This may seem
incomprehensible, but it can be explained if one considers what were
perceived as Hitler's enormous triumphs in Germany and abroad.
That fed into the stylization of the Führer as a divine savior who
negated the perceived injustice of the Treaty of Versailles and allowed
(non-Jewish) Germans to once again feel proud of their country.

On March 7, 1936, slightly more than three years after becoming
German chancellor, Hitler held a speech in the Reichstag in which
he claimed that in the short time of his reign, Germany had regained
its "honor," having "rediscovered a faith, overcome its greatest economic crisis and finally begun a new cultural renaissance."[479] In an
election twenty-two days later, the Nazi Party received 98.9 percent
of the votes. Even though the polling was by no means democratic,
there was no doubt, as historian Ian Kershaw writes, that the majority
of Germans stood behind their Führer. Even today, people who experienced Hitler recall the prewar years of Nazi Germany as a "good" or
"pleasant" time. And the concrete, palpable achievements credited to
Hitler were indeed impressive. Kershaw writes: "To most observers,
both internal and external, after four years in power the Hitler regime
looked stable, strong, and successful."[480]

POW Vetter was referring to precisely these qualities. The fact that the Third Reich was collapsing did not automatically diminish Hitler's status. He remained the primary figure with whom Germany identified precisely because they *distinguished* him from National Socialism and the other party elites. Vetter articulated the entire emotional power carried by the Third Reich—everything non-Jewish Germans saw in the National Socialist project and were prepared to invest in it emotionally. Germans' faith in their own greatness, which Hitler personified, seemed to pay dividends even up until the final days of World War II.

Vetter and Wöffen weren't the only POWs to judge the historical achievement of the Führer independently of Germany's defeat and collapse. SS Brigadeführer Kurt Meyer, for instance, proclaimed:

MEYER: In my opinion the FÜHRER hasn't been quite himself since the winter of 1941 and 1942, as a result of all the happenings. He gets some sort of attacks of hysteria. Despite all that I must say, that he achieved an incredible amount after Germany collapsed and even if the whole REICH collapses once more, he is responsible for a tremendous awakening in the German people; he gave them back their self-confidence.[481]

This sort of emotional investment yielded fine returns—at least until the first deadly wartime winter in Russia in 1942. Feelings of national greatness based on the seeming and empirical triumphs of the Nazi regime were a fantastic payoff on the emotions and energy Germans invested in the Third Reich. Author W. G. Sebald wrote of such feelings "in August 1942, as the vanguard of the 6th Army reached the Volga River and more than a few Germans dreamed of settling after the war in the cherry gardens of an estate alongside the quietly flowing Don."[482] The emotional component involved in the proposition of a better future thanks to the National Socialist project explains why trust in the system and faith in the Führer grew continually until the system began to break down.

German national pride entailed faith in a rosy future and an assertion about Germans themselves, embodied by the Führer and the Nazi project, which united people to the extent that even those who initially had been critical or skeptical of the project were gradually integrated into the community. Psychologically, any misgivings about having chosen the wrong leader and system would have meant devaluing oneself. Thus faith in the Führer persisted even as hopes for final victory disappeared. Moreover, we can observe the same dialectic principle of self-reinforcing conviction in Adolf Hitler himself. His initial successes caused him to believe that he was indeed appointed by divine providence to lead Germany to the global dominance it was predestined to achieve by the laws of nature and race. Hitler, to follow Kershaw, increasingly became the victim of the myth of his own significance, and Hitler's *Volk* set such extraordinary emotional stock in its faith in the Führer and itself that, as though on the commodities market, it had difficulty finding an exit strategy when its stock began plummeting. Just as the cult of personality surrounding the Führer exempted Hitler from any sort of criticism and transformed him into a superhuman savior, the German populace believed itself capable of anything under his leadership.

For that reason, the faith in the Führer that POWs articulated in the surveillance protocols was far greater than their trust in the system, and many of the prisoners drew the same sort of seemingly contradictory distinctions as Vetter and Wöffen.[483] The notion that much of what went on in the government and particularly in the war happened behind the Führer's back and against his will allowed soldiers to maintain their belief in Hitler even as the Nazi system eroded and the war was being lost. This perspective still persisted after the war. Even today, some three generations after 1945, every banal incident in the Führerbunker has the status of a historical event. Moreover, soldiers saw the personnel surrounding their leader—Himmler, Göring, Goebbels, Julius Ley, and Martin Bormann—as much the same circle of sometimes ridiculous characters we do today. Himmler was perceived as a demonic figure, whose SS succeeded in gaining a fatal influence over the system and the war. Göring, mostly referred to as "Hermann," was a familiar, reliable fellow who acted on his convictions and, in most soldiers' eyes, had lamentably little clout with Hitler. Goebbels was alternately the "imaginative politician" or "the cripple" with an impressive intellect. Ley was seen as a dilettante, bigoted, corrupt profiteer, while Bormann appeared as an inscrutable but definitely threatening gatekeeper controlling access to Hitler. This is more or less how all these men continue to be seen.

As the psychological warfare specialists who interviewed German POWs in the 1940s discovered, this basic constellation of Nazi leadership figures with its stereotypes and images already existed before the war was lost and set the tone for how Goebbels and company were viewed after the war.[484] It is astonishing, when one reads the surveillance protocols, how constant the clichés about the other leading Nazis remained before and after German military defeat.

THE FÜHRER

Not surprisingly, in quantitative terms, the person POWs talked about most often in the protocols was Hitler, followed by Göring, Himmler, and Goebbels, and then at some remove Ley, Baldur von Schirach, Walter von Brauchitsch, and others. In this regard, the protocols reflected the amount of popular attention the individual leadership figures commanded during the Third Reich. Moreover, faith in the Führer is a running trope in the POWs' conversations. "There is only one HITLER and whatever he wants will be done," pledged one soldier,[485] while another intoned, "If HITLER no longer lived then I should not desire to live."[486] Soldiers' trust in their Führer was blind and boundless. "If the Führer has said it, you can rely on it," one POW assured his listeners. Another asserted: "HITLER has done it wonderfully. He has kept all his promises. We all have the fullest confidence in him."[487] In November 1940, a lieutenant said: "I am perfectly convinced that we'll win the war. Absolutely certain. HITLER will not tolerate BERLIN being bombed by American a/c [aircraft]."[488] And a private confessed that when confronted with bad news: "I console myself with the words of the Führer, he has taken everything into account."[489]

Germans had emphatic faith not just in the Führer as a person but in the predictions he made. "I am not a rabid National Socialist," said one Luftwaffe first lieutenant in 1941, "but when HITLER says that the war will end this year, then I believe it."[490] Even Stalingrad, as doubts first emerged in Germany's ability to achieve final victory, did not dispel Germans' trust in Hitler. For example, a low-level officer named Leska complained, "The outlook for us isn't rosy," whereupon his interlocutor, Private Hahnfeld, responded, "Yes, but the FÜHRER has always known that it is a struggle for our very existence."[491] A conversation between two sergeants was very similar:

LUDWIG: Things look appalling in RUSSIA!
JONGA: That's just your imagination. It's no longer a question of gaining territory but of who wins the war of morale. If the Rus-

sians imagine we're weak, then they've made a mistake. Don't forget what a marvellous head ADOLF has on his shoulders.[492]

Regardless of rank and function, German soldiers' faith in the Führer seems to have been genuine. Often their statements give the impression that the speaker feels he has a personal relationship to Hitler. That is not unlike today's pop stars, who seem beyond reach and blessed with something extraordinary, yet still remain strangely familiar and intimate. The propagandistic staging of Hitler's public appearances, indeed the presentation of the whole National Socialist system, was thoroughly modern. It's hard to imagine Winston Churchill receiving thousands of love letters, as Hitler did, or getting 100,000 congratulatory telegrams, as was the case when Göring's daughter was born.

The myth of the simple-hearted, benevolent, and yet mysterious and omnipotent Führer was bolstered and updated by countless rumors. Hitler also cultivated the image of the diva with his screaming style of oratory, his ascetic eating and drinking habits, and his legendary outbreaks of temper, which allegedly once included biting a hotel carpet.[493] POWs who could boast of special proximity to the Führer, for example, those who were once seated near him or called to report directly to him on military matters, described those encounters in immense detail and always with reference to Hitler's special qualities. Those stories were intended to imply an intimate familiarity with the Führer, and news about Hitler, whether first- or secondhand, was a topic that guaranteed a rapt audience. One recurring trope was Hitler's hypnotic ability to put others under his sway.

A somewhat different picture emerges from actual encounters with the Führer, such as related by Ludwig Crüwell, the commander of the Wehrmacht's Panzer Army Africa, to an eagerly attentive stool pigeon:

CRÜWELL: I am convinced that a great part of the FÜHRER'S success as Party Leader is accounted for by pure mass suggestion. It's bound up with a kind of hypnotism, and he can exercise this on a great many people. I know people who are undoubtedly superior to him mentally and who yet fall under his spell. I cannot explain why it doesn't affect me. I mean, I know perfectly well that he carries a superhuman burden of responsibility; what he said to me about AFRICA was astonishing, but I can't say that (I was influenced). One outstanding thing is his

hands — he has beautiful hands. You don't notice it in the photographs. He has the hands of an artist. I always looked at his
hands; they are beautiful hands, and there is nothing common
about them — they are aristocratic hands. In his whole manner,
there is nothing of the little man about him. What surprised me
so much — I thought he would fix me with an eagle eye — I don't
mean I expected a long speech but . . . "Allow me to present
you with the Oakleaves," in a quiet voice, you understand. I
had pictured <u>that</u> quite differently.[494]

In addition to being deeply impressed with Hitler, Crüwell offers evidence for his personal acquaintance with the Führer by using the sort
of details that can only be observed in proximity, and those details, the
general asserts, were different than he had imagined. In Crüwell's tale,
the *personal Führer* is even more fascinating than the hypnotic one.
The story is unintentionally comic in the sense that Crüwell denies
falling under Hitler's hypnotic spell while describing the Führer as if
he were the savior incarnate. Crüwell's narrative is one of expectations and how they were surpassed. Hitler is not only astonishing; he
is astonishing in an unexpected way.
    Telling stories of this sort was a way for the speaker to distinguish
himself as someone special who had been allowed to come so close to
the Führer. Crüwell's interlocutor offers a relatively sober commentary:

WALDECK: All his notions are prompted by his feelings.

Crüwell immediately recognized this as a challenge and responds:

CRÜWELL: If he wants to influence his people, then he must
    behave naturally. If he considers the impression he wants to
    give, then it's bad. I know very good soldiers who have always
    sought out someone on whom to model themselves. That's
    always bad. He has an elastic step. He is very nicely dressed,
    quite simply, with black trousers and a coat. Rather more grey
    than this one, it's not field grey. I don't know what kind of
    material it is, and unlike GÖRING, he wears no decorations![495]

Crüwell interprets Hitler's tendency to follow his gut instincts as a sign
of authenticity and a part of what makes him convincing. The general

then continues his narrative with intimate details about the Führer's ostentatiously displayed asceticism and humility. Excerpts like this make it clear how much Hitler's reputation for charisma programmed people's encounters with him, and how the unexpected impression the Führer made fueled further stories. Encounters with Hitler were self-fulfilling prophecies; faith in the Führer, an emotional perpetuum mobile.

The significance of Hitler as a public figure who was alternately regarded as a savior and something of a pop star became particularly apparent when Germany celebrated France's capitulation. The official festivities in Berlin were supposed to commence at 3 p.m. on July 6, 1940. Hundreds of thousands of people had been waiting for hours to give the Führer a rousing reception. The crowds constantly urged Hitler that afternoon to appear on his balcony. It was the height of his military success and his fame, and he was the embodiment of the German *Volk*'s inflated self-image: " 'If an increase in feeling for Adolf Hitler was still possible, it has become reality with the day of the return to Berlin,' commented one report from the provinces. 'In the face of such greatness,' ran another, 'all pettiness and grumbling are silenced.' Even opponents of the regime found it hard to resist the victory mood. Workers in the armaments factories pressed to be allowed to join the army. People thought final victory was around the corner. Only Britain stood in the way. For perhaps the only time during the Third Reich there was genuine war-fever among the population."[496]

Two years on, the euphoria was over. The campaign against Britain had proven much more difficult than anticipated, and the invasion of the Soviet Union had not only ratcheted up the brutality of the fighting, but pushed the prospect of a rapid end to the war into an indeterminate future. German defeat at Stalingrad only reinforced the nascent doubts Germans had begun to feel. What if the war should be lost?

CONCERNS ABOUT DEFEAT

WALDECK: If we lose the war, all the FÜHRER'S achievements will be forgotten.

CRÜWELL: Some things will remain for ever. They will last for hundreds of years. Not the roads—they are unimportant. But what will last is the way in which the state has been organised, particularly the inclusion of the working man in the state and no one has ever done that before.[497]

The continuation of Waldeck and Crüwell's dialogue makes it clear that the latter sees the Führer's historical importance as distinct from the outcome of the National Socialist project. But for others, faith in the Führer served as an antidote to doubts about whether the war would end happily for Germany. Colonel Meyne, for instance, asserted in June 1943: "The FÜHRER is a man of genius, he is certain to find some way out down there."[498] Statements like these were, of course, inspired by the belief that the war could still be won, and the speculations many soldiers engaged in were above all concerned with *when* that victory could be expected. This sort of confidence increasingly crumbled after Stalingrad, yet that didn't affect people's faith in Hitler. "The FÜHRER said: 'We shall take STALINGRAD,' " asserted a Sergeant Kotenbar on December 23, 1942, at a point when the 6th Army had been surrounded for more than a month, "and you can depend on it, we shall take STALINGRAD."[499]

Others, for instance, Sergeant Wohlgezogen, were finding it difficult by this point to maintain their faith in final victory. His statements continually hint at doubts:

WOHLGEZOGEN: My God if we lose! . . . I don't believe we shall ever lose the war—although we . . . . . in RUSSIA—ADOLF won't give in! Not until he is down to the last man, even if the whole human race is destroyed! He knows what it means, if we lose! He will end up by using gas—he doesn't care what he does.[500]

Two aspects of Germans' faith in Hitler are clearly recognizable in statements like these. Responsibility for one's own welfare is delegated to a person who knows how to achieve the desired end and possesses the means and the lack of scruples to do so. And, perhaps more interestingly, the figure of the omnipotent Führer serves to dispel the doubts the speaker otherwise would have.

Wohlgezogen is on the verge of articulating doubts about Germany's prospects of victory before brushing them aside by reflexively summoning up a mythic image of the Führer: "ADOLF won't give in!" This excerpt and others manifest the cognitive dissonance that arises when events deviate from expectations. Emotionally, cognitive dissonance produces deep feelings of dread, if events are negative and unchangeable. Since such feelings are hard to bear, and reality itself cannot be altered, the only way to correct the dissonance is to change one's perception and interpretation of reality.[501] This basic need is quite commonplace. People who live near nuclear power plants, for instance, tend to regard atomic energy as less dangerous than people who live at a greater distance. Smokers who are well aware of the health risks they are subjecting themselves to develop theories as to why the personal danger is not so great. They tell themselves that they are really moderate smokers, or that their father lived to the age of eighty-six, or that people die of other things besides lung cancer. These strategies of minimizing dissonance allow people to live with situations that are other than what they would prefer.

Germans' maintenance of their faith in the Führer was just such a means of reducing dissonance, but it also required a continuous level of emotional investment. The more dubious Germany's prospects looked, the more intense Germans' belief in their leader had to be. Conversely, the psychological significance of the Führer figure showed how much Germans had already invested in such belief. Doubting the ability and power of the Führer would have devalued that investment. For this reason, Germans tended to conflate the destiny of their leader and their own fates:

> BACH: GERMANY'S last chance is to win this war. If we don't win it, then there will be no more Adolf HITLER either. If the Allies are able to carry out their plans, then it will be all up with us. You can imagine how the Jews will triumph then! Then, we shall not simply be shot, we shall die in the most brutal way.[502]

A similar example is a conversation between two Luftwaffe lieutenants in March 1943:

> TENNING: There is a great deal at stake. If we win this war, it will be a threefold victory. Firstly it's the triumph of the National Socialist idea, secondly a triumph for Germans, thirdly a triumph over Versailles.
> V. GREIM: My only fear is that we shall become too soft, too languid again.

TENNING: Not if we come over to ENGLAND, we shan't be then.
The air force alone will never win this war. We realised that a
long time ago, but the English haven't done so yet.

V. GREIM: If we were to lose, we should never find another man
like the FÜHRER. He was unique.

TENNING: Yes, that's true.[503]

Similar sentiments also cropped up among generals in June 1943:
"We can't deny that if HITLER had remained, shall we say, what he
was . . . we could not have helped backing him up wholeheartedly and
we would be looking forward to a happy time, there's no doubt about
that."[504]

Faith in the Führer was often linked with the idea that Hitler had
personally ordered many details of how the war was waged. Many
soldiers felt themselves to be personally dependent on his ability to
make correct decisions. Luftwaffe First Sergeant Duckstein claimed:

DUCKSTEIN: The FÜHRER personally . . . . our sorties.

KASSEL: Did he order the sorties?

DUCKSTEIN: No, he didn't do that but he stopped one sortie.

KASSEL: Why?

DUCKSTEIN: As in precautionary measure in case there was
something else afoot. It has happened several times that the
FÜHRER has personally interfered with our sorties.

KASSEL: How do you know the FÜHRER did that?

DUCKSTEIN: Because he takes an interest in everything.[505]

It is clear from this dialogue that First Sergeant Kassel finds it unusual
that Hitler would have personally ordered the sorties of Duckstein's
unit. Duckstein, in turn, invents or cites reasons to make what he has
said seem plausible. His final argument, that Hitler concerns himself
with everything, serves to reduce cognitive dissonance by reinvesting
trust. The more Duckstein claims that the Führer is personally concerned, the more intensely Duckstein himself has to believe that idea.

As confidence in German victory disintegrated, many soldiers
also developed a sense of sympathy with Hitler, which was based on
conspiracy theories. "I'm sorry for the FÜHRER, the poor devil never
sleeps peacefully," one POW said. "His intentions were good, but what
a government!"[506] Another seconded that sentiment:

> ERFURTH: How frightful! What trouble that <u>poor</u> man (HITLER) takes and how he is always disappointed! The way everyone lets him down![507]

This, too, was a way of making reality cohere with wishful thinking and expectations. Even high-level officers were not immune to this way of thinking, as dialogue between Major Ulrich Boes and one of his peers demonstrates:

> BRINCK*: Yes, what is the FÜHRER doing all the time?
> BOES: He? He's working—hard, in fact.
> BRINCK: I beg your pardon?
> BOES: He's working quite hard.[508]

THE FÜHRER IS NO LONGER HIMSELF

> "Throughout the world we have made only enemies, not one single friend. GERMANY alone to rule the world! ADOLF is the twilight of the Gods."[509]

In light of the theory of cognitive dissonance, it is hardly surprising that, even after the German debacle at Stalingrad, POWs would say things like: "We are sure to win the war. I should like to see the person who would refuse to fulfill any demand of the FÜHRER."[510] It is interesting to see how soldiers resolved such sentiments with their nagging doubts as to Hitler's military acumen. On June 28, 1942, at the start of the Wehrmacht's second major offensive in southern Russia, two Luftwaffe lieutenants racked their brains over what was going on inside the Führer:

> FRÖSCHEL: How can HITLER have changed so much? I used to have great respect for him.
> WAHLER: Now one begins to doubt him.
> FRÖSCHEL: I simply can't understand how it could have happened.
> WAHLER: It's perfectly clear—he tricks everyone and takes over everything himself. He investigated everything himself, he supervises everything personally, he knows everything. And with time he must imagine that he's indispensable, and that we

couldn't continue to exist without him. It is of course possible that this has become a disease with him.

FRÖSCHEL: I always have the feeling that he has been forced into it, that he is no longer a free agent. That would, to a great extent, exonerate him.

WAHLER: No, it wouldn't because he is the FÜHRER, and is therefore perfectly free. What we're coming to in GERMANY is not National Socialism, but tyranny. For he is the FÜHRER. In every one of his speeches he stresses that he is the man. Very well then, he has a free hand and needn't hesitate to get rid of people like HIMMLER and GOEBBELS. And if he's afraid of these people, then he's no FÜHRER. If he can't rid himself of them, and says: "I must keep the people who were with me on the 9th of November" [date of the Munich putsch], he must nevertheless understand that he is the FÜHRER. He gets rid of everybody else, so why doesn't he get rid of men whom everybody hates?

FRÖSCHEL: Perhaps he really is suffering from overwork.

WAHLER: I think, too, that his nerves are in a pretty bad state.

FRÖSCHEL: And that he is no longer master of the situation. Without realising it, he lets other people direct his notions. I really cannot understand—and he used to be my ideal. To think that he should suddenly be found wanting in this way! Perhaps it is due to egotism.

WAHLER: His actions don't support that theory. His last speech—the one about the German legal systems—contradicts the idea.

FRÖSCHEL: It's just possible that egotism and self-importance enter into it on my side and prevent me from acknowledging that I have been so mistaken in a man.

WAHLER: Anyway it is clear that he has changed to an enormous degree.

FRÖSCHEL: Yes, and I still believe that it is not his real self.

WAHLER: Perhaps it is an impersonator; perhaps he himself died long ago.[511]

This dialogue perfectly illustrated how the mechanism of dissonance reduction functions. The speakers transfer blame for any doubts about the Führer and their own emotional investment in him onto external factors. Psychological circumstances or conspiratorial activities here are what caused the change in Hitler's personality. The Führer,

Wahler and Fröschel posit, is no longer figuratively or even, in the impersonator idea, literally himself. Interesting, too, is the fact that Fröschel himself acknowledges the possibility that psychological factors are preventing him from acknowledging the truth. In so doing, he describes the mechanism of dissonance reduction. But the final turn in the conversation offers a much more satisfying explanation, that the real Hitler has been replaced by an actor, allowing the two men to maintain their faith in the Führer even when they have lost all faith in his actions.

Private Költerhoff had a far less extravagant explanation for Hitler's behavior: "The FÜHRER himself is not the worst. There are many things which simply never come to his ears."[512] The idea that Hitler was being kept in the dark was one of the most common German legends, especially as the war neared its end. Sergeant Gamper also proposed that the truth about the course of the war was being withheld from Hitler:

> GAMPER: I spoke to a journalist who was at the FÜHRER's head-
> quarters and he told me some appalling things about the FÜH-
> RER. KEITEL controls the FÜHRER's headquarters. Before his
> "Generals" or anyone get to ADOLF to make a report they are
> given detailed instructions by KEITEL [as to] what they are to
> say, how they are to say it, and only then are they allowed into
> ADOLF's presence. For example, if a "General" had to report
> that a withdrawal was necessary, at the time when the first with-
> drawals occurred, when people weren't yet accustomed to the
> idea of Germans withdrawing, they had to say the following:
> "My FÜHRER, I considered it better not to hold that position
> but to move to here. That is to say, not that we are withdrawing,
> but because the positions there are more favourable." Whereas
> that was entirely untrue, they had been flung out.[513]

Sergeant Müss used the same language. Hitler's behavior, he posited, was becoming increasingly strange because he was hermetically sealed off from the truth:

> MÜSS: I too have always had the impression that they have
> deceived the FÜHRER at every turn. For example, they say that
> ADOLF sometimes sits down at the table with a large position

map in front of him and stares at it. Nobody is allowed to dis-
turb him, even if reports of the utmost importance come in.
Sometimes he sits at the table for six, seven or ten hours in
an attitude of deep meditation. Sometimes matters of utmost
importance come in and are all dealt with by KEITEL. But he
sits there staring at his map and goes into a frenzy, more or less
crazy. He shrieks and raves and socks people in the jaw and
so on.[514]

Such theorizing usually held that Hitler was being systematically
deceived. SS Hauptsturmführer Born and Sergeant Wolf von Helldorf,
the son of the president of the Berlin police, named the guilty parties:

HELLDORF: My father [the police president of Berlin] had unlimited access because he always told him what he thought directly
without any crawling. The Führer appreciated that a lot.
BORN: Back then, I think it was near CHARKOV, Standartenführer
Krumm (Kumm?) received the oak cluster, and Krüger, I think.
In any case it was two or three people, and a Hauptsturmführer. At the award ceremony, the Führer must have asked something special. In any case, these three men fell silent and looked
at each other. The Führer noticed that something wasn't right.
They received orders to report to him the following day for a
discussion. They spent no less than three hours with the Führer
and laid everything out of the table, with total honesty.
HELLDORF: That's what the Führer is lacking.
BORN: It's said one of them gave him a real shock.
HELLDORF: The Führer is fully isolated. He exists on what three
or four people tell us. He depends on them and they . . . well, I
don't want to use any hard words but . . .
BORN: Who are the three people.
HELLDORF: It's BORMANN, one of the worst figures there is
among us. Then, on the military side of things there's KEITEL,
and politically . . . in the same company is GOEBBELS.
BORN: Strangely, until now, it's always been the case that the
REICHSFÜHRER [HIMMLER] is permanently with him.
HELLDORF: The REICHSFÜHRER is half to blame.
BORN: Consciously or not, the Führer has never been in agree-
ment with all these Jewish actions. I know that for a fact. A lot of

the time no one told him what was going on and instead . . . did
it on their own authority. The Führer isn't as terribly extreme
and terribly sharp as he's depicted.[515]

Even a high-ranking officer like Field Marshal Erhard Milch put
forth a variation of this conspiracy theory. In May 1945, he proposed:

MILCH: The FÜHRER in 1940/41 was not the man he was in 1934/35,
   but was completely confused, and had completely wrong ideas
   and followed these wrong ideas. He must have been made ill,
   I'm convinced of that, though of course too much responsibility is enough to make you ill on its own.[516]

In another example, a POW regretted that the constant manipulation
of Hitler unjustly diminished his historical significance. But even more
lamentable was the fact that the misinformation of the Führer had
led to things for which the German military was now going to be held
responsible. Major General Reiter articulated this fear:

REITER: He was a historical figure; only history will be able to
   give him his proper due; one must first hear all that happened;
   we have heard nothing. Those incompetent fools who never
   told the FÜHRER that he was being lied to in reports etc! We,
   too, shall be blamed for that, you can be sure of that.[517]

Higher-ranking officers, for example, Major General Gerhard Bassenge, were particularly concerned about being held responsible for
the things that had been carried out with or without Hitler's knowledge:

BASSENGE: We have been completely deceived by our FÜHRER.
   We were . . . . . . with completely wrong assumptions—the path
   was forced on us. The oath was sworn in 1933, when HINDEN-
   BURG was still there, and when conditions were quite different.
   After one year things were quite different—by then we had
   taken the oath![518]

Soldiers' disappointment that the future was almost certainly not
going to be as bright as had been promised revealed the emotional

significance of the National Socialist project and their faith in the Führer. Colonel Reimann, for instance, was clearly frustrated:

> REIMANN: It had all gone so well. It was all so marvellous and so perfect, and then with that damned RUSSIA it all went awry. There are two people who didn't know that in RUSSIA it is cold in winter; one was NAPOLEON BONAPARTE, and the other was the FÜHRER, the dilettante general, but everyone else knew.[519]

THE FÜHRER AS FAILURE

> "What is the difference between CHRIST and HITLER? With CHRIST one died for all." (Laughter.)
> *Lieutenant General Friedrich von Broich, July 1943*[520]

After the 6th Army capitulated in Stalingrad in February 1943, doubts began to multiply as to whether final victory was still possible. Even if the majority of soldiers did not point the finger of blame at Hitler, the number of statements critical of him grew. "I must admit that ADOLF isn't all he should be, for instance, his treatment of the Jews isn't right," a Private First Class Harnisch complained.[521] Colonel Helmuth Rohrbach even believed: "Apparently the FÜHRER doesn't listen to our generals, it's lamentable. One man can't be a politician, a statesman and a general at the same time. That's madness."[522]

In 1944, Sergeant Doetsch and First Sergeant Bräutigam arrived at a remarkable conclusion considering their socialization as young fighter pilots:

> DOETSCH: A few days before these new raids on LONDON began, some bigwig came to see us and made a speech. I can't remember who he was, but he behaved like a hysterical woman.
> BRÄUTIGAM: Was it perhaps the leader of operations in ENGLAND?
> DOETSCH: That's possible. He shouted: "Set fire to their houses, so that I can go to the FÜHRER and say the GAF has been over ENGLAND again." He actually implored us: "You mustn't fail, put your last ounce into it!" He was quite hysterical.
> BRÄUTIGAM: Yes, taking after the FÜHRER.

> DOETSCH: When you think what a dreadful mess HITLER has
> made of things, as a good German you can't help coming to the
> conclusion that he really ought to be shot.
> BRÄUTIGAM: You are right there, but one must not say so.
> DOETSCH: I certainly won't say so to the people here.[523]

Of course, most of the critical remarks about Hitler contained remnants of personal sympathy and traces of faith. For instance, a sharpshooter named Caesar pondered what he would do if he were to encounter the leaders of his country:

> CAESAR: I've been wondering what I would do if I were to meet
> HITLER and his friends in flight. I decide that I would say to
> them: "I can't do anything for you, but I won't tell anyone that
> I've seen you here. There's a path through the wood there, so
> go and hide in the bushes." The only exception I might possibly
> make would be HIMMLER.[524]

Two recent master's theses that have analyzed the statements of POWs of all ranks interned at Fort Hunt in the United States have come to another conclusion.[525] Faith in the Führer tended to recede drastically among the lower ranks after Normandy while generally being maintained further up the hierarchy. This is another indication that the personal identification and emotional investment stabilized people's trust in Hitler. But these indices need to be pursued. The reverse and difficult-to-grasp side of faith in the Führer is what does *not* occur in the POWs' conversations: political reflection about what went wrong. In fact, the depoliticization of German soldiers would seem to be one of National Socialism's most lasting achievements.

Soldiers tended to see what was happening as not their affair, but the business of their omnipotent Führer and his circle of helpers, whom the soldiers saw alternately as philistine, corrupt, incompetent, or criminal. They did not, in the main, have a political opinion on the National Socialist state, the dictatorship, or the persecution of Jews. The criticism they put forth was aimed at the personal traits of Nazi bigwigs and occasionally at individual policies. But it was very rare for the POWs to engage in political debates about decisions or perspectives. Clear differences in position or opinion seldom emerge. This is one of the central results of totalitarian rule. It creates a mental lack of alternatives and makes people fully dependent on the charismatic leader, to whom they stay true even when their mutual downfall is inevitable. As the protocols reveal especially with respect to higher-ranking officers, politics is replaced by faith. And since faith in the Führer was simultaneously a faith of Germans in themselves, every threat to positive images of Hitler was also a threat to the project in which people had invested so much energy and emotion. The fear was that this project would turn out to be utterly worthless.[526]

Ideology

THÖNE: I expect you have heard about the treatment of the Jews in RUSSIA. In POLAND the Jews got off comparatively lightly. There are still Jews in POLAND living there. But in the occupied parts of RUSSIA there aren't any left.

V. BASSUS: Were the ones in RUSSIA considered more dangerous?

THÖNE: More hatred—they were not dangerous. I am not letting any cat out of the bag by telling you this. I think I can safely say that all Jews in RUSSIA, including women and children, were shot without exception.

V. BASSUS: Wasn't there some compelling motive for it?

THÖNE: Hatred was the compelling motive.

V. BASSUS: Hatred by the Jews—or?

THÖNE: By us. It isn't a reason, but it is actual fact.

First Sergeant von Bassus and Lieutenant Thöne,
February 2, 1944[527]

The laconic nature of the above exchange is what makes it so remarkable. While Bassus looks for reasons for the destruction of European Jews, Lieutenant Thöne repeatedly points out that the phenomenon needs no justification. Hatred is enough of a spark, without any further motivation such as the alleged danger represented by Jews or their purported hatred for Germans. Even more astonishing is Thöne's assertion that German hatred is not a reason, but a sheer fact. It's hard to imagine a clearer formulation of what autotelic violence is, and it points up one finding about the deep psychological effect of National Socialist ideology on the soldiers subjected to surveillance. Ideology was not prominent among the things that occupied soldiers' minds. Many soldiers may have been perfectly willing to use violence to solve the alleged "Jewish question," but an astonishing number of them were explicitly against it. But for all of them, the existence of the question was a given, regardless of whether they as individuals thought the Nazis' anti-Jewish policies were good or bad, right or wrong.

THE SPECTRUM OF OPINION

In April 1943, after reading the nineteenth-century German poet Heinrich Heine, First Lieutenant Fried remarked: "They say that the Jews weren't able to master the German language in literature and so on. But the 'Journey through the Harz' is marvellous."[528]

A few months earlier a low-level officer named Wehner* declared: "When I meet a Jew I could shoot him out of hand. The number of Jews we killed in POLAND! We did them in mercilessly."[529]

Both statements were made around roughly the same time by two members of the same branch of the military, the Luftwaffe. So is it fair to say that Fried represented humanistic Germany whereas Wehner was an anti-Semitic ideological warrior? Our material provides no evidence that enjoying Heine's "Journey Through the Harz" was any indication of whether or not someone was capable of murdering Jews. Conversely, of course, we can conclude that Wehner was fanatic enough to refuse to read books by Jewish authors (his other statements confirm this). The juxtaposition of these two excerpts indicated the spectrum of opinion expressed in the protocols about Jews and racism in general. On the one hand, the transcripts contain praise for Heine and Jewish doctors, chemists, and physicists as well as emotional rejections of the Holocaust and the persecution of Jews in general.[530] On the other, the protocols are also full of theories about a global Jewish conspiracy, including "Jewified" England and America, as well as tales of glee after killing Jews.[531] In short the transcripts contain just about everything under the sun. Moreover, contradictory opinions were not only expressed by two or more POWs in dialogue. As we saw in the section on the Holocaust, single individuals often used seeming mutually exclusive arguments and expressed diametrically opposed perspectives. "The Nazis are worse swine than the Jews,"[532] remarked one POW, while another opined, "The Japanese are the Jews of the east."[533]

Some statements indicate how far the anti-Semitic imagination was given free rein:

> ERFURTH: I always disliked seeing the Jewish women from GER-
> MANY who had to clean the streets in RIGA. They still kept on
> speaking German. It was revolting! That should be forbid-

den, and they should not be allowed to speak anything but
Yiddish.[534]

Other utterances were nothing short of absurd: "I am the ping-pong
champion of Western Germany. But I am out of practice. I gave up
the game after a typical Jew-boy—sixteen years old—had beaten me.
Then I said to myself: 'That is certainly not real sport!' "[535] Conversations about racial issues or "the Jews" have the same basic structure
as other exchanges. Remarks are interjected, and stories told, before
the POWs change the subject. Such conversations aimed primarily
at establishing consensus and did not admit of one side insisting on
a point, doggedly asking questions, or arguing. In the main, a unity
of perspective and political evaluation was quickly established, and
in any case soldiers did not see topics dealing with Jews as particularly important. If the topics were broached, soldiers usually had an
opinion, but no one seems to have been particularly eager to bring
them up.

That impression is confirmed by a detailed analysis carried out by
Alexander Hoerkens, who examined the role of ideology in two thousand pages of transcripts from the protocols. He determined that less
than one fifth of the excerpts concerned political, racial, or ideological topics.[536] The everyday routine of the war was far more important
to POWs. With a few notable exceptions, the "Jewish" topic was just
another subject of conversation, and it was treated as such by both
hard-core anti-Semites and enthusiastic exterminators and those who
were generally repulsed by Nazi crimes. When the talk did turn to the
mass executions, the conversation was often about fears of reprisals:
"Don't you think that the shooting of all those Jews, of women and
children, will be avenged? My brother, who is an infantryman, has told
me a lot about how they were pushed into the graves before they were
really dead."[537]

Just as there were some committed National Socialists who thought
the persecution of Jews was a historical mistake, there were also clear
anti-Nazis who thought anti-Semitism was the party's only reasonable
policy. Two soldiers, for instance, got quite hot under the collar when
discussing "the Nazis":

HÖLSCHER: It is obvious that from the very first, from 1933, they
    were preparing for war. And even if they said in their speeches

a score of times: "We don't want any war, ask the mothers, and ask the wounded"—those were HITLER's words—what I say to myself, what I believe, is that that was a sheer lie. He lied! He, who so often said he didn't want war!

V. BASTIAN: What I always said was, then why does he talk so much about it; it's perfectly obvious that we Germans don't want war at all, that we aren't at all in a position to conduct a war, and that we're fed up with it.

HÖLSCHER: He meant exactly the opposite, he wanted war. I can't help laughing when I hear them abusing each other about who's responsible for the war ... HITLER was already well-known for his brutalities through his S.A. and S.S. men, through their brawls at public meetings. They accomplished everything by beating people up. HITLER says himself: "National Socialism means fighting."

V. BASTIAN: Yes, fighting, that's what it means.

HÖLSCHER: That means they never stop fighting, it's a perpetual fight, an ever-lasting brawl. The individual counts for nothing, the Fatherland is everything. They said to themselves: "We'll just show the fools of 1919 what can be made of GERMANY." Say what you like, the man's crazy. What he does can only be done by a man who has terrific nerve and exceptional stamina and who has absolutely no regard for losses ...

V. BASTIAN: At any rate, I have still no idea of where the Nazis are going to land us in the end. That swine with his brown shirt![538]

From this excerpt one would expect such frank critics of the Nazi regime to be against the party's anti-Semitic policies. But the conversation takes the following turn:

HÖLSCHER: No, there's no telling, but there's quite a lot of good in it, I'll admit—it's all right about the Jews. I don't think the racial problem has been at all badly handled.

V. BASTIAN: Our racial policy is excellent, also the Jewish question, and the entire legislation for preserving the purity of German blood. That law is really first-class.

Today, the argumentative mix found in the protocols is dumbfounding. One reason is the very nature of everyday conversations. As the nineteenth-century German author Heinrich von Kleist already sensed, much of what we think only gets "finished" in the act of speech.[539] Opinions and attitudes do not simply exist a priori of concrete social interactions, like objects in a drawer that one can take out at will. Often, thoughts first coalesce in conversation, one word following the other, and they do not exist for very long. Under the influence of mood, a need for consensus, or a misapprehension, or because the conversation is just idle chatter, people sometimes try out opinions or thoughts that they will discard the next time they converse with someone. For that reason, real arguments are rare in the protocols, despite the fact that the men concerned did not come together of their own free will, and the amount of time they were forced to spend together would otherwise encourage conflicts. Of course, there were a few genuine arguments of the "I beg to differ" variety[540] and at least one running feud of the sort that can happen between people sharing an apartment.[541] This shows that arguments were in fact recorded and thus happened very rarely. As in all other everyday conversational situations, soldiers might agree with an opinion only to reject it in their next conversation, and the desire to establish a relationship was often far more significant than the content of what was said.

COHERENT PICTURES OF THE WORLD

The vagaries of human conversation make it difficult to determine how deeply anchored bits of National Socialist ideology were in the consciousness of POWs. We can only say for sure that ideology played a role in absolutely unambiguous statements. An example is this one by nineteen-year-old navy midshipman Karl Völker:

> VÖLKER: I know what the Jews did. About 1928 or 1929 they carried off the women and raped them and cut them up and the blood—I know of many cases—every Sunday in their synagogues they sacrificed human blood, Christian blood. The Jews are past masters at whining, the women are even worse than the men. I saw it myself that time we smashed up the synagogue. There were any number of corpses there. Do you know what they do? They lay the corpse on a sort of bier. Then they come with these things, stick them in and suck the blood out.

They make a small hole in the belly, then they leave the poor wretch five or six hours till he's dead. I'd gladly do in thousands of them, and even if I knew that only one amongst them was guilty I would still do them all in. The things they do in the synagogue! No one can whine like a Jew, but he can be a thousand times innocent, he'll still be done in. And the way they slaughter the calves! Don't talk to me about the Jews! Never in my life have I enjoyed anything more than the time when we smashed up the synagogues. I was one of the most fanatical there, when I saw the mutilated corpses lying there. You could see them there with small tubes in them. They were women, and were full of holes.

SCHULTZ: Where did they get the women from?

VÖLKER: At that time, where we lived, a certain number were simply missing. They were all with the Jews. There was one case of a woman who always had to fetch things from a Jew; he had a shop. The Jew told the woman she should come in and see him as he had something for her. There were five Jews standing there—they undressed her. There was a subterranean passage from the shop to the synagogue. Their doctrine tells them that the best deed they can do is to sacrifice Christian blood. Every Sunday they butchered somebody. It takes three to four hours. And how many of them had been raped! I now have no money. We shot them all mercilessly. There certainly will have been some innocent ones amongst them, but there were some guilty ones too. It doesn't matter how much good you do, if you've got Jewish blood, that's enough![542]

Völker was the classic ideological warrior of the sort Daniel Goldhagen envisions: a willing executioner, driven by delusional eliminatory and pornographic visions of violence, who gave his all to exterminate Jews. Völker's tales, which elicit a skeptical response from his listener, are most likely the result of an intensive study of the SS magazine *Der Stürmer* and anti-Semitic group training in the Hitler Youth. Such stories may seem completely bizarre, but the speaker here both believes in and draws conclusions from them. People like Völker did indeed exist.

In the minds of most of the POWs, though, National Socialism was something different than the piecemeal, if internally consistent, theory about the "eternal laws of life" one can read out of the writings and speeches of everyone from Nazi ideologue Alfred Rosenberg to Hitler himself. Hoerkens's analysis concludes, on the basis of conversations between 621 soldiers, that the majority tended to view Nazi racial policies negatively and that only 30 of them could be described as ideological warriors. Junior officers, above all lieutenants, made up the lion's share of this minority. They were still children in 1933 and thus had been socialized most intensely by the Third Reich.[543] It is among them that we can best speak of a Nazi picture of the world.

When the rest of the soldiers talk about politics, race, Jews, and related topics, it is not a coherent worldview but rather a patchwork of diverse and often contradictory fragments. Committed National Socialists were able to tell stories full of empathy about Jews they had known personally and express dismay at the "scandalous treatment" of the minority by a "cultured people." At the same time, there was a basic level of agreement with Nazi racial policies, as the example of navy W/T operator Hammacher in May 1943 shows:

HAMMACHER: This Jewish question ought to have been treated quite differently. There shouldn't have been this persecution. Instead we ought to have introduced laws quite calmly and quietly, laying down that only so-and-so many Jews were to be allowed to practise as lawyers and so on. But as things are, all the exiled Jews have quite naturally worked very hard against GERMANY.[544]

Examples concerning the "Jewish actions" have already revealed that soldiers could be critical of the methods employed for mass executions, while feeling indifferent to or even supportive of the executions themselves. The same applied to ideology and racism in general. Negative opinions predominated on these topics. "I have always been opposed to those SS swine," a Lieutenant Oehlmann opined. "I was always against the persecution of the Jews, too. One should have been able to exile the Jews but one shouldn't have treated them like that."[545] This was hardly a fundamental rejection of anti-Semitic policies, although views on the topic grew more and more critical as confidence in victory dissolved. "It will be a disgrace being a German after the war," one POW complained. "We'll be as much hated as the Jews were."[546] "The greatest mistake was the expulsion of the Jews," seconded another. "That and particularly the inhuman treatment," agreed a third.[547]

In general, we can assume that such topics were most often broached by those who objected to the persecution and execution of Jews, while those to whom the Final Solution seemed necessary would have spoken up less often. Phrases liked "international" or "world Jewry" or "Jewified" England and America—together with stereotypes such as Jews being "work-shy"—occur with regularity. The reference frame of categorical inequality and the everyday anti-Semitic practice clearly had a deep psychological effect on POWs. Nonetheless, it still remains largely uncertain what that meant for the men's perception and behavior in concrete situations. The capacity of attitudes and mental dispositions to inspire action is often overrated. They only predispose individuals to anti-Semitic behavior in extreme cases, such as the navy man cited above. It would require intense analysis of concrete situations to determine whether someone killed Jews out of anti-Semitic conviction or as a result of group dynamics. Sometimes, peer pressure made people into mass murderers without any sort of individual motivation on their own part. This conclusion is supported by evidence from the Wehrmacht, including the various positions and situations in which soldiers found themselves. Anti-Semitism may have been one basis for what they did when they battled, retreated, fought against partisans, and spent their free time, but it was not a sole motivation. As exemplified in POWs' remarks about the Jewish ghettos, many of the men felt some empathy with the victims and were shocked at their living conditions: "These Jews were doing hard labour there at the main airport and were treated badly, like animals."[548] But that sympathy did not have any consequences in terms of the question of whether they would carry out or refuse an order to secure a ghetto.

For instance, a Lieutenant Rottländer told of a friend who had suffered after having participated in a mass execution:

> ROTTLÄNDER: They annihilated whole villages there. Whole villages of Jewish people were driven out mercilessly: holes were dug and then they had to shoot them. He said it was difficult enough at the beginning, but afterwards his nerves were absolutely shattered. They had to cover the bodies over afterwards and some of them were still moving in the hole, children and all. He said: "Even though they were Jews, it was dreadful."

Rottländer's listener, Lieutenant Borbonus, has an immediate response: "Well, what on earth can you do if it is ordered by higher authority?"[549]

When there was sufficient distance between the speaker and the events described, POWs related news of atrocities in much the same tone that people today talk about child soldiers in Africa or bestial deeds of the Taliban. We may find certain acts terrible, but our frame of reference for atrocities is abstract and doesn't have much to do with our own lives or those of our interlocutors. An engineer who designs mobile phones does not perceive himself as being connected with the fact that coltan, essential to modern telecommunications, is strip-mined in war-torn Congo. Likewise, soldiers were not personally affected if Jews were being slaughtered *somewhere else by others*. The same distance applies, mutatis mutandis, for ideological and racist concepts. It is unclear how such concepts related to what they did in World War II. Take, for example, Heinrich Skrzipek, chief quartermaster of U-187:

> SKRZIPEK: Cripples ought to be put out of the way painlessly. They wouldn't know everything about it and in any case they don't get anything out of life. It's just a question of not being sensitive! After all we aren't women! It's just because we are sensitive that we get so many blows from our enemies . . . And exactly the same with mental-defectives and half-wits. Because the half-wits are the very people who have very large families and for one mental-defective you could feed six wounded soldiers. Of course you can't please everybody. Several things don't suit me, but it's a question of the good of the people as a whole.[550]

Even if most of the racist stereotypes used in the protocols are anti-Jewish, the things POWs said reflected the entire spectrum of Nazi prejudice. Stereotypes are applied to Germany's allies ("Those yellow monkeys aren't human beings; they are still animals";[551] "The Italians themselves don't know what they want. They're a stupid race"[552]) and its enemies ("I can't even look on a Russian as a human being";[553] "Poles! Russians! There's a lousy crowd working in there"[554]) alike.

Racism could even serve as the basis for a surprisingly melancholic statement on the postwar future: "One thing is obvious: EUROPE will perish, regardless of whether the Germans or the English are beaten, as these two races are the props of culture and civilisation. It is tragic that such prominent races should have to fight each other instead of fighting Slavdom together."[555] Stereotypes and prejudices are constant elements of cultures, and they shape individuals' orientation and group social practice.[556] In a society in which categorical inequality directs state policy, is considered a scientific standard, and is bolstered by massive propaganda, collective stereotypes are cemented. Nonetheless, as our sources show, this did not happen to the extent that Goebbels, Himmler, or Hitler would have liked and that Holocaust research long declared it did. Ideology is merely the basis of attitudes, and we know little about whether those attitudes in fact inspired action.

Conversely, we can say that the ideology of fundamental human inequality made antisocial behavior toward oppressed groups seem acceptable and even desirable. That is why sympathy with adversaries and victims, although present in protocols, was the exception and not the rule.

Astonishingly, a concept that does not occur at all in our sources is the idea of the *Volk* community. Considering how much attention has been given to this psychosocial category in recent research on Germans in the Third Reich, it is surprising that soldiers never once refer to what should be a central aspect of their mentality.[557] Nor does the concept crop up in other sources, such as reports on state-sponsored "Strength Through Joy" vacations and other Nazi social provisions. This is even more baffling since the *Volk* community reflected civilian and not military organizational structures. The complete absence of this phrase should make future researchers skeptical about the extent to which such integrative elements permeated Nazi society.

All in all, in terms of soldiers' mentality, we cannot say that the majority felt they were waging an "eliminatory" or a "racial" war. Above all, they were oriented around a military and wartime frame of reference in which ideology played only a subordinate role. But they also waged war within the frame of reference of their society, a National Socialist one, which in certain situations led them to act in radically inhumane fashion. Nonetheless, to perpetrate atrocities— and this is what is most disconcerting—soldiers did not need to be either racist or anti-Semitic.

MILITARY VALUES

Far more important than ideology for soldiers' perceptions and inter-pretations, and thus for their concrete decisions and actions, was their military value system. It was firmly integrated into their frame of reference. Germany's militaristic tradition had greatly eased the incorporation of millions of men into the Wehrmacht. They were already familiar with the system of norms that awaited them in the barracks. Although most of them were conscripts, they were more than willing as a rule to adapt to the military framework and carry out their tasks as well as they could. Skilled carpenters, bookkeepers, and farmers wanted to become good tank drivers, gunners, and infantrymen. This meant learning the concrete basics of the military craft, perfecting the use of weapons, and becoming obedient, disciplined, and hard. They wanted to achieve victories, demonstrate bravery and a willingness to sacrifice, and fight down to the last bullet in case of defeat. Ever since the wars of 1864–71 had unified the German nation, there had been a broad consensus in German society about what soldiers were supposed to be.

Germans' sense of positive identification with the armed forces was reinforced both by Germany's military triumphs early on in World War II and by internal structures within the Wehrmacht that promoted meritocracy. All soldiers were given the same food to eat, all were eligible for the same medals, and all were encouraged to take on responsibility, if they demonstrated leadership qualities. The high degree to which soldiers identified with the military is evident in countless conversations among POWs. They loved talking about how their units were structured and armed, how various forms of organization had fared in combat, what sort of training they had received, how their weapons worked, and what sort of promotions and distinctions they had earned. The POWs presented themselves as masters of their trades, committed, proud of their units and weapons, and irritated when things did not go according to plan. The military was viewed as something self-evident, as a world to which one belonged and in which one had found one's true place.

Nonetheless, soldiers accepted norms and values like obedience, bravery, and devotion to duty so unquestioningly that they rarely mentioned them explicitly. The only ones who did so were high-ranking officers who had reason to reflect on general questions about normative issues. Colonel General Hans-Jürgen von Arnim, for instance, remarked: "A soldier who doesn't stand firm is no soldier, and the more confused things are around him, the firmer he must stand—mentally."[558] Arnim was referring to the obedience and devotion to duty. These were all the more necessary in difficult times, as he himself had just experienced in the course of German defeat in Africa. Colonel Reimann, who was interned with Arnim in Trent Park, described the Wehrmacht's mental corset in even more vivid terms: "We would do what our superiors, who have one star more [say]. We would do what our superior officers ordered us." Reimann added that it was a "racial peculiarity of the Germans, when they are soldiers, that they obey orders."[559] Whether or not Germans were particularly and excessively obedient, though, is an open question.

In any case, obedience was seen as a higher virtue than reflecting on whether military actions made sense. Captain Hartdegen, for example, said of his time in the staff of a tank training division in Normandy in 1944: "We used to sit down together in the evening with the 'General' and his senior commanders, and we always used to say: 'Has the FÜHRER gone mad—these orders which he demands of us.' We carried them out, just because we had been properly educated."[560] Irmfried Wilimzig, a critic of the Nazis who was interned at Fort Hunt in the United States, concurred: "Orders are orders, that's self-evident, especially at the front."[561] Although the Wehrmacht also tried to teach soldiers to think and act for themselves, obedience remained one of its most important norms. Refusing an order was considered an utterly unacceptable deviation, which threatened the very foundation of the army. The imperative to obey bound soldiers together less because they were afraid of being punished than because it was a firmly anchored rule in their frame of reference. Major Leonhard Mayer told a bunkmate in a U.S. POW camp about the following incident at the Battle of Cherbourg:

> MAYER: It's the difficult situation an officer gets into. For example, there was this case. Today, if an officer who wants to do his duty is guided by healthy common sense and is able to weigh up certain things against one another, that officer can face a thankless destiny.
>
> As the commander of a combat troop, I had the task of main-

taining our position regardless of the circumstances. That was my order and I carried it out. But it wasn't as if I as a commander hid away in my bunker, although I could have done so. 70 to 80 percent of the time I was up front with my troop. We were taking a heavy battering from artillery. Guys were falling in droves. I soon noticed a certain exhaustion although they conducted themselves without fault. But enemy propaganda leaflets dropped from above, about conditions as a POW and such, had made a certain impression on my men. At the same time the order came, and it was announced everywhere, to give shirkers a push. So I had to push my men with every means at my disposal. If I didn't, it would have been unjust toward my topmost superiors. Still, you feel a human emotion. You tell yourself: You have to push these poor men forward, even if it's pointless. We had no support from heavy artillery, or the Luftwaffe. We could only engage in hand-to-hand combat.

AHNELT: What kind of a unit was it? Bavarians?

MAYER: Half Bavarian and half from Frankfurt. The men behaved pretty well, but about 20 percent were shirkers. Not common everyday shirkers. People whose nerves were so shot they couldn't do anything. Now imagine that Germany doesn't lose the war. It's possible that I would be put up in front of a military tribunal and asked why I didn't hold my position two hours longer.

The smartest thing, Mayer asserts, would have been to flee in the face of a hopeless situation. But he had orders to hold his position for three days:

MAYER: On the one hand, the wounded lay dying, lined up like herring, men with whom I'd served together for years. On the other hand, I had my duty. I'd like to write a book about it, if I get a typewriter some day here. Now I'm in a POW camp, and my tragedy is symptomatic of the overall tragedy. That's the thanks you get for all your work. I worked like a lunatic because I've been trained to carry out my duty, orders have to be followed. Regardless of political connections. I would have acted the same, if I'd been in the Red Army.

I would have had time to get out of the line of fire. A few

months ago, I could have gone to Munich. I was close to becoming a regimental commander. But I didn't want to desert my post before the invasion. That's what's tragic.[562]

Major Mayer found himself in a moral dilemma, faced with what he calls a "thankless destiny." He had to choose between following orders and trying to preserve the lives of comrades whom he had known for years and for whom he was responsible. He wanted to be a good commander who stood by his men and shared their suffering, and he realized that more and more of them were being killed because he as a commander refused to break off the one-sided battle. But disobeying orders was out of the question. Obedience and duty were his highest priority. This becomes especially evident in his remark that he would have behaved exactly the same had he been a member of the Red Army. Only when his troop was down to the last thirty men, Mayer reports later on in the protocols, did he give up the fight. Otherwise, they would have all been simply slaughtered. It was impossible for him to violate orders until his unit had, for all practical purposes, ceased to exist and his own life was jeopardized. Technically speaking, though, he had not followed instructions down to the letter. For that reason, he thinks he could theoretically be brought up for court-martial.

We do not know the details of how Mayer's unit really behaved in battle in June 1944. It's possible that he also suffered pangs of conscience because in reality some of his men had deserted or surrendered long before he was down to his last thirty soldiers, as he claimed. Nonetheless, his anecdote is an example of the immense importance that the officer corps, in particular, attached to obedience and duty. Only in extreme emergency situations, at the very last second, one could say, was it possible for them to break free from this reference frame. Interestingly, politics had very little influence on the attitudes of men like Mayer. There was no shortage of critics of the regime who complained about the misfortune the Nazis had brought down upon Germany and yet were outraged when infantrymen surrendered without any stiff resistance.[563]

In soldiers' frames of reference, bravery was just as universal a virtue as obedience and sense of duty. Bravery was the primary reflection of an individual's performance insofar as most soldiers, unlike Luftwaffe pilots, could not measure themselves on the basis of enemies killed or tanks destroyed. Land warfare was the sum of many smaller parts, and there were no concrete results of individual actions. Bravery was the only criterion. The standard against which infantrymen were judged was their ability to keep fighting and carry out their tasks under the most difficult circumstances.

For example, a First Lieutenant Gayer reported about his deployment on the Italian Front:

> GAYER: I was first sent into operation near CASSINO, and we were in operation for a few weeks on the ORSOGNA front. Although in that case I noted as "Kompanie" commander and was in fact near ARIELLE (?) south of PESCARA. We were completely wiped out by artillery fire. My "Kompanie" consisted of twenty-eight Germans and thirty-six Italians. The Italians ran away. The Italian "Leutnant" was the first to go. We stayed there for about ten days.[564]

Gayer's story contrasts the behavior of his own soldiers with that of the Italians, among whom even the *lieutenant* ran away. By contrast, the Germans, if Gayer is to be believed, held out for ten days before the unit was wiped out by murderous artillery fire. The image of soldiers courageously fighting on under the most difficult, deadly conditions recurs throughout the surveillance protocols.

Combat soldiers, especially those who had been part of elite units, told these sorts of stories most frequently. One of the most drastic narratives came from SS Standartenführer Hans Lingner, one of the few high-ranking SS officers to be captured by the Allies during the war. He reported proudly about the deeds of an Untersturmführer in his division:

> LINGNER: For three whole days he and eighteen men defended a locality which was being attacked from all sides by half a regiment. I actually experienced how one MG pinned down whole sectors. Then we carried out a counter-attack and rescued them. They were the remnants of a rescue "Abteilung" which was 180 men strong before and now had only those eighteen men left. Those were still the good old types![565]

The norm of fighting bravely on instead of surrendering can also be identified among noncombatants from the Wehrmacht. For instance, the POWs who complained most vehemently about the quick German capitulation in Paris on August 25, 1944, were army administrators.[566]

Bravery, obedience, and devotion to duty were the major determining factors of how soldiers' behavior was perceived,[567] and this matrix of values remained stable over the entire course of the war. Individual biographical and political elements played almost no role whatsoever. Military values were just as important to those with Ph.D.'s in philosophy as to people who had worked in banks or bakeries—and just as significant for committed Social Democrats as for passionate Nazis. As much as the 17 million members of the Wehrmacht may have differed from one another socially, they consistently shared the same military value system during their time of service.

There were, however, interesting nuances between various branches of the military and soldiers who used different sorts of weaponry. Conversations between navy men emphasized bravery, pride, hardness, and discipline more than talk between airmen and army men did. First Lieutenant Hans Jenisch reported about the loss of U-32 in October 1940: "When our U-boat sank I heard a few shouts of 'Heil Hitler,' and some cheering in the distance, but some cried pitifully for help. Horrible! But there are always one or two who do that."[568] A private told in the same vein of the sinking of the blockade runner MS *Alstertor*: "During the fight we had some prisoners down under one of the hatches, and a guard was posted outside the door with pistol drawn and commanded not to open the door till the order was given. The officer who was to give the order was killed. The ship keeled over, but the guard remained standing there at his post, and neither he nor any of the prisoners got out. That's what's called doing one's duty!"[569]

There are many other examples of this sort illustrating the importance of military virtues in the stories told by navy POWs. Similar statements can be found among servicemen from other military branches, but there was good reason why they occurred so frequently among sailors. German navy men had rebelled against their commanders near the end of World War I, and the navy was, from the beginning of World War II, the least important branch of the German military. On September 3, 1939, the commander in chief of the navy, Grand Admiral Erich Raeder, deemed the coming struggle against Britain, a traditional sea power, to be so hopeless that all German sailors could do was "die with honor."[570] Raeder's mood soon improved, and at one point he even believed that a blockade could bring England to its knees, but the navy leadership was also forced to try to bolster morale in special ways. Displaying particularly good morale was the navy's lone trump card, the one way it had of achieving recognition within the state and the Wehrmacht in general. Nonetheless, as of 1943, the German navy descended into military insignificance. German battleships and destroyers were far inferior technologically to American and British warships, and the German navy lacked the necessary fuel to properly train sailors, so the Allies won almost all of the battles at sea. Notable successes failed to materialize. The Allies negated a slight German advantage in E-boats and U-boats with better radar and sonar technology. And the longer there was no positive news to report and the larger the enemy's matériel and personnel advantage became, the more fighting became a value for its own sake.[571] The Nazi leadership respected the navy in this regard,[572] and the alleged extraordinary morale among German sailors was one of the main reasons Hitler chose Grand Admiral Dönitz to succeed him as Reich president.

Down to the Final Bullet

"The German gives up, if it's hopeless."[573]

Especially in critical situations, military virtues were supposed to encourage soldiers to keep fighting to the very end. The model soldier was the one who battled, as the cliché had it, down to the very last bullet. Indeed, Wehrmacht regulation number 2 read: "It is expected of every German soldier that he prefers to die with a weapon in his hand to being captured. But in the vagaries of battles, even the bravest man may have the misfortune to be taken captive by the enemy."[574] In the first half of World War II, even if soldiers were made to swear an oath that they would sacrifice their lives for the Third Reich, the military leadership did not interpret this regulation literally.[575] If a battle was lost from a tactical standpoint, soldiers were allowed to surrender. Fighting on was considered senseless, even if individual infantrymen still had ammunition in their belts.

Yet as the war turned for the worse, the German military leadership became more radical in its demands that soldiers fight on until the bitter end. In the final phase of the war, this trope became emblematic for the Wehrmacht as a whole. The German setbacks before Moscow in the winter of 1941–42 were the beginning of a transition whereby soldiers were no longer just supposed to fight until a battle had been decided, but to continue "fanatically" until they were killed.

On December 16, 1941, Hitler reacted to the deteriorating situation of Army Group Center on the Eastern Front by ordering: "Commanders, unit leaders and officers are to take personal steps to force troops to engage in fanatic resistance in holding their positions, without regard to enemy breakthroughs on the flanks or from the rear."[576] Field Marshal Wilhelm Keitel added ten days later: "Every foot of territory is to be fought for with every ounce of energy."[577] Military commanders on the ground initially welcomed these general orders in the belief that they would help quell panic among exhausted soldiers. But opposition quickly arose when the orders were put into concrete practice. Colonel Erich Hoepner remarked: "Fanatic will alone isn't enough. . . . The fanatic resistance that's being demanded only leads to the sacrificing of defenseless troops."[578] German generals refused to accept stand-and-die commands because the death of their soldiers on the battlefield, under the conditions the army was facing, did not promise to yield any military advantages. Hitler remained adamant, however, and replaced those commanders who did not submit to his dictates. Hitler credited his uncompromising order for the fact that the Soviet counteroffensive before Moscow was halted in February 1942. That counterstrike was the first crisis faced by the Wehrmacht, and Hitler was convinced that it made military sense to sacrifice troops in precarious situations.[579] Henceforth, he demanded that soldiers fight fanatically, down to the last bullet, no matter how critical their situation, and he insisted that his commands be carried out to the letter. On November 3, 1942, when Field Marshal Erwin Rommel wanted to withdraw from El Alamein in Egypt, the dictator explicitly forbade any sort of retreat. "Strength of will shall win out over the stronger battalion," Hitler wrote. "There's no other path to show your troops other than victory or death."[580] With support from his superior, Albert Kesselring, Rommel refused to follow this suicide command and ordered his troops to retreat. He was not principally concerned with saving the lives of individual soldiers. In other situations, Rommel had no scruples about sending men to their certain deaths. In April and May 1941, he had ordered part of his forces to launch a militarily irrational attack on the stronghold of Tobruk in Libya and accused Lieutenant General Heinrich Kirchheim of being a coward for refusing to sacrifice his men. But by November 1942, Rommel could see no military sense in having his divisions hold out in their current positions. Hitler had a different opinion. His command that German troops hold their ground in Africa had a narrow military goal and a larger aim. On the one hand, the dictator believed that sheer force of will could hold back the British 8th Army. And on the other hand, he saw a deeper meaning in soldiers sacrificing their lives. In Hitler's mind, the willingness to do so was a precondition of national unity.[581]

Rommel's disobedience prevented German tank divisions in Africa from being completely destroyed in November 1942. He was subsequently transferred and thus did not witness their ultimate end in Tunisia in May 1943. Hitler strictly ruled out Rommel's suggestion that Army Group Africa be withdrawn to Europe and instead ordered the troops to fight to the death. Knowing all too well what was being asked of him, the commander of the German Afrika Korps, Hans Cramer, relayed by radio on May 9, 1943: "Ammunition gone. Weapons and equipment destroyed. DAK [German Afrika Korps] fought until unable as per orders."[582] Cramer was taken prisoner by the British and interned in Trent Park. Because he suffered from serious asthma, the plan was to repatriate him in February 1944. But he soon began to wonder how, if he returned to Germany, he would explain to Hitler "why things collapsed so quickly." What worried him the most was that the command to fight to the last bullet had not been carried out: "My division commanders asked me over and over whether this could be changed, and I said 'No.' . . . But the end looked as though we had surrendered with bullets in our guns, in our machine guns and our tanks." The idea of "to the last bullet," Cramer told fellow POW General Crüwell, "is relative. You could just as well say 'to the last tank-busting grenade.' "[583] Cramer refused to enter into a fight "with pistols against tanks" or a "final infantry battle" that seemed to make no military sense. Once the battle had been decided from a tactical perspective, he had "handed over" his troops to the enemy—something he did not want to admit to the Führer. Crüwell advised him not to speak of "handing over," but rather only of the "end."[584]

If General Cramer suffered from pangs of conscience about not completely fulfilling his duty, Colonel Meyne was positively outraged about the form the "final battle" took in Tunisia. It was, he complained, unprecedented in German military history, a capitulation that was "depressing" in a way the German defeat at Stalingrad had not been. The demise of the 6th Army had been sad, Meyne opined, but "they fought to the last, allowed themselves to be fired on from all sides in the tightest space and held out for who knows how long. Only when nothing more was possible, did they capitulate." The situation in Africa, Meyne said, was completely different. "It is shattering how many officers give up fighting," Meyne complained. "They simply lose desire. They've had enough." The Führer's command to fight down to the last bullet had been passed on to the Wehrmacht's African divisions, but they had only answered "Where is the ammunition?" In the end, on May 8, 1943, the supreme commander of the 5th Tank Army, Lieutenant General Gustav von Vaerst, had simply ordered: "Pleinouvoir—as long as you can, and then stop."[585]

The POWs' tales suggest that most officers interpreted the order to fight until the last bullet in terms of conventional military logic. Hitler, meanwhile, had divorced himself from traditional tactics. He wanted to see sacrifice for its own sake. Goebbels took a similar view in June 1944, when he wrote: "We are not fighting down to the last bullet for the sake of our own lives. We're fighting down to the last drop of blood or breath. . . . There's only one either-or situation, life or death."[586] The Wehrmacht adapted to this apocalyptic rhetoric. In summer 1944, officers in charge of the Atlantic bunkers had to swear an oath to defend their position to the last man.[587] Excuses such as not having any ammunition or supplies would lead to them being "relieved [of command] in the sharpest fashion."[588] On July 21, 1944, Field Marshal Günther von Kluge reported to Hitler about the hopeless military situation in Normandy: "We will hold our positions, and if no support arrives to improve our situation, then we'll have to die with honor."[589] These lines were no doubt intended to placate the Führer and conceal Kluge's knowledge of two failed plans to assassinate Hitler. But Kluge's report does show what the highest-ranking German military officers believed the Führer wanted to hear. As the Allies advanced to the borders of Germany proper in fall 1944, the Wehrmacht chiefs of staff officially introduced "a duty to go down fighting."[590] Field commanders were forbidden to capitulate even when the tactical situation was hopeless.[591]

It remains to be seen whether the idea of truly fighting down to the bitter end really was anchored in the frame of reference of mid-level officers and ordinary soldiers. Regulations governed nearly everything in soldiers' lives, from the cut of their uniforms to the use of weapons and conduct in battle. But there were no regulations governing capitulation. No rules stated when and how one was allowed to surrender. The ideas of the military leadership remained largely abstract to low-ranking soldiers in the heat of battle. Defeat on the battlefield was a moment of disorientation, in which group behavior became especially important. Soldiers fought as one, and mostly they were captured in groups.

First Sergeant Renner of Luftwaffe Reconnaissance Regiment 7, for instance, was unwilling to fight down to the last bullet in the Battle of Cherbourg in June 1944:

> RENNER: We still had any amount of explosive, we could have held out for at least three or even five days more. But I did all I could to prevent that . . . Then I withdrew and went out on to the battle field and went on firing again so to speak, but into the blue, of course. Then I seized the opportunity to get back to the "Bunker" where I started to "mutiny," at least that's what it's called. I said: "Well, if things are going like this, comrades and gentlemen, whoever is married and loves his wife" —
>
> Despite the intense bombardment I stood in front of the "Bunker" and started to talk . . . . . "Do you want to die out there for a senseless fight, now that it is hopeless? Come on, let us get out." Finally I led the way out in the heaviest of bombardments, carrying the white flag."[592]

Renner repeatedly returned to German lines and saved the lives of 282 men, who became POWs. This case is a perfect example of how soldiers oriented themselves around how their comrades behaved. Renner had enough authority to assert himself against those who wanted to defend their positions to the last man. As soon as the first soldiers began to follow him, the ice was broken, and more and more began surrendering. Because the commanding officer was hiding in his bunker, Renner could exploit his men's lack of orientation and show them a way out. This story would no doubt have turned out differently had a charismatic officer taken the lead and ordered the men to fight down to the last bullet.

Soldiers' will to survive and the group dynamic of combat situations explain why, even during the early victorious phase of World War II, units of up to two hundred men sometimes surrendered, refusing, much to the dismay of the Nazi leadership, to fight to the last.

Yet soldiers' occasional violation of a military norm does not mean that the "last bullet" trope failed to establish itself.[593] The surveillance protocols show that it was anchored as a central point of orientation in German soldiers' frame of reference and did influence their behavior.

For example, a Captain Gundlach from the 716th Infantry Division reported the following about soldiers defending their positions in the village of Ouistreham in Normandy on June 6, 1944:

> GUNDLACH: We were in the "Bunker" there, of course we defended ourselves and coped with the situation. I happened to be the senior officer there. So I took over the command and we defended ourselves to the last. When some of my men fainted, owing to the fact that we got no more air into the "Bunker," and so they wanted to force us out with flame-throwers, I said: "No, we can't have that." Then we were taken prisoner.[594]

In his account, Gundlach continued to fight regardless of whether he could actually inflict any damage on the enemy. After the British began using flamethrowers and soldiers started passing out due to the heat and lack of oxygen, though, he felt he had done his duty. Gundlach fought up until a recognizable point, the moment when his men became incapable of defending themselves, before saying "No, we can't have that." Private First Class Lorch of the 266th Infantry Division tells much the same story about his capture near Saint-Lô in mid-July 1944. Initially his unit was forbidden to surrender. But "when our ammunition ran out," Lorch related, "our commander said: 'Now they can go kiss our asses.' "[595]

Conversations among POWs taken captive during the German defense of Cherbourg in late July 1944 illustrate the relevance of the "fighting-to-the-bitter-end" idea as a norm for action. The soldiers knew that the loss of the city meant a huge setback for the Wehrmacht. And they repeatedly insisted both that the stronghold could not be defended by a ragtag and poorly equipped force, and that they themselves were not to blame for its *rapid* fall. Instead soldiers accused others of not fighting until the end. Colonel Walter Köhn, for example, said:

> KÖHN: A "Leutnant" said to me: "What are we going to do about the ammunition tunnel?" So I said: "Blow up the opening to it. There's nothing else we can do." Then afterwards we 'phoned

up and said that we had blown up the opening, but had previously called them to see whether there were still German soldiers or anything inside. A hundred-and-fifty men came out of there. They were hiding away in a corner at the back, and had been there for days. A hundred-and-fifty men! "Well, what have you done with them?" "I sent them into action immediately. They had no arms. I collected up some arms and sent them into action, and when I had done so, looked round, and they had all cleared off again."[596]

The surveillance protocols are not the only source in which members of the Wehrmacht speak with outrage at the behavior of German soldiers at Cherbourg as a violation of military norms. With obvious annoyance, the port commander navy captain Hermann Witt relayed to Paris that a Major General Sattler had needlessly surrendered with four hundred men.[597] What irritated Witt was not capitulation in and of itself, but the fact that Sattler allegedly gave up without a compelling reason. For Witt, that was a sign of a total moral collapse. "It was JENA and AUERSTÄDT all over again," he complained a short time later as a POW, referring to Prussian troops' historic defeats in the Napoleonic Wars.[598] Saving soldiers' lives in a lopsided battle was of no concern to many officers in Cherbourg. It was noted with satisfaction that the unit under the command of First Lieutenant Hermann Keil had held out to the very end at Cap de la Hague: "One can only say that our troops behaved in a most exemplary manner right to the last moment; their morale and behaviour were excellent."[599]

Most soldiers showed at least a theoretical desire to hold out to the last. Nonetheless, situational factors, personal dispositions, and group dynamics often led to flexible interpretations of what that meant. Witt, the last man to surrender at Cherbourg, claimed he had fulfilled this ideal, as did Brigadier Botho Elster, who surrendered together with his twenty-thousand-strong troop at the Loire bridge in Beaugency on September 16, 1944, without firing a shot. Elster argued that he and his men had done everything they could to push through to the east, and that failings by the military high command had left him with no means of waging an honorable battle against the enemy.[600]

Regardless of how they had actually behaved, soldiers stylized their actions as fighting to the bitter end. One example of this is the bold tones used in radio messages by high-ranking officers to their superiors, shortly before they capitulated. The verbal noise such exchanges produced allowed both sides to tell themselves they were conforming to norms. And in fact, some of the men involved received coveted medals or promotions for their behavior.[601]

The need to depict one's own conduct as honorable automatically led soldiers to differentiate their own behavior from that of others. Soldiers occasionally accused comrades from other branches of the military, or those of different ranks, of cowardice. One private, for instance, complained in July 1944: "The officers at CHERBOURG were a cowardly lot. One of them was to come before a court-martial of Naval Civilian officials because he intended deserting. They never even got as far as the proceedings because those officers were in their shelters and hadn't the nerve to come out. The whole thing was dropped on that account. They had, however, the nerve to issue orders like: 'We'll fight to the last man!' "[602] The private blamed the officers for his unit's defeat: "At CHERBOURG our officers had packed their trunks days beforehand in readiness to be taken prisoner. If our officers hadn't been such cowards, CHERBOURG would never have fallen the way it did."[603] Officers, of course, put things precisely the other way around. Colonel Köhn, for instance, complained, "When the CO and the officer were there the men held out, but the moment they had gone . . ."[604] After the Wehrmacht rapidly lost Paris, some officers carped that they, the officers, had been the only ones who defended German control of the city. They, in the officers' own accounts, could at least say with good conscience that they had fought to the last.[605]

The arguments used were similar throughout the ranks, but the surveillance protocols demonstrate that the need to portray one's own conduct as conforming to military norms increased the higher ranked an individual was. As a POW, Witt even used letters to his wife to report in secret codes to Grand Admiral Dönitz about his battle on the breakwater at Cherbourg.[606] Other high-ranking officers boasted that their troops had been the last ones to capitulate.[607] Major General Erwin Menny, who was captured by Canadian troops in Falaise and sent to a U.S. POW camp, noted in his diary in November 1944:

MENNY: I am horrified at how few of the more than 40 generals I have met in captivity personally fought to the end. It goes without saying that every soldier and general, above all, tries everything, even things that seem hopeless. If you're lucky, you can do the impossible. How often did my men and I escape being surrounded or other dire situations, although we had long reconciled ourselves to dying? The fact that I alone, with two other men, survived unwounded was pure chance or a miracle. I can do without being admired by the enemy, but I'd rather English newspapers wrote that I defended myself with bitter resolve and preferred death to capture. I will never understand how a general can "capitulate."[608]

In Menny's eyes, generals were subject to special rules of conduct. A general was supposed to fight to the last, preferably with a weapon in his hand, and seek out death rather than being captured. If he capitulated at all, then only after being wounded. Menny added with pride that he had refused to raise his hands when he surrendered.

Generals Thoma and Crüwell, despite being diametrically opposed in their politics, reacted with similar outrage when they read in Trent Park of Field Marshal Friedrich Paulus allowing himself to be taken prisoner in Stalingrad. "I should have blown my brains out. I am bitterly disappointed, bitterly disappointed!" Crüwell fumed, before adding, "I think the fact that you and I were captured is a different matter and there is no comparison."[609] Both men stress that they battled to the end before falling into enemy hands. Thoma reported that gunfire had forced him out of his tank and that an enemy bullet had passed through his cap. But the fashion in which Paulus had surrendered had nothing heroic about it. In Thoma's and Crüwell's minds, Paulus had violated the norm in two respects. Thoma opined:

> THOMA: It's impossible for the Commander to go on living in such circumstances. It's just the same as if all the men on a ship were lost or three sailors or so were saved and the Captain and First Officer—the whole business is quite incomprehensible to me, because I know PAULUS. It must have been that his nerves and everything were completely shattered. But it is un-soldierly and it upsets me as a soldier.[610]

But the two men agreed that Italian generals had behaved far more disgracefully at the battle of El Alamein. Whereas Thoma claimed to have barely escaped from his tank with bullet holes in his uniform, the Italian generals "arrived in full dress with all their baggage. The

English officers in CAIRO laughed at them. They arrived looking like COOK's tourists with their luggage containing their peacetime uniforms. They immediately put on their peacetime uniforms. I immediately said: 'Please don't put me with them.' "[611]

The expectation that high-ranking officers would lead by example and fight to the death also recurs throughout official Wehrmacht daily reports. On July 3, 1944, for example, one report read: "In heavy defensive fighting, the commanding generals, Lieutenant General Martinek and Artillery General Pfeiffer, together with Major General Schünemann, fulfilled their duty and died a hero's death, fighting at the vanguard of their troops."[612]

Significantly, soldiers' reflections on this topic rarely, if ever, include thoughts about whether their behavior was useful in an operative sense. Thoma never paused to consider what benefit it would have for him as a commanding general to be present on the most advanced line, and Menny never mulled over the question of whether his attempted escape was sensible or whether it merely condemned more of his men to death. Nor did Captain Gundlach ponder whether holding out in his bunker near Ouistreham did anything to delay the advance of British forces. Fighting sui generis needed no justification. Those who conformed to the norm, or at least told themselves they did, could feel good about themselves as soldiers and avoid recriminations following defeat.

Germany's worsening fortunes only began to influence standards of normal soldierly behavior late in the war. The crushing defeat at Normandy may have convinced many soldiers that the war was lost, but they continued to believe that soldiers should fight bravely down to the very end. Only after the failed Ardennes Offensive did this imperative lose currency, as most soldiers realized that unconditional surrender was the only option, and Hitler largely lost his mythic aura.[613] Masses of soldiers commenced a "tacit strike," as General Edwin Graf von Rothkirch reported on March 9, 1945, in Trent Park: "They just sit there and do nothing when the Americans arrive."[614]

This tendency should not, however, obscure the fact that some soldiers, depending on their situation and personal disposition, did put up fierce resistance to advancing Allied troops well into April 1945. If the social fabric of a combat unit remained intact, and if the soldiers felt they were still well equipped, they fought far more fiercely than one would expect in the final days of a lost war. An example was the performance of 2nd Navy Infantry Division south of Bremen in April 1945. The division consisted of leftover ships' crewmen with little combat experience. Badly trained and equipped, they nonetheless fought with great energy and absorbed huge losses.[615]

The higher an individual was ranked, the more difficult it was for him to divorce himself from the framework of military values. In Trent Park, German generals argued quite emotionally about what the Wehrmacht should do in the face of the catastrophic military situation. In late January 1945, General Heinrich Eberbach concisely summed up the basic poles of opinion:

> EBERBACH: Yes, but everyone has a different conception of the word "Fatherland." One man thinks: "The moment has come when we must capitulate regardless of the conditions, in order to preserve the essential being of the German race." The other man thinks: "Things are now so desperate that the best thing for what remains of the German race is to fight to the bitter end, so that at least some respect may be wrung from the enemy, and so that that German race may at some future date rise again with whatever is left, by virtue of this fight to the death." Those are the two conceptions. One cannot say that one is wrong, this one is right.[616]

Admittedly, once the Allies succeeded in crossing the Rhine in late March 1945, most soldiers distanced themselves from the idea of fighting with honor down to the final bullet. "I used to think it was wrong to lay down your arms, that it would cause a crack in popular morale that would bode ill for the future," admitted General Ferdinand Heim in late March 1945. "But now it has to end. It's simply insanity."[617] Heim reached this conclusion in the relatively idyllic surroundings of Trent Park. Generals at the front may have had similar thoughts, but their subjective perceptions of how much room for maneuver they enjoyed varied, so they did little to resist the apocalyptic fantasies of the military high command. The fact that Germany's collective military suicide was only partial came down to the reality that fighting to the last man presumed that one was capable of fighting at all. No one, neither the troops nor the officers, wanted to face tanks with only rifles in their hands. If there were no effective means to combat the enemy, German soldiers simply stopped fighting. They did this in Russia in 1941, in Normandy in 1944, and in the Rhineland in 1945.

The only exceptions were a handful of elite units in the Waffen SS, the military wing of the organization, who took their instructions to fight to the final bullet more literally. It is striking how few SS men British and American forces succeeded in capturing either in France or Germany. American and British reluctance to take any SS prisoners cannot, by itself, explain this phenomenon. Another explanation is that many, if not all, SS units continued to fight in the sort of hopeless situations in which regular troops laid down their arms. Wehrmacht soldiers observed this fanaticism with ever greater disbelief. Sacrificing their own lives, observed Lieutenant Colonel von der Heydte, was a manifestation of the "false ethics, that faithful into death complex," which the SS, like Japanese kamikazes, cultivated among their ranks.[618]

With the exception of the Waffen SS, German ground forces possessed enough common sense to give up fighting when they were no longer able to put up an organized and effective defense. Soldiers simply refused to sacrifice their lives in such situations. Sacrifice to no military end was not part of their universe of norms. Becoming a casualty had to serve some sort of instrumental value. If there was no purpose in dying, soldiers tended to lay down their arms, especially on the Western Front, since it was not considered dishonorable to surrender to the Allies.

Such patterns of behavior can be seen again in the battle for the fortress of Saint-Malo. When German troops were surrounded in the citadel there, the commandant, Colonel Andreas von Aulock, let it be known that "everyone should prepare to die and remind himself that you can only die once. It was a battle to the last, to the point where we were supposed to sacrifice ourselves." That was how Georg Neher described the situation to a bunkmate in the U.S. POW camp Fort Hunt. "The day before we surrendered he ordered the sappers to lay landmines here and there. They weren't aimed at the Americans, but us. Of course, we didn't do that. . . . We had survived up until then and done ourselves proud on the battlefield, and now we were supposed to die a pathetic death. I would have rather thrown a grenade in the colonel's bunker." But to the soldiers' relief, they determined that "Aulock wasn't serious. It was all bluster. He never intended to die. He just said what he did so he would be mentioned a couple of times in the Wehrmacht reports and be promoted to general. He wanted to be interned as a general and a bearer of the [Iron Cross with] oak leaves."[619] Aulock achieved his ends. Reports of the colonel's heroic persistence delighted Hitler, who remarked that Aulock should serve as a model for all other garrison commandants. Aulock got his Oak Leaves and the promise he would be promoted to major general. Ironically, due to a clerical error, it was Aulock's brother Hans and not Aulock himself who ended up getting promoted.

Even high-ranking officers like this colonel did not fight to the bitter end, although some of them felt pangs of conscience about being captured alive by their enemies. "Strictly as a soldier, I have nothing to be ashamed of," said Lieutenant General Wilhelm von Schlieben, the fortress commandant at Cherbourg, shortly after he was interned. "I simply say that things would have ended more happily, if I'd died."[620] It would have been a "historical deed," Schlieben added, if he had thrown himself into the machine gun fire. Rear Admiral Walter Hennecke, one of Schlieben's fellow POWs, reported that the latter had indeed tried to end it all. Hennecke had hindered his fellow officer by arguing "That's tantamount to suicide. There is no point to it."[621]

Colonel Hans Krug, who was captured by British landing forces in Normandy on June 6, 1944, had a mind-set similar to Schlieben's:

> KRUG: I am quite resigned to the fact that things went badly with me—only that I have been taken prisoner! I wonder whether I shall be blamed for that? Whether they won't consider that I should have given my life. The order states: "Everyone surrendering a strongpoint will be sentenced to death. It is to be held to the last shot and the last man."[622]

As British forces surrounded Krug's bunker, he had called his division commander over a still functioning telephone connection and asked for instructions. But the commanding general refused: " 'Do whatever you consider right.' I said: 'Won't you give an order, sir?' 'No, I can't survey the situation.' I said that to him too. He said: 'No, you act according to your conscience!' " Krug was bewildered. He had accepted orders to defend his position to the last man, and now he was supposed to decide for himself. He didn't know what to do, although the hopelessness of his military position was obvious. He later formulated his dilemma as follows: "If it affects the prestige of the FÜHRER and the REICH, then we shall carry out this order. Or isn't it more important for me to save these valuable young lives from completely useless destruction."[623] In the end, Krug surrendered, but he continued to have pangs of conscience about not falling in battle.

The urge to fight until the bitter end was even stronger on the Eastern Front. German soldiers' fear of the Red Army, encouraged by Nazi propaganda, and the brutality of the war as it was waged on both sides did not make internment as a POW seem like a very attractive prospect. "Then there's another point which rather bothers me personally, and that is the following," reflected General Cramer. "It also has to do with my experience in RUSSIA about which you also know. It is of course a fact that the final fighting in AFRICA was not so intense as that in RUSSIA, because the soldiers know that to be a PW in ENGLAND is bearable in contrast to being killed in RUSSIA."[624] In addition to the last battles in Tunisia, Cramer had personally experienced the collapse of southern German lines on the Eastern Front after Stalingrad had been surrounded. He was thus in a position to compare the Wehrmacht's two greatest military catastrophes in the years 1942 and '43, and there was undeniable truth to his observation, as countless other examples show.[625] German soldiers' fear of the Red Army meant that many of them refused to capitulate in the final year of the war. When surrounded in places like Tarnopol, Vitebsk, Budapest, Poznan, and finally Berlin, the last defenders of the Third Reich often preferred the most hair-raising attempts to break through to their own lines to the option of simply surrendering. In so doing, thousands of soldiers marched to their own deaths like lemmings. Had they capitulated, most of them would have survived.[626] Nowhere in the West, neither in Cherbourg and Saint-Malo nor Metz and Aachen, did German soldiers show the same reluctance to surrender. But such reluctance was only a tendency, not an iron rule. Hundreds of thousands of Wehrmacht troops did allow themselves to be captured on the Eastern Front. The estimated number was 860,000 from 1941 to 1944.[627]

DYING WITH HONOR

The German navy developed a relationship all its own to the trope of fighting down to the last bullet. As we have seen, the German navy command, ever conscious of the shame of the sailors' rebellion of 1918, had placed utmost priority upon making amends in World War II. The fatalist command that navy men be ready to "die with honor" followed immediately upon Britain's entry into the war, which few of the top leaders had expected.[628] Navy Commander in Chief Raeder may have covered up the 1939 case of the crew of the MS *Admiral Graf Spree* sinking their own ship to avoid a lopsided battle with the British and save their own skins. But he also ordered that in future German warships were to battle to victory or go down with flags flying.[629] There are numerous examples of navy commanders demanding this sort of sacrifice from their men during the course of the war. And Raeder's successor, Dönitz, placed even more emphasis on "dying with honor" in the second half of the conflict.

For example, in November 1942, when Dönitz learned that Captain Hans Dietrich von Tiesenhausen, commander of U-331, had waved the white flag in order to save his helpless vessel from enemy aircraft, he immediately condemned the action and promised to have the captain court-martialed upon his return to Germany. "There can be no doubt in the Navy," Dönitz fumed, "that waving a white flag or taking down one's flag is equivalent to dishonorable surrender . . . and a violation of the venerable military and seaman's principle of preferring to go down with honor rather than lowering one's flag." In Dönitz's view, the commander should have sunk his own vessel after exhausting his capacity to do battle rather than heading for the African coast in order to better the chances of saving his crew. "Officers are to be instilled with the uncompromising rigor to regard the honor of the flag as more important than the lives of individuals," Dönitz added. "There is no such thing as raising a white flag in the German Navy, either at sea or on land."[630]

It had become a general trend during the nineteenth century for warships to refuse to surrender, and the same behavior can be found in various navies in the first half of the twentieth.[631] In Germany, Hans Bohrdt's painting *The Last Man* had provided an iconic image of this idea during World War I. Bohrdt's work was a stylized representation of a naval battle off the Falkland Islands in December 1914, in which sailors from the capsized cruiser MS *Nuremberg* had supposedly held up German flags to approaching British warships, and subsequently drowned.[632]

During World War II, the German navy leadership cultivated the cult of fighting to the last bullet in special ways. In late March 1945, to Dönitz's satisfaction, Hitler ordered that fortifications in Western Europe should be placed under the command of navy officers. "Many fortresses have been surrendered without fighting to the bitter end," Hitler noted, "but never a [German] ship."[633] In his political testa-

Hans Bohrdt (1857–1945): The Last Man. *Contemporary postcard.
(The painted original went missing in 1916.)*

ment, Hitler even wrote that the navy had completely lived up to his idea of honor for German officers, that "the surrender of territory or a city is intolerable and above all troop commanders are responsible for leading by example and sacrificing their own lives to do their duty."[634]

Naturally, we should ask here how much such statements actually reflected reality, and how much wishful thinking. In spring 1944, German naval forces in the North Atlantic were barraged with orders and warnings that stressed the importance of repelling the coming invasion and getting sailors to sacrifice their lives. Dönitz even ordered submarines to surface and ram enemy ships if necessary.[635] But that command remained just words. In practice, Dönitz was careful about deploying his resources, for instance only sending submarines into the English Channel if there was a good chance they could carry out their missions successfully. He never again spoke of them ramming enemy ships, and the only sailors sent on what amounted to suicide missions were small close-combat units, who used hastily improvised weapons like human torpedoes, boats packed with explosives, and, as of 1945, tiny, two-man submarines. Losses among pilots of one-man torpedoes were horrendous and in no way justified by military results. Yet news of the willingness with which young German sailors sacrificed their lives got around, making its way even to Imperial Japan's ambassador, who compared their bravery to that of the kamikaze pilots.[636]

A closer look reveals that what actually happened at sea was considerably more ambivalent than navy captains made it seem in their final radio messages. For example, on May 27, 1941, when the battleship *Bismarck* was sunk, Admiral Günther Lütjens radioed: "We're fighting to the final shell. Long live the Führer." Yet that was an exaggeration. In reality the *Bismarck* kept battling until the heavy artillery on board was disabled. One hundred fifteen men from a crew of 2,200 survived. In this respect, Lütjens behaved in much the same way as Rear Admiral Heinrich Ruhfus in Toulon. Both knew how their respective lopsided battles would end, yet neither wanted to give up without a fight. Ruhfus tried to gain time in order to destroy the port, while Lütjens seized the opportunity to inflict damage on British ships. But when his artillery was put out of commission after a short exchange of fire, the crew of the *Bismarck* began preparing to abandon ship. Many died as British navy men subjected the defenseless vessel to a barrage of gun and artillery fire. Before they sank their own ship, around a thousand *Bismarck* crew members escaped overboard. But high seas and fear that German submarines might be lurking prevented British sailors from launching an efficient rescue operation.

German navy men lived in a world of military commands in which orders to sacrifice their lives and battle "fanatically" played a particularly central role. And the rhetoric used by the navy leadership definitely had an effect on ordinary sailors. In conversations among navy POWs, concepts of discipline, pride, and honor occur much more frequently than in the chatter between army soldiers:

> WILJOTTI: I knew a Motor Torpedo-Boat commander I had a lot
> to do with. They were sent out against an overwhelming enemy
> force. They fought like lions during the invasion. But a pack of
> dogs means death for the rabbit. We had around 22 boats. 17 of
> them sunk with everyone on board. Orders.[637]

When sailors talked about their own ships, there was a noticeable change in their perspective. They fought tooth and nail until their equipment no longer functioned, and under no circumstances did they want their own vessels to fall into enemy hands. Sailors also took great care to destroy top secret material. Yet none of them would have thought of voluntarily going down with their ships to avoid being captured by the enemy. And whether a ship went down with flags flying was chiefly a concern of official, stylized propaganda. Once a sailor's ship had been sunk, he had done his duty, and he would try to save his own life, whether or not the flag was still flying. As in the army, there were limits to the willingness of German navy men to sacrifice their own lives. The fact that so many vessels were lost with all hands on deck had more to do with the nature of naval warfare than with the selflessness demanded by the German navy leadership. Even if a crew succeeded in getting off board, rescues were relatively rare. For instance, in 1944, the crew of a Canadian amphibious plane, the *Sunderland,* reported that it had sunk a German U-boat off the west coast of Ireland and that the crew were swimming around in the water. Someone took a photo of fifty-seven German sailors, and then the plane circled a few times and headed back to its home base. None of the submarine crew survived. U-625 was one of 543 German ships that went lost together with its entire crew. Dönitz used such horrendous losses to argue for the special morale maintained by submarine crews.[638] But in their own words, one finds little evidence of the fanaticism and contempt for death Dönitz praised in his speeches. German sailors followed orders and tried to be brave. But more than anything they wanted to survive.

"I WOULDN'T HAVE RAMMED ANYONE. IT'S SHEER IDIOCY. LIFE MAYN'T BE MUCH, BUT ONE DOES CLING TO IT AFTER ALL."[639]

The radicalization of the German political and military leadership did not have the same sort of effect on the Luftwaffe as it did on the army and the navy. In the face of dissipating morale in 1944–45, pilots were ordered to redouble their intensity in battle. This was especially the case with fighter pilots, whom Göring increasingly accused of cowardice.[640] In fall 1943, the idea of using kamikaze pilots was first broached. Luftwaffe doctor Theo Benzinger and glider pilot Heinrich Lange formulated it in a memorandum: "The military situation justifies and demands that naval targets be fought with extreme means like manned missiles whose pilot voluntarily sacrifices his life." The authors knew that this would represent "a form of warfare that is fully new in Europe." But the benefits of conventional attacks were disproportionate to the number of pilots getting shot down. If airmen were going to lose their lives anyway, the authors reasoned, why not take the greatest number of the enemy with them?[641]

In September 1943, Field Marshal Erhard Milch, the second most important leader in the Luftwaffe, discussed this suggestion with his subordinate officers. Plans were hatched to crash planes loaded with

Attack on U-625 on March 10, 1944. A few moments later the submarine was hit and sank. (Imperial War Museum, London, C-4289)

The crew of U-625 succeeded in clambering aboard one-man life rafts. But bad weather came up a bit later, and all were lost at sea. (Imperial War Museum, London, C-4293)

explosives into enemy warships or fighters packed with ammunition into enemy bomber formations. But Milch had scruples about sending pilots on "suicide missions." It would be better, he reasoned, if pilots dove toward enemy targets and then ejected with parachutes before impact. But the general view of the Luftwaffe leadership was that kamikaze missions were unnecessary, and suggestions like Benzinger and Lange's were never put into practice.

Hanna Reitsch, the well-known female test pilot, was friends with Benzinger and Lange and took the opportunity while visiting Hitler's Berghof residence to tell the Führer about their idea. But Hitler was having none of it and personally intervened in July 1944 to prevent thirty-nine pilots from crashing their Fw 190 fighter bombers into an Allied armada in the Baie de la Seine.

In fall 1943, when it was again proposed to crash special "suicide aircraft" into enemy ships, Luftwaffe fighter officer Hans-Günther von Kornatzki formulated the idea of an airborne "storm attack." In his vision, fearless fighter pilots would bring down Allied planes by simply ramming them in the air. Over the course of the war, this had happened on a number of occasions—either by accident or after a conscious decision on the part of pilots. There was a decent chance for the pilot to survive by ejecting with a parachute. The task was to coordinate such chance events. The commanding general in charge of fighter pilots, Adolf Galland, was open to the idea of a "storm attack" but didn't think much of the hair-raising spectacle of pilots purposely ramming enemy planes. In May 1944, when the first "storm fighters" were initiated into this new type of mission, they had to swear that they would attack the enemy from extremely short range and, if they failed to shoot him down, physically ram his aircraft. Three such units were formed in the course of 1944, each one containing around fifty specially modified Fw 190s. Yet despite the fact that the oath taken by the pilots emphasized their willingness to ram enemies, it rarely happened in practice. If the planes were able to get that close to the enemy, they could usually shoot him down using artillery. Still, on occasion, German pilots did ram Allied bombers. About half of them lost their lives.

The surveillance protocols show that Luftwaffe pilots did not consider ramming sorties suicide missions, but as an especially clever way of adapting aerial warfare, which was becoming ever more extreme.[642] Any means were legitimate if they increased the number of enemy kills. Luftwaffe POWs didn't even show any particular outrage at rumors of a new ordinance stipulating that any airmen returning home without an enemy kill or at least damage to their aircraft would be court-martialed.[643]

Colonel Hajo Hermann felt that, since conventional fighter planes were too few in number to stop the Allied daytime bombardments of Germany, the defense of the Reich needed to be radicalized. In fall 1944, he came up with the perfidious idea of having one or two thousand young pilots ram their fighters into an American bomber squadron. The shock that the U.S. Air Force would feel from this "massive blow," Hermann felt, would buy Nazi Germany some breathing room. Experienced pilots, who would be needed later in the war, would be exempt from the mission.

When Luftwaffe general and former ace pilot Adolf Galland learned of the plan, he asked Hermann whether he was going to be part of the mission, to which Hermann replied in the negative. After that Galland saw no point in discussing the idea any further. "He's second on my list of criminals," Galland later remarked as a POW.[644]

In January 1945, though, Galland succeeded in getting an audience with Hitler. Hitler's Luftwaffe adjunct subsequently had let it be known that the Führer had the highest respect for men who were willing to volunteer for such ramming missions. No soldier would be ordered to take part, but it was felt there would be enough volunteers. By the end of the month, Göring had signed off on a call for young pilots to volunteer for a mission that, at the cost of one's own life, might turn the tide in the war. Two thousand young men allegedly stepped forward. Three hundred of them were selected and informed that the plan was for them to crash into American bombers en masse. Many were surprised. They had expected to be going after bigger targets like aircraft carriers or battleships and found their lives too valuable to be sacrificed to destroy a single B-17 Flying Fortress. Those responsible for training them explained that this wasn't a suicide mission per se. Pilots would be allowed to eject from their planes once they had rammed their targets. On April 7, 1945, 183 pilots purposely crashed their aircraft into an American bomber unit over Magdeburg. The Wehrmacht reported four days later that the pilots' "fearless willingness for self-sacrifice" had destroyed more than 60 enemy aircraft. In reality the number was 23. Of the 183 German aircraft that had taken off, 133 had been shot down, and 77 pilots lost their lives.

What is particularly interesting is that suggestions to commence "self-sacrificial missions" did not come from the highest levels of German political and military leadership, who otherwise never tired of demanding that soldiers fight until death. While hundreds of thousands of ground troops fell because of Hitler's command to hold out whatever the costs, the Führer could not bring himself to order the Luftwaffe to approve a suicide mission for dozens of pilots. And the ramming sortie of April 7 wasn't a kamikaze mission in the narrow sense, since pilots could escape by parachute. Sixty percent of those involved did in fact survive. This was a much higher quotient than applied to submarine crews on the most risky missions.

Another variation of "self-sacrificial missions" was tried out in April 1945. On January 31 of that year, the Red Army had crossed the Oder and established itself on that river's western banks. The German army had tried but failed to destroy the bridgeheads. The Luftwaffe was told to use any means to achieve this end in order to disrupt the Soviet advance on Berlin. On March 5, the idea was put forward of destroying the bridges over the Oder with a self-sacrificial mission, but first the Luftwaffe tried to accomplish this aim by conventional means. After that, too, failed, the German air force resorted to suicide sorties. Some of the former volunteers were recalled, and others stepped forward of their own free will. On April 17, one day after Soviet troops launched their major assault on Berlin, the first pilots crashed their planes into the bridges over the Oder. From a military standpoint, though, the mission was completely senseless since pontoon bridges could be repaired very quickly.

All in all, Hitler's ideas of military sacrifice were astonishingly contradictory. He demanded that soldiers fight down to the final bullet and the last man. His orders forbade any retreats or premature surrenders, promoting fanaticism as the key to ultimate victory. Yet even as he thundered that "every bunker, every block of houses in every city and every German village must become a fortress before which either the enemy bled to death or the occupants perished in hand-to-hand combat,"[645] he also accepted that survivors did exist. In the case of the failed defense of the German stronghold of Metz, he even commissioned a special armband in recognition of those who had taken part. He would have no doubt approved if the veterans of Metz had shot themselves with their final bullets. But he did not enforce his stand-and-die demands, although hundreds of thousands of soldiers who had followed to the letter his commands to hold out had lost their lives. Hitler was indifferent to the number of dead. He considered massive casualties to be part of the destiny of the German people, locked in a struggle for total victory or total defeat. Nonetheless, he shied away from explicitly ordering suicide commandos, just as he didn't demand poison gas be used as the final stage of a total war.

ITALIAN WEAKLINGS AND RUSSIAN BEASTS

The reference frame of German soldiers firmly anchored the virtues of following orders, doing one's duty, and fighting bravely to the last, and this ethos made itself apparent throughout the stories soldiers told about their own battle experiences—and even more so when they discussed comrades, enemies, and allies.

With few exceptions, German soldiers in all three military branches had an extremely negative view of Italians. Wehrmacht troops had difficulty understanding Italian behavior, which they perceived as tantamount to an unwillingness to fight. Their commentary was correspondingly dismissive. Italian behavior was a "tragedy."[646] "If only those blasted Italians . . . would do something," one POW carped.[647] Other telling excerpts from the protocols: "They have no self-confidence";[648] "They're in a blue funk";[649] they "were a frightful lot!"[650] "The dirty dogs," groused another German soldier, "give themselves up if they have the slightest trouble!"[651] "They're so terribly soft," concurred someone else.[652] Militarily, Germany's Italian allies were seen as useless. "You can only consider 130,000 Italians equal to about 10,000 Germans," reckoned one POW.[653] Another joked that every Italian tank carried with it a white flag,[654] while someone else quipped that "if [our enemies] were only the Italians then the B.D.M. [the League of German Maidens] and the old peasants from the CHIEMSEE would be quite enough."[655] German soldiers mocked Benito Mussolini's pretensions: "The Italians are supposed to be descended from the Romans, but the Romans would have achieved more with spears and shields than they have!"[656] In short, German soldiers found that Italians "are the worst soldiers we have anywhere in EUROPE."[657]

A few Italian units did come off slightly better in the judgments of their allies. The Italian paratrooper division "Folgore" may have been poorly equipped, "but at least they were men."[658] And there was one situation in which Italian fighters did perform up to scratch: "Under German leadership they (the Italian soldiers) are excellent," a Sergeant Funke reported about the battles in Tunisia in April 1943. "At ENFIDAVILLE in the retreat they received the order: 'Young Fascists will die where they stand.' Thirty Italians held out there for three days."[659] Some POWs also mentioned poor Italian equipment and supplies as mitigating factors. But of the eighty-four German generals interned at Trent Park, only one brought this up. The ratios were similar at other British facilities and in American POW camps.

No doubt, the negative view of Italians as soldiers, which established itself as early as 1941 and which was also on ample display in official files and in field posts and soldiers' diaries, exaggerated the situation. But it was not entirely untrue. The stereotype was based on experiences on the battlefield, where Italian units often crassly failed to live up to German standards, or British ones for that matter.

Military virtues were also the criteria German soldiers used to evaluate their other allies. Slovak soldiers were second only to members of the Wehrmacht; Romanians were "very good, notably better than they were in the last war"[660] and "not at all bad soldiers."[661] Spanish mercenaries also came in for praise: "The Spanish Legion is very good—the only thing is that they're a frightful mixture, but from the military point of view they're good soldiers."[662] Hungarians, however, were deemed "a worthless lot" since they were perceived to have simply run away from the Russians.[663]

German soldiers used the same reference frame to judge their enemies. Wehrmacht soldiers had the greatest respect for the British, who were seen as "tough and brave opponents" who fought fairly.[664] In Dunkirk and Greece, British troops had fought fantastically. They were "excellent airmen"[665] and "tough guys" . . . "like us."[666] "Put a British soldier in a German uniform and you won't notice the difference," one soldier for the Wehrmacht's Afrika Korps thought.[667] Yet higher-ranking officers didn't always join in the praise: "If the English get a few hits, they just clear off, and they don't go to it—like our people do, and when they do, they're very clumsy."[668] The commander of the Wehrmacht's 1st Paratroop Division even opined about Allies in Italy: "In their whole attitude toward the war, the masses of the enemy won't be able to absorb heavy losses in the long term."[669]

American troops were less admired than the British because their victories were allegedly only the result of their material advantages, which Wehrmacht soldiers considered unfair. As soldiers, U.S. troops were "cowardly and petty";[670] they hadn't "any idea what real hard warfare means";[671] "they cannot endure privations";[672] and they were "inferior to [Germans] in close combat."[673] "The American swine," scoffed one POW, "take to their heels if they're really attacked."[674] Again in conjunction with fighting in Italy, one general concluded: "Generally speaking, the Americans, with a few exceptions, are considered poorer fighters because they lack driving force and have no desire."[675]

By contrast, German soldiers had enormous respect for their Russian adversaries, whose capacity for sacrifice and brutality was a source of fear. A sample of opinion: "Those people have a terrific toughness of spirit and body";[676] "They fight to the very last, the Russians, my God, they can fight";[677] "You wouldn't believe how fanatically the devils fought."[678] Nonetheless, precisely because they seemed to display such contempt for death, Russians often struck Germans as soulless, oxlike, fighting beasts. Crüwell related: "Near UMAN, in that first battle of encirclement in the UKRAINE, my tanks literally had to crush the people to death because they wouldn't give themselves up. Just imagine that."[679] Still, Crüwell had high regard for Red Army soldiers because they fought so brutally. Higher-ranking German officers still thought there was no way a soldier who battled tirelessly and fiercely for his country could be a bad soldier. That was in keeping with the militaristic ethos of the Wehrmacht. A Major Blunt from the Luftwaffe related how 125 Russian bombers attacked a German bridgehead over the Berezina River near Bobruysk in 1941. German fighter pilots shot down 115 of the planes. But for Blunt, the Russian attack was neither senseless nor insane. On the contrary, the incident only proved what "grand fliers" the Russians were.[680]

German soldiers saw Italians as cowardly, Russians as death-defying, British as tough, and Americans as soft, and with very rare exceptions these estimations did not change over the course of the war. The initial battles set the tone that continued until 1945, aside from a few expansions and variations. Only when the tide began to turn against Germany did subtle shifts occur. For instance, in the second half of the war, as the Red Army began advancing, ever more quickly, to the borders of Germany proper, Germans tended to emphasize Russian soldiers' brutality over their bravery.

Bravery in battle was also a key criterion for evaluation of one's own comrades. No one liked "staff wallahs."[681] Those who weren't actively engaged in combat opened themselves up to accusations of cowardice, and one's superiors were expected to lead the vanguard. One POW complained:

> PRINCE HEINRICH XLII of REUSS was my "Abteilungskomman-deur." He was a major in 1940, a Lieutenant Colonel in 1942—all due to his connections. As soon as the battle of KIEV began, this gentleman withdrew and became ill. As soon as the battle of KIEV had been won and we had settled down in the town, he turned up again. When the battle down in the CRIMEA started, that man was nowhere to be seen. When we were in SIMFEROPOL, after two or three weeks of quiet, he turned up again. When things got going at SEVASTOPOL, during the winter of 1943, he was ill again, his weight shrank to under 100 lbs, he looked so wan, and then he left. He is generally looked upon as a rather degenerate type of man.[682]

A positive counterexample was Colonel Claus von Stauffenberg:

> VIEBIG: He's frightfully smart, and extraordinarily intelligent—at any rate that's how he has always been described to me. That's to say he's a German officer type; just as much a fighting man as a General Staff Officer with incredible energy, considerate and thorough.[683]

Although Major Viebig thoroughly condemned Stauffenberg's role in the failed attempt to assassinate Hitler, he was full of praise for the count as a military personality. Significantly, Viebig saw Stauffenberg as a combat soldier, even though the latter had only spent three months at the front. General staff officers were often viewed critically, but Stauffenberg's "energy," combined with the fact he had been seriously and visibly wounded in Tunisia, outweighed any skepticism his rank might have brought with it.

Soldiers also approved of Field Marshal Rommel for his energy, even though they otherwise perceived him as an ambivalent figure. "He was impressive as a soldier," opined a Colonel Hesse. "He was no great leader but he was a *real soldier*, an intrepid, very brave man, very harsh, even towards himself."[684]

Cowardice and Desertion

Soldiers had an almost exclusively negative view of those who failed to conform to the ideal of the brave warrior, those who were thought to have fled without a fight or even gone over to the enemy. As of summer 1944, there was no end to the conversations in British and American POW camps about excessive numbers of cowards in the German ranks. A Lieutenant Zimmermann from the 709th Infantry Division recalled driving along a country road from Cherbourg to the front: "Troops were already streaming along the road in any order: Labour Service, Flak and a few infantrymen. I said: 'Boys, don't run away, don't make the bloody affair even worse than it is.' "[685] Zimmermann knew that Cherbourg would soon be lost, but he still felt that order should continue to rule and that soldiers should bravely fight on. The fact that German soldiers were retreating pell-mell made the inevitable defeat even worse, as it undermined the core of Zimmermann's belief in what it meant to be a soldier.

Very rarely, and only among nonofficers, did soldiers admit that they had considered abandoning their positions and running away. A Private Leutgeb told a bunkmate about the battle in Normandy:

LEUTGEB: We had one thousand rounds per MG. You can imagine how long that lasts; we had no ammunition left. We had some damned Sudeten German there, the "Unteroffizier," and I said to him: "What are we supposed to do here, we haven't got any ammunition left, so let's make off, we can't do any more good." "What the hell do you mean?" he said. I would have made off, but I didn't want to do it because of my pals. Then we got mortar fire, which was simply indescribable. In the third Gruppe, only the machine-gunner was left alive.[686]

In soldiers' eyes, the only thing worse than someone who refused to fight was someone who deserted. Major Heimann recalled a case from the battles for Aachen:

HEIMANN: I had three "Bataillons" up there which only needed to retreat by night. Actually only the staff of my local defence "Bataillons" returned consisting of fifteen men; the rest had gone over to the enemy. They were men of forty to fifty years old, who felt quite safe in the "Bunker," but then said: "We're not going into the open field positions." We were supposed to defend AACHEN with people like that![687]

In their conversations, POWs treated desertion as something unthinkable. "I could never have done it myself and I don't think any men from GERMANY proper would ever desert, only Austrians and all those Volksdeutsche [ethnic Germans from outside Germany proper]," asserted one lieutenant in late December 1944.[688] It was rare for soldiers to directly address the topic before the end of 1944. One exception: "I shall probably be sentenced to death, but it's better to be alive under sentence of death for desertion, than to be lying dead on the battlefield."[689] Interestingly, the soldier who said this was a member of the SS division "Frundsberg." By July 1944, the German situation was so miserable that even the Waffen SS was no longer a monolithic bloc of fanatic political warriors. In order to avoid accusations of shirking and cowardice, most German soldiers who had deserted concealed that fact and sought to portray their behavior as conforming to military norms. They had only given up because the war was *now* lost and it *no longer* made sense to keep fighting. Hopelessness was named far more often as a reason for desertion than any political motivations. This may have been due to the POWs' communicative situation: especially while being held prisoner, individuals were not permitted to question military values.[690]

Very few soldiers articulated any doubts at all about the war itself or Germany's attacks upon its neighbors. Even a deserter like Alfred Andersch, later a well-regarded German author, who abandoned his post near Rome on June 6, 1944, displayed a thoroughly positive attitude toward the Wehrmacht and military virtues.[691] That shows how deeply even those men who had the courage to break free from the framework of the Wehrmacht had internalized the military value system. It was only as of spring 1945 that increasing numbers of soldiers dared to speak frankly and unashamedly about desertion:

TEMPLIN: All people can talk about these days is taking off, whether you can just run away and how best to do it. The afternoon we were taken captive, we were sitting in a basement waiting. There was a lot of shooting nearby, and at any moment, we thought a shell will hit the basement. We were 15 men, and we were just sitting there, and no one dared to say: We'll just sit here and wait to be taken prisoner. But the Americans simply wouldn't come. And that evening some infantrymen showed up and said, "Come on, you can leave here now." And we had to follow them. Otherwise we would have taken off. The infantry, the lieutenant were already gone by the afternoon. They blew up the bridge, but we just sat there. I wasn't afraid at all.

FRIEDL: Yes of the Germans, but not of the Americans. The Germans, that was a lot worse, the uncertainty. Everyone thinks differently about how he acts. Everyone thinks: "If only the time would come," and then comes the officer, and you carry out orders just so. That's what's tragic about the situation.[692]

The official punishment for showing cowardice in the face of the enemy or for desertion was, with very few exceptions, death, and German military tribunals were not shy about enforcing this rule. Some 20,000 German soldiers were given the death penalty—about the same number as in Imperial Japan. By comparison, only 146 American soldiers were put to death, while it is estimated that 150,000 Soviet ones were executed.[693]

The number of men executed as deserters increased as final defeat began to loom, rising dramatically in fall 1944. Up until that point, soldiers seemed to have accepted the death penalty as a perfectly normal punishment for desertion or even cowardice in the face of the enemy. In December 1943, Lieutenant Hohlstein of 15th Tank Division talked about his experiences two years previously in Russia. His bunkmate First Sergeant von Bassus inquired about the conditions surrounding the winter of crisis before the gates to Moscow in 1941–42. Hohlstein pointed out that there had been deserters:

HOHLSTEIN: Yes. There are always some individual cases. People who had been in the fighting in RUSSIA right from the beginning and had marched most of the time in the swamps and forests and mud and everything, who had been through that dreadful autumn and then experienced the cold and then the Russian break-through, of course became pessimistic and said: "It's all up now, now, our number's up." In order to get to the rear more quickly, several men threw away their arms, their rifles and so on, which is in itself not very serious, but they were condemned to death. They had to be, because it just had to be made clear to them that a thing like that simply couldn't be done.[694]

Bassus was astonished that Wehrmacht soldiers had deserted as early as 1941. Both men consoled themselves with the idea that these had been only isolated cases, and they agreed that deserters definitely deserved the death penalty.

The protocols contain numerous first- and secondhand descriptions in the period up until late 1944 of executions of soldiers who had supposedly shown cowardice or deserted. As was the case with reports about the executions of partisans, the tales rarely called forth astonishment, outrage, or negative reactions. Listeners were mostly interested in gory or unusual details. Otherwise, the stories were part of the everyday realities of war. Several generals tried to prove their toughness by describing how they lined up soldiers "against the wall" at the front. These officers were by no means fanatic Nazis. Lieutenant General Erwin Menny reported about his assignment in Russia in 1943:

> MENNY: I had just taken over a "Division" there, which had newly come from NORWAY, so that it was as yet fresh, and still good. The enemy broke through, simply because a few fellows had run away. Immediately I insisted on fetching the deputy judge advocate general from the Staff at the rear and brought him to the front—his knees were knocking together with fright—and we tried the men directly behind the place where the enemy had broken in and sentenced them immediately and shot them at once, on the spot. That went round like wildfire and the result was that the main defensive line was in our hands again at the end of three days. From that moment on there was quite good order in the "Division." It acted as a deterrent, at any rate no one else ran away <u>unnecessarily</u>. Of course a thing like that is contagious, it is demoralizing when everyone runs away.

The only response from Menny's interlocutor, Schlieben, was a question: "Where was that?"[695]

Success

Of the 17 million men who served in the Wehrmacht, around 80 percent of them were directly involved at some point in the fighting. Nonetheless, not every one of them had the same opportunity to demonstrate heroism, achieve a great victory, or be part of a battle. There were large numbers of radio operators, fuel coordinators, and airplane mechanics—an infantry division even included bakers, butchers, and medical orderlies, who never fired a shot. Their lives were fundamentally different from those of an infantry foot soldier, tank driver, or fighter pilot. Wehrmacht soldiers wanted one thing above all: to be able to do their jobs well, whatever they were. A mechanic who worked on submarines or a sapper in Stalingrad wanted to perform as well as he had in civilian life as a bookkeeper, farmer, or carpenter. And the ethos of wanting to do good work wasn't the only thing these men transferred to their military lives. They also maintained the same tendency as in any organization to criticize poor working conditions or senseless procedures and orders.

In this sense, Major Alfred Gutknecht complained about administrative inefficiencies that hindered him in his function:

> GUTKNECHT: It was the same on the CHANNEL ISLANDS, that was enough to make anyone despair too; there was an incredible number of vehicles there—in the first place there were private cars, on the islands in any case. That's beyond me, for the islands are only small. There weren't so many lorries. Then each of them, the army, the GAF, the navy and the "Todt" Organisation, brought their lorries to the islands. So I suggested that they should be combined, that's to say that armed forces transport pools should be formed, including the "Todt" Organisation. It was not possible, and even Feldmarschall von RUNDSTEDT did not assert his authority.[696]

One spoke in much the same tones about fighting on the front—only there, inefficiency could be fatal for large numbers of soldiers. Major

Frank from the 5th Paratrooper Division, for instance, objected to the conditions under which his battalion had to attack during the Ardennes Offensive:

> FRANK: Right on the very first day of the offensive we stormed
> FÜRDEN, it was a fortified village. We got to within 25 m. of the
> "Bunker," were stopped there and my best "Kompaniechefs"
> were killed. I was stuck fast there for two and a half hours, five
> of my runners who returned were all shot. Then, for two and
> a half hours, always on my stomach, I worked my way back,
> by inches. What a show for young boys, making their way over
> a plain and without support of heavy weapons! I decided to
> wait for a forward observation officer. The "Regimentskom-
> mandeur" said: "Get going, take that village—there are only
> a few troops holding it." "That's madness," I said to my "Regi-
> mentskommandeur." "No, no, it's an order. Get going, we must
> capture the village before evening." I said: "We will too. The
> hour we lose waiting for the forward observation officer I will
> make up two and three times over afterwards." Then there
> were assault guns available. I said to him: "At least give me the
> assault guns, to come in from the north and destroy their 'Bun-
> ker.' " "No, no, no." We took the village without any support
> and scarcely were we in it when our heavy guns began firing
> into it. I brought out one hundred and eighty-one PW alto-
> gether. I rounded up the last sixty and a salvo of mortar shells
> fell on them from one of our mortar "Brigaden," right into the
> midst of the PW and guard troops. After twenty-two hours our
> own artillery was still firing into the village. Our liaison was a
> <u>complete</u> failure. We had tanks as well, they were <u>never</u> used
> in conjunction with the infantry, all the tanks were recklessly
> thrown away. On the one hand the tanks were thrown away,
> on the other hand the assault guns were thrown away, and the
> infantry too, but if there had been a little co-operation, if those
> one or two hours had been allowed each time to prepare it,
> then it would have been wonderful.[697]

Major Frank craved success. He wanted to conquer Fürden as quickly and with as few losses as possible and then press on westward. Bad coordination, he felt, doomed those ambitions. Yet although he char-acterized the attack on Fürden as "insanity," Frank followed orders and carried it out. The alternative was simply unthinkable. And he described taking the village, "without any support," and capturing 181 POWs as a personal triumph. He had successfully carried out his mission, even if the Ardennes Offensive as a whole failed, with German forces suffering heavy casualties. The fault, however, wasn't Frank's, but rather that of the "mid-level leadership." If Frank had been allowed to do things his way, everything would have been "wonderful."

There are countless tales in the surveillance protocols in which speakers emphasized their own achievements within the overall context of a catastrophic defeat. They occur with roughly the same frequency with which stories about the company or the boss crop up in everyday peacetime conversations. Narratives of this sort do not just document the role played by the ideal of "doing a good job" in the perceptions and interpretations of historical actors. They also show that professionalism was a major factor in how soldiers positioned and saw themselves. Civilian and wartime jobs were structurally and psychologically similar. In their narratives, soldiers cited concrete results to reinforce the proposition that they did a good job. Indicators of military success were the number of POWs captured, as in Major Frank's story, as well as tanks and planes destroyed, ships sunk, and enemies killed. The head of the German navy's coastal battery at Longues-sur-Mer, Lieutenant Herbert, waged a hopeless battle against the invading Allied armada on June 6 and 7, 1944. Just four days later, in a POW camp, he encountered Colonel Hans Krug, who had led an army regiment in the same episode of the war:

> HERBERT: I should like to report to you, sir, that I have sunk a cruiser.
> KRUG: Hearty congratulations!
> HERBERT: I am extremely proud of having achieved that before being taken prisoner. I didn't know it myself. But I have had it confirmed from three sides here.
> KRUG: Has the "Batterie" been taken?
> HERBERT: Yes, the "Batterie" has gone. They shot up one gun after the other from the sea. But I still kept firing with one gun at the end . . . I had a splendid Flak "Zug" there. My Flak "Zug" shot down sixteen aircraft.[698]

In Herbert's mind the success of having sunk a cruiser, of having kept on fighting down to the last gun, and of having achieved sixteen hits outweighed the fact that the Wehrmacht's most modern shore battery had not been able to hinder the landing of British troops. Indeed, the battery was destroyed by one British and one French cruiser. We have no way of reconstructing why Herbert thought he had sunk a cruiser. It is possible that the British spread misinformation that the lieutenant gladly used, or he may have just been lying in an attempt to impress his interlocutor. In reality, he had not even managed to hit either warship. In addition, we know from British sources that this shore battery surrendered on June 7, 1944, after barely putting up a fight. Herbert's claim to have fought to the last was pure fiction.

Through the protocols, the narrative tendency is to describe surrounding conditions as particularly dire in order to make one's own deeds seem more significant. A Lieutenant Simianer asserts that an irresponsible regiment commander had deployed his battalion without heavy artillery and sent them to battle British tanks in July 1944. Yet although his unit had only four bazookas, Simianer claimed that he and his men had destroyed four tanks, and he himself two — which was no doubt considered a notable achievement.[699] The upshot of the story was that, although Simianer was burdened by an incompetent superior officer and insufficient equipment, he still did his duty with aplomb.

Stories of this sort served two functions: to vent frustration with the inadequacies of military leadership and military material while raising one's own status as someone who had achieved success despite inauspicious circumstances. Such narratives are by no means unique to the military. Similar tendencies of perception and presentation can be found in all work situations.

DECORATIONS

Medals and awards were even better evidence of one's own achievements than wild adventure stories. As we have seen, Hitler and the leadership of all three branches of the armed forces created the most varied system of military honors among all the nations involved in World War II, establishing a hierarchy of status within the Wehrmacht. Frontline fighters, whose medals and badges made them instantly recognizable as such, enjoyed the highest social prestige. This system of incentives, an extension of its predecessor from World War I, was firmly anchored in the frame of reference of soldiers of all disciplines and ranks and had significant impact on what they perceived as success. In soldiers' conversations, people were often identified by the medals they had been awarded, along the lines of: "Have you heard anything of Oberst BACHERER, the holder of the Knight's Cross?"[700]

It was a source of shame to have served without having won a medal. "I shall be a laughing-stock when I get home," lamented First Lieutenant Herz of the Afrika Korps. "In the first place I've been captured unwounded, and then I haven't even got the Iron Cross, Class I."[701] Heinrich-Hans Köstlin, whose E-boat was rammed by a fellow German vessel during defensive maneuvers in February 1942 and subsequently sank, was plagued by similar concerns: "As Ps/W we ought to be given some sort of award, otherwise it won't be fair to people like us. My pals will now become officers and will get the E-boat badge and the E.K.1. If later on we go to a training school, it will be possible to see at a glance that they were in the war. But I haven't anything. You get the E.K.1 after fifty sorties."[702]

The desire to earn accolades was especially strong in units whose successes were measurable. Luftwaffe fighter and bomber pilots spoke endlessly about the number of kills and missions they had as well as the decorations they had been awarded. Particularly in the first phase of the war, in which the quality of German training and warplanes led to quick success, airmen's thinking was dominated by fame and public acknowledgment. In the navy, too, where the tonnage of ships sunk was the dominant criterion, soldiers' attention revolved around decorations. Revealingly, Lieutenant Otto Kretschmer fretted intensely as a POW over whether his last radio message had reached Dönitz. Along with the regrettable fact that he had had to abandon ship, Kretschmer wanted his superior to know about his successes on his final mission, which had made him Germany's top submarine commander.[703]

Reports from the naval command reveal that submarine duty was popular because sailors had excellent chances to be decorated. Almost half of Knight's Cross recipients in the navy served aboard submarines, and U-boat commander Günther Prien was the first publicly celebrated hero of Nazi propaganda.[704] While a Knight's Cross was beyond most soldiers' reach, it was a matter of pride to wear the insignia of one's unit. And the chances of doing that by serving on a submarine were significantly better than in other units, especially at the start of the war, when losses were relatively small. The commander of U-473, Captain Heinz Sternberg, is reported to have told his crew in 1943: "We need twice twenty-one days to get the U-boat badge. I should like to have a U-boat badge. As I've been doomed to sail in a U-boat anyway I should also like to have the badge."[705] But Sternberg's wishes did not come true. His ship was sunk on its second mission, and Sternberg was killed.

Statistically, sailors were far more likely to survive aboard surface vessels. But that sort of service was far less popular as of 1942; because of lack of fuel and the navy leadership's fears of unacceptable losses, many German warships lay idle in ports. How were they supposed to prove their mettle and collect accolades, sailors reasoned, if they didn't carry out any operations against the enemy? Navy Private Birke, for instance, who survived the sinking of the battleship *Scharnhorst* in 1943, complained that he had been at sea since August 1940 and still hadn't gotten an Iron Cross.[706]

The pressure to fight and win medals was enormous. As the *Scharnhorst* raised its anchor on December 25, 1943, in the northern Norwegian fjord of Alta and set sail to attack a British convoy, the mood was jubilant. Finally the sailors were going to see some action. Few of them realized that they were being sent on a virtual suicide mission. The *Scharnhorst* was sunk the following day, and only thirty-six men from a crew of nearly two thousand survived. They were brought to the Latimer House POW camp, where they proudly told of their mission.

"Four destroyers should have been sufficient to sink us," a Private Bohle related. "There were nine ships in all. The SCHARNHORST had to fight a lone battle from 12.30 hours to 20.00 hours. And if the destroyers hadn't been there, they wouldn't have sunk us. It's actually hard to realise: twenty-six thousand tons of steel and iron and two thousand men all gone! It's a miracle how they stood up to it for so long, for we received a hell of a lot of hits. There were seven to eight torpedo hits alone. I would never have thought a ship could withstand seven torpedo hits. We were definitely hit seven times. The last three put the finishing touches. The first ones didn't affect us at all." Private Backhaus, another survivor of the *Scharnhorst,* added: "After the last three, we suddenly developed a list. What a performance the engines put up!"[707] The two navy men noted with pride that their commanding officers had followed the course of the battle via radio. "The war has ended for us," noted a further survivor named Alsen with regret. "I should like to have been in it longer."[708]

Gaining medals that proved one's bravery at the front was even more important to staff officers and generals than to ordinary soldiers. The general chief of staff of the army, Franz Halder, was completely humiliated by Hitler in a heated argument on August 24, 1942. "What can you tell me about the troops," the Führer fumed, "as someone who was sitting in the same chair in World War I and yet who has failed to even earn the black insignia for being wounded in combat?"[709] Hitler was prodding the deepest wound in the egos of many of the Wehrmacht's top leaders: never having proved themselves in frontline combat.

Many of the top Wehrmacht generals had been staff officers in World War I and had thus never been wounded, and it was Hitler's will that that situation not be repeated in World War II. Proving one's mettle at the front was supposed to be part of everyone's career, even for staff officers. The idea that generals, too, should be prepared to fight personally was one consequence of this change in the military frame of reference. But not every general took the imperative as seriously as Walther von Reichenau, who swam half naked across the Weichsel River with his men during Germany's invasion of Poland and earned an assault badge as a field marshal in Russia.[710] Most generals focused on status symbols more in keeping with their class: the Knight's Cross and rapid promotion. Major General Hans Sattler, whose career had suffered a setback when his will to fight was questioned in 1941, turned up his nose at this attitude, carping: "An adjutant who was present there told me that he said: 'The worst people are the generals; if they are not promoted or given accelerated promotion and awarded the Knight's Cross, they are discontented.' What do you think of that, that's what SCHMIDT says."[711]

The weight carried by the most prestigious decorations among high-ranking officers is clearly evident in the conversations between the sixteen generals who were captured in Tunisia in May 1943. Colonel General Hans-Jürgen von Arnim, the last commander of the German-Italian troops in northern Africa, attracted pity from his colleagues because he had not even been given the Knight's Cross with Oak Leaves, while Rommel had been awarded the one with Diamonds.[712] The POWs in Trent Park also whispered of General Hans Cramer: "He had been recommended for it, but he didn't get it, and as a result he is furious that he didn't. He has made every possible effort to get it, and he'll get it yet."[713] When Lieutenant General Gotthart Franz received word in August 1943 that he was to be awarded the

Knight's Cross for his service in Tunisia, he fastened his Iron Cross First Class around his neck even before the International Red Cross delivered his new medal. Bursting with pride, he wrote home that he could now look his family in the eye again.[714] Not everyone in the POW camps was lucky enough to receive retrospective decorations. Lieutenant General Menny wrote in his diary, with a sigh, that he no longer had any chance of receiving the much coveted Oak Clusters. It was better if officers had already racked up all the medals they wanted before they were captured. General Bernhard Ramcke boasted to his fellow detainees that he had received the highest accolades for bravery in both World Wars I and II.

A high-ranking, frontline officer without a sufficient number of medals was sure to be eyed with suspicion by his peers. For this reason, shortly after his arrival in Trent Park, the fortress commander of Aachen, Colonel Gerhard Wilck, felt compelled to justify himself: "I was CO of a 'Regiment' in the east. I was in NORWAY for a long time, that's why I have relatively few decorations."[715]

There is also photographic evidence of the importance of decorations for feelings of personal pride. In November of 1943 and 1944, inmates posed for group photos that were then sent home as Christmas cards to their families. While some of them simply donned their uniforms, without any decorations, others preferred to appear in front of the camera wearing all their medals.

The Iron Cross was a permanent topic of discussion among POWs of all ranks. Everyone had a comrade or a relative who had received the Iron Cross, First or Second Class, and since soldiers were perennially oriented around others' achievements, this created social pressure. If a soldier had not been awarded the decoration, an explanation was required. The simplest sort of justification was that others had unfairly received the medal or that the person in question had performed just as well as his peers, but had been unjustly neglected. Endless discussions were held about the criteria by which the medals were awarded. As early as February 14, 1940, when World War II was barely six months old, Navy First Lieutenant Fritz Huttel complained:

> HUTTEL: In this war they're not handing out so many Iron Crosses as in the last. The U-boat officers especially are getting very few Iron Crosses. A U-boat commander has to make two raids and sink at least 60,000 tons before he gets the Iron Cross

The inmates at Trent Park, November 1944. Standing (left to right): General von Choltitz, Colonel Wilck, General Ramcke, Major General Eberding, Colonel Wildermuth; sitting (left to right): Lieutenant General von Heyking, Lieutenant General von Schlieben, Lieutenant General Daser. (BA 146–2005–0136)

1st Class. After the first raid we only got the U-Boat badge, whereas there are people on the outpost boats in the Baltic who have been given the Iron Cross. Those people have done nothing and know nothing about sailoring. We've had the hell of a time with U 55 for weeks and yet we don't get the Iron Cross. The dissatisfaction at the unjust distribution is great.[716]

Huttel's complaints were baseless. Submarine officers had the best chance of anyone at being decorated, and U-55 had been sunk on its maiden mission. The officers had had no chance to distinguish themselves. Nonetheless, Huttel felt the need to justify why he had not been decorated. Complaints of this sort were by no means restricted to the navy. Luftwaffe officers were also constantly griping. For example, in July 1940, after Germany's successful campaign against France, one Luftwaffe sergeant complained: "At ROTTERDAM all parachutists got E.K.2 and E.K.1, although they only fought for three days. I've been an aviator since the beginning of the war and have got nothing. An aviator who has no E.K. after the war will be looked down upon."[717]

Along with the never-ending criticism that the criteria for decoration were either too lax or too strict, recriminations abounded that medals were handed out on the basis of rank and not achievement. Common soldiers and low-ranking officers often felt their superiors were pulling strings to gain accolades. "I can surely put in for the E.K.1 after 33 Active Service flights," registered one low-ranking officer bitterly. "The officers get one after 3 flights and what do we get? We don't get one Iron Cross. We get shot in the spine (literally—the iron in the cross)."[718] Meanwhile high-ranking officers complained that they did not get enough recognition from Hitler because of his National Socialist worldview.[719] In their view, members of the Waffen SS were disproportionately decorated for political reasons. "The SS get their badges, not for what they've done, but for their political and moral attitude," griped navy lieutenant Günther Schramm.[720]

It is no doubt true that medals were sometimes handed out for political reasons alone, but those were exceptional cases. In general, there is no evidence for the frequent claim that members of the Waffen SS were more often decorated than others. "Abuse" was far more common within the Wehrmacht, where accolades were sometimes handed out for nonexistent achievements. For example, during Germany's campaign against Norway, the Luftwaffe awarded Knight's Crosses to five bomber pilots who had fictitiously claimed to have sunk enemy ships.[721] The veracity of airmen's often grotesquely exaggerated claims could have been easily checked against navy radio surveillance. But for obvious reasons, the Luftwaffe leadership did not want to diminish the air force's prestige in the interest of the truth.[722]

The German navy was equally prone to willful credulity when it came to kill reports by submarine commanders. Some officers were notorious for exaggerated tonnages sunk and still received medals. Part of common navy parlance was the expression "Schepke tonnage"— a reference to the fact that commander Joachim Schepke routinely overestimated the tonnage of the ships he had sunk. Rolf Thomsen was another commander whose reports were absurdly optimistic, and he received the Knight's Cross with Oak Leaves for his efforts. On two patrols, for example, he claimed to have sunk a destroyer, two corvettes, six freighters, and an escort carrier. There was only proof of one of these vessels having been truly sunk. Late in the war, when there were few triumphs to cheer, the navy leadership was eager to believe positive reports from their commanding officers.[723] Although no one could reconstruct whether or not Thomsen was intentionally lying, many people believed he was an empty boaster—a reputation that dogged him even as a navy officer after World War II for the Federal Republic of Germany.

Inflated reports by German navy men, however, paled in comparison to those of Enzo Grossi, an Italian submarine commander, who claimed to have sunk two American battleships in the southern Atlantic in 1942 and who was awarded the Gold Medal for Bravery by Mussolini and the Knight's Cross by Hitler. Nazi newsreels repeatedly featured the courageous commander peering bare-chested through his periscope.[724] After the war, it emerged that Grossi hadn't sunk any ships at all. Right-wing circles in Italy refused to accept this, spreading a conspiracy theory that the Americans had constructed replicas of the two battleships Grossi had destroyed in an attempt to cover up their losses. Grossi's medal for bravery was revoked posthumously.[725]

All in all, Wehrmacht soldiers accepted the system of incentives created by the political and military leadership with very little criticism and integrated it into their personal frames of reference. The surveillance protocols show that the lure of medals and other decorations was an excellent motivational tool. The only griping centered around whether specific accolades had indeed been awarded fairly and whether superior officers were applying award criteria consistently. Bearers of the Knight's Cross who put on too many airs were jokingly referred to as "tin collars,"[726] and there was minor criticism about the design of certain medals. "The Knight's Cross set with diamonds is a frightful thing," complained one Luftwaffe lieutenant. "You give diamonds to a woman but not to a fighter pilot."[727] The preponderance of decorations also came in for sarcasm. "It's only the Captains of the BERLIN river steamers who have no special decoration," scoffed one submarine officer in November 1940.[728] Jokes about Göring were particularly popular, especially after he became the sole recipient of the special "Grand Cross of the Iron Cross" in July 1940. On February 1, 1945, First Lieutenant Hartigs of Luftwaffe Fighter Wing 26 asked ironically: "Don't you know the 'mammoth cross'? At the end of this war, in which we shall be victorious, GÖRING is going to get the Mammoth Cross of the Grand Cross with Diamonds on an S.P. mounting."[729]

ITALIANS AND JAPANESE

Wehrmacht soldiers may have differed from one another in a number of respects, but their basic frame of reference remained quite consistent. It is only when we begin to make international comparisons that we discover major differences in this regard. The central point of reference for Italian soldiers, for instance, was neither the nation nor the state nor indeed the military itself. Italian fascism pushed corruption and nepotism to the extreme. Italian historian Amedeo Osti Guerrazzi writes: "Other countries—for example England or Germany, closed ranks in an hour of great peril and rallied around institutions, performing a feat of utmost resistance on behalf of a cause they saw as crucial to the welfare of the entire collective. By contrast, in Italy, the social network completely collapsed, as in times of extreme crisis, the attitude became 'every man for himself.' "[730]

Italian soldiers never succeeded in finding any great sense of purpose in doing battle. They lacked not only a positive self-image, but also military triumphs and an officer corps that could communicate values such as bravery, devotion to duty, and steely resilience. The officer corps was seen as an incompetent, cowardly clique, whose members had attained their posts through nepotism, not merit. Italian officers were only enthusiastic about war, the prevailing view held, as long as they themselves didn't have to fight. Their main motivation, if we believe a conversation between two Italian POWs in the British camp Wilton Park, was personal enrichment:

> FICALLA: The officers were a gang of thieves, you had to protect the men against them grimly; from colonels downwards; after a bombardment of MARSALA, the whole of one of my artillery N.O. pushed off in lorries to loot the town, and I reported that. Apart from those who did it on a big scale, even the junior officers, the lieutenants and second lieutenants used to do it; when the meat ration for the troops arrived, they would pinch whole beefsteaks which they ate in their quarters or sent home as presents etc.—I heard all sorts of stories about that. And then there was the soap—they used to take ten cakes home when they went on leave, and sugar too etc.
>
> SALZA: I was told that by the Americans and the English, and some of our men told us about it too.

> FICALLA: The men all know about it too, but no divisional com-
> mander. I couldn't punish every case because there were so
> many things one never saw. When that is the sort of atmo-
> sphere prevailing, it doesn't make any difference if the troops
> are good, as our men are on the whole.[731]

Appeals to the bravery of common Italian soldiers were cheap and
likely fell on deaf ears. Italian POWs recorded in the surveillance protocols repeatedly state that the officers were the first to flee when the
going got rough.[732] Admiral Priamo Leonardi, the commander of the
fortifications at Augusta, opined: "If people see that the whole H.Q.
staff pushes off somewhere else they say: 'Why should we stay here?
Are we really such fools? Let's all push off.' "[733] Leonardi himself
doesn't seem to have been particularly concerned about defending
Augusta, admitting that he had considered slinking away disguised as
a civilian. "In the end," he reasoned, "if everyone else marches off,
there's no reason the admiral shouldn't flee as well."[734]

Some German generals may have thought and behaved in similar
fashion. Major General Sattler, for instance, had tried to flee the fortifications at Cherbourg in a speedboat in 1944, and when his escape
failed, he immediately capitulated. Still, it would have been unimaginable for him to confess his lack of heroism to his fellow POWs. Members of the Wehrmacht and in particular high-ranking officers always
tried to depict themselves as professional, upstanding soldiers. No one
would have dared raise questions, as Leonardi voluntarily did, about
the core of every true soldier's self-image, his own bravery.

The conversations of lower-ranking Italian POWs, too, show how
much their perception of the war differed from that of their German
allies. Planes shot down, ships sunk, and decorations won play no significant role in their discussions, and the same is true for concepts like
honor, bravery, and the "fatherland."[735] Italian POWs focused on the
hair-raising deficiencies that became apparent with every major military engagement. For instance, in March 1943, a lieutenant colonel
captured in Tunisia related: "Our army has become a mere gang of
adventurers. They should all be brought to trial, at least from a military stand-point. And I should be in with [Italian supreme commander
in North Africa] General BATISTICO himself. I wish an inquiry could
be opened into all their doings in AFRICA: how they behaved in various circumstances; it was disgraceful! Nearly everybody in the army

will tell the same sad story of corruption and disorganization. It would almost be better if we had the English or the Russians in ITALY."[736]

The Italian military leadership and the Italian state were perceived as being so corrupt and incompetent that they, and not the Allies, were sometimes considered the true enemies. From the point of view of ordinary Italian soldiers, only a "fesso" (idiot) would sacrifice himself for a system that did not represent one's own interests in the slightest.[737]

The only Italian soldiers who told stories of a type comparable to those of Wehrmacht soldiers were members of the special forces.[738] Paratroopers, fighter pilots, and submarine crewmen did tend to talk about their own achievements, their weaponry, and the challenges they had to overcome to fulfill their missions. It was important for them to be seen as good soldiers, corruption and incompetence notwithstanding, and they often spoke of ideals such as bravery and devotion to duty. In this vein, a U-boat officer of the watch remarked in 1941: "One must win the war, and do one's part even if one is anti-fascist."[739] In April 1942, in a conversation between two Italian pilots, one did invoke instances of heroism in battle: "We scored a direct hit and when we came back on the scene there was no more cruiser to be seen. So many of our people wanted to change their jobs because torpedo-carrying aircraft are so dangerous. This last time we were to be in the air for six hours. We were to do BEYROUTH, PORT SAID, ALEXANDRIA. CAIRO. Our pilots are very young, but amazingly brave. They throw themselves on their targets. We did four torpedoes at RHODES. Do you know Captain BUSSATI? He was a torpedo aircraft ace."[740]

Members of these units often made the impression of being the most committed fascists. On August 31, 1943, after running through the list of their own achievements, two submarine captains discussed the general situation: "Had we had four or five divisions of young Fascists like those who fought in AFRICA, those English Gentlemen could never have landed! Just look—in AFRICA fourteen tanks with crews of young Fascists went out to fight a hundred and forty English tanks, and I can well believe it!"[741]

Bravery seems to have been an important point of reference for committed fascists. Nonetheless, in contrast to their German counterparts, they refused to fight to the bitter end when all seemed lost. For them, World War II was effectively decided when the Allies captured

Sicily. The only choice was to sue for peace. The vast majority echoed the sentiments of Italian commander and short-lived prime minister of fascist Italy Pietro Badoglio: " 'We must end the war with honour.' He is an old soldier, and he will never accept unconditional surrender."[742] In fact, Italy never capitulated unconditionally, but negotiated an armistice with the Allies. The two submarine captains were probably not all that proud of the chaotic end to Italy's participation in World War II, which saw the Italian king and Badoglio fleeing. What's important, however, is that Italian POWs had no stake in any apocalyptic scenarios about fighting down to the last bullet or drop of blood.

Yet despite all the differences, we should not overlook a certain amount of common ground in the values of German and Italian soldiers. Italian soldiers were noticeably impressed by the superior fighting ability of their German allies, who were otherwise not very well liked.[743] With reference to the conquest of Crete, one Italian navy man remarked: "It's phenomenal! The Germans are the only ones who fight through to the end; even if they are cut to pieces they go on until they have smashed through. Neither we Italians, nor the Japanese, and still less the English, can do it."[744]

The soldier quoted here could only arrive at this sort of conclusion if he valued bravery and persistence in battle as well as military success. Moreover, conversations about the shameful conditions in their own army, including cowardice among their commanders and corruption, suggest that many Italian soldiers regarded such deficiencies as deviations from what should have been the military norm.[745] When Italian soldiers were well equipped and competently led, they also showed signs of being willing to fight bravely.

Nonetheless, men like Field Marshal Giovanni Messe had no desire for camaraderie with German detainees in his British POW camp. On the contrary, he maintained that Italians were completely incompatible with their German allies. In so doing, he arrived at a flattering explanation for Italian military failings: "They [the Germans] haven't got [a soul]. We are generous, and in reality we are incapable of hatred. Our mentality is like that, that is why I have always maintained that we are not a warlike people. A warlike people knows how to hate."[746]

By any standards, the Japanese were more soldierly and oriented toward traditional military virtues than the Italians. The most important Japanese military codes of behavior—the Gunjin Chokuyu, Senjinkun, and Bushido—formed a unique frame of reference that required soldiers to demonstrate loyalty, bravery, daring, and, above all, absolute obedience. Retreat was forbidden, and soldiers were never supposed to surrender. These values were also effective in practice because they were based on the deeply rooted conviction in Japanese society that any sort of imprisonment was dishonorable. Being taken captive brought shame not only on oneself, but one's family as well. For this reason, countless Japanese soldiers preferred to commit suicide rather than fall into enemy hands. As an American GI wrote from New Guinea in 1944, the Japanese ethos was to achieve victory or die trying, so that Japanese troops were incapable of giving up or allowing themselves to be taken prisoner.[747] In the years up until March 1945, American troops succeeded in capturing only around 12,000 Japanese POWs—a tiny number compared to the millions of soldiers in European internment camps.[748]

Such facts alone hardly provide a differentiated picture of Japanese soldiers' frame of reference. Interrogation protocols and war diaries show that Japanese soldiers' will to survive was in fact sometimes more powerful than their sense of cultural duty. In addition, the American practice of not taking Japanese POWs meant that fear of being killed or tortured by the Americans created a fear of capitulation. The shame of capitulation alone, according to historian Hirofumi Hayashi, would not have prevented Japanese soldiers from laying down their arms, had they not been convinced they would have been killed or tortured if they did so.[749] Even in the relatively early phase of the war, fall and winter 1942, the Battle of Guadalcanal had shown that the Japanese weren't always willing to charge to their deaths, weapons drawn. Mostly, situational factors were what prevented Japanese soldiers from capitulating.

Moreover, interrogations of POWs in Burma suggested that behind their facade of discipline and obedience, Japanese soldiers thought about the same sorts of issues as their German allies at the time. Among the major points of reflection were the rapidly worsening course of the war in 1944 and '45, the diminishing respect enjoyed by the military leadership, insufficient supplies, and the disappointing performance of the Japanese air force. Other parallels were the tendency of Japanese soldiers to be apolitical and the comparatively high morale and confidence in the navy versus the army. As was the case with the Wehrmacht, this may have been down to the fact that navy men experienced a different sort of war than ground troops.

A comparison between German, Italian, and Japanese soldiers shows that cultural factors had significant influence on their respective frames of reference. What from the Japanese perspective was a model soldier was an idiot for Italians and a partly admired, partly despised fanatic for Germans.

THE WAFFEN SS

This book focuses on the soldiers of the Wehrmacht, but we shouldn't forget that the Nazi Party had an army of its own, the Waffen SS, of which there were some 900,000 members over the course of the war.[750] One interesting question is to what extent the perception and interpretations of Waffen SS fighters differed from those of regular soldiers. Himmler was always at pains to stress the special character of his men. Nonetheless, it's impossible to overlook the fact that shared experiences of frontline fighting created tighter and tighter personal relationships and tended to erase differences. By November 1944, an SS Brigadeführer in a tank division, Kurt Meyer, would state: "I don't believe that there is any difference at all today between the SS and the army."[751] How much truth was there to this statement? Did the war truly override Himmler's best efforts at forming an elite National Socialist troop that not only wore different uniforms than the regular army, but also had a different mind-set?

At the Nuremberg War Crimes Trials, prosecutors had no doubts as to the special status of the Waffen SS, declaring it a criminal organization. Prominent SS generals like Paul Hausser, Wilhelm Bittrich, and Meyer vehemently protested against this ruling, which had far-reaching consequences for their own fates. In contrast to regular army servicemen, former Waffen SS men were denied pensions, and a number of avenues for advancement in postwar society and the military were closed off to them. An advocacy group founded in 1949 named the Mutual Assistance Association of Former Members of the Waffen SS (HIAG) spared little effort in trying to show that SS men had been "soldiers like all others." (A former SS general published a book with this title in 1966.) This argument fell flat because even in the immediate postwar years it was well known that the Waffen SS had committed a multitude of war crimes and had remained an integral part of the SS, whose role was not limited to doing battle on the front lines. Moreover, the Waffen SS was an excellent scapegoat for absorbing blame for crimes against humanity, in particular ones associated with the Holocaust, so that the Wehrmacht itself could be exonerated. We have now known for some years, of course, that the Waffen SS was not the sole perpetrator of war crimes. Considering that historical research, especially in the past ten years, has cast considerable blame on the Wehrmacht, the question has become even more pertinent: Was there any difference between the two entities?[752] Was the Wehrmacht perhaps not every bit as fanatical, radical, and criminal as the Waffen SS? Was the postwar debate perhaps not just part of a carefully staged diversion intended to create a myth of the "clean" Wehrmacht? Were the Waffen SS and the Wehrmacht not both components of one and the same fighting community, in which differences in mentality were quickly smoothed over by the common experience of battle?

RIVALRIES

In summer 1934, then commander in chief of the German military Werner von Blomberg accepted the creation of SS military units as a way of repaying Hitler for emasculating a dangerous Wehrmacht rival, the SA. Initially, Waffen SS men were few in number and had little military significance. With the beginning of World War II, however, they unmistakably began to compete with the Wehrmacht. The relationship of the two organizations at that point was especially tense. Regular army men, officers as well as ordinary soldiers, looked down their noses at the newly formed fighting troop. A conversation from July 1940 between an army sergeant and an SS Rottenführer illustrates the subjective feelings of competition experienced by men serving in the two organizations:

> SERGEANT: It was the same in POLAND. Many of the S.S. were
> stood against the wall for disobedience by the army command-
> ers. And the "Germania" regiment was a complete failure. The
> "Germania" made the most terrible mess of things.
> SS ROTTENFÜHRER: Well, an army officer told me that the S.S.
> were the best infantry regiments in Germany. And it was an
> officer (who said it)!
> SERGEANT: Well, with us they said exactly the opposite. They

said that the officers were no good at all and were the biggest fatheads!

SS ROTTENFÜHRER: Yes, don't I just know those young 'Wehrmacht' subalterns, who've bought their position—the contemptible rats!

SERGEANT: Balderdash! Certainly, if everything that happened in POLAND became known in the Army, there might be an awful row.

SS ROTTENFÜHRER: Well, if I find an officer telling such tales, he won't live long.

SERGEANT: The scraps between the "S.S." and the "Wehrmacht" will never end!

SS ROTTENFÜHRER: What happened in POLAND? One mustn't talk about the casualties. But I can at least tell you that our "S.S." formations had heavy losses! And the Army left us in the lurch! It was lamentable! At any rate the "S.S." will never again be subordinate to the Army, that is clear! To give some decrepit old general the right of doing whatever he likes with an "S.S." regiment! They gave us the dirtiest work . . . . (interrupted).

SERGEANT: Well, I suppose you're not trying to insinuate that the other infantry regiments had no losses? They lost just as heavily as the "S.S."—[you] can take that from me! Well, anyway on the Western front the "S.S." did nothing decisive.

SS ROTTENFÜHRER (shouting): You don't know anything!

SERGEANT (also shouting): Oh, but I do! Every child knows that!

SS ROTTENFÜHRER: You don't know it. The "S.S." fought just as bravely (interrupted) . . . . . .

SERGEANT: But it did nothing decisive.

SS ROTTENFÜHRER (quite excited): Of course, of course, only the Army . . . . . but you seem to forget who commands in GERMANY to-day—the Army or the Party. You've seen what happens to the Army bosses—people like BLOMBERG etc. . . . and FRITSCH, if they aren't willing to pull their weight.

SERGEANT (annoyed): Well, you seem to think that the party and the "S.S." rule GERMANY and the Army has to play second fiddle! That is where you are entirely wrong! You think the "S.S." can do whatever it likes! But in BELGIUM it was in a hole, so they sent for us.

SS ROTTENFÜHRER: We were not in a hole at all. Ask anybody

as to what the "S.S." did at DUNKIRK and on the SCHELT. You can't imagine it!

SERGEANT: Well, at any rate the Army is still the decisive factor.

SS ROTTENFÜHRER: And, without us, it would be wiped out.

SERGEANT: Well then, we must abolish the Army and only have "S.S." units. My height is 1.72 (m), perhaps they'll take me!

SS ROTTENFÜHRER: Well, the "S.S." regiments, "Deutschland," "Germania" and "Adolf Hitler" are certainly the best infantry regiments in GERMANY.[753]

The exchange is full of stereotypes on both sides. The SS man's reference to "subalterns" who purchased their positions and "decrepit old general" reflected a distorted version of the Wehrmacht as the direct descendant of the old Imperial Army. The army man's accusations of the SS's inflated self-image and "fathead" officers revived the classic Wehrmacht objection that Nazi soldiers were unprofessional. Significantly, both speakers use the same criteria for evaluating military achievement. The main factor is bravery, which itself is measured in numbers of casualties. The army sergeant counters the argument that the SS troops suffered heavy losses with the statement that Wehrmacht regiments had incurred just as many casualties elsewhere. For the sergeant, that was proof of equivalent courage. Both men also claim that their organization is a central pillar of the German state. The SS man explicitly defines the Waffen SS as a part of the party that rules the country, while the army sergeant sees the Wehrmacht as a power of its own within German society.

The Wehrmacht was extremely critical of the Waffen SS's military performance in both the Poland and France campaigns. But modest fighting efficiency was by no means a problem unique to the SS. It tended to affect all of the army divisions formed at the start of the war as well. Many of these divisions "failed," as General Erich von Manstein wrote.[754] At the same time, the lack of professionalism among SS ranks was perfect fodder for Wehrmacht criticism. Over time, as the Waffen SS did indeed become more professional, the rivalry cooled off. Increasingly, Wehrmacht soldiers came to appreciate the merits of the Waffen SS as an elite troop. Nonetheless, the bickering never ceased entirely, and in official correspondence the two sides constantly accused each other of irregularities. The Wehrmacht, for instance, repeatedly complained that Waffen SS soldiers were insufficiently trained, while SS men reproached the Wehrmacht for allegedly having lukewarm morale.[755]

Although heavy losses and the massive expansion of the Waffen SS changed the force's structure, basic differences in *social* structure persisted between it and the Wehrmacht.[756] Wehrmacht soldiers perceived SS men as "others," and that impression was reinforced by their appearance. The tattoos of blood groups on their forearms and camouflage uniforms with SS runes carried a symbolic significance that should not be underestimated. Initially mocked as "SS tree frogs," SS men were immediately recognizable and as such distinguishable from regular army soldiers. Their difference, impossible not to register, spurred on the rivalry between the two military organizations, and their competition for attention and recognition never ceased entirely. General Crüwell, for instance, was outraged that an SS division had received the honorary name "Prince Eugen," after the Austrian general who conquered Belgrade in 1717, although his men had conquered the Serbian capital and felt his division had earned the appellation. Wehrmacht soldiers also complained that medals were handed out far more liberally within SS divisions. "Supposing, we'll say, an infantry division got twenty Iron Crosses, Class 1 for some affair or other, then the S.S. undoubtedly got forty," Crüwell groused.[757] "They are treated quite differently." Another thing that rankled the Wehrmacht was the speed with which "morbidly ambitious" SS men were promoted.[758] In particular, the meteoric career of Kurt Meyer, who was made a division commander with the rank of major general at the age of thirty-four, occasioned considerable resentment. In addition, the Waffen SS received better equipment and vehicles[759] and rations.[760] Wehrmacht officers also viewed with envy the fine "human material" made available to SS divisions. "Even in 1943 the army only got old crocks from home," complained Major General Christoph von Stolberg-Stolberg. "The SS got, first of all, their volunteers, then secondly they got 4% of the best recruits, and then as well as that they take all the people away from the schools. That's to say, the SS was blessed with nearly 100% officer cadets, and the army had none at all."[761]

But SS divisions were not the only ones who were generously decorated, well equipped, and regularly replenished with select young personnel. Elite units within the Wehrmacht also enjoyed such privileges. One good example is the armored grenadier division "Greater Germany," which the Wehrmacht leadership purposely built up as an army "praetorian guard" to complete with the Waffen SS.[762] There were also

Two Waffen SS soldiers in camouflage uniform, date unknown.
(Photographer: Weyer; BA 10 III Weyer-032-2BA)

a number of elite units within the Luftwaffe as well as paratroopers
and the armored division "Hermann Göring." All enjoyed special status. Members of these groups were also perceived as "others," thanks
to their special uniforms and helmets and the favoritism many claimed
was shown to them when decorations were handed out.[763] Their arro-
gant behavior also engendered resentment. "The famous or infamous
Hermann Göring Division," Colonel Hans Reimann complained
while speaking of his time in Tunisia, "was there, a lot of swine, nothing but puffed up—the officers were so loud-mouthed that young pup-
pies and the older ones as well, they were so loud-mouthed that you
simply didn't know what sort of people they were; at the first attack
they were scattered and ran away so fast from the tanks that we had
to stop them!"[764]

BRAVERY AND FANATICISM

Applying great effort and skill, Nazi propagandists promoted the
image of the Waffen SS as a "fanatic" fighting troop with an incred-

A group of German soldiers in Normandy in summer 1944.
Their helmets and uniforms distinguish them as paratroopers.
(Photographer: Slickers; BA 101 I-586-2225-16)

ible "capacity for sacrifice," and these categories crop up regularly in
the surveillance protocols. Wehrmacht soldiers generally agreed that
SS troops were "bullish" extremists, heedless even of death, marching
forward into the crossfire to the strains of "Deutschland über alles"
and suffering "terrible," "insane," and "senseless" losses.[765] "One regiment, the Standarte Germania, had 2500 men killed in three months,"
reported a horrified Luftwaffe sergeant.[766]

Most of the generals interned at Trent Park had fought on the Eastern Front in 1941 and '42, which is where they first encountered the
Waffen SS. They, too, told of senseless sacrifices among SS units:

> UNKNOWN: I will just tell you about one scene which I myself wit-
> nessed with my own eyes—otherwise I shouldn't speak about
> it. That was during the winter fighting, when four Russian
> divisions, a Guards cavalry division, two Guards infantry divi-
> sions and one other division, broke through the neighbouring
> division on my left wing. I now formed a defensive flank. My
> front was like this, and the defensive flank projected like this,
> it formed an acute angle—ridiculous. I was right in the centre
> at a distance of 4 km. with my battle headquarters, at a dis-
> tance of 2 km. from both fronts. In order to form the defensive

flank, I got as a second unit an S.S. battalion, that is, it wasn't much more than a glorified company. The company consisted of about a hundred and seventy-five men, a few heavy machine guns and two mortars. There was one Hauptsturmführer von BENDEN, a grand fellow who had also been in the World War. These fellows had been acting as a protective division in the rear and had engaged guerrillas. They were then withdrawn and sent up to the front. I gave them orders to take the village of VOLCHANKA (?). As they hadn't any heavy weapons, I gave them two light machine guns and three anti-tank guns, which I also immediately withdrew. The attack was begun. I couldn't believe my eyes, how quickly the attack proceeded, it developed splendidly, we advanced against the village and met with fire. Suddenly BENDEN stood up in his car and drove up to the head of his battalion and the battalion fell in and marched on in step against the village.

BÜLOWIUS: . . . . complete madness.

UNKNOWN: They had nine officers. Out of these nine, seven were killed or wounded. Out of a hundred and seventy infantrymen, about eighty were lost. They took (?) the village . . . . . Afterwards they held the village with eighty men for a whole week, or rather they had to leave it once and got back again. In the end they had twenty-five men left. Yes, it was an absolute scandal. I gave him a troop of quick-firing (?) guns, he didn't fire a round, not a single round. (I said), "You must fire, von BENDEN." — "Nonsense, we can take it this way too." Utter madness.[767]

Most listeners reacted to tales like this in the same way as Lieutenant General Karl Bülowius did, by declaring SS behavior completely senseless.

The truth of such narratives was never doubted. Everyone accepted them as plausible. But SS units weren't the only ones who were imagined to have incurred horrendous and senseless losses. Upon hearing such a story from SS Hauptsturmführer Benden, Major General Fritz Krause remembers one of his own:

KRAUSE: But I have had the experience with G.A.F. units . . . . from both battalions, the only two which then

existed, they were G.A.F. field divisions. They arrived somewhere there at five in the morning after a 16 km. night march
through snow and ice. Then they took the infantry—at that time
it was the Korps KNOBELSDORF—and sent it to the left wing
of an assault group which was being formed. The attack commenced at five o'clock straight from the column of march, they
didn't even have time to take their greatcoats off. They went
off to the attack without any anti-tank guns or machine guns,
nothing at all. They set off and advanced about 1½ to 2 km.,
suffering only a few losses. A Russian tank attack developed
and mowed the people down. And from those two battalions
there were 480 killed, of which quite 300 had been squashed
as flat as this book by the tanks. And countless wounded. Both
battalions annihilated.[768]

Many soldiers had tales of hair-raising operations that had cost hundreds of men their lives. Typically, though, heavy losses among Wehrmacht units were explained with reference to inexperience among the
field commanders or the troops themselves, while losses among the
SS were the result of "utterly misconceived recklessness."[769] Interestingly, the protocols don't contain any stories about Waffen SS units
who suffered particularly light casualties. Although many soldiers, in
particular navy and Luftwaffe men, never had anything at all to do
with the Waffen SS, they believed in the intimidating images of their
rivals as elite hotshots, who had been specially selected and trained,
and who had no fear whatsoever of being killed.[770]

At first glance, Himmler's soldiers seem to have fulfilled his
demands for the ultimate sacrifice. Himmler had decreed in 1941 that
there should be no such thing as a "captive SS man." They were the
"keepers of honor, the keepers of the fighting power of the division.
They have a duty to draw their pistol on a comrade, if necessary, and
force him to overcome his fear even in the face of giant onrushing
tank. It may happen that a regiment or battalion shrinks to a fourth or
a fifth of its original size. But it is beyond the realm of possibility that
this fourth or fifth finds itself unable or unwilling to keep attacking. . . .
As long as there are 500 men in a division, those 500 men are capable
of attacking."[771] In 1944 Himmler called for an attitude similar to that
of Japanese soldiers, among whom only 500 POWs from a force of
300,000 had been captured.[772]

The voices of SS men in the surveillance protocols initially seem to confirm Wehrmacht soldiers' view of them as unswerving fanatics. Members of the Waffen SS related how their superiors drove them forward at gunpoint or summarily executed Wehrmacht soldiers who tried to retreat.[773] When the commander of the SS division "Hitler Youth," Kurt Meyer, encountered a demoralized Wehrmacht general in Trent Park, he boasted: "I wish a lot of the officers here could command my 'Division,' so that they might learn some inkling of self-sacrifice and fanaticism. They would be deeply and profoundly ashamed."[774] Meyer's radicalism had already shocked Wehrmacht officers at a training seminar in fall 1943. One of the participants remembers him declaring, after a third glass of wine, that "the soldier must become a heathen, fanatic fighter who hates every Frenchman, Englishman and American (or whatever nationality the enemy has) so that he wants to jump at the enemy's throat and drink his blood. The soldier has to hate every [enemy], every one must be his mortal foe. Only so can we win the war."[775]

For Standartenführer Hans Lingner, who joined the SS early on and fought on the Eastern Front and in Normandy, the will to fight was inherently linked with the greater meaning of sacrifice. Lingner told a fellow POW, a regular army captain:

> LINGNER: We have all been brought up from the cradle to consider LEONIDAS' fight at THERMOPYLAE as the highest form of sacrifice for one's people. Everything else follows from that, and if the whole German nation has become a nation of soldiers, then it is compelled to perish; because by thinking as a human being and saying "It is all up with our people now, there's no point in it, it's nonsense," do you really believe that you will save the sacrifice of an appreciable number of lives? Do you think it will alter the peace terms? Surely not. On the other hand it is established that a nation which has not fought out such a fateful struggle right to the last has never risen again as a nation.[776]

Hitler and Himmler would have used pretty much identical formulations. Lingner's and Meyer's attitudes are in many respects typical for the perspective of the Waffen SS as a whole. It was no accident, for instance, that two regular army POWs in February 1945 expressed their belief that the SS would battle to the last and withdraw to the Alps to fight "a kind of partisan war."[777]

Nonetheless, historian Rüdiger Overmans has shown that the percentage of Waffen SS who fell in battle was not significantly higher than that in the regular army.[778] Indeed, when we take a closer look at the numbers, SS casualty figures are nearly identical to those for Wehrmacht tank divisions or Luftwaffe paratroopers. As long as the front remained intact, there seems to have been little difference in behavior between various elite units. So why did Wehrmacht soldiers perceive the Waffen SS as a fanatic fighting force that had suffered disproportionate casualties?

If we analyze reports of losses, it emerges that in phases of German retreat and defeats, such as in France in August 1944, significantly fewer Waffen SS soldiers were taken as prisoners of war than members of regular army or Luftwaffe units. The fact that the Allies tended to simply execute SS men does not fully explain this phenomenon.[779] Apparently members of certain SS units did more often prefer to fight to the death rather than try to save themselves by capitulating.[780] This was only a *tendency,* and not an absolute rule—otherwise, the percentage of fatalities among the Waffen SS would have been markedly greater than within the regular army. Still, the tendency did partially confirm the image of the fearless SS warriors from Nazi propaganda and established it, in simplified form, in Wehrmacht soldiers' frame of reference. Yet ironically, regular soldiers' fixation upon the putatively high losses among the Waffen SS allowed them to question the SS units' supposed bravery. While regular army men did not doubt the daring of SS troops, normally a positive quality in their system of values, they also believed that the SS provoked "unnecessarily" large numbers of casualties. In this way, regular army POWs could avoid taking a purely positive view of SS soldiers. There were battles, of course, in which SS troops had achieved successful results without inordinate numbers of casualties,[781] but stories of this sort did not fit in with the predominant Wehrmacht narrative and were thus left untold.

Some of those whose views were recorded in the protocols do reveal a more differentiated picture of the Waffen SS, including doubts as to whether they truly were more willing to fight to the death. General Cramer recalled the mood among three units of the Waffen SS during the defense of Charchow Ksiezy in Poland in February 1943: "They are just as fed up. They were more or less compelled, too, they didn't . . . at all of their own free will. They took part in all the dirty work and they are just as fed up as we are."[782] Whether or not this was a fair assessment of the three newly deployed regiments, "Leibstandarte Adolf Hitler," "The Reich," and "Death's Head," is an open question. The point is that there was more to the Waffen SS than fanaticism and willingness to sacrifice, as is evidenced by the decision by these three units to defy a command by Hitler and withdraw from the Polish town. One of the units also attracted the ire of General Erhard Raus six months later for operating "listlessly." Raus even tried, unsuccessfully, to get the division leader, SS Brigadeführer Heinz Krüger, stripped of his command.[783]

Further reports from other battles also suggest that Waffen SS men were not invariably prepared to make the ultimate sacrifice. General Heinrich Eberbach opined that the "Leibstandarte Adolf Hitler" regiment in Normandy fought "worse than ever before."[784] That estimation is supported by Allied sources and by the relatively small number of decorations handed out.[785]

Interestingly, one of the few POWs who admitted to desertion in the British protocols was an SS man named Reichheld from the division "Frundsberg."[786] Moreover, a statement by SS Obersturmführer Otto Woelcky from the "Leibstandarte Adolf Hitler" division reveals a striking lack of fanaticism from an officer who joined the SS early on. In September 1944, Woelcky's unit was ordered to help defend the West Wall of the Siegfried Line between Germany and France. In a village behind the line of bunkers, he was quartered at the house of a woman who asked him a question:

WOELCKY: "Tell me, what are you actually going to do here?" I told her: "We are going to man the West Wall here." So she said: "Man the West Wall? Is a stand going to be made here?" I said: "Of course a stand is going to be made here." I said: "At last we've got somewhere where we can establish ourselves a bit, where we can form a front." Then she said: "That's hellish. We were all so glad, because we thought that the Americans would advance quickly and that we should get it over at last, and now you came here, and there will be fighting here, and all we have will be smashed up again! What are we to do, where are we to go? Everything we have will be shot to bits!" Of course at first I was just flabbergasted. I said: "Now listen to me, you can go

away from here; in fact you'll have to." I said: "Things will get
pretty uncomfortable anyhow. You are 2 km. to the rear of the
'Bunker' here, and that means you'll have to count on shelling
or bombing every day." So she said: "Well, where are we to
go? We have no means of moving all our belongings." I said:
"Of course you can't take all your worldly goods, that would be
impossible." Well, I could understand that attitude about the
evacuation. But then she started: "We have been lied to, and
cheated for five years, and promised a golden future, and what
have we got? Now war has come upon us again, and I just can't
understand how there can be one German soldier left who will
fire another shot" and so on. I picked up my brief-case, put it
under my arm, and went out of the house. Actually I should
have taken some action against the woman, but I could well
understand her feelings.[787]

We have no way of knowing whether Woelcky's tale was true or not.
But the fact that he was taken prisoner a few days later near the village of Prüm in western Germany speaks for its veracity. Apparently,
Woelcky felt little desire to fight "to the last gasp of breath." Woelcky
had joined Hitler's praetorian guard in 1933. But by the final year of
war, he divorced himself from the SS frame of reference, showing
understanding for the war fatigue of a civilian and refusing to take
action against her defeatism.

The surveillance protocols reveal that SS men maintained surprisingly heterogeneous views of the war. At the same time, there was
an unmistakable *tendency* toward radicalism, which we will discuss
shortly.

Another common explanation for heavy casualties among the
Waffen SS, in addition to their fanatic readiness for sacrifice, was their
lack of professionalism. There are numerous complaints about this in
official Wehrmacht files.[788] It is difficult today to evaluate whether they
had any real basis, but their frequency suggests that they weren't completely spurious. The Waffen SS, however, wasn't the only target. Official Wehrmacht correspondence is full of griping about often absurd
forms of alleged misbehavior by the army and the Luftwaffe as well.
Moreover, there were countless instances in which Wehrmacht members praised the achievements of the Waffen SS. Sergeant Grüchtel,
who piloted transport aircraft to and from Stalingrad, reported about

the collapse of the southern wing of the Eastern Front in the winter of 1942–43: "We were all convinced in January and February that things would go badly in RUSSIA. The Russians were hot on our heels. We had already packed our bags in SABROSHI (?), the Russians were 6 k. from the airfield, half of the UKRAINE had already been lost. Then on the 19th (?) February ADOLF arrived in person. From then on things went well. Then the S.S. Leibstandarte arrived. I didn't think much of them till then, but the fellows set about it damned well."[789]

With reference to the battles in Normandy in summer 1944, a primary group leader from the Organisation Todt, the Third Reich's corps of engineers, opined:

> VETTER: Without belittling the army, and with the exception of some of the elite regiments in the army, it's an actual fact that the only troops with any real dash nowadays are the paratroopers and the SS.[790]

The Allies more or less confirmed these assessments, writing with "respect" of the SS division "Hitler Youth."[791] And the veteran armored division commander General Heinrich Eberbach also regarded the SS group as "excellent" and "illustrious."[792]

All in all, in terms of fighting morale and professionalism, the Waffen SS was a heterogeneous institution, as was the case for all other branches of the military. Its military achievements, even in the narrow sense, can by no means be reduced to the cliché "fanatic but unprofessional." The Waffen SS fought in much the same way as other elite units. An occasionally greater willingness to follow orders to the letter and fight to the death is the lone, if significant, difference between SS men and regular soldiers.

CRIMES

Wehrmacht soldiers defined the difference between themselves and the Waffen SS not only in terms of defiance of death, but brutality as well. It is somewhat surprising how widespread this view was among army, navy, and Luftwaffe men.

"The difference between Waffen S.S. and other troops is that they are rather more brutal and that they never take prisoners," said one

Luftwaffe gunner in January 1943.[793] A war correspondent agreed that this was the standard procedure: "The S.A. troops, the 'ADOLF HITLER' bodyguard and the 'Death's Head' 'Standarte' never take prisoners, they shoot them."[794] A navy radio operator offered a moral assessment: "In POLAND it was all right for them to kill captured Poles, because the Poles had killed and burnt captured German airmen, but I think it's wrong that the S.A. troops should have killed innocent French prisoners."[795] The moral standard here was clear. There was nothing wrong with shooting captured soldiers in reprisal, but it was unjust to kill innocent civilians. It is unclear where this radio operator, who fell into British hands after U-99 sank on March 7, 1941, got his information. It could well have been secondhand, which would be an indication how early the Waffen SS accrued its ambiguous reputation.

News of war crimes committed by the Waffen SS in France apparently spread like wildfire. A Luftwaffe reconnaissance specialist told of a friend who was in the SS "Death's Head" Division:

He once told me that in the campaign in the West they took no coloured prisoners whatever. They simply put up a machine-gun and mowed them all down. Perhaps those are the men who are now bringing the German soldier into disrepute. On the Western front, he said, they were really feared. The French didn't realize that a difference was made between French and coloured troops, so that whenever the French caught sight of those "Death's Head" units, they bolted before them in holy terror.[796]

The SS man appears to have boasted about his unit's misdeeds in order to underscore the Waffen SS's feared reputation, and the "Death's Head" Division was the unit that committed the greatest number of war crimes during the campaign against France. Among them were the murder of 121 British POWs near Le Paradis as well as several mass executions of non-Caucasian soldiers from the British colonies. It was apparently standard practice in this division not to take any black prisoners.[797]

Wehrmacht POWs agreed that the Waffen SS had acted no differently in Russia. On the contrary, reports of SS crimes against civilians and POWs there were even more frequent:[798]

KÜRSTEINER: The SS dragged wounded Russians along with them during the winter campaign in RUSSIA, they thrashed and hit and beat them on the road with their rifles, ripped open all their clothes, undressed them, left them stark naked and shovelled snow over them; they shovelled the snow off again, plunged their bayonets in and out of their hearts. Those are things which nobody would believe if you told them; the SS did that! That was the SS![799]

This excerpt exemplifies how Wehrmacht POWs used talk about Waffen SS misdeeds to imply that the regular army had nothing to do with any war crimes. Captain Alexander Hartdegen from the staff of the Wehrmacht 3rd Tank Division reported, for instance, that his division commander had explicitly prohibited any executions of prisoners, causing "trouble with [the SS division] 'Viking' because we didn't shoot the PW."[800] The speaker in this case seems very eager to protest his own innocence: "I can tell you, quite honestly, that I have not taken part in any shooting throughout the whole war. Not in the regiments I was in either. No such thing occurred in AFRICA; we promised 'fair play' there, sometimes we even exchanged: tins of sardines for cigarettes with the English there. Thank God that sort of thing never occurred in our case."[801]

We can no longer determine whether such statements were true. What is beyond doubt is that the fighting in Africa was relatively fair, and POWs were not executed. The clear contrast Hartdegen draws between the "good" Wehrmacht and the "evil" Waffen SS is one that we encounter often in the protocols, and it occurs with special frequency in stories about the fighting in France in summer 1944. Numerous army and Luftwaffe POWs recount Waffen SS war crimes during this time. Men from SS division "Götz von Berlichingen" were reported to have shot all American POWs,[802] while the "Hitler Youth" Division was said to have taken no prisoners at all.[803] Men from the division "The Reich" were described as shooting two American medics they captured with the words: "Well, one of them was certainly a Jew, he looked Jewish, and the other one was also."[804]

Sergeant Voigt from the Army Signal Battalion told of "horrific" scenes he had witnessed as the German military retreated from France:

VOIGT: In the end there were twenty-five of us left, and we had a few SS men with us. If you don't keep them in check they will kill anyone. We went into a French farm at night to get some food. Those fellows (SS) wanted to take away practically all

that the farmer had left. Then later we run across a few French
and they (SS) completely smashed in the skull of one of them.[805]

War crimes in France are attributed almost exclusively to the Waffen
SS. There is scarcely any mention in the surveillance protocols of comparable abuses by Wehrmacht soldiers.[806] This conforms to the picture
emerging from the latest research, which has found little evidence
of Wehrmacht or Luftwaffe war crimes on this front and attributes
responsibility for the most grievous abuses to the Waffen SS.[807]

It is hardly surprising, then, that the Waffen SS never shed the reputation for extreme brutality that began to coalesce in 1939–40. Alleged
eyewitnesses repeatedly connected SS men with the murder of women
and children, which was nearly always condemned as violating the military ethos.[808] While a POW, Major Hasso Viebig met the first general
staff officer of the Wehrmacht's 58th Armored Corps, under which the
SS division "The Reich" served for a time. Conversations with a Major
Beck opened Viebig's eyes:

> VIEBIG: Because of his activities in FRANCE, Major BECK (PW)
> knows how the SS behaved. He knows of several cases, which
> of course he didn't mention here. I was told here that the SS
> shut French women and children up in a church and then set
> the church on fire. I thought that was just propaganda but
> Major BECK told me: "No, it's true. I know they did it."[809]

Viebig's narrative refers to the massacre of Oradour, in which a company from the division "The Reich" murdered 642 men, women, and
children.

Few Wehrmacht POWs tried to maintain differentiated views when
it came to war crimes. In April 1945, Franz Breitlich was conversing
with his bunkmate Helmut Hanelt in the American POW camp Fort
Hunt. Breitlich tells of how Russian civilians had been mowed down
by tanks and machine gun fire. "Our troops really carried out some
business," Breitlich generalizes. "The vanguard of the Wehrmacht not
so much, but when the SS arrived, they really did some business."[810]

It is interesting that Breitlich initially speaks of "our" troops, only to
immediately qualify his statement by saying it was the SS, and not the
Wehrmacht, who really got down to "business." Very few soldiers went
so far as to imply there was little difference between the Wehrmacht

and the SS. One was Colonel Eberhard Wildermuth, who came from a relatively left-wing political background:

> WILDERMUTH: In carrying out the mass executions the SS did things which were unworthy of an officer and which every German officer should have refused to do, but I know of cases where officers did <u>not</u> refuse, and <u>did</u> do them, those mass executions. I know of similar things which were done by the army, and by officers.
>
> We dissociate ourselves in that way from these people, but they could immediately confront us and say: "But if you please, in this instance the German Hauptmann So-and-so, or the German Oberst So-and-so did exactly the same thing as the SS."[811]

Wildermuth was no doubt well informed on the topic of war crimes as he had served on practically every front and had good connections to the German resistance. At the very least, he had witnessed Wehrmacht crimes in Serbia in 1941.[812] But the conclusions he drew were the exception to the rule. Most Wehrmacht officers simply denied that their troops had ever been involved in crimes of such serious dimensions.

In so doing, some even partially defended the SS. When Colonel Meyne, as a POW, was confronted with stories about the Waffen SS burning down villages, he replied: "They don't do that sort of thing, they are purely fighting troops, there is nothing against them. It must have been those S.S. Security Divisions, or something like that, about whom those stories were told." A bit later, he added: "Of course there has been a lot of dirty business there, but it is quite clear to us that the Russians actually murdered all Germans there. There's no doubt at all about it."[813] According to Meyne's logic, the SS may have committed some crimes, but they were justified as a response to the Red Army killing German prisoners. Meyne was one of the few POWs who saw little difference between the Waffen SS and regular army soldiers. To support this view, he needed to differentiate between those who fought on the front line and the Security Service men in occupied territories. The distinction was specious, but that's not the point. It's more interesting to take a closer look at Meyne's perspective.

Meyne's only experience with the Waffen SS came, as far as we can tell, at the beginning of Operation Barbarossa. As the commander of an independent artillery division, his men and the SS division "The Reich" were both subordinate to the Wehrmacht 2nd Armored Group. The SS men fought side by side with regular Wehrmacht forces against the Red Army, carrying out the same orders and sharing the same experiences. From the perspective of an army officer, it was probably nothing extraordinary that civilians were killed in this phase of the war, especially as the Eastern Front was witnessing a general eruption of brutality. In July 1941, war crimes were occurring in practically all army divisions. The SS division "The Reich" was nothing special in this regard.[814] Thus, in Meyne's eyes, this group was more like a regular infantry division than, for instance, the SS Cavalry Brigade, who murdered thousands of civilians in the Pripet swamps. That was why Meyne saw the Waffen SS as examples of normal "fighting troops," who had not dramatically violated any ethical lines.

Up until now, we have only discussed the recorded conversations of Wehrmacht POWs, and it may be questionable whether they are a reliable source of information about war crimes perpetrated by the Waffen SS. Perhaps SS men were a screen onto which regular army men projected their own crimes. Navy private Lehmann, for instance, described how his unit discovered a secret radio transmitter at the home of an elderly French gentleman near Canisy, whereupon they "put him up against the wall and knocked him down." Lehmann also claimed that Germans were popular among the occupied French people, and that it was only the SS who had made "a mess of things" so that "people didn't like this very much."[815] Lehmann clearly uses the idea of unacceptable SS behavior to excuse himself from any blame for French people's hostility toward their German occupiers. Yet according to official Wehrmacht policy, the elderly French gentleman would have to have been tried by a military tribunal and not simply gunned down.

Most reports about Waffen SS atrocities are so general that it is impossible to confirm them. Given the countless crimes committed by Wehrmacht members, doubts can exist as to whether the Waffen SS was even uniquely brutal. So it is a stroke of luck that the British devoted considerable energy to listening in on the inner thoughts of Himmler's political soldiers. In conversations with other SS men as well as members of the Wehrmacht, they chatted about the war crimes they had committed with what appears today to be astonishing ease.

Excerpts like this from the protocols give us a rare interior look at the mind-set of the Waffen SS.

For example, an SS Untersturmführer recounted the following from his time on the Eastern Front:

> KRÄMER: I have experienced it in RUSSIA at OREL. An MG 42 was set up in the main aisle of a church. Then the Russian men, women and children were made to shovel snow; then they were taken into the church, without knowing at all what was happening. They were shot immediately with the MG 42 and petrol was poured on them and whole place was set on fire.[816]

Krämer was one of two thousand officers transferred in 1943 from the "Leibstandarte Adolf Hitler" to the newly formed "Hitler Youth" Division, and they had an enormous influence on the character of that unit.

A young SS man named Röthling fought in an armored grenadier regiment, where he came into contact with the veterans of the "Leibstandarte" Division: "Our 'Zugführer' said that in RUSSIA they always assembled about a hundred Russian PW and then made them march ahead over the mine-field. They made them blow up their own mines."[817] In France, they had been forced to make do with cows, Röthling then joked. Discussing his experiences in Normandy, Röthling described his superior to a fellow POW, a regular army private first class:

> RÖTHLING: If the people here know what we have done to their PW we shouldn't live much longer either. [The PW] was first interrogated a bit. If he said anything that was all right; if he didn't say anything, that was all right too. They would let him go, and then fire fifty rounds with the MG when he was ten paces away, and that would be the end of him. Our CO always used to say: "What am I to do with the swine? We haven't got enough to eat for ourselves." Our CO had to pay dearly for all his sins against us. He died a miserable death by being shot in the stomach on the last day.[818]

Röthling did not see himself as a perpetrator of war crimes. On the contrary, he says that his superior had sinned "against us." This curious narrative moment can perhaps be explained by the fact that war crimes were usually not carried out by seventeen-year-old new recruits to the "Hitler Youth" Division, but by the veteran officers.

Röthling's stories are not the only narrative evidence of the crimes of the "Hitler Youth" Division in Normandy. Even by Waffen SS standards, this division had a reputation for being not only particularly courageous, but especially brutal. "These were boy-scout types and the sort of swine who think nothing of cutting a man's throat," Lingner remarked in February 1945.[819]

Even more explicit were descriptions of fighting partisans in southern France, as told by an SS man to an army paratrooper:

> FÖRSTER: They had it in for us, "Division Das Reich," because in the TOULOUSE (?) region we had killed more partisans than we took prisoner. We may perhaps have taken twenty of them prisoner and they were only for interrogation. Then we tortured these twenty too, so that they died.
>
> Then when we marched up north, we marched via TOURS. They completely wiped out a "Wehrmachtskompanie" (?) there . . . . . . we caught one-hundred-and-fifty at one go and hanged them in the street.
>
> BÄSSLER: But then I can't understand how they could kill off one-hundred-and-fifty at once.
>
> FÖRSTER: We saw them lying there with their eyes poked out and their fingers cut off. With those one-hundred-and-fifty partisans, whom we hanged, the knots were tied in front, not behind. If the knot is behind, the spine is broken immediately, but in this way they suffocate slowly. That tortures them.
>
> BÄSSLER: The SS know everything; they have already tried everything out.
>
> FÖRSTER: Just think of it. If they kill one-hundred-and-fifty of our fellow soldiers, then we know no quarter. That was the only time that I was in favour [of killing anyone]. We don't do anything to anyone, but if anyone does anything to us, then we are . . . [820]

Förster is happy to chat about atrocities committed by his unit. When Bässler criticizes the number of partisans executed and the gruesome nature by which they were hanged, Förster claims that it was done out of solidarity for fallen comrades, and this was the only time he had been in favor of such reprisals. The event Förster is probably describing was the execution by the division "The Reich" of ninety-nine men in the southern French village of Tulle, after the SS men had discovered the bodies of sixty-nine Wehrmacht soldiers killed by the French resistance.[821] As we have observed before, the trope of retribution is used to justify acts of inhumanity, indeed barbarity. It is interesting that Förster exaggerates the number of victims. This is a typical means of making a story more interesting. It also shows that numbers of dead were a way of impressing listeners with one's story. Figures were part of the narrative aesthetic of violence.

The surveillance protocols conclusively illustrate the nonchalance with which Waffen SS men spoke about war crimes. Historical research explains this attitude as the result of ideological indoctrination and brutalization during training, both of which were also closely connected to the concentration camp system.[822] Evidence for this view can be found in statements by SS men throughout the surveillance protocols.

Kurt Meyer, one of the most prominent Waffen SS officers in the camps, did not bother at all to conceal his political orientation from the Wehrmacht generals. He had adopted National Socialism like a religion from a young age and dedicated himself to the ideology, saying a person could only give his heart once in life.[823] Lingner, on the other hand, tried to explain his beliefs:

> LINGNER: National-Socialism is racial doctrine put into practice, that is, all those who by their character and also to some extent in their outward appearance promise to become people of value—the basic idea of these people is equivalent to National-Socialism, if unadulterated by education. It can only be a combative action-loving one, never an out-and-out selfish one. Those fellows are Germans and whatever they think or do will always be right as it is <u>for</u> Germany. No need to change that.
>
> I am convinced there is hardly anything to be said against National-Socialism as such, against its basic idea. It represents a German tendency absolutely. That some so-called Nazis like WEBER at MUNICH and lots of others behaved like swine, is a different story. Who can tell whether a true cult of

National-Socialism wouldn't have been able to prevent this war![824]

Men like Meyer and Lingner were not just paying lip service to Nazi ideology. Along the lines of Himmler, they truly saw themselves as political soldiers, whose task it was to school their men in Nazi ideas:

> LINGNER: I am of the opinion that an army must in some way be equipped politically, otherwise it isn't in a position to withstand a mortal struggle like this one. If one lets the ordinary soldier get drawn into the war, and for several years, without pumping into him in the crassest way the necessity for the whole struggle, then one meets with no success. In that respect the Russian education is exemplary.[825]

There is considerable evidence that Lingner wasn't the only Waffen SS leader to attempt the sort of ideological indoctrination he felt was lacking in the regular armed forces. Beginning in September 1940, unit leaders were officially responsible for both the military *and* political training of SS soldiers.[826]

Of course, the desire to indoctrinate soldiers doesn't mean that even all members of the Waffen SS were completely infused with National Socialist ideology. As historian Jürgen Förster has shown, the means needed for political indoctrination—from instruction material to qualified teachers—were often lacking.[827] And results often lagged behind expectations:

> RÖTHLING: We had a political lecture every Sunday, about the origin of the "Hitler Youth" movement and all that sort of stuff.
> Our CO would arrive: "Look here boys, you know I haven't got many magazines or books about political things. I don't possess a radio, and I don't feel much like it anyhow. I've got enough work to do during the week. 'Heil Hitler.' The session is over."[828]

Political education, of course, is only one aspect of ideological conditioning. Indeed, lectures are but the smallest part of the latter. Far more important is the construction of an ideologically charged frame of reference. Practice is the most significant factor in forming attitudes.

A young German did not become a committed SS man only by reading pamphlets. He had to be bound up in a network of common practices. This point is often overlooked when analysts draw conclusions about the ideologization of a group from the existence of political concepts and education. It is easy for individuals to maintain distance from mottos and rules they are forced to write out over and over. It is much harder for them to divorce themselves from things of which they have been a part. For this reason, National Socialist commemoration ceremonies and parties to mark the winter and summer solstices, the Party's own judicial system,[829] and the special rules applying to marriage[830] played a far greater socializing role than education in organizations like the SS.

Röthling, in any case, had much more vivid memories of those sorts of events. He recalled that he had been instructed as to the appropriate marriage behavior and told that he should try to find an Aryan "girl" and ensure that there were "future generations."[831] An additional factor bolstering personal identification was the cult of hardness that was encouraged by brutal elements within young men's SS training. An SS man named Langer from the "Hitler Youth" Division recalled: "In the Waffen SS you couldn't do anything if an 'Unterführer' hit you during the training. The purpose of the training is to make you just as they are; it's pure sadism."[832]

Ideological conditioning helped create the sense that one was part of "the Führer's elite troop" with a duty "to set a good example to the army."[833] The older generations of SS "Führer corps" made sure this spirit was transferred to the new recruits in 1943. Even if the armored grenadier divisions "Reichsführer SS" and "Götz von Berlichingen" were far from elite fighting units, their officers did succeed in molding an SS spirit renowned for its extreme brutality. The "Reichsführer SS" division made its name with a number of massacres in Italy,[834] while "Götz von Berlichingen" left behind a trail of blood in France, when it executed 124 civilians in the village of Maillé on August 25, 1944.[835] The division was also responsible for numerous other atrocities, including the execution of American POWs on the command of Oberscharführer Fritz Swoboda.

The Waffen SS was a heterogeneous institution, encompassing both the Dachau commandant and later general Theodor Eicke as well as the future Nobel Prize laureate author Günter Grass. There is evidence of internal criticism, particularly from the lower ranks, as well as occasional proof that SS officers refused to carry out particularly gruesome orders. Obersturmführer Woelcky was one example of the latter. Another was twenty-four-year-old Obersturmführer Werner Schwarz, the company commander of the 2nd Company of the SS Panzergrenadierregiment "The Führer." As a POW, he told an army first lieutenant:

> SCHWARZ: Ten people had to be shot for each one of the men killed. They <u>had</u> to be; it was an order; and three for each of the wounded. I had four men wounded in the last operation; we set fire to a house, but I didn't allow any shootings. I told my CO: "We don't achieve anything by that; we should get terrorists, <u>those</u> are the people we should shoot. But I'm not in favour of shooting civilians."
>
> I was supposed to carry out measures against one village. I told my CO: "I'm not going to do it." "Why not?" I didn't want to say: because I am too soft-hearted, but I really am; I couldn't do it. So the . . . . . was called off . . . I was the most harmless fellow in the "Bataillon."[836]

Schwarz may, of course, have been trying to cover his tracks, but there are some indications that his story was true. In summer 1944, Schwarz's division was indeed ordered to carry out reprisals against civilians. But the battalion commander passed that task on to another division, perhaps after Schwarz's protest.[837]

Yet despite the presence of men like Woelcky and Schwarz, assuming their self-descriptions were accurate, the general tendency was that the core of Waffen SS leaders and officers were more radical than their Wehrmacht counterparts. Another indication of this is the fact that they maintained faith in ultimate German victory far longer than their regular army equivalents. An example is Untersturmführer Pflughaupt of the "Leibstandarte Adolf Hitler" division, who was captured by the British in fierce fighting around Caen in July 1944. He was deeply impressed by British artillery superiority, yet believed nonetheless that "the FÜHRER needs four to six weeks for mounting the reprisal weapon, which can fire accurately, so as to eliminate the (enemy) artillery, and that we must just hold out that long, and then we could go over to the attack."[838] Although he himself had seen how an offensive by three SS divisions was stopped within a kilometer, he could not imagine that the Führer would not have an ace up his sleeve. Given that he had experienced the massive British counteroffensive Goodwood, it is hard for us to see how he could conclude: "As soon as the English artillery is eliminated . . . the English retreat."

By this point in the war, no Wehrmacht officer was comparably optimistic.[839] Indeed, of the eighty Waffen SS officers interned in British and American POW camps, none thought the war had been lost before February 1945. Nor did they make any remarks critical of Hitler or his regime. Even more remarkably, none of the two hundred SS men of all ranks who were interned ever made critical statements about Wehrmacht war crimes, even though that sort of criticism hailed down in the other direction. It is hardly plausible that members of the SS knew nothing of Wehrmacht atrocities—the two wings of the military worked together far too closely for that. It appears that the frame of reference for what was considered normal, necessary, and encouraged differed from one group to the other. Within the Wehrmacht, there was a consciousness that certain acts were criminal, although that knowledge was not sufficient motivation for refusing to carry them out. There were a number of social and pragmatic reasons for continuing even when one realized standard boundaries were being transgressed. As a result Wehrmacht soldiers developed a number of social and personal strategies for reducing the resulting cognitive dissonance.

Within the core units of the Waffen SS, we find a unique amalgamation of racism, callousness, obedience, willingness for personal sacrifice, and brutality. Individually, all these elements can be identified within the Wehrmacht as well. It is easy to identify a rabid anti-Semite such as Gustav von Mauchenheim, the notorious commander of the 707th Infantry Division, who murdered some 19,000 civilians in the Soviet Union in 1941.[840] One can also prove that individual Wehrmacht units, particularly elite ones, were responsible for numerous atrocities. The 1st Mountain Division or the 4th Tank Division, for instance, executed large numbers of prisoners and civilians.[841] Additionally, there were plenty of units that defended their positions down to the last man. But in the Wehrmacht, instances of radicalism never coalesced into a stable, coherent whole. Regular army units were more heterogeneous in their perceptions and actions than the Waffen SS. It was only isolated regiments and battalions in specific phases of the war that stood out as excessively brutal. The political spectrum within the Wehrmacht was also broader than in the Waffen SS. In the elite division "Grossdeutschland," committed Nazis like Major Otto-Ernst Remer fought side by side with men like Colonel Hyazinth von Stachwitz, apparently a critic of the Nazi system.

The units of the Wehrmacht that most closely resembled the Waffen SS were the paratrooper divisions.[842] They put on similar elitist airs, were distinguished from the rest of the Wehrmacht by their uniforms, had numerous committed Nazis in their ranks, and tended toward radicalism.[843] Recalling his experiences in Normandy in 1944, Colonel Kessler described paratroopers as virtual barbarians whose excesses were covered up by the military brass: "The SS and the paratroops, too, behaved *like swine*. Back at AVRANCHES they blew up the jewellers' safes with hollow charges."[844] Yet even paratroopers paled in comparison to the Waffen SS in terms of their use of violence against women and children, their belief in final German victory, and their willingness to keep fighting down to the last round of ammunition.[845]

Ultimately, in comparison to the Wehrmacht, the Waffen SS was not only comprised of different sorts of people with a manner and a frame of reference all their own. It also had a different relationship to the most extreme sorts of violence.

Frame of Reference: War

Before we turn to the question of how National Socialist the Wehrmacht's war really was, let us summarize the key points of individual soldiers' frame of reference. The decisive factors in their *basal orientation*—the way in which they perceived and interpreted events—were the military value system and their immediate social environment. Differences of ideology, background, education, age, rank, and branch of service mattered little on this level. The exceptions were the differences just discussed between the Waffen SS and regular Wehrmacht soldiers.

Cultural ties reinforce this conclusion. These include, above all, ties to a canon of military virtues, the accompanying official and perceived responsibilities, and the accolades one could receive for carrying out one's duty. As we saw in our brief comparison of German, Italian, and Japanese soldiers, each group had a specific national frame of reference. This helps explain why some German soldiers continued to fight even after they knew the war was lost.

On the other hand, soldiers in the concrete situations in which they had been deployed often *did not* know that the war was lost, or if they did, were unable to comprehend what defeat meant. Moreover, the issue of whether the war was still winnable was sometimes irrelevant to soldiers trying to carry out a specific task, be it holding their position, avoiding capture by the enemy, or saving the lives of subordinates. Knowledge of the larger context does not automatically rule out actions independent of that knowledge. As a general rule, interpretations and decisions in concrete situations are usually made without reference to the "big picture." Thus, it is not surprising that most of the soldiers whose voices we encounter in the surveillance protocols seem ignorant of the larger context.

Disorientation results when things run contrary to their *expectations,* for example, when enemy success stories dispelled Germans' initial euphoria after their easy early triumphs and their premature fantasies about final victory, and their confidence began to erode. Yet as we have seen, disappointments scarcely altered soldiers' desire to perform their military tasks. The futility of the endeavor as a whole did not change the frame of reference, in which individuals' roles and responsibilities were defined. On the contrary, complaints about the inadequacy of the military leadership and the material at their disposal grew precisely because soldiers continued to *want* to do their jobs well.

As we observed in examples of extreme violence, sexual attacks, racist convictions, and quasi-religious faith in the Führer, *temporally specific contexts of perception* influenced the perspective, interpretations, and actions of soldiers. This is why, from today's vantage point, soldiers related and listened to stories of the most extreme brutality with such nonchalance. Understanding the context also helps us understand why many German soldiers maintained such a seemingly irrational faith in the Führer so late in World War II.

Role models and the desire to set a good example influenced soldiers' behavior perhaps more than any other factors. Indeed, we almost have to conclude, tautologically, that "soldierliness," as it was imagined and enacted in group practice, directed individual perceptions and actions. That is the reason foot soldiers subjected their superiors' behavior to such close scrutiny and vice versa. The internalized canon of military virtues provided the matrix for a subtle, continual evaluation of one's own behavior as well as that of comrades and enemies.

War-specific *interpretive paradigms*—for example, the ideas that war is hell, casualties are inevitable, and different rules obtain in combat than in civilian life—are omnipresent. War was the arena in which soldiers existed, and it was from within this world that they perceived POWs, civilian populations, partisans, forced laborers, and everyone else they encountered. As we saw with the examples of mass execution of supposed partisans, there was often no clear distinction between soldiers' interpretations of their situation and their justifications for their actions. The violence of war opened up an interpretive and behavioral freedom that did not exist in civilian life. The power to kill and rape others, to be cruel or merciful, as well as all the new possibilities soldiers had, can be traced back to the opening of an arena of violence and its accompanying interpretive paradigms.

Official duties were a decisive influence on soldiers' lives and behavior, as we saw with deserters late in the war, who still felt the need to justify what from our perspective seems like a perfectly rational decision. The same holds true of *social duties*. Frontline soldiers felt an almost exclusive sense of duty to their comrades and their superiors who formed their social units. What girlfriends, wives, or parents thought of what soldiers experienced and did was irrelevant. Soldiers' immediate social environments compelled them to act in certain ways. Abstract concepts like a "global Jewish conspiracy," "Bolshevist promotion of genetic inferiority," or even the "National Socialist *Volk* community" played only an ancillary role. As a rule German soldiers were not "ideological warriors." Most of them were fully apolitical.

Personal dispositions no doubt played a role in how soldiers saw, evaluated, and dealt with events, but the specific details are only visible in individual case studies, which are beyond the scope of this book. Initial studies of this sort suggest that soldiers' perceptions were heterogeneous. This is true even of generals, who because of their long military service were often seen as a homogeneous group.[846] Nonetheless, soldiers' diverse and often diametrically opposed views of the war were rarely reflected in their actions. In war, soldiers tended to behave alike, regardless of whether they were Protestants or Catholics, Nazis or regime critics, Prussians or Austrians,[847] university graduates or uneducated people.

In light of these findings, we should be even more skeptical of intentionalist explanations of Nazi atrocities. Studies devoted to collective biography may highlight motivations,[848] but they also tend to exaggerate the formative role of ideology at the expense of actual practice. Group-specific practices are a much more enlightening source for explaining extremely violent behavior by soldiers than cognitive rationale and personal categories.

In our view, the decisive factor in the atrocities discussed in this book was a general realignment from a civilian to a wartime frame of reference. It is more significant than all issues of worldview, disposition, and ideology. These are primarily important in determining what soldiers saw as expected, just, bewildering, or outrageous. They did not dramatically influence how they actually behaved. This conclusion may seem somewhat lapidary in light of the atrocities soldiers committed, but war creates a context for events and actions in which people do things they never would have otherwise. Within this context, soldiers could murder Jews without being anti-Semites and fight fanatically for the fatherland without being committed National Socialists. It is high time to stop overestimating the effects of ideology. Ideology may provide reasons for war, but it does not explain why soldiers kill or commit war crimes.

The actions of the workers and artisans of war are banal, indeed just as banal as the behavior of people existing under heteronomous circumstances—in companies, government offices, schools, or universities—always are. Nevertheless, this very banality unleashed the most extreme violence in the history of humanity, leaving behind 50 million casualties and a continent devastated in many respects for decades to follow.

How National Socialist Was the Wehrmacht's War?

"We are the war. Because we're soldiers."

Willy Peter Reese, 1943

The murder of POWs, the execution of civilians, massacres, forced labor, plunder, rape, the perfection of deadly technology, and the mobilization of society were all characteristics of World War II. But they were not new. New were the dimensions and the quality of these phenomena, which went beyond anything previously experienced in human history. In terms of the modern age, new was the revocation of limits on violence, culminating in the industrialized mass murder of European Jews. But it is not our aim here to offer a retrospective evaluation of the character of World War II. The central questions we would pose are: what was specific to the perceptions and actions of German soldiers at this point in time, and what elements can be found in other twentieth-century wars?

These two questions form a prism through which we in the present can look back on the past. And that being the case, another question emerges: what aspects of World War II, and in particular Wehrmacht soldiers' perceptions and deeds, are specifically National Socialist or specific to this particular armed conflict?

Who Gets Killed

On July 12, 2007, two American helicopter crews opened fire on a group of civilians in the Iraqi capital of Baghdad. Among them was Reuters news agency photographer Namir Noor-Eldeen. As a video titled "Collateral Murder" later published on the WikiLeaks website would show,[849] most of those fired on were killed instantly. One person, apparently seriously wounded, tried to crawl his way to safety. When a delivery truck arrived, and two people tried to help

Source: WikiLeaks

the wounded man, American helicopter crews resumed fire. Not only were the would-be rescuers killed in the barrage. A short time later, it emerged that two children who happened to be in the truck were also seriously wounded. The attack was launched after the helicopter crews believed they saw people in the first group carrying weapons. When the identification was confirmed, they opened fire, and the rest took its course.

The entire event transpired in a matter of minutes, and the protocol of the GIs' radio conversations is revealing:

00:27 Okay we got a target fifteen coming at you. It's a guy with a weapon.
00:32 Roger [acknowledged].
00:39 There's a . . .
00:42 There's about, ah, four or five . . .
00:44 Bushmaster Six [ground control] copy [I hear you] One-Six.

00:48 . . . this location and there's more that keep walking by and one of them has a weapon.

00:52 Roger received target fifteen.

00:55 K.

00:57 See all those people standing down there.

01:06 Stay firm. And open the courtyard.

01:09 Yeah roger. I just estimate there's probably about twenty of them.

01:13 There's one, yeah.

01:15 Oh yeah.

01:18 I don't know if that's a . . .

01:19 Hey Bushmaster element [ground forces control], copy on the one-six.

01:21 That's a weapon.

01:22 Yeah.

01:23 Hotel Two-Six; Crazy Horse One-Eight [second Apache helicopter].

01:29 Copy on the one-six, Bushmaster Six-Romeo. Roger.

01:32 Fucking prick.

01:33 Hotel Two-Six this is Crazy Horse One-Eight [communication between chopper 1 and chopper 2]. Have individuals with weapons.

01:41 Yup. He's got a weapon too.

01:43 Hotel Two-Six; Crazy Horse One-Eight. Have five to six individuals with AK47s [automatic rifles]. Request permission to engage [shoot].

01:51 Roger that. Uh, we have no personnel east of our position. So, uh, you are free to engage. Over.

02:00 All right, we'll be engaging.

02:02 Roger, go ahead.

02:03 I'm gonna . . . I can't get 'em now because they're behind that building.

02:09 Um, hey Bushmaster element . . .

02:10 He's got an RPG [rocket-propelled grenade]?

02:11 All right, we got a guy with an RPG.

02:13 I'm gonna fire.

02:14 Okay.

02:15 No hold on. Let's come around. Behind buildings right now from our point of view. . . . Okay, we're gonna come around.

02:19 Hotel Two-Six; have eyes on individual with RPG. Getting ready to fire. We won't . . .

02:23 Yeah, we had a guy shoot—and now he's behind the building.

02:26 God damn it.

The tragic fate of the people on the ground begins at the moment when a helicopter crew member thinks he recognizes a weapon. From this point on, the group, which the helicopter crews watch from a distance via video monitors, becomes a target, and the intention to focus on and destroy this target is preprogrammed. It only takes a few seconds for other crew members to identify further weapons. Almost instantaneously an armed individual becomes a whole armed group. Equally quickly, the weapon becomes an AK-47 and then a rocket-propelled grenade launcher. When the first helicopter receives permission to attack, the group disappears from view behind a building. At that point, from the soldiers' perspective, the only thing that matters is to get their sights back on their targets, and one of the people deemed to be carrying a weapon is perceived as having fired a shot. Precisely because the group has disappeared behind a building, the U.S. soldiers' desire to "incapacitate" them as quickly as possible becomes overwhelming. Any remaining doubt about whether these people actually are "insurgents" and whether they really are carrying weapons is rendered moot. The soldiers have defined the situation, and that definition calls for a set procedure.

Group thinking and mutual confirmation of what is perceived replaced the factual situation with an imagined one. Viewers watching the video now don't see what the soldiers see. But the viewer doesn't bear the burden of having to make decisions. What happens in the video may unfold before his eyes, but it has nothing to do with him. The task of U.S. helicopter crews as well as ground troops, however, is to battle insurgents. Every person on the street is perceived under this condition. Moreover, every suspicion those on the street raise, for whatever reason, carries a fatal tendency to be confirmed by further indications. When a group of people that has seemingly been clearly identified then disappears from view, soldiers perceive extreme danger. From that point on everything is directed toward combating the target:

02:43 You're clear.

02:44 All right, firing.

02:47 Let me know when you've got them.

02:49 Let's shoot.

02:50 Light 'em all up.

02:52 Come on, fire!

02:57 Keep shoot, keep shoot. [keep shooting]

02:59 keep shoot.

03:02 keep shoot.

03:05 Hotel . . . Bushmaster Two-Six, Bushmaster Two-Six, we need to move, time now!

03:10 All right, we just engaged all eight individuals . . .

03:23 All right, hahaha, I hit [shot] 'em . . .

Within the blink of an eye, eight people are dead, and one seriously wounded. The attack itself has confirmed the definition of the situation beyond any doubt. A combat situation does in fact exist, whereas before it was simply imagined.

The video caused a sensation when it was illegally made public in 2010, since it depicted American GIs killing a group of defenseless civilians from the air without being in any real danger. Yet upon closer examination it is completely unspectacular. Everything shown happens within the frame of reference "war" and carries a certain degree of inevitability. The "Collateral Murder" video is a perfect illustration that the consequences are real whenever people define a situation as real. The soldiers have a task, and they are trying to carry it out. In order to do that, they see the world through professional eyes. Everyone down below is suspect. Part of seeing the world professionally is exchanging impressions with others, and the tendency is that observations and comments that have been made once will be confirmed. Thus a single weapon becomes many, and passersby become combatants. One can call this phenomenon a "dynamic of violence," an instance of "group thinking," or a "path dependency." In practice, all these elements come together with fatal consequences for eleven people within the space of a few minutes.

But the procedure is by no means over when the targets are destroyed. On the contrary, the soldiers take stock of their work:

04:31 Oh, yeah, look at those dead bastards.

04:36 Nice . . .

04:44 Nice.

04:47 Good shoot.
04:48 Thank you.

What might appear to outsiders, and the media who reported on the video, as sheer cynicism is nothing other than professional acknowledgment after a job well done. The soldiers' mutual congratulations once again make it clear that, from their perspective, they have destroyed completely legitimate targets.

The other side's casualties are almost always regarded as fighters, partisans, terrorists, or insurgents. We recall here the rule among U.S. troops from the Vietnam War "If it's dead and Vietnamese, it's Vietcong,"[850] as well as the Wehrmacht soldiers who justified killing women and children by saying they were "partisans." It is the violent act following the definition that confirms the definition's accuracy. In this way, violence serves as proof that one has correctly assessed a situation. The "Collateral Murder" video clearly illustrates how violence transforms a murky situation, in which men suffer from a lack of orientation and don't know what to do, into something crystal clear. When all the targets are dead, order has been restored. Once the procedure has been set in motion, any further details will be seen in light of the original definition. The delivery truck with the men who are trying to help the wounded civilians to safety *is* an enemy vehicle. And as a logical extension, the would-be rescuers *are* further terrorists.

Even the fact that there were children in the vehicle, who were badly wounded by American gunfire, can be made to confirm the original definition of the situation:

17:04 Roger, we need, we need a uh to evac [evacuate] this child. Ah, she's got a uh, she's got a wound to the belly.
17:10 I can't do anything here. She needs to get evaced . . .
17:46 Well it's their fault for bringing their kids into a battle.
17:48 That's right.

We see how enormous the power of definition is. In this case, child casualties are not even considered collateral damage, let alone evidence of a grievous or indeed any mistake made by the U.S. helicopter crews. The wounded children are just one more piece of evidence of how perfidious the "insurgents" are since they don't even hesitate to take their kids into battle.

Source: WikiLeaks

THE DEFINITION OF ENEMIES

At one point in the "Collateral Murder" video, one of the helicopter gunners says of the injured man trying to crawl away, "Come on, buddy. All you gotta do is pick up a weapon." Here, too, we see the convergence of violence and the confirmation that it was justified. The gunner wants the man to behave according to the soldiers' definition of the situation, as an insurgent, so that they can kill him. We observed the same mode of self-fulfilling prophecy in relation to World War II soldiers' treatment of supposed partisans. In that case, it was the ammunition allegedly found on victims that justified executing them as "terrorists."

This is a general characteristic of violence in war. The behavior of those defined as the "enemies" confirms the legitimacy of that designation. This has nothing to do with stereotypes, prejudices, or "worldviews." The only characteristic of "target persons" that counts is that they pose a threat. Any indication to that effect provides sufficient reason to kill. In the Vietnam War, soldiers feared that even babies could be carrying concealed hand grenades. In World War II, children could be considered partisans, just as in the Iraq War they could be regarded as insurgents.

In a voluminous study of the dynamic of violence in the Vietnam War, historian Bernd Greiner cited a series of examples of the "self-evident" identification of enemies. The simplest one was that anyone who tried to flee was automatically an enemy who should be shot. The attempt to escape confirmed suspicions that an individual was a Vietcong.[851] Somewhat more complicated is the discovery of "evidence." When examining the surveillance protocols, we highlighted the story of the presence of ammunition being used to distinguish supposed partisans from civilians. The same procedure, however illogical it was, was applied in the Vietnam War, where GIs sometimes razed villages in which they had previously deposited Soviet-made ammunition as proof of a Vietcong presence there. The U.S. 9th Infantry Division killed a total of 10,899 people but only secured 748 weapons. That suggests that 14 civilians were murdered for every true Vietcong eliminated. As a justification, soldiers often claimed that the Vietcong were killed before they could go get their weapons.[852]

It was difficult for American soldiers in Vietnam to precisely identify enemies since the Vietcong waged a guerrilla war. Not knowing whether they were confronted with incognito fighters, men and women, or harmless civilians, created a huge challenge. The lack of orientation soldiers feel in a "war without fronts," or what we today would call asymmetrical warfare, underscores the compulsive need soldiers feel to establish certainty, particularly under violent conditions. Precisely in situations in which soldiers do not face standard sorts of battle, but can be killed in irregular attacks, explosive traps, and ambushes, their ability to orient themselves is a precondition for survival. Ambush situations also make soldiers feel helpless. As one present-day German sergeant serving in Afghanistan described it: "If you're ambushed, things get hectic. You require a phase of orientation. Who is being shot at from where? It feels awful, to say the least. The enemy is always at an advantage since he chose the place of the attack and is familiar with it. . . . I was also glad if I could alight from my vehicle. You may lose some cover, but you're a much smaller target. And you can act on your own terms again, decide whether to shoot back or hide."[853] Only when a situation of clarity has been restored about who the enemies are do soldiers once again feel secure. Fatally, violence is precisely the means by which orientation can be regained most simply, quickly, and unambiguously. A successful act of violence removes the gray areas.

This was the reason why the Wehrmacht most often engaged in acts of extreme violence against innocent civilians in the context of fighting partisans. It is beyond question that the POWs in the surveillance protocols operated under the assumption that in the battle against presumed partisans, one was allowed to kill, burn down villages, and terrorize civilians. The threatening chimera of the "Franc-tireur," the irregular fighter, had already played a prominent role in the Franco-Prussian War of 1870–71, and it was an established Wehrmacht doctrine to nip any incipient guerrilla activity in the bud with brute force.[854] Thus, internalized cultural factors combined with objective uncertainty to make the use of "ruthless severity" seem unavoidable and normal.

It is unique to the conditions of war that the definition of the enemy justifies all acts taken as a result of that definition. In this respect, the way the Wehrmacht waged war was no different from the way many fighting forces have. This perspective applies equally to war between sovereign states and asymmetrical warfare. The parties at war have the right to define who is and isn't an enemy. The perennial argument that one was only trying to defend oneself against an enemy bent on world domination or enamored of senseless violence is a standard element of war crimes trials or interviews and personal testimonies. It's the excuse perpetrators use to justify why they did certain things. At the moment when violence occurs, though, it needs no justification. Or as the leader of a German mobile medical unit in Afghanistan formulated things: "You feel great rage in battle. You don't have much time to think. That only comes later."[855]

The decisive point in the example of the U.S. helicopter crews' behavior is this: entirely unrelated to historical, cultural, and political circumstances, the definition of a specific situation and all the actors present in it establishes the frame of reference for everything that happens subsequently. Group thinking and the dynamic force of unfolding violence ensure that the ending is almost always deadly.

REVENGE FOR WHAT WAS AND COULD BE DONE TO US

The analogy of killing can be extended by definition all the way to the level of genocide. The murder of Jews was also defined as an act of self-defense, at least by racial theorists and those who helped arrange the Holocaust. Only here the subject of the fear and aggression was a whole community and not an individual. It is no accident that Jews about to be killed were also described as partisans, that is: irregular enemies it was permissible to eradicate. As one Wehrmacht soldier remarked, "Where there's a Jew, there's a partisan."[856]

Killing under the guise of self-defense also occurs in other cultural and historical contexts. The genocide carried out by the Hutu against Tutsi in 1990s Rwanda was preceded by forms of perception and interpretation that American historian Alison Des Forges vividly described as "accusation in a mirror." In a kind of putative genocidal fantasy, one side accuses the other of planning to completely annihilate it. This schema of mirror-image accusations is not just a psychosocial phenomenon. It is also an explicitly promoted propaganda method. With the help of this technique, as one source quoted by Des Forges asserts, "the side actually terrorizing the other will accuse its enemy of terrorizing it."[857] The logical corollary to spreading fantastic fears of being threatened is to create a willingness for self-defense among the party that feels itself under threat. Every form of murderous attack and systematic annihilation can also be perceived as a necessary act of self-defense.

This emerges very tangibly in the motif of "revenge" that plays such a prominent role in narratives of war, irrespective of cultural, historical, or geographical context. Indeed, we have to speak of a narrative trope here. The basic story, as exemplified in countless novels, films, and oral war stories, begins with a soldier relating how a close friend died in battle in an especially horrible or treacherous way. From that moment on, the story usually concludes, the protagonist decided to pay the enemy back in kind. Occasionally this narrative figure is augmented with a promise made to the dying friend by the storyteller. In any case, personal trauma legitimizes the protagonist's lack of mercy toward the enemy. It was in this sense that one American soldier in Vietnam told his father in a letter that total destruction was the only way to deal with the Vietcong and confessed that he could never have imagined feeling such hatred.[858]

Psychiatrist Jonathan Shay, who worked with a number of Vietnam veterans, reported that the desire to revenge the death of a buddy inspired some GIs to reenlist for additional tours of duty.[859] One of them was author Philip Caputo: "Finally, there was hatred, a hatred buried so deep that I could not then admit its existence. I can now, though it is still painful. I burned with a hatred for the Viet Cong and with an emotion that dwells in most of us, one closer to the surface than we care to admit: a desire for retribution. I did not hate the enemy for their politics, but for murdering Simpson, for executing that boy whose body had been found in the river, for blasting the life out of Walt Levy. Revenge was one of the reasons I volunteered for a line company. I wanted a chance to kill somebody."[860]

These sorts of desires for revenge, which ascribe the necessity of horrific and brutal actions to experiences of loss, can be generalized. With allusions to the biblical idea of an eye for an eye and a tooth for a tooth, the enemy's behavior can be defined as a transgression that demands a payback in kind. In World War II, for instance, an American GI wrote home about the requisitioning of German apartments: "It's a really rough deal and these Krauts are getting a good belly full of their own medicine."[861] Desire for revenge was one of the central themes in a comprehensive study of American soldiers' attitudes during World War II made by a group of authors under the direction of Samuel A. Stouffer.[862]

Not all soldiers, of course, were able to live out their desires for vengeance against those they considered their enemies. Sometimes, they were hindered by comrades or sudden, unexpected feelings of empathy for the adversary. The desire to perform one's tasks efficiently can also act as a counterweight, as is evident in a letter from a senior German staff medic in Afghanistan: "At the very latest when the alarm sounds for the second time in a bunker, even the greatest philanthropist will develop desires for bloody revenge. The simplest solution in military terms, the one favored by soldiers here, is a major artillery counterstrike. Technically speaking, this is no big problem. You locate the target, point your guns and fire away. It takes less than a minute. The first time the enemy shelled us they had bad luck, but the Taliban aren't stupid. The next time they attacked, they used longer cables and fired their rockets from a spot next to a kindergarten."[863] Yet even such reflections and observations about the potentially self-defeating nature of desires for revenge, comparable to those in all situations of war,[864] underscore the significance of the vengeance motif in the daily lives of soldiers.

TAKING NO PRISONERS

During World War II, POWs were treated in radically different fashions. Some were dealt with according to a strict interpretation of the

SOLDIERS

Geneva Convention, while others were put to death en masse. While only 1 to 3 percent of Anglo-American POWs died in German captivity, 50 percent of Red Army prisoners perished[865]—a figure that exceeded even the high numbers of Allied soldiers who died in Japanese captivity. The Wehrmacht decision to let Russian POWs starve to death, which soldiers discussed in the surveillance protocols, was something that went beyond the normally accepted boundaries of war and can only be understood in the context of the Nazi campaigns of annihilation. That is the reason why German POWs were disgusted at how Russian prisoners were being treated and even sympathized with them.[866] Although most German soldiers never came into contact with German POW camps, many had witnessed the transport of prisoners from the front lines and had a good idea of how captured enemies were being mistreated. The German soldiers remained mere witnesses, though, with scant opportunities for changing what they found objectionable.

The situation was different on the battlefield. Here, practically every foot soldier was an active participant who decided for himself whether or not to kill his enemy. In the heat of battle, questions of whether an enemy taken prisoner would be allowed to live were subject to constant renegotiation. Gray areas could persist for hours or even days, especially when the troops that had taken prisoners became embroiled in new battles.

Depending on the situation, enemies who surrendered were sometimes shot without any further ado. But that was unique neither to the Wehrmacht nor to the Nazi approach to war. Examples of POWs being executed go all the way back to antiquity, although the dimensions expanded dramatically in the twentieth century. In other wars as well, there were standing official and unofficial orders to "take no prisoners," and even when no such instructions existed, it was often more expedient for soldiers to simply kill enemies rather than have to disarm, care for, transport, and guard them. Reports about such executions often read "shot while attempting escape" or simply "no prisoners taken." In World War I as well, POWs were killed out of revenge or simple jealousy, since many soldiers resented the fact that they would have to fight on, while the lives of the prisoners were presumably safe—or because keeping POWs was inconvenient or dangerous.[867] The same was true in the Korean and Vietnam wars, and we can assume nothing has changed in the Afghanistan and Iraq wars either.

Situational conditions in war often establish rules that violate those of the Geneva Convention. Soldiers may consider it inadvisable or superfluous to burden themselves with POWs, opting simply to eradicate them. This phenomenon occurred in all theaters of World War II, although with varying frequency. In those areas where fighting was particularly fierce, the numbers of POWs executed rose. Because of the prevailing cult of toughness, elite units were more likely to kill enemies who tried to surrender. The U.S. 82nd Airborne Division in Normandy, for example, did not behave all that differently in this regard than the SS division "Götz von Berlichingen."[868]

The greatest eruptions of violence in World War II occurred in the Soviet Union and the Pacific. But extreme violence was also part of everyday life in the relatively "normal" European theaters of war in France and Italy,[869] and it was perpetrated by both sides: " 'Even in hopeless situations,' reported American Joseph Shomon, who saw many bodies as the commander of a graves registration unit, 'the Germans would usually fight to the last, refusing to surrender. [Then] when their ammunition was gone, they were ready to give up and ask for mercy [but because] many American lives had been lost in this delay, our troops often killed the Germans.' "[870] According to historian Gerald Linderman, the most frequent reason for American GIs to shoot German POWs was to avenge their own lost comrades. But Linderman also cites intentional and not just situational factors. Sometimes soldiers were ordered not to take any prisoners,[871] and they were more likely to execute captured soldiers who conformed to Nazi stereotypes, yelled "Heil Hitler," or belonged to the Waffen SS.[872] For instance, four years after the fact, Ernest Hemingway still told with pride how he had boldly shot a captive member of the Waffen SS.[873]

To briefly summarize: A lot of what appears horrible, lawless, and barbaric about war crimes is actually part of the usual frame of reference in wartime. For that reason, stories about cruelty don't attract any more attention in the World War II German surveillance protocols than they do in reports and commentaries by U.S. soldiers who served in Vietnam. Such instances of cruelty rarely seem like anything spectacular to the majority of soldiers as long as they are not called to answer for themselves before a court of law. Such violence is instrumental in nature. It's hardly any surprise, then, that it occurs in war.

War as Work

Work is a crucial social activity in all modern societies. What we do is embedded within a veritable universe of desired end results, defined largely by people other than ourselves, be they bosses or those who set the rules for institutions, businesses, or military units. In the context of work, individuals per se only bear particular responsibility for that precise part of the total process to which they contribute. Ironically, division-of-labor arrangements are precisely what relieve individuals of accountability for what they do or are prepared to do. Commercial airplane pilots or reserve policemen can become murderers who kill civilians. Likewise, aviation companies, oven producers, or academic departments covering pathology can become instruments of genocide. Matrixes of social functions and institutions store up human potential like batteries.[874] Never is this more apparent than in wartime. When societies are mobilized to fight a total war, institutions, businesses, and organizations that normally work harmlessly toward their respective peacetime goals become "essential to the war effort." That's because they can easily redirect their potential.

Seen from the historical perspective, cases in which swords have been beaten into plowshares are far less common than vice versa. Modern division of labor, with its focus on instrumental reason, can serve almost any purpose imaginable. In their analysis of letters German soldiers sent home from the Eastern Front, historians Ute Daniel and Jürgen Reulecke cited Jens Ebert's thesis that war is accepted as long as it can be articulated in terms of peacetime, workplace values such as diligence, endurance, persistence, duty, obedience, and voluntary subordination: "The only thing that changes on the frontline or as part of a special commando is the content of one's work, not one's attitudes toward work itself or the way it is organized. In this sense, the soldier is a 'worker of war.' "[875]

This sort of work-oriented understanding of war is also clearly expressed in a letter sent home by a U.S. Marine captain to his mother during the Vietnam War. In it, he tries to justify his decision to extend his tour of duty and explain why killing enemies is an appealing job, carrying a lot of responsibility. "Here there is a job to be done. There are moral decisions made every day. My experience is invaluable. This job requires a man of conscience. The group of men that do this *must* have a leader with a conscience. In the last three weeks we killed more than 1,500 men on a single operation. That reflects a lot of responsibility. I am needed here, Mom."[876]

When war arises, the participants don't have to reconfigure their psyches, overcome themselves, or be specially socialized in order to be able to kill. The context in which they do the things they do only needs to be altered. For soldiers who only do the sorts of things they were trained for anyway, nothing at all changes except the fact that the context becomes deadly serious. Thus, as a number of examples have shown, the transitional phase from training and practice to actual war not only surprised and frightened soldiers. It also excited and fascinated them. In no case, however, did the definition of what they were supposed to do, what they were there for, change.

Pride in the fruits of one's labor and descriptions of what one has achieved are not the only way in which people express that war is work, and that they see it as such. The idea is also articulated in acknowledgment that the enemy, too, has done a "good job." In the surveillance protocols, one vivid example of this was the appreciation German POWs had, all Nazi propaganda about Bolshevik inferiors notwithstanding, for the skill of Red Army soldiers. The same was true for German soldiers viewed from the perspective of the enemy.[877] Nonetheless, soldiers' perceptions of one another were also formatted by cultural stereotypes. For Germans, Red Army soldiers were courageous warriors and masters of improvisation. But those positive images were clouded by stereotypical beliefs in inherent Russian brutality and lack of self-preservation instincts.[878] Since Japanese soldiers treated POWs with extreme brutality, American GIs also came to view "Japs" as inhuman enemies. Other aspects of Japanese behavior were equally incomprehensible to U.S. soldiers: the practice of killing their own wounded or POWs who had been released, or of refusing to be saved by GIs when their ships were sunk. This radicalized the way American soldiers perceived their enemies, expanding upon already existing cultural stereotypes. For that reason, the word "Jap" had extremely nasty, and occasionally racist, connotations that were absent from the relatively harmless term "kraut."[879]

The Group

Cultural differences prevent soldiers of all nationalities from perceiving war universally. In soldiers' own eyes, not all soldiers are created equal. Differentiations people make in peacetime persist during war. What distinguishes war from peace, and remains constant from war to war, is camaraderie. The group plays an extraordinarily important role. Without it, individual soldiers' behavior in wartime would be incomprehensible. Soldiers never act on their own. Even sharpshooters or fighter plane aces, who have only themselves to rely upon, are still parts of a group that remains together before and after battle. Samuel Stouffer's previously discussed study from 1948 thus concludes that the group has far more influence over individual soldiers' behavior than ideological convictions, political views, and personal motivations.[880]

This conclusion does not just apply to the military. Edward Shils and Morris Janowitz, for instance, emphasize that the Wehrmacht's ability to do battle was based not on National Socialist fervor, but on the need to satisfy personal needs within the context of group relationships.[881] Moreover, this aspect of the Wehrmacht's organization was supported by modern management and personnel techniques.[882] A soldier's immediate social environment decides how he perceives and interprets war, and the parameters by which he targets and evaluates his own actions. Every member of a group sees himself as he believes others see him. That, as Erving Goffman has shown in his "stigma" study, provides the most powerful motivation for people to conform to the norms of the group. [883] In war, for an indeterminate length of time and under the most extreme conditions, the soldier is part of a group he can neither leave nor seek out according to his own personal preference. That is completely different from civilian life, in which people select their own groups. The lack of alternatives to the group a soldier is part of and helps comprise makes it an all-decisive normative and practical entity, especially as battle is a life-or-death situation. To paraphrase a sentiment often expressed in American combat briefings in Vietnam: I don't know why I'm here, and you don't know why you're here, but let's try our best to do a good job and stay alive.[884]

Such sentiments underscore the importance of one's comrades for everything that happens and is thought or decided during war. This far outweighs the significance of any worldviews, convictions, or historical inevitabilities, which might have provided the external conditions leading to the war itself. The internal reality of war, as it presents itself to soldiers, is the group. That is how war appeared to Vietnam veteran Michael Bernhardt, who refused to participate in the My Lai massacre and was subsequently ostracized. The only thing that counted, Bernhardt later recalled, was how people thought of you in the here and now, how people in your immediate surroundings regarded you. Bernhardt's unit was his entire world. What they thought was right, *was* right; what they thought was wrong, *was* wrong.[885]

The German soldier Willy Peter Reese would have agreed with Bernhardt:

> Just like winter clothing covers up almost all of you except for your eyes, the fact of being a soldier only allowed space for tiny bits of individuality. We were in uniform. Not only were we unwashed, unshaven, full of lice and sickness. We were corrupted in our souls, little more than the sum of our blood, guts and bones. Our camaraderie arose from our forced dependency on one another and from living together in the closest of confines. Our humor was cruel toward others, black, satiric, obscene, biting, angry. It was a game played with casualties, brains blown out, lice, pus and excrement. A nothingness of the soul. . . . We had no belief to carry us, and any philosophy only existed to help us see the world in somewhat lighter terms. The fact that we were soldiers was enough to justify any crimes and corruption and was sufficient basis for an existence in hell. . . . We were of no significance, and neither were starvation, frostbite, typhus, dysentery, people freezing to death or being crippled and killed, destroyed villages, plundered cities, freedom and peace. Individuals were least important of all. We could die without a care.[886]

Willy Peter Reese was killed shortly after he wrote these words. His words resonate with another universal truth of war: *reasons don't matter.*[887]

IDEOLOGY

One of the major themes of literary and cinematic meditations on war—from Erich Maria Remarque and Ernst Jünger to Francis Ford

Coppola's *Apocalypse Now*—is that ideology and all other larger reasons behind war are irrelevant. Indeed, apart from a small percentage of ideological warriors, one central characteristic of soldiers is their distance from and disinterest in the causes that led to their present situation. This is true not only when everything is falling apart, as in Reese's description. It also applies to situations of victory. Soldiers' attention is primarily focused on things at hand, the plane just shot down or the village just taken—and not abstractions like "the conquest of living space in Eastern Europe," "the defense of Bolshevism," or the "yellow peril." Things like that form the backdrop of war and the arenas of battle connected with it. But they rarely provide the concrete motivation for soldiers' interpretations and actions in any given situation.[888]

That fact runs all the way through the twentieth century. The signature psychosocial experience of World War I was disillusionment at the fact that there was nothing heroic or ideological about the hail of shrapnel soldiers endured as part of trench warfare. Fundamental senselessness was a feeling shared by American troops in Korea, Vietnam, and Iraq, and by all the nations involved in Afghanistan. Indeed, it was augmented as the rationale behind those wars became increasingly abstract. Why should you fight far away from home for the freedom of people who despise you? Why defend populations and stretches of territory that have nothing to do with you personally?

With reference to the Vietnam War, one U.S. sergeant wrote to a friend: "Of course Americans are dying, and I would not belittle anyone who served 'with proud devotion' and faith in this enterprise. It may not have been a terribly wrong theoretical idea at one time. But the foreign introduced offensive, the consequent corruption and then the contempt that developed between people and groups—it makes a mockery of the 'noble' words used to justify war. It belies the phony enthusiasm with which those words may be delivered. It's now a war of survival."[889]

Today, a German captain serving with the 373rd Paratroopers Battalion in Kunduz says: "At the start, we wanted to achieve something, for example, taking some territory from the enemy. But after the death of my men, we sometimes ask ourselves whether it's worth it. Why risk our lives, when the Taliban will immediately reappear as soon as we're gone? We're fighting for our lives and our mission, if we even still have one. But in the end in Kunduz, we're above all fighting for sheer survival."[890]

Soldiers' statements about their experience of war frequently show strong similarities and points of overlap. Andrew Carroll, the founder of the Legacy Project, a volunteer initiative aimed at collecting and preserving correspondence by U.S. veterans of all foreign wars, has said that the similarities and not the differences stand out when one compares letters by American soldiers with correspondence written by their German, Italian, and Russian counterparts.[891]

At the beginning of World War II, German soldiers were far less prone to see the conflict as senseless. Quick German victories were followed by relatively long periods of respite, and Wehrmacht soldiers thought that they would personally benefit from Germany's war of conquest.[892] But by fall 1941, when success stories became rarer and long, drawn-out battles increasingly taxed German troops, "world-view" rationales and motivations declined in importance. The predominant feeling among soldiers was that they had been abandoned to a monotonous endeavor which had little to do with their own lives, although their own survival depended on it. There is not one sociological study of World War II that fails to emphasize the relatively minor role played by ideology and abstract convictions in the daily practice of war. Group dynamics, technology, space, and time set the parameters that mattered to soldiers and allowed them to orient themselves. Given the dominance of the here-and-now, the only difference between what soldiers did and what people in modern societies always do, when confronted with a task that they are supposed to carry out, was the fact that the former entailed life or death. If you work for an energy, insurance, or chemical company, "capitalism" as such does not help you perform your job, and if you're a policeman handing out a speeding ticket or a court bailiff repossessing a flat-screen television from a debtor, you don't think that you are upholding the values of freedom and democracy. You're only carrying out a duty you have been charged with. Soldiers do their jobs in war using violence. That's all that distinguishes their actions from those of other workers, employees, and government officials. The results of soldiers' work are also different: casualties and destruction.

MILITARY VALUES

The immediate social environment, the modern work ethic, and fascination with technology may indeed yield something like a "universal soldier." At the same time, different perspectives exist on war and violence, and we can identify nationally specific elements in the formation of military frames of reference. For the Wehrmacht in World War II, these elements included concepts of honor, toughness, and sacrifice to a degree that no longer applies within today's German military.[893] Even World War I did not see such an extreme emphasis on the idea of being duty-bound.[894] Although the dividing lines may be blurry, Wilhelmine Germany, the Weimar Republic, the Third Reich, and today's Federal Republic all featured different sets of military values.

The differences are even greater in the international arena, as our brief comparison of Nazi Germany, Fascist Italy, and Imperial Japan showed. The central values for Wehrmacht soldiers were bravery, obedience, devotion to duty, and emotional hardness. Those were the key factors determining how soldiers perceived and evaluated their own behavior.[895] This frame of reference, already in place during peacetime, remained remarkably stable throughout World War II.

But even though soldiers began with this core set of values, they arrived at differing views on the ultimate sense of the war. A committed Nazi saw things differently than a former communist, and the same was true for a fifty-two-year-old general and a twenty-three-year-old lieutenant. Their basic understanding of the military, though, remained the same, and in battle it was irrelevant how soldiers' individual values had been formed, as long as they stuck to the core virtues as a guide for their interpretations and actions. Men like Axel von dem Bussche and Otto-Ernst Remer, both highly decorated battalion commanders, hardly differed in terms of their military ethos, even though the former was a major figure within the German resistance, and the latter was responsible for smashing the anti-Nazi opposition in Berlin.

The consequences that emerged from this positively charged canon of values were far-reaching. Few people seriously questioned either the Wehrmacht or the war itself, even if they believed Germany was heading for defeat or were outraged by atrocities. The idea that a soldier had to do his duty under all circumstances was so firmly anchored in soldiers' frame of reference that it could only be shaken by the immediate prospect of death or complete military defeat. The imperative to act according to military norms only ended when the Wehrmacht order collapsed and soldiers could no longer see any sense in sacrificing their lives for a lost cause. Self-sacrifice for its own sake was never a part of the classic military canon of values, and the Nazi leadership had little success over the course of the war in radicalizing soldiers' attitudes.

Biographical factors no doubt influenced how individuals interpreted the war. But quantitatively speaking, such differences were marginal and got smoothed over by the daily experience of battle in much the same way as differences in social class. Only at the core of the left-wing and Catholic milieus did the military canon of values possess less appeal.[896] Far more influential in shaping individuals' attitudes and behavior were military formations. Elite units, for instance, had their own variations on the military frame of reference, although they affected perceptions of the war far less than soldiers' actions and consequences. What mattered for elite soldiers was action. An elite fighter was supposed to prove his mettle in battle, and not just talk about it. In each branch of the military and each class of weaponry, specific identities crystallized. They in turn were heavily influenced by concrete events and experiences. The trope of fighting to the death, for instance, was interpreted in significantly different ways by an infantry soldier, a fighter pilot, and a submarine helmsman.

VIOLENCE

Violence is practiced by all groups, men and women, educated and uneducated people, Catholics, Protestants, and Muslims, if cultural and social situations make it seem sensible. Exercising violence is a *constructive* social act. That is to say, perpetrators use it to achieve goals and create realities. They compel others to bend to their will, distinguish those who belong from those who are excluded, increase their own power, and take possession of the property of those vanquished. Violence is also destructive, of course, and not just for its victims.

Yet none of this argues for the persistent myth that violence is always bubbling, waiting to be released, just below the thin crust of civilization. All these reflections imply that groups of human beings have perennially chosen the option of violence when it seemed likely to promote their own survival. In fact, civilization is not some sort of thin crust. Ever since modern nations introduced the principle of a state monopoly on the legitimate use of force, meaning that every private act of violence can be punished, the use of violence has dramatically declined. This bit of progress brought on by civilization has allowed for the level of freedom enjoyed by the citizens of democratic societies today. Yet that does not mean violence has been eradicated. It has only taken on a different form. It does not mean that individuals or groups never violate the state's monopoly or that democratic states per se refrain from exercising violence. The frame of reference for violence in the modern age is different from that in nonmodern cultures—that is all. The question is not one of violence and its absence, but of its proportions and the means by which it is regulated.

A sufficient reason for people to decide to kill other people can be the feeling that their existence is threatened, that violence is being legitimately demanded of them, or that it makes some sort of political, cultural, or religious sense. This applies not just to violence in the course of a war, but to other social situations as well. For this reason, the violence practiced by Wehrmacht soldiers was not as a rule more "National Socialist" than the force used by British or American soldiers. The only cases in which the violence can be seen as National Socialist were those instances where it was directed against people who could under no circumstances be seen as a military threat: the murder of Soviet POWs and, above all, the extermination of European Jews. War, as is the case with all genocides, created the framework in which the constraints of civilization were revoked. It also created the large number of Wehrmacht soldiers who would eventually serve as "assistant executioners." The Holocaust did not define the character of World War II. Nonetheless, as the most extreme form of violence in human history, the Holocaust has influenced and formed people's views of that war. This historically unique crime still dominates our understanding today of history's most deadly war, an exorbitant explosion of violence that claimed 50 million lives. Yet the majority of the victims died in the violence of World War II, not as a result of the Holocaust. All the wars waged in the meantime have shown that it is inappropriate to show outrage or surprise that people are killed and maimed when there is war. If there is war, that's the way it is.

It would be more productive to ask whether and under what circumstances people can refrain from killing. That would put an end to the ostentatious demonstrations of horror at the crimes and violence against innocent civilians every time states decide to wage war. Civilian casualties are inevitable because the frame of reference "war" promotes actions and creates temporary structures in which violence, in either a total or partial sense, can no longer be constrained and limited. Like every form of social behavior, violence has its own specific dynamic. This book is full of illustrations of what that dynamic is.

Will it ever be possible for a historical or sociological analysis of violence to develop the sort of moral neutrality a quantum physicist maintains toward an electron? Will such analysis ever be able to describe violence as a social possibility with the same detachment as political scientists approach elections and parliaments? As products of the modern age, history and social sciences are duty bound to follow certain basic assumptions. That's why they encounter such difficulty when confronted with phenomena that challenge those assumptions.

If we cease to define violence as an aberration, we learn more about our society and how it functions than if we persist in comforting illusions about our own basically nonviolent nature. If we reclassify violence in its various forms as part of the inventory of possible social actions among communities that have come together for mutual survival, we will see that such groups are also always potential communities of annihilation. Modernity's faith in its own distance from violence is illusionary. People kill for various motives. Soldiers kill because it's their job.

APPENDIX

The Surveillance Protocols

"Know your enemy."

Sun Tsu (500 B.C.)

For as long as there have been wars, combatants have tried to spy on their enemies to gain a decisive advantage. By the late nineteenth century, the world was becoming ever more interconnected, and technological revolutions in transportation and the media increased the possibilities for human knowledge to the extent that surveillance work was professionalized. The first modern secret service arose in Britain, and the world's other major powers were quick to establish intelligence agencies of their own. During World War I, complexly structured institutions began collecting and evaluating information from a broad variety of sources. That entailed decoding radio messages, carrying out aerial surveillance, and interrogating POWs. Classic forms of spying temporarily faded in significance.

Learning from past experience, the British War Ministry began in March 1939 to set up special interrogation centers for POWs in case the country had to go back to war.[897] For the first time, it was planned to bug POWs' cells and systematically eavesdrop on what they said. The idea wasn't new. In 1918, an interrogation center with hidden microphones was ready to go operational, before being halted by the armistice that ended World War I. With the establishment of the Combined Services Detailed Interrogation Centre (CSDIC) on September 26, 1939, the idea was revived. After being temporarily located in the Tower of London, the center moved to the estate of Trent Park in the north of Britain's capital. Latimer House and Wilton Park were added as facilities in 1942. In July of that year, the entire CSDIC moved to Latimer House. Wilton Park was used to house Italian POWs.[898] Trent Park became a long-term internment facility for German staff officers.[899]

A drawing of Trent Park made by Lieutenant Klaus Hubbuch.
(Neitzel Archive)

The Americans adopted the British system of interrogations and surveillance, and the Allies soon established a network of secret cross-continental Interrogation Centers.[900] Those on the Mediterranean and in the United States were particularly significant. By summer 1941, the War Department in Washington had already decided to build such centers, and over the course of 1942, two of them, run jointly by the U.S. Navy and Army, became operational. Japanese POWs were sent to Camp Tracy in California, while Fort Hunt in Virginia housed German POWs.

Only a small percentage of the approximately one million German POWs captured by the British and the Americans were brought to these special facilities. After subjecting captives to a multipart interrogation process on the front lines and further behind them, Allied intelligence officers selected POWs who seemed to possess especially interesting information for additional surveillance. Nonetheless, their numbers were relatively large. From September 1939 to October 1945, 10,191 German POWs and 563 Italian ones were transferred through the three English surveillance camps. The length of time they stayed there varied from a few days to three years. The CSDIC (U.K.) made 16,960 protocols from the conversations of German POWs, and 1,943 from Italian prisoners.[901] All in all, these documents totaled some

48,000 printed pages. From various locations near the Mediterranean, Cairo, Algiers, and Naples, 538 protocols were made covering conversations between 1,225 German soldiers.[902] A large number of reports have also survived of conversations between 3,298 German POWs at Fort Hunt.

The British material consists of word-by-word transcriptions in German varying in length from half a page to twenty-two pages, usually accompanied by English translations. For reasons of secrecy, the names of those conversing were omitted until 1944. They were usually identified only by their rank and official position. Nonetheless, it was possible to reconstruct most of their names. Unfortunately, the British documents contain no information about individual biographies. Those from Fort Hunt are more revealing, since American intelligence subjected German POWs not only to covert surveillance but to interrogations and questionnaires as well. This was in accordance with the innovative idea of using surveys to research Wehrmacht morale. In addition, so-called Personal Record Sheets listed all the main data historians today need to reconstruct individual biographies. There are additional documents such as POWs' own descriptions of their past and reports noting intelligence officers' special observations. All the documents prepared by the personnel at Fort Hunt were collected in a file devoted to the individual POW so that interrogation officers could always refer to the data when questioning prisoners.[903] Organized alphabetically according to the prisoners' names, the so-called 201 files eventually encompassed more than 100,000 pages.[904] The core of this material, the surveillance protocols, amounted to some 40,000 pages.

The scope of the British and American reports is indeed impressive. But two questions arose as to the quality of the information they contain:

1. How representative was the group of soldiers whose words were recorded?
2. Did the POWs know they were being spied upon? How frank and unencumbered were the conversations contained in the protocols?

Interestingly, the social makeup of the POWs was different in British and American surveillance camps. The Allies were dividing up the work. The British mainly eavesdropped on high-ranking officers and

C. S. D. I. C. (U.K.)

S. R. REPORT

IF FURTHER CIRCULATION OF THIS REPORT IS NECESSARY IT MUST BE
PARAPHRASED, SO THAT NEITHER THE SOURCE OF THE INFORMATION NOR
THE MEANS BY WHICH IT HAS BEEN OBTAINED IS APPARENT.

S.R.G.G. 739

M 170 - Generalmajor (Chief Artillery Officer: German Army Group AFRICA)
                                        Captured TUNISIA 9 May 43
M 179 - Generalmajor (GOC 10th Pz. Division) Captured TUNISIA 12 May 43
M 181 - Generalmajor (GOC 164th Division) Captured TUNISIA 13 May 43
A 1201 - Generalmajor (GOC Air Defences TUNIS and BIZERTA) Captd TUNISIA 9 May 43

Information received: 1 Jan 44

GERMAN TEXT

? M 179: Ich habe einmal in diesem Kriege Menschen erschiessen lassen müssen
          und zwar zwei, die sind ...... gefasst worden als Spione und auch
          nach Aussagen von den Einwohnern aktiv, ... diese Leute waren nun
          so brave offene Leute, teils ältere Gefreite, die waren wachsbleich,
          denen war das so ekelhaft. Da kam der Adjutant heran und sagte, der
          ist für heute völlig fertig, der läuft bloss 'rum und ist also bei-
          nahe irre, weil ihm das so auf die Nerven gegangen sei.

? M 170: ...... haben sie öfters die Kuriere zwischen SALONIKI und SOFIA auf
          diesen langen Strassen angefallen und wenn das passierte, wurden diese
          Nachbars(?)dörfer dem Erdboden gleich gemacht, da wurde alles -
          Weiber, Kinder und Männer, zusammengetrieben und niedergemetzelt.
          Hat mir auch der Regimentskommandeur erzählt - BRÜCKENMANN, ja.
          Der hat einmal erzählt, wie viehisch das war. Da wurden sie in einen
          Pferch getrieben, dann hiess es: "Nun schiesst darauf." Natürlich
          brachen sie zusammen nach vielem Gebrüll - auch die Kinder - und
          waren natürlich noch nicht tot. Da musste nachher ein Offizier hin-
          gehen und musste denen einen Genickschuss geben. Dann haben sie sie
          alle in die Kirche geschleppt und haben sie einzeln herausgeholt und
          haben sie immer zu dritt erschossen. Das haben sie nun drin gehört,
          haben sich noch verbarrikadiert und haben Widerstand geleistet; da
          haben sie ...... die Kirche abbrennen müssen, weil sie nicht herein-
          kamen. Der sagte, es wäre viehisch, diese Abschlachterei, obwohl -

?   : Es waren auch andere da ......

?   : Nein, nein, ... griechische(?) Dörfer.

?   : Das war aber vom Heer aus befohlen ......

?   : Das war vom Heer aus.

                                                                        /2

*A surveillance protocol from Trent Park. (The National Archives,
London)*

navy and Luftwaffe men. Around one half of the POWs in Fort Hunt,
on the other hand, were simple foot soldiers from the German army.
A third were low-ranking officers, and only around a sixth, staff officers.[905] The British thus concentrated on the Wehrmacht elite, while
Americans focused on ordinary men.

Admittedly, this material does not come from a representative cross section of the Wehrmacht and the Waffen SS. In order for that to have been the case, all of the 17 million members of the German armed forces would have to have had an equal statistical likelihood of being interned in one of the surveillance facilities. That was of course not the case. For example, there were no POWs who had fought exclusively on the Eastern Front. Conversely, members of combat units, and in particular submarine and Luftwaffe crew members, were overrepresented.

Nonetheless, the soldiers subjected to surveillance covered a broad spectrum. Practically every type of military curriculum vita is represented, from navy frogmen to administrative generals. The men in question fought on all the fronts of the war, articulated a variety of political views, and were members of the most diverse sorts of units. Whereas letters sent home from the front usually skew our perspective toward better-educated soldiers, whose correspondence was more likely to be preserved, the protocols feature the voices of soldiers of whom no other documentary evidence has survived.

Naturally, the question arises of whether the POWs might have known they were being listened in on. That would cast doubt upon the authenticity of the information they provide. They must have at least suspected that the British and Americans would want to tap into what they knew, and they could have consciously spread disinformation. In fact, Allied methods of intelligence gathering were hardly unknown in Germany. A POW named Franz von Werra, who had been briefly interned at Trent Park, managed to escape British custody and reported back in detail about English interrogation techniques.[906] On June 11, 1941, the German Military Intelligence Service issued guidelines about how Wehrmacht soldiers were to behave if captured by the British. They included warnings about potential spies in German uniform and concealed microphones. The authors of the guidelines explicitly stressed that the enemy had repeatedly obtained valuable information via such channels.[907] In November 1943, as part of the first exchange of POWs, Lieutenant Commander Schilling returned to Germany and briefed his superiors about his and others' experiences with British interrogation. In this way, the Wehrmacht supreme command learned the names of a number of spies who were working with the British. They also heard that the generals in Trent Park "were too open and cavalier in their mutual conversations, neglecting the need for caution." Again, it was stressed that German soldiers should beware of spies and covert surveillance should they happen to be captured.[908]

The protocols, however, strongly suggest that most German POWs forgot all about these warnings and prattled on heedlessly with their comrades about their military experiences. For instance, there are repeated references in conversations between NCOs and ordinary soldiers to the Nazi propaganda film *Warriors Behind Barbed Wire*[909] as well as cautionary remarks not to reveal information to the enemy. But in the same breath, the speakers would then discuss matters they had concealed during interrogations,[910] dictating secrets directly into a waiting microphone. It never occurred to most soldiers that they could be under covert surveillance—a fact confirmed by the self-incriminating statements they made concerning atrocities.[911] No doubt, some soldiers kept their mouths shut, perhaps because they suspected their quarters might be bugged.[912] But most just threw caution to the wind after a short time. The need to share their thoughts with comrades was greater than the dictates of prudence.[913]

We must recall that the Allies used a number of clever tricks to tap the knowledge of their enemy. German exiles and cooperative POWs were used to steer conversations,[914] and POWs of the same rank but different divisions and units were housed together. These methods proved very successful. Submarine navigators from various vessels swapped stories about what they had experienced, and Luftwaffe officers recalled battles and compared notes about the technical details of their aircraft. Soldiers were often transferred to the camps only a few days after they had been captured, and many were still in a state of shock from the often dramatic circumstances in which they had been taken prisoner. That increased their need to talk. After all, many had narrowly escaped being killed. There was no difference in the behavior of officers and ordinary soldiers on this score.

The interrogation reports from Fort Hunt demonstrate just how cooperative many POWs were. A surprising number of them simply told everything they knew in hope of getting better treatment or— far more rarely—to damage the Nazi regime.[915] Some dictated data like exact measurements to the interrogating officers; others made sketches of military facilities in Germany or construction plans for weaponry. Most of the POWs hesitated to cooperate to that extent, but only censored themselves with reference to tactical and technical specifics. On questions of politics, conditions in Germany, or morale in the Wehrmacht, they were entirely forthcoming. These men were equally open when conversing with one another. To the delight of Allied intelligence officers, the only taboo was talking about one's own feelings.

British and American intelligence, of course, did not devote such enormous energy to collecting this information for the benefit of later generations of historians. So what sort of results did the surveillance yield? Intelligence gathered during World War II was highly complex, and decisions were never made on the basis of a single source. Interrogation and eavesdropping on POWs was part of the Human Intelligence Division, which was only a part, if a key one, of a whole intelligence network. Over the course of the war, the Allies succeeded in gaining insights into all aspects of the Wehrmacht, including the condition, tactics, and morale of Germany's fighting forces and the technical specifications of their weaponry. The enormous potential of human intelligence became obvious for the first time during the Battle of Britain, and after that it was unthinkable that it would not be part of the process of information gathering. The most spectacular success recorded by human intelligence was probably information that proved crucial to Britain's successful defense against the V1 and V2 rockets. A conversation between Generals Thoma and Crüwell had given the decisive tip.[916]

There is no doubt that the energy invested in surveillance of POWs was worthwhile, and the Allies knew only too well that they had built up an effective system for gathering human intelligence. For that reason the surveillance files were not made available to prosecutors at the war crimes trials in Germany. The Allies' own methods of gathering intelligence were, at all costs, to be kept secret.[917]

ACKNOWLEDGMENTS

A book like this is the result of many people's research and would not exist without the support of numerous colleagues.

Our most profound gratitude goes out to the Gerda Henkel and Fritz Thyssen Foundation for financing our research group. Dr. Michael Hanssler, Dr. Angela Kühnen, Dr. Frank Suder, and their teams were extremely committed in assisting us. They and their institutions are impressive examples of how research can be funded in a goal-oriented, efficient, uncomplicated, and cordial manner.

We would like to thank Prof. Dr. Michael Matheus, the director of German Historical Institute in Rome, for helping us with the grant application, supporting work on the project in Italy, and for organizing a conference in April 2008, where we were able to present some of our findings to our Italian colleagues. We are also very grateful to Dr. Lutz Klinkhammer for his work on the Italian part of the project. The Institute for Advanced Study in the Humanities in Essen was not only a central research location, but a generous host for workshops, conferences, and lectures. That helped us make progress in an extremely inspiring, interdisciplinary atmosphere.

We would also like to acknowledge those who worked on the project—Dr. Christian Gudehus, Dr. Amedeo Osti Guerrazzi, Dr. Felix Römer, Dr. Michaela Christ, Sebastian Gross, MA, and Tobias Seidl, MA—for three years of intense and constructive research. They formed an excellent team, and it was a joy to work with them. In June 2008, Dr. Richard Germann of Ludwig Boltzmann Institute for Historical Social Science in Vienna joined our ranks. To him we owe numerous bits of information about the socio-biographical background of the POWs who were put under surveillance as well as about Austrians in the Wehrmacht. Dr. Dietmar Rost provided us with a number of excellent pieces of advice concerning American soldiers.

We were very pleased that our work on this project spilled over into university instruction, and that a number of MA theses were written on this topic. With their work, Falko Bell, Nicole Bögli, Stephanie

Fuchs, Alexander Hoerkens, Frederik Müllers, Anette Neder, Katharina Straub, Martin Treutlein, Daniela Wellnitz, and Matthias Weusmann all made important contributions to the project, and we thank them sincerely for their commitment and interest.

We also received valuable tips, advice, and support from Dr. Alexander Brakel, Dr. Christian Hartmann, Prof. Dr. Gerhard Hirschfeld, Dr. Johannes Hürter, Prof. Dr. Michael Kißener, Prof. Dr. MacGregor Knox, Dr. Peter Lieb, Dr. Timothy Mulligan, Dr. Axel Niestlé, Prof. Dr. Andreas Rödder, Dr. Thomas Schlemmer, Dr. Klaus Schmider, and Adrian Wettstein. Dr. Jens Kroh, Manuel Dittrich, Dr. Sabine Meister, Vanessa Stahl, and Florian Hessel were very helpful in preparing the manuscript and deserve our gratitude. Finally, we would like to thank the S. Fischer publishing house for their faith in us and above all Prof. Dr. Walter Pehle for his customarily expert and careful editing.

Sönke Neitzel and Harald Welzer, December 2010

Notes

Abbreviations

AFHQ	Allied Forces Headquarters
BA/MA	German Federal Archive/Military Archive, Freiburg i.Br.
CSDIC (UK)	Combined Services Detailed Interrogation Centre (U.K.)
GRGG	General Report German Generals
HDv	Official Germany Army Reports
ISRM	Italy Special Report Army
I/SRN	Italy/Special Report Navy
KTB	Wartime Diary
NARA	National Archives and Records Administration, Washington, D.C.
OKW	Wehrmacht Supreme Command
PAAA	Political Archive, German Foreign Ministry
SKl	German Naval Command
SRA	Special Report Air Force
SRCMF	Special Report Central Mediterranean Forces
SRGG	Special Report German Generals
SRIG	Special Report Italian Generals
SRM	Special Report Army
SRN	Special Report Navy
SRX	Special Report Mixed
TNA	The National Archives, Kew Gardens, London
USHMM	United States Holocaust Memorial Museum
WFSt	Wehrmacht General Staff

1. The research group worked under the direction of Dr. Christian Gudehus and consisted of Dr. Amedeo Osti Guerrazzi, Dr. Felix Römer, Dr. Michaela Christ, Sebastian Groß, and Tobias Seidl. More detailed analyses can be found in Harald Welzer, Sönke Neitzel, and Christian Gudehus, eds., *"Der Führer war wieder viel zu human, viel zu gefühlvoll!"* (Frankfurt/Main: Fischer, 2011).
2. SRA 2670, 20 June 1942, TNA, WO 208/4126.
3. SRA 3686, 20 February 1943, TNA, WO 208/4129.
4. A further influence on the concept of the frame of reference was the work of French sociologist Maurice Halbwachs, who was murdered in the Buchen-

wald concentration camp. He pointed out the formative influence of the social framework ("cadres sociaux") in memory.

5. It is unclear precisely how many people panicked. *The New York Times* ran a story on 31 October 1938 entitled "Radio Listeners in Panic, Taking War Drama as Fact," and reported on various incidents, in which an entire block's worth of people fled their apartments. The article did not use the phrase "mass panic," although a significant number of people certainly did mistake fiction for fact.

6. Gregory Bateson, *Ökologie des Geistes* (Frankfurt/Main: Suhrkamp, 1999).

7. Alfred Schütz, *Der sinnhafte Aufbau der sozialen Welt: Eine Einleitung in die verstehende Soziologie* (Frankfurt/Main: Suhrkamp, 1993).

8. Erving Goffman, *Rahmenanalyse* (Frankfurt/Main: Suhrkamp, 1980), p. 99.

9. Kazimierz Sakowicz was a Polish journalist who began documenting the mass murder of Lithuanian Jews in 1941. Rachel Margolis and Jim Tobias, eds., *Die geheimen Notizen des K. Sakowicz: Dokumente zur Judenvernichtung in Ponary, 1941–1943* (Frankfurt/Main: Fischer, 2005), p. 53.

10. Williamson Murray and Allan R. Millet, *A War to Be Won: Fighting the Second World War* (Cambridge: Harvard University Press, 2001), p. 360.

11. Norbert Elias, *Was ist Soziologie?* (Munich: Juventa, 2004).

12. Cited in Rolf Schörken, *Luftwaffenhelfer und Drittes Reich: Die Entstehung eines politischen Bewusstseins* (Stuttgart: Klett-Cotta Verlag, 1985), p. 144.

13. Raul Hilberg, *Täter, Opfer, Zuschauer: Die Vernichtung der Juden, 1933–1945* (Frankfurt/Main: Fischer, 1992), p. 138.

14. Martin Heinzelmann, *Göttingen im Luftkrieg* (Gottingen: Die Werkstatt, 2003).

15. Norbert Elias, *Studien über die Deutschen* (Frankfurt/Main: Suhrkamp, 1989).

16. Michel Foucault, *Überwachen und Strafen* (Frankfurt/Main: Suhrkamp Verlag, 1994).

17. Erving Goffman, *Asyle: Über die Situation psychiatrischer Patienten und anderer Insassen* (Frankfurt/Main: Suhrkamp, 1973).

18. Rolf Schörken recalled of his experiences as a sixteen-year-old assistant anti-aircraft gunner: "In the school classes of this age group, pupils who displayed a mixture of intelligence, sporting prowess and social skills normally had the most say.... Now, the antithetical type of pupil took control: those who had grown more quickly and were simply more physically powerful than the others. Intelligence of the sort promoted in school, to say nothing of being educated, almost became negative traits and were punished with ridicule and scorn. Anyone who dared read a serious book or listened to serious music was a lost cause.... These new shapers of opinion create a pressure, indeed a compulsion to conform that knew no corrective limits. The fact that we were all part of the Wehrmacht did little to counteract this. In reality, being connected to the Wehrmacht was what enabled people to completely let themselves go in battle." See Schörken, *Luftwaffenhelfer und Drittes Reich.*

19. Harald Welzer, "Jeder die Gestapo des anderen: Über totale Gruppen," in *Stadt der Sklaven/Slave City,* Museum Folkwang, ed. (Essen, 2008), pp. 177–90.

20. Room Conversation, Schlottig–Wertenbruch, 10 August 1944, NARA, RG 165, Entry 179, Box 540.
21. Raul Hilberg, *Die Vernichtung der europäischen Juden* (Frankfurt/Main: Fischer, 1990), p. 1080.
22. Karl E. Weick and Kathleen M. Sutcliffe, *Das Unerwartete managen: Wie Unternehmen aus Extremsituationen lernen* (Stuttgart: Schaeffer-Poescher, 2003).
23. Gerhard Paul, *Bilder des Krieges, Krieg der Bilder: Die Visualisierung des modernen Krieges* (Paderborn: Schoeningh Verlag, 2004), p. 236.
24. SRM 564, 17 June 1944, TNA, WO 208/4138.
25. Wolfram Wette, ed., *Stille Helden—Judenretter im Dreiländereck während des Zweiten Weltkriegs* (Freiburg: Herder, 2005), pp. 215–32.
26. Harald Welzer, *Täter: Wie aus ganz normalen Menschen Massenmörder werden* (Frankfurt/Main: Fischer Verlag, 2005), p. 183.
27. GRGG 217, 29–30 October 1944, TNA, WO 208/4364.
28. There has been much written about the fact that more than 60 percent of the participants in the Milgram experiment were willing to subject what they believed was a fellow participant to a presumably lethal dose of electricity. The experiment was duplicated in more than ten other countries, and the results remained comparable. What has attracted less attention is the fact that the percentage of people who blindly obeyed instructions sank when the experiment was varied. This strongly suggested that social immediacy has a strong influence on obedience. If there was contact between the "learner" and the "teacher," for instance, if they were in the same room or the "teacher" had to press the "learner's" hand onto an electrified surface, the percentage of those who blindly followed instructions sank to 40 and 30 percent respectively. The significance of social proximity also emerges when "teachers" and "learners" were friends, acquaintances, or family members. In these cases, the percentage of blind obedience dropped to 15 percent, and "disobedient" subjects tended to break off the experiment significantly earlier than in other variations of the Milgram test.
29. Edward A. Shils and Morris Janowitz, "Cohesion and Disintegration in the Wehrmacht in World War II," *Public Opinion Quarterly* 12, no. 2 (Summer 1948).
30. Morton Hunt, *Das Rätsel der Nächstenliebe* (Frankfurt: Suhrkamp Taschenbuch, 1988), p. 77.
31. Cited in ibid.
32. Sebastian Haffner, *Geschichte eines Deutschen. Erinnerungen, 1914–1933* (Munich: Der Hoerverlag GmbH, 2002), p. 105.
33. Harald Welzer, Sabine Moller, and Karoline Tschuggnall, *"Opa war kein Nazi": Nationalsozialismus und Holocaust im Familiengedächtnis* (Frankfurt/Main: Fischer, 2002), p. 75.
34. Sebastian Haffner also wrote: "The strange and disheartening thing was admittedly that, beyond the initial shock, the first grand announcement of a new mood of murder in all of Germany occasioned a flood of discussions—but about the 'Jewish question' and not the anti-Semitic question. It was a

trick the Nazis also used successfully in a number of other 'questions.' By publicly threatening someone else—a country, a population or a group of people—with death, they prompted a general discussion of the other's right to existence instead of their own. Such discussions actively questioned the value of others' lives. Suddenly, everyone felt competent and justified in having and spreading an opinion about Jews." Haffner, *Geschichte*, p. 139ff.

35. Welzer, *Täter*, p. 161ff.
36. Peter Longerich, *Davon haben wir nichts gewusst! Die Deutschen und die Judenverfolgung 1933–1945* (Munich: Siedler, 2006), p. 25ff.
37. Saul Friedländer, *Das Dritte Reich und die Juden: Die Jahre der Verfolgung 1933–1945* (Munich: Deutsche Taschenbuch Verlag, 1998), p. 24.
38. Michael Wildt, *Volksgemeinschaft als Selbstermächtigung: Gewalt gegen Juden in der deutschen Provinz, 1919–1939* (Hamburg: Hamburger Edition, 2007).
39. Peter Longerich, *Politik der Vernichtung: Eine Gesamtdarstellung der nationalsozialistischen Judenverfolgung* (Munich: Piper Verlag, 1998), p. 578.
40. Raphael Groß, *Anständig geblieben: Nationalsozialistische Moral* (Frankfurt/ Main: Fischer Verlag, 2010); Welzer, *Täter*, p. 48ff.
41. Saul Friedländer, *Das Dritte Reich und die Juden: Die Jahre der Verfolgung, 1933–1945* (Munich: Deutsche Taschenbuch Verlag, 1998), p. 24.
42. The average age of the leaders within the party and the state was thirty-four and forty-four respectively. See Götz Aly, *Hitlers Volksstaat: Raub, Rassenkrieg und nationaler Sozialismus* (Frankfurt/Main: Fischer Verlag, 2005), p. 12ff.
43. Ibid. The quote is from the English translation, *Hitler's Beneficiaries: Plunder, Racial War and the Nazi Welfare State* (New York: Metropolitan Books, 2007), p. 11.
44. See Lutz Niethammer and Alexander von Plato, *"Wir kriegen jetzt andere Zeiten"* (Bonn: Dietz Verlag J. H. W. Nachf, 1985); Harald Welzer, Robert Montau, and Christine Plaß, *"Was wir für böse Menschen sind!" Der Nationalsozialismus im Gespräch zwischen den Generationen* (Tübingen: Edition Diskord, 1997); Welzer, Moller, and Tschuggnall, *Opa*; Eric Johnson and Karl-Heinz Reuband, *What We Knew: Terror, Mass Murder and Everyday Life in Nazi Germany* (London: Basic Books, 2005), p. 341; Marc Philipp, *Hitler ist tot, aber ich lebe noch: Zeitzeugenerinnerungen an den Nationalsozialismus* (Berlin: Bebra Verlag, 2010).
45. Aly, *Volksstaat*, p. 353ff.
46. Hans Dieter Schäfer, *Das gespaltene Bewußtsein: Vom Dritten Reich bis zu den langen Fünfziger Jahren* (Gottingen: Wallstein, 2009), p. 18.
47. Ibid., p. 12.
48. Wolfram Wette et al., eds., *Das Deutsche Reich und der Zweite Weltkrieg*, Vol. 1 (Stuttgart: Metzler Verlag, 1991), p. 123ff.
49. For an international comparison of militaristic discourse from the mideighteenth century to the outbreak of World War II, see Jörn Leonhard, *Bellizismus und Nation: Kriegsdeutung und Nationsbestimmung in Europa und den Vereinigten Staaten, 1750–1914* (Munich: Oldenbourg Verlag, 2008).

50. For a concise account, see Brian K. Feltman, "Death Before Dishonor: The Heldentod Ideal and the Dishonor of Surrender on the Western Front, 1914–1918," lecture manuscript (University of Bern, 10 September 2010). See Isabel V. Hull, *Absolute Destruction: Military Culture and the Practices of War in Imperial Germany* (Ithaca: Cornell University Press, 2005); Alan Kramer, *Dynamic of Destruction: Culture and Mass Killing in the First World War* (Oxford: Oxford University Press, 2007); Alexander Watson, *Enduring the Great War: Combat, Morale and Collapse in the German and the British Armies, 1914–1918* (New York: Cambridge University Press, 2008).

51. Watson, *Enduring*, p. 3. The trope of fighting to the last bullet was very powerful throughout the nineteenth century. It is reflected in the 1873 painting *Les Dernières Cartouches* by Alphonse de Neuville, which heroically stylized the defense of the Bourgerie in Bazeilles near Sedan and was enthusiastically received all over France.

52. Rüdiger Bergien, *Die bellizistische Republik: Wehrkonsens und "Wehr-haftmachung"* in *Deutschland, 1918–1933* (Munich: Oldenbourg Wissen-schaftsverlag, 2010). For the international context, see Stig Förster, ed., *An der Schwelle zum Totalen Krieg: Die militärische Debatte um den Krieg der Zukunft, 1919–1939* (Paderborn: Schoeningh, 2002).

53. Jürgen Förster, "Geistige Kriegführung in Deutschland 1919 bis 1945," in *Das Deutsche Reich und der Zweite Weltkrieg*, Vol. 9/1, Militärgeschichtliches Forschungsamt, ed. (Munich: Deutsche Verlags-Anstalt, 2004), p. 472.

54. Sabine Behrenbeck, "Zwischen Trauer und Heroisierung: Vom Umgang mit Kriegstod und Niederlage nach 1918," in *Kriegsende 1918: Ereignis, Wirkung, Nachwirkung*, Jörg Duppler and Gerhard P. Groß, eds. (Munich: Oldenbourg, 1999), p. 336ff.

55. Karl Demeter, *Das Deutsche Offizierskorps, 1650–1945* (Frankfurt/Main: Bernard & Graefe, 1965), p. 328.

56. See also Christian Kehrt, *Moderne Kriege: Die Technikerfahrungen deutscher Militärpiloten, 1910–1945* (Paderborn: Schoeningh Verlag, 2010), p. 228.

57. Sönke Neitzel, *Abgehört: Deutsche Generäle in britischer Kriegsgefangen-schaft, 1942–1945,* 4th edition (Berlin: List Taschenbuch, 2009), pp. 452, 456, 435, 449, 440.

58. BA/MA, Pers 6/6670.

59. BA/MA, Pers 6/9017.

60. Neitzel, *Abgehört*, p. 457.

61. BA/MA, Pers 6/770. Freiherr von Adrian-Werburg received a similar evalua-tion; see 2 September 1943, BA/MA, Pers 6/10239.

62. Neitzel, *Abgehört*, p. 442.

63. Ibid., p. 468.

64. BA/MA, Pers 6/6410.

65. Neitzel, *Abgehört*, p. 462.

66. Cited in Förster, "Geistige Kriegführung im Deutschland 1919 bis 1945," in *Das Deutsche Reich*, Vol. 9/1, p. 554. On Dönitz, see Dieter Hartwig, *Großad-miral Karl Dönitz: Legende und Wirklichkeit* (Paderborn: Schoeningh, 2010).

67. Report of Activity, Schmundt, 24–25 June 1943, p. 75.

68. See also the evaluations of Generals Friedrich von Broich and Walter Bruns in Neitzel, *Abgehört,* pp. 432, 434.

69. Heribert van Haupt, "Der Heldenkampf der deutschen Infanterie vor Moskau," *Deutsche Allgemeine Zeitung,* Berlin afternoon edition No. 28 (16 January 1942), p. 2.

70. Hubert Hohlweck, "Soldat und Politik," *Deutsche Allgemeine Zeitung,* Berlin edition No. 543 (13 November 1943), p. 1ff.

71. Erich Murawski, *Der deutsche Wehrmachtbericht* (Boppard: Boldt, 1962): 21 July 1944, p. 202; 3 August 1944, p. 219; 4 August 1944, p. 222; 19 August 1944, p. 241, 2 November 1944, p. 349; 3 November 1944, p. 351. On sacrifice, see 3 November 1944, p. 350; on the fanaticism of the Waffen SS, see 27 February 1945, p. 495; 30 March 1945, p. 544.

72. For example, Order No. 52 of 28 January 1944. See Walter Hubatsch, ed., *Hitlers Weisungen für die Kriegsführung, 1939–1945: Dokumente des Oberkommandos der Wehrmacht* (Uttingen: Doerfler im Nebel-Verlag, 2000), p. 242.

73. Johannes Hürter, *Hitlers Heerführer: Die deutschen Oberbefehlshaber im Krieg gegen die Sowjetunion 1941/42* (Munich: Oldenbourg Verlag, 2006), p. 71.

74. In contrast to World War I, the Grand Cross was not used as a decoration for bravery. Although it was mentioned in a statute of decorations as an acknowledgment for decisive actions that changed the course of battles, Hermann Göring was the only person ever to receive one. That was to underscore his position as the Führer's designated successor. There apparently were plans to award Heinrich Himmler one as well for his role as the commander of the Army Group Weichsel. But since he failed in that task, he was not decorated. Therefore, in World War II, the Grand Cross was a decoration for Nazi leaders who carried out military functions.

75. For exact statistics, see http://www.ritterkreuztraeger-1939–45.de/Sonstiges /Statistiken/Statistiken-Startseite.htm.

76. Manfred Dörr, *Die Träger der Nahkampfspange in Gold. Heer: Luftwaffe. Waffen-SS* (Osnabruck: Biblio Verlag, 1996), p. xviii.

77. Christoph Rass, *"Menschenmaterial": Deutsche Soldaten an der Ostfront: Innenansichten einer Infanteriedivision, 1939–1945* (Paderborn: Schoeningh Verlag, 2003), p. 259ff. See also Christian Hartmann, *Wehrmacht im Ostkrieg: Front und militärisches Hinterland, 1941/42* (Munich: Oldenbourg Wissenschaftsverlag, 2009), pp. 189–201.

78. For more information on cases that led to convictions, see Rass, *"Menschenmaterial,"* pp. 256–58.

79. René Schilling, *"Kriegshelden": Deutungsmuster heroischer Männlichkeit in Deutschland, 1813–1945* (Paderborn: Schoeningh Verlag 2002), pp. 316–72.

80. Hartmann, *Wehrmacht im Ostkrieg,* p. 198.

81. See Ralph Winkle, *Der Dank des Vaterlandes: Eine Symbolgeschichte des Eisernen Kreuzes, 1914 bis 1936* (Essen: Klartext, 2007), p. 345ff.

82. SRA 177, 17 July 1940, TNA, WO 208/4118.

83. This became especially clear in the discussions surrounding the ordinances. Felix Römer, "Im alten Deutschland wäre ein solcher Befehl nicht möglich gewesen: Rezeption, Adaption und Umsetzung des Kriegsgerichtsbarkeitserlasses im Ostheer, 1941/42," *VfZG* 56 (2008), pp. 53–99.

84. James Waller, *Becoming Evil: How Ordinary People Commit Genocide and Mass Killing* (Oxford: Oxford University Press, 2002).
85. SRA 75, 30 April 1940, TNA, WO 208/4117. All subsequent quotations from this file.
86. See Jochen Böhler, *Auftakt zum Vernichtungskrieg: Die Wehrmacht in Polen, 1939* (Frankfurt/Main: Fischer, 2006).
87. Jan Philipp Reemtsma, *Vertrauen und Gewalt: Versuch über eine besondere Konstellation der Moderne* (Hamburg: Hamburger Edition, 2008).
88. Harald Welzer, *Verweilen beim Grauen* (Tübingen: Edition Diskord, 1998).
89. Mary Kaldor, *New and Old Wars: Organised Violence in a Global Era* (Cambridge: Polity Press, 2006); Herfried Münkler, *Über den Krieg: Stationen der Kriegsgeschichte im Spiegel ihrer theoretischen Reflexion* (Weilerswist: Velbrück, 2003).
90. One of the most prominent and frequently read works of this sort is Johanna Haarer's *Die deutsche Mutter und ihr erstes Kind* (The German Mother and Her First Child). It was first published in 1934 and was reprinted after the war without the word "German" in the title.
91. SRA 3616, 31 January 1943, TNA, WO 208/4129.
92. Böhler, *Auftakt*, p. 181ff.
93. Ibid., p. 185
94. See Kehrt, *Moderne Krieger*, pp. 403–7.
95. Donald E. Polkinghorne, "Narrative Psychologie und Geschichtsbewußtsein: Beziehungen und Perspektiven," in *Erzählung, Identität und historisches Bewußtsein: Die psychologische Konstruktion von Zeit und Geschichte: Erinnerung, Geschichte, Identität*, Jürgen Straub, ed. (Frankfurt/Main: Suhrkamp, 1998), pp. 12–45. See also the excellent study by Stefanie Schüler-Springorum, *Krieg und Fliegen: Die Legion Condor im Spanischen Bürgerkrieg* (Paderborn: Schoeningh Verlag, 2010), pp. 159–70, 176–80.
96. Svenja Goltermann, *Die Gesellschaft der Überlebenden: Deutsche Kriegsheimkehrer und ihre Gewalterfahrungen im Zweiten Weltkrieg* (Stuttgart: Dt. Verlag, 2009).
97. SRA 2642, 15 June 1942, TNA, WO 208/4126.
98. SRA 3536, 9 January 1943, TNA, WO 208/4129.
99. SRA 5538, 30 July 1944, TNA, WO 208/4134. The description refers to the "Vercors" mission from 21 July to early August 1944; cf. Peter Lieb, *Konventioneller Krieg oder NS-Weltanschauungskrieg? Kriegführung und Partisanenbekämpfung in Frankreich, 1943/44* (Munich: Oldenbourg Verlag, 2007), pp. 339–50.
100. SRA 1473, 1 April 1941, TNA, WO 208/4123.
101. SRA 180, 18 July 1940, TNA, WO 208/4118. This story refers to a false report made by a Stuka pilot, who claimed to have sunk a British battleship with a 250-kilogram bomb. It was common for soldiers to exaggerate their own successes. See Sönke Neitzel, *Der Einsatz der deutschen Luftwaffe über dem Atlantik und der Nordsee, 1939–1945* (Bonn: Bernard & Graefe, 1995), p. 40.
102. SRA 620, 26 September 1940, TNA, WO 208/4119.
103. SRA 3849, 18 March 1943, TNA, WO 208/4129.
104. SRA 623, 26 September 1940, TNA, WO 208/4119.

105. SRA 2600, 8 June 1942, TNA, WO 208/4126.
106. Klaus A. Maier et al., *Das Deutsche Reich und der Zweite Weltkrieg*, Vol. 2 (Stuttgart: Deutsche Verlag, 1979), p. 408.
107. SRA 2600, 8 June 1942, TNA, WO 208/4126.
108. Paul, *Bilder des Krieges, Krieg der Bilder*, p. 238.
109. SRA 2636, 15 June 1942, TNA, WO 208/4126.
110. Ibid.
111. SRA 2678, 19 June 1942, TNA, WO 208/4126.
112. SRA 3774, 6 March 1943, TNA, WO 208/4129.
113. Ibid.
114. SRA 3983, 6 May 1944, TNA, WO 208/4130.
115. SRA 828, 26 October 1940, TNA, WO 208/4120.
116. There were in fact cases on all war fronts of pilots being killed while parachuting to the ground. They were particularly frequent in the last phase of aerial warfare over Germany. American fighter pilots killed at least one hundred of their German counterparts in this fashion. Klaus Schmider, "The Last of the First: Veterans of the Jagdwaffe Tell Their Story," *Journal of Military History* 73 (2009), pp. 246–50. See also SRA 450, 4 September 1940, TNA, WO 208/4119; SRA 5460, 16 July 1944, TNA, WO 208/4134.
117. SRX 1657, 17 March 1943, TNA, WO 208/4162.
118. Ernst Jünger, *Kriegstagebuch, 1914–1918,* Helmuth Kiesel, ed. (Stuttgart: Klett-Cotta, 2010), p. 222.
119. SRA 4212, 17 July 1943, TNA, WO 208/4130.
120. For background on the activities of German destroyers in the Bay of Biscay, which led to the death of Leslie Howard on 1 June 1943, see Neitzel, *Einsatz der deutschen Luftwaffe,* pp. 193–203.
121. SRX 2080, 7 January 1945, TNA, WO 208/4164.
122. SRX 179, 13 March 1941, TNA, WO 208/4158.
123. Room Conversation, Kneipp–Kerle, 22 October 1944, NARA, RG 165, Entry 179, Box 498.
124. SRN 2023, 28 July 1943, TNA, WO 208/4146. There is no way of reconstructing what the navy private is referring to.
125. SRN 1758, 6 May 1943, TNA, WO 208/4145.
126. SRN 322, 15 May 1941, TNA, WO 208/4142.
127. SRX 120, 23 July 1940, TNA, WO 208/4158. Scheringer refers here to the attack on Convoy OA 175 on 1 July 1940. On his final mission, he hit four ships weighing some 16,000 gross tons.
128. Michael Salewski, *Die deutsche Seekriegsleitung,* Vol. 2 (Munich: Bernard & Graefe Verlag, 1975); Werner Rahn et al., *Das Deutsche Reich und der Zweite Weltkrieg,* Vol. 6 (Stuttgart: Deutsche Verlags-Anstalt, 1990).
129. SRN 626, 9 August 1941, TNA, WO 208/4143.
130. SRX 34, 10 February 1940, TNA, WO 208/4158.
131. KTB SKl, Teil A, 6 January 1940, S. 37, BA-MA, RM 7/8.
132. SRX 34, 10 February 1940, TNA, WO 208/4158.
133. Stephen W. Roskill, *Royal Navy: Britische Seekriegsgeschichte, 1939–1945* (Hamburg: Stalling, 1961), p. 402ff.

134. See, e.g., Roger Chickering and Stig Förster, "Are We There Yet? World War II and the Theory of Total War," in *A World at Total War: Global Conflict and the Politics of Destruction, 1937–1945,* Roger Chickering, Stig Förster, and Bernd Greiner, eds. (Cambridge: Cambridge University Press, 2005), pp. 1–18.

135. For more information and an international comparison, see Stig Förster, ed., *An der Schwelle zum Totalen Krieg: Die militärische Debatte über den Krieg der Zukunft, 1919–1939* (Paderborn: Schoeningh Verlag, 2002).

136. See also Adam Roberts, "Land Warfare: From Hague to Nuremberg," in *The Laws of War: Constraints on Warfare in the Western World,* Michael Howard, George J. Andresopoulos, and Mark R. Shulman, eds. (New Haven: Yale University Press, 1994), pp. 116–39.

137. Cited in Joanna Bourke, *An Intimate History of Killing* (London: Granta Books, 1999), p. 182.

138. SRGG 560, 14 November 1943, TNA, WO 208/4167.

139. Directly after World War II, two American international law experts acknowledged that only "political and military, rather than legal, considerations" could have held back the German occupying forces. See Lester Nurick and Roger W. Barrett, "Legality of Guerrilla Forces Under the Laws of War," *American Journal of International Law* 40 (1946), pp. 563–83. This statement is all the more telling since it came directly after the war from lawyers who were also members of the U.S. Army with little reason to sympathize with the Third Reich. We owe this reference to Klaus Schmider, Sandhurst.

140. On this discussion, see Lieb, *Konventioneller Krieg,* pp. 253–57. See also Jörn Axel Kämmerer, "Kriegsrepressalie oder Kriegsverbrechen? Zur rechtlichen Beurteilung der Massenexekutionen von Zivilisten durch die deutsche Besatzungsmacht im Zweiten Weltkrieg," *Archiv des Völkerrechts* 37 (1999), pp. 283–317.

141. SRA 3444, 28 December 1942, TNA, WO 208/4128.

142. Harry Hoppe (11 February 1894–23 August 1969), commander of Infantry Regiment 424 of the 126th Infantry Division, received the Knight's Cross on 12 September 1941 for the conquest of Schlüsselburg.

143. Room Conversation, Kneipp–Kehrle, 23 October 1944, NARA, RG 165, Entry 179, Box 498. Franz Kneipp was apparently deployed in 1941 with the SS Police Division. Eberhard Kerle was a radio operator. We know little more about him.

144. Ibid.

145. SRA 818, 25 October 1940, TNA, WO 208/4120.

146. SRA 4758, 24 December 1943, TNA, WO 208/4132.

147. SRA 5643, 13 October 1944, TNA, WO 208/4135.

148. Welzer, *Täter,* p. 161.

149. Herbert Jäger, *Verbrechen unter totalitärer Herrschaft: Studien zur national-sozialistischen Gewaltkriminalität* (Frankfurt/Main: Suhrkamp, 1982).

150. SRX 2056, 14 November 1944, TNA, WO 208/4164.

151. SRA 5628, 28 September 1944, TNA, WO 208/4135.

152. SRA 5454, 8 July 1944, TNA, WO 208/4134.

153. SRX 2072, 19 December 1944, TNA, WO 208/4164.
154. Carlo Gentile, *Wehrmacht, Waffen-SS und Polizei im Kampf gegen Partisanen und Zivilbevölkerung in Italien, 1943–1945* (Paderborn: Schoeningh, 2011).
155. Lieb, *Konventioneller Krieg*, p. 574.
156. SRA 5522, 25 July 1944, TNA, WO 208/4134.
157. SRA 5664, 30 November 1944, TNA, WO 208/4135.
158. For example, Lieutenant William Calley, who was sentenced to life imprisonment for his role in the My Lai massacre (the sentence was commuted a short time later), is quoted as saying: " 'The old men, the women, the children—the babies—were all VC or would be VC in about three years,' he asserted, continuing, 'And inside of the VC women, I guess there were a thousand little VC now.' " See Bourke, *Intimate History*, p. 162.
159. SRA 2957, 9 August 1942, TNA, WO 208/4127.
160. Jochen Oltmer, ed., *Kriegsgefangene im Europa des Ersten Weltkrieges* (Paderborn: Schoeningh, 2006), p. 11.
161. Georg Wurzer, "Die Erfahrung der Extreme: Kriegsgefangene in Rußland 1914–1918," in Oltmer, ed., *Kriegsgefangene im Europa des Ersten Weltkrieges*, p. 108.
162. Christian Streit, *Keine Kameraden: Die Wehrmacht und die sowjetischen Kriegsgefangenen, 1941–1945* (Stuttgart: Deutsche Verlags-Anstalt, 1980); Alfred Streim, *Sowjetische Gefangene in Hitlers Vernichtungskrieg: Berichte und Dokumente* (Heidelberg: C. F. Müller Juristicher Verlag, 1982); Rüdiger Overmans, "Die Kriegsgefangenenpolitik des Deutschen Reiches, 1939 bis 1945," in *Das Deutsche Reich und der Zweite Weltkrieg*, Vol. 9/2, Militärgeschichtliches Forschungsamt, ed. (Munich, 2005), pp. 804–24.
163. Cited in Felix Römer, " 'Seid hart und unerbittlich…' Gefangenenerschießung und Gewalteskalation im deutsch-sowjetischen Krieg, 1941/42," in *Kriegsgreuel: Die Entgrenzung der Gewalt in kriegerischen Konflikten vom Mittelalter bis ins 20. Jahrhundert*, Sönke Neitzel and Daniel Hohrath, eds. (Paderborn: Schoeningh Verlag, 2008), p. 327.
164. Ibid., p. 319.
165. SRM 599, 25 June 1944, TNA, WO 208/4138. See also SRA 2671, 19 June 1942, TNA, WO 208/4126; SRA 2957, 29 August 1942, TNA, WO 208/4127; SRX 1122, 22 September 1942, TNA, WO 208/4161.
166. Hartmann, *Wehrmacht im Ostkrieg*, pp. 542–49.
167. Johannes Hürter, *Ein deutscher General an der Ostfront: Die Briefe und Tagebücher des Gotthard Heinrici, 1941/42* (Erfurt: Sutton Verlag, 2001).
168. SRM 1023, 15 November 1944, TNA, WO 208/4139.
169. Dieter Pohl, *Die Herrschaft der Wehrmacht: Deutsche Militärbesatzung und einheimische Bevölkerung in der Sowjetunion, 1941–1944* (Munich: Oldenbourg Verlag, 2008), p. 205; Hartmann, *Wehrmacht im Ostkrieg*, pp. 523–26.
170. SRM 49, 24 February 1942, TNA, WO 208/4136.
171. On the execution of 180 Russian POWs because no means of transport were available, see SRA 2605, 10 June 1942, TNA, WO 208/4126.
172. SRX 2139, 28 April 1945, TNA, WO 208/4164. Walter Schreiber, born 15 July 1924 in Großaming/Steyr Land, joined the Waffen SS in 1942 and served in

the "Leibstandarte Adolf Hitler" in the area around Charkow in spring 1943. He is perhaps referring to an incident from this period. A passionate National Socialist, he joined a frogman commando unit in July 1944. On 7 March 1945 he was captured in fighting around the bridge at Remagen. Michael Jung, *Sabotage unter Wasser: Die deutschen Kampfschwimmer im Zweiten Weltkrieg* (Hamburg: Verlag E. S. Mittler & Sohn GmbH, 2004), p. 74.

173. SRA 4273, 14 August 1943, TNA, WO 208/4130; cf. Room Conversation, Müller–Reimbold, 22 March 1945, NARA, RG 165, Entry 179, Box 530.

174. SRA 2957, 9 August 1942, TNA, WO 208/4127. See SRA 5681, 21 December 1944, TNA, WO 208/4135.

175. SRA 5681, 21 December 1944, TNA, WO 208/4135; SRA 4742, 20 December 1943, TNA, WO 208/4132; SRA 2618, 11 June 1942, TNA, WO 208/4126.

176. GRGG 169, 2 August–4 August 1944, TNA, WO 208/4363.

177. Christian Hartmann, "Massensterben oder Massenvernichtung? Sowjetische Kriegsgefangene im 'Unternehmen Barbarossa': Aus dem Tagebuch eines deutschen Lagerkommandanten," *VfZG* 49 (2001), pp. 97–158; Hubert Orlowski, *"Erschießen will ich nicht": Als Offizier und Christ im Totalen Krieg. Das Kriegstagebuch des Dr. August Töpperwien* (Dusseldorf: Gasterland Verlag, 2006); Richard Germann, "'Österreichische' Soldaten in Ost- und Südeuropa, 1941–1945: Deutsche Krieger—Nationalsozialistische Verbrecher—Österreichische Opfer?" (Ph.D. dissertation, University of Vienna, 2006), pp. 186–99.

178. SRA 2672, 19 June 1942, TNA, WO 208/4126.

179. Ibid.

180. SRM 735, 1 August 1944, TNA, WO 208/4138. See also SRA 5681, 21 December 1944, TNA, WO 208/4135.

181. SRA 4791, 6 January 1944, TNA, WO 208/4132.

182. Room Conversation, Krug–Altvatter, 27 August 1944, NARA, RG 165, Entry 179, Box 442.

183. Interrogation Report, Gefreiter Hans Breuer, 18 February 1944, NARA, RG 165, Entry 179, Box 454.

184. See, e.g., SRA 2672, 19 June 1942, TNA, WO 208/4126; SRA 5502, 21 July 1944, TNA, WO 208/4134; SRGG 274, 22 July 1943, TNA, WO 208/4165; SRGG 577, 21 November 1943, TNA, WO 208/4167; Room Conversation, Lehnertz-Langfeld, 14 August 1944, NARA, RG 165, Entry 179, Box 507; Room Conversation, Gartz–Sitzle, 27 July 1944, NARA, RG 165, Entry 179, Box 548.

185. SRGG 1203 (C), 6 May 1945, TNA, WO 208/4170.

186. SRA 3966, 26 May 1943, TNA, WO 208/4130.

187. During the night of 26 July 1942, the Jewish residents of Przemyśl were collected from their houses by the SS. At around 5 a.m., the local commander, Max Liedtke, called SS Untersturmführer Adolf Benthin and insisted that those Jewish men who worked for the Wehrmacht be exempted from deportation. He threatened to file a complaint with the general staff, whom he had already informed by radio about what was going on. Without waiting for a response, Liedtke's adjutant Albert Battel sealed off the only entrance to the

Jewish ghetto. SS men were threatened with machine guns if they tried to pass. Battel's justification was that a state of emergency had been declared in Przemyśl. This was legally correct, although the act was still a major humiliation and provocation of the SS. The SS then contacted a high-ranking officer in Cracow to get the state of emergency lifted. It being clear that the SS would soon prevail, Battel had some 90 workers and their families transferred from the ghetto to the commander's headquarters. He also allowed 240 further people hide in the headquarters' basement. Battel and Liedtke's assessment of the situation was correct. The state of emergency was lifted, and on 27 July, the SS continued their so-called resettlement operation.

188. Wolfram Wette, *Retter in Uniform: Handlungsspielräume im Vernichtungskrieg der Wehrmacht* (Frankfurt/Main: Fischer Taschenbuch Verlag, 2003).

189. Some 1,400 Jews were murdered in three phases — July, August, and November 1941 — in Daugavpils. Israel Gutman, Eberhard Jäckel, Peter Longerich, and Julius H. Schoeps, eds., *Enzyklopädie des Holocaust,* Vol. 1, p. 375.

190. SRGG 1086, 28 December 1944, TNA, WO 208/4169.

191. See Frank Bajohr and Dieter Pohl, *Der Holocaust als offenes Geheimnis: Die Deutschen, die NS-Führung und die Alliierten* (Munich: C. H. Beck Verlag, 2006); Peter Longerich, *"Davon haben wir nichts gewusst!" Die Deutschen und die Judenverfolgung, 1933–1945* (Munich: Siedler, 2006); Harald Welzer, "Die Deutschen und ihr Drittes Reich," *Aus Politik und Zeitgeschichte,* 14–15 (2007).

192. SRGG 1086, 28 December 1944, TNA, WO 208/4169.

193. Ibid.

194. See Welzer, Moller, and Tschuggnall, *Opa,* p. 35ff.; Angela Keppler, *Tischgespräche* (Frankfurt/Main: Suhrkamp Verlag, 1994), p. 173.

195. SRGG 1086, 28 December 1944, TNA, WO 208/4169.

196. Ibid.

197. Ibid.

198. Ibid.

199. Ibid.

200. Surviving material and his numerous statements in the surveillance protocols allow us to reconstruct the biography of Hans Felbert in detail. As early as 3 June 1940, he was relieved of his regimental command for not leading his troops with the necessary "hardness" against the enemy. Starting in June 1942, as a field commander in Besançon, he clashed repeatedly with the SS Security Service. He was, however, unable to prevent the execution of forty-two partisans there. Felbert surrendered while retreating with his men in the face of French troops. For that, Hitler sentenced him, in absentia, to death. There were reprisals against his family. British intelligence agents considered him a dedicated opponent of National Socialism. Neitzel, *Abgehört,* p. 443. Bruhn was part of the anti-Hitler conspiracy. He and his men occupied the Berlin City Castle on 20 July 1944 and he was a witness for the prosecution at the Nuremberg Trials. See Neitzel, *Abgehört,* p. 434.

201. In 1942 Kracow-Plaszów was expanded into a forced labor camp, and in 1944 it became an extermination camp. In summer 1944, with Kittel present in the city, 22,000 to 24,000 were interned there. Some 8,000 people were murdered

in the camp. Israel Gutman, ed., *Enzyklopädie des Holocaust: Die Verfolgung und Ermordung der europäischen Juden*, Vol. 2 (Berlin: Argon Verlag, 1993), p. 118ff.

202. SRGG 1086, 28 December 1944, TNA, WO 208/4169.

203. GRGG 265, 27 February–1 March 1945, TNA, WO 208/4177.

204. Frederic Bartlett, *Remembering: A Study in Experimental and Social Psychology* (Cambridge: Cambridge University Press, 1997); Harald Welzer, *Das Kommunikative Gedächtnis: Eine Theorie der Erinnerung* (Munich: Beck, 2002).

205. SRGG 1158 (C), 25 May 1945, TNA, WO 208/4169.

206. This account is in line with perpetrators' testimony at postwar trials. See Welzer, *Täter*, p. 140.

207. Jürgen Matthäus, "Operation Barbarossa and the Onset of the Holocaust," in *The Origins of the Final Solution: The Evolution of Nazi Jewish Policy, September 1939-March 1942*, Jürgen Matthäus and Christopher Browning, eds. (Lincoln: University of Nebraska Press, 2004), pp. 244–309.

208. See Welzer, Moller, and Tschuggnall, *Opa*, p. 57.

209. We owe this reference to Peter Klein.

210. See Andrej Angrick, *Besatzungspolitik und Massenmord: Die Einsatzgruppe D in der südlichen Sowjetunion, 1941–1943* (Hamburg: Hamburger Edition HIS Verlag, 2003); Andrej Angrick et al., eds., " 'Da hätte man schon ein Tagebuch führen müssen.' Das Polizeibataillon 322 und die Judenmorde im Bereich der Heeresgruppe Mitte während des Sommers und Herbstes 1941," in *Die Normalität des Verbrechens: Bilanz und Perspektiven der Forschung zu den nationalsozialistischen Gewaltverbrechen*, Helge Grabitz et al., eds. (Berlin: Edition Hentrich, 1994), pp. 325–85; Vincas Bartusevicius, Joachim Tauber, and Wolfram Wette, eds., *Holocaust in Litauen: Krieg, Judenmorde und Kollaboration* (Cologne: Boehlau Verlag, 2003); Ruth Bettina Birn, *Die Höheren SS- und Polizeiführer: Himmlers Vertreter im Reich und in den besetzten Gebieten* (Düsseldorf: Droste Verlag, 1986); Peter Klein, ed., *Die Einsatzgruppen in der besetzten Sowjetunion, 1941/42: Tätigkeits- und Lageberichte des Chefs der Sicherheitspolizei und des SD* (Berlin: Hentrich, 1997); Helmut Krausnick and Hans-Heinrich Wilhelm, *Die Truppe des Weltanschauungskrieges: Die Einsatzgruppen der Sicherheitspolizei und des SD, 1938–1942* (Stuttgart: Deutsche Verlags-Anstalt, 1981); Konrad Kwiet, "Auftakt zum Holocaust. Ein Polizeibataillon im Osteinsatz," in *Der Nationalsozialismus: Studien zur Ideologie und Herrschaft*, Wolfgang Benz et al., eds. (Frankfurt/Main: Fischer, 1995), pp. 191–208; Ralf Ogorreck, *Die Einsatzgruppen und die "Genesis der Endlösung"* (Berlin: Metropol, 1994).

211. SRA 2961, 12 August 1942, TNA, WO 208/4127.

212. SRA 4583, 21 October 1943, TNA, WO 208/4131.

213. SRN 2528, 19 December 1943, TNA, WO 208/4148.

214. SRM 30, 27 January 1942, TNA, WO 208/4136.

215. SRA 3379, 8 December 1942, TNA, WO 208/4128.

216. At the end of his autobiographical writings, Höss took stock: "Today I can see that the extermination of Jews was fundamentally wrong. It was precisely in this act of genocide that Germany attracted the hatred of the entire world.

It did not serve the cause of anti-Semitism. On the contrary, it helped Jewry take a step toward its final goal." Martin Broszat, ed., *Rudolf Höß: Kommandant in Auschwitz: Autobiographische Aufzeichnungen des Rudolf Höß* (Munich: Deutsche Verlags-Anstalt, 1989), p. 153.

217. Hannah Arendt, *Eichmann in Jerusalem: Ein Bericht von der Banalität des Bösen* (Leipzig: R. Piper & Co. Verlag, 1986).

218. Christopher R. Browning, *Ganz normale Männer: Das Reserve-Polizeibataillon 101 und die "Endlösung" in Polen* (Reinbek: Rororo, 1996), p. 243.

219. Robert J. Lifton, *Ärzte im Driten Reich* (Stuttgart: Ullstein Tb. Auflag, 1999).

220. SRA 4604, 27 October 1943, TNA, WO 208/4131.

221. Arendt, *Eichmann,* p. 104.

222. SRA 4604, 27 October 1943, TNA, WO 208/4130.

223. See Welzer, *Täter,* p. 266; and "Internationaler Militärgerichtshof," ed., in *Der Prozess gegen die Hauptkriegsverbrecher,* Vol. 29 (Nuremberg: International Military Tribunal, 1948), p. 145.

224. In Odessa, some 99,000 Jews were murdered, most of them by Romanian soldiers. *Enzyklopädie des Holocaust,* Vol. 2, p. 1058ff.

225. On the Night of Broken Glass in Vienna, see Siegwald Ganglmair and Regina Forstner-Karner, eds., *Der Novemberpogrom 1938: Die Reichskristallnacht in Wien* (Vienna: Museen der Stadt Wien, 1988); Herbert Rosenkranz, *Reichskristallnacht: 9. November 1938 in Österreich* (Vienna: Europa Verlag, 1968).

226. GRGG 281, 8 May–9 May 1945, TNA, WO 208/4177.

227. SRA 5444, 8 July 1944, TNA, WO 208/4134.

228. Room Conversation, Swoboda-Kahrad, 2 December 1944, NARA, RG 165, Entry 179, Box 552.

229. SRA 4820, 13 January 1944, TNA, WO 208/4132.

230. Lvov was home to the Janowska concentration camp, which did not, however, have gas chambers. Estimates of the number of people murdered there range from tens of thousands to 200,000. *Enzyklopädie des Holocaust,* Vol. 2, p. 657ff. The nearest gas chambers were located at the Belzec concentration camp, some seventy kilometers to the northwest. From mid-March to December 1942, as many as 600,000 Jews, "gypsies," and Poles were murdered there. On the murders of Jews in Galicia, see Thomas Sandkühler, *"Endlösung" in Galizien* (Bonn: Dietz, 1996).

231. We can no longer reconstruct how much Ramcke knew about the Holocaust. The fact that he only fought for around four weeks, in February and March 1944, on the Eastern Front in Ukraine would suggest his knowledge was limited.

232. GRGG 272, 13 March–16 March 1945, TNA, WO 208/4177.

233. Welzer, *Täter,* p. 158ff.

234. Kutno was conquered by German troops on 15 September 1939. In June 1940, the Jewish population was confined to a ghetto, where they lived under terrible conditions. In March and April 1942, the ghetto was dissolved, and its inhabitants killed at the Kulmhof extermination camp. Evidence has yet to emerge of any mass executions of Jews in Kutno.

235. GRGG 272, 13 March–16 March 1945, TNA, WO 208/4177.

236. Ibid.
237. In her book *Eichmann in Jerusalem,* Hannah Arendt wrote of Eichmann's complete inability to conceive of what he had done. It is possible, though, that her impression was mistaken, based as it was on Eichmann's indolence and indifference during his trial. It's more likely that the normative standards Eichmann followed in tirelessly carrying out his duties at the Main Office for Reich Security simply deviated from those that normally apply elsewhere. Eichmann was guided by National Socialist morality. Postwar conservative German politician Hans Karl Filbinger implicitly pointed to those standards as a justification for his own role as a navy judge in handing out death sentences, when he said: "What was just back then cannot be unjust today."
238. SRM 33, 31 January 1942, TNA, WO 208/4136.
239. SRA 3313, 30 October 1942, TNA, WO 208/4128.
240. Taumberger is presumably talking here about the subterranean facility at Gusen, Austria, where the Messerschmitt 262 fighter jet was supposed to be produced.
241. SRA 5618, 24 September 1944, TNA, WO 208/4134.
242. Welzer, Moller, and Tschuggnall, *Opa,* p. 158.
243. Room Conversation, Müller–Reimbold, 22 March 1945, NARA, RG 165, Entry 179, Box 530.
244. William Ryan, *Blaming the Victim* (London: Pantheon, 1972).
245. Broszat, ed., *Rudolf Höß,* p. 130.
246. Daniel Jonah Goldhagen, *Hitlers willige Vollstrecker: Ganz gewöhnliche Deutsche und der Holocaust* (Munich: Siedler, 1996), p. 462ff.; Browning, *Ganz normale Männer,* pp. 154, 332.
247. See Welzer, Moller, and Tschuggnall, *Opa,* p. 57.
248. Cited in Browning, *Ganz normale Männer,* p. 34
249. Welzer, *Täter,* p. 132ff.
250. Hilberg, *Die Vernichtung,* p. 338ff.
251. Ibid., p. 339.
252. SRN 852, 11 March 1942, TNA, WO 208/4143; Heinz-Ludger Borgert, "Kriegsverbrechen der Kriegsmarine," in *Kriegsverbrechen im 20. Jahrhundert,* Wolfram Wette and Gerd R. Ueberschär, eds. (Darmstadt: Wissenschaftlicher Burgergesellschaft, 2001), pp. 310–12; *Enzyklopädie des Holocaust,* Vol. 2, p. 859ff.
253. SRA 4759, 25 December 1943, TNA, WO 208/4132.
254. SRM 1163, 5 January 1945, TNA, WO 208/4140.
255. SRA 3948, 16 April 1943, TNA, WO 208/4130.
256. SRN 720, 25 December 1941, TNA, WO 208/4143.
257. SRCMF X 16, 29 May–2 June 1944, TNA, WO 208/5513; conversation between M 44/368 and M 44/374, cited in Anette Neder, "Kriegsschauplatz Mittelmeerraum: Wahrnehmungen und Deutungen deutscher Soldaten im Mittelmeerraum" (Master's thesis, University of Mainz, 2010), p. 70.
258. SRA 554, 18 September 1940, TNA, WO 208/4119.
259. SRA 5264, 14 May 1944, TNA, WO 208/4133.
260. SRA 2947, 10 August 1942, TNA, WO 208/4127.

261. Room Conversation, Quick–Korte, 23 July 1944, NARA, RG 165, Entry 179, Box 529.
262. GRGG 169, 2–4 August 1944, TNA, WO 208/4363.
263. Room Conversation, Schulz–Voigt, 16 June 1944, NARA, RG 165, Entry 179, Box 557.
264. SRA 554, 18 September 1940, TNA, WO 208/4119; Lieb, *Konventioneller Krieg,* pp. 15–19.
265. SRA 3966, 26 April 1943, TNA, WO 208/4130.
266. SRM 410, 16 December 1943, TNA, WO 208/4137.
267. SRM 423, 24 December 1943, TNA WO 208/4137.
268. SRM 892, 15 September 1944, TNA, WO 208/4139.
269. SRM 975, 20 October 1944, TNA, WO 208/4139.
270. SRA 5852, 3 May 1945, TNA, WO 208/4135.
271. Room Conversation, Goessele–Langer, 27 December 1944, NARA, RG 165, Entry 179, Box 474.
272. Room Conversation, Drosdowski–Richter, 11 January 1945, NARA, RG 165, Entry 179, Box 462.
273. SRM 659, 18 July 1944, TNA, WO 208/4138.
274. Room Conversation, Müller–Reimbold, 22 March 1945, NARA, RG 165, Entry 179, Box 530.
275. Room Conversation, Hanelt–Breitlich, 3 April 1945, NARA, RG 165, Entry 179, Box 447.
276. GRGG 232, 8–11 December 1944, TNA, WO 208/4364. On euthanasia and earlier ideas of eugenics in Wilhelmine and Weimar Germany, see Ernst Klee, *"Euthanasie" im NS-Staat: Die Vernichtung lebensunwerten Lebens* (Frankfurt/Main: Fischer Verlag, 1985).
277. SRGG 782, 21 January 1944, TNA, WO 208/4167.
278. SRGG 495, 21 October 1943, TNA, WO 208/4166.
279. For more detail, see Felix Römer, *Kommissarbefehl: Wehrmacht und NS-Verbrechen an der Ostfront, 1941/42* (Paderborn: Schoeningh Verlag, 2008).
280. GRGG 271, 10–12 March 1945, TNA, WO 208/4177.
281. SRGG 679, 20 December 1943, TNA, WO 208/4167.
282. SRM 877, 7 September 1944, TNA, WO 208/4139.
283. SRM 633, 11 July 1944, TNA, WO 208/4138.
284. Welzer, *Täter,* p. 218ff.; Groß, *Anständig geblieben.*
285. Broszat, ed., *Rudolf Höß,* p. 156.
286. SRA 3249, 9 October 1942, TNA, WO 208/4128.
287. SRA 4880, 27 January 1944, TNA, WO 208/4132.
288. SRA 5702, 6 January 1945, TNA, WO 208/4135.
289. Charlotte Beradt, *Das Dritte Reich des Traumes* (Frankfurt/Main: Suhrkamp, 1981).
290. Helmut Karl Ulshöfer, ed., *Liebesbriefe an Adolf Hitler: Briefe in den Tod: Unveröffentlichte Dokumente aus der Reichskanzlei* (Frankfurt/Main: VAS, 1994).
291. SRGG 1133 (C), 9 March 1945, TNA, WO 208/4169.
292. GRGG 272, 13–16 March 1945, TNA, WO 208/4177.

293. Room Conversation, Meyer–Killmann, 17 August 1944, NARA, RG 165, Entry 179, Box 516.

294. SRA 3468, 30 December 1942, TNA, WO 208/4128.

295. Ibid.

296. SRA 4174, 14 July 1943, TNA, WO 208/4130.

297. SRA 4232, 20 July 1943, TNA, WO 208/4130.

298. SRA 591, 23 September 1940, TNA, WO 208/4119.

299. SRA 179, 17 July 1940, TNA, WO 208/4118.

300. SRA 4652, 4 November 1943, TNA, WO 208/4132.

301. SRA 3259, 13 October 1942, TNA, WO 208/4128.

302. SRA 687, 4 October 1940, TNA, WO 208/4120.

303. SRA 3035, 24 August 1942, TNA, WO 208/4127.

304. SRA 3891, 28 March 1943, TNA, WO 208/4129.

305. SRA 3915, 29 March 1943, TNA, WO 208/4130.

306. Ulf Balke, *Der Luftkrieg in Europa: Die operativen Einsätze des Kampfgeschwaders 2 im Zweiten Weltkrieg*, Vol. 2 (Bonn: Bernard & Graefe, 1990), p. 524.

307. SRA 5108, 27 March 1944, TNA, WO 208/4133. See also Ernst Stilla, "Die Luftwaffe im Kampf um die Luftherrschaft" (Ph.D. dissertation, University of Bonn, 2005), pp. 236–43.

308. SRA 4663, 5 November 1943, TNA, WO 208/4132.

309. Stilla, *Die Luftwaffe*, pp. 232–36.

310. SRA 2570, 3 June 1942, TNA, WO 208/4126.

311. SRA 1503, 13 April 1941, TNA, WO 208/4123.

312. SRN 625, 9 August 1941, TNA, WO 208/4143.

313. SRA 4156, 10 July 1943, TNA, WO 208/4130.

314. SRA 1503, 13 April 1941, TNA, WO 208/4123.

315. Klaus-Michael Mallmann, Volker Rieß, and Wolfram Pyta, eds., *Deutscher Osten, 1939–1945: Der Weltanschauungskrieg in Photos and Texten* (Darmstadt: Wissenschaftlicher Buchgesellschaft, 2003), p. 155.

316. Regina Mühlhäuser, *Eroberungen, sexuelle Gewalttaten und intime Beziehungen deutscher Soldaten in der Sowjetunion, 1941–1945* (Hamburg: Hamburger Edition, 2010). On sexual violence, see also Birgit Beck, *Wehrmacht und sexuelle Gewalt: Sexualverbrechen vor deutschen Militärgerichten* (Paderborn: Schoeningh, 2004).

317. SRN 2528, 19 December 1943, TNA, WO 208/4148.

318. Angrick, *Besatzungspolitik und Massenmord*, p. 450.

319. Bernd Greiner, *Krieg ohne Fronten: Die USA in Vietnam* (Hamburg: Hamburger Edition, 2007).

320. Angrick, *Besatzungspolitik und Massenmord*, p. 150.

321. Ibid., p. 448.

322. Willy Peter Reese, *Mir selber seltsam fremd: Die Unmenschlichkeit des Krieges: Russland, 1941–44*, Stefan Schmitz, ed. (Munich: Claassen Verlag, 2003).

323. Angrick, *Besatzungspolitik und Massenmord*, p. 449.

324. SRA 1345, 21 February 1941, TNA, WO 208/4123.

325. Mühlhäuser, *Eroberungen,* p. 186.

326. Ibid., p. 187.

327. USHMM, RG-31 002M, Rolle 11, 3676/4/105, Bl. 16 f. 25 February 1942, cited in ibid., p. 214.

328. SRA 753, 14 October 1940, TNA, WO 208/4120.

329. SRA 4819, 12 January 1944, TNA, WO 208/4132.

330. SRA 2871, 4 August 1942, TNA, WO 208/4127.

331. Room Conversation, Sauermann–Thomas, 5 August 1944, NARA, RG 165, Entry 179, Box 554.

332. See Michaela Christ, "Kriegsverbrechen," in Welzer, Neitzel, and Gudehus, eds., *"Der Führer."*

333. Room Conversation, Kruk–Böhm, 12 June 1944, NARA, RG 165, Entry 179, Box 504.

334. SRA 2386, 12 December 1941, TNA, WO 208/4126.

335. SRA 4903, 30 January 1944, TNA, WO 208/4132.

336. SRX 1937, 2 February 1944, TNA, WO 208/4163.

337. SRN 809, 23 February 1942, TNA, WO 208/4143.

338. SRA 1227, 1 February 1941, TNA, WO 208/4122.

339. SRA 712, 8 October 1940, TNA, WO 208/4120.

340. Diziplinarbericht der 8. Zerstörerflottille "Narvik" für die Zeit vom 1. Juli 1942 bis 1. September 1943, BA/MA, RM 58/39.

341. Room Conversation, Müller–Reimbold, 22 March 1945, NARA, RG 165, Entry 179, Box 530.

342. Room Conversation, Czosnowski–Schultka, 2 April 1945, NARA, Box 458, p. 438ff.

343. Mallmann, *Deutscher Osten;* Mühlhäuser, *Eroberungen.*

344. Room Conversation, Held–Langfeld, 13 August 1944, NARA, RG 165, Entry 179, Box 506.

345. Room Conversation, Kokoschka–Saemmer, 15 June 1944, NARA, RG 165, Entry 179, Box 500.

346. Philipps O'Brien, "East Versus West in the Defeat of Nazi Germany," *Journal of Strategic Studies* 23 (2000), p. 93.

347. See the seminal study by Kehrt, *Moderne Krieger.*

348. SRA 172, 15 July 1940, TNA, WO 208/4118.

349. SRA 4130, 1 July 1943, TNA, WO 208/4130.

350. SRA 3748, 26 February 1943, TNA, WO 208/4129.

351. SRA 4135, 3 July 1943, TNA, WO 208/4130.

352. See Lutz Budraß, *Flugzeugindustrie und Luftrüstung in Deutschland, 1918–1945* (Düsseldorf: Droste Verlag, 1998).

353. SRA 510, 11 September 1940, TNA, WO 208/4119.

354. SRA 496, 10 September 1940, TNA, WO 208/4119.

355. SRA 4063, 5 June 1943, TNA, WO 208/4130.

356. SRA 5467 15 July 1944, TNA, WO 208/4134.

357. SRA 5710, 11 January 1945, TNA, WO 208/4135; Josef Priller, *Geschichte eines Jagdgeschwaders: Das J.G. 26 (Schlageter) 1937–1945* (Stuttgart: Motorbuch Verlag, 1956), pp. 265, 335.

358. Mäckle got lost while flying a Ju 88 on a mission over the North Sea and accidentally landed in the English town of Woolbridge. His mistake hand-delivered Germany's latest nighttime fighter jet technology to the British. Gebhard Aders, *Geschichte der deutschen Nachtjagd, 1917–1945* (Stuttgart: Motorbuch Verlag, 1978), p. 250.

359. What was meant was probably the Me 210, which the Luftwaffe planned to introduce in 1940. The schedule was continually put back because of technical problems, and the model was ultimately abandoned. Rüdiger Kosin, *Die Entwicklung der deutschen Jagdflugzeuge* (Bonn: Bernard & Graefe, 1990), pp. 135–38.

360. SRA 117, 12 June 1940, TNA, WO 208/4118.

361. SRA 117, 12 June 1940, TNA, WO 208/4118.

362. SRA 3273, 16 October 1942, TNA, WO 208/4128.

363. SRA 3069, 30 August 1942, TNA, WO 208/4127.

364. SRA 4516, 11 September 1943, TNA, WO 208/4131. The stories refer to the He 219.

365. SRA 3069, 30 August 1942, TNA, WO 208/4127.

366. SRA 3307, 26 October 1942, TNA, WO 208/4128.

367. SRA 3943, 13 April 1943, TNA, WO 208/4130. In December 1941, a private spoke of having seen the He 177, the aircraft that was supposed to fly to America. SRA 2371, 6 December 1941, TNA/WO 208/4126. See also SRA 5545, 29 July 1944, TNA, WO 208/4134. See also Room Conversation, Krumkühler–Wolff, 26 August 1944, NARA, Entry 179, Box 566. The talk there is also of an aircraft supposedly to be used to drop propaganda leaflets on New York. Navy Lieutenant Josef Bröhl of U-432 spoke of a jet plane that would be used for the leaflet mission. SRN 1629, 11 April 1943, TNA, WO 208/4145.

368. See Karl Kössler and Günther Ott, *Die großen Dessauer: Die Geschichte einer Flugzeugfamilie* (Planegg: Aviatic-Verlag GmbH, 1993), pp. 103–5.

369. Peter Herde, *Der Japanflug: Planungen und Verwirklichung einer Flugverbindung zwischen den Achsenmächten und Japan, 1942–1945* (Stuttgart: Steiner, 2000).

370. SRA 3950, 17 April 1943, TNA, WO 208/4130.

371. SRA 2992, 12 August 1942, TNA, WO 208/4127.

372. SRA 3465, 30 December 1942, TNA, WO 208/4128, mentions the principle behind the flying missile Me 163.

373. SRA 4235, 20 July 1943, TNA, WO 208/4130.

374. SRA 4709, 15 December 1943, TNA, WO 208/4132.

375. SRA 4880, 27 January 1944, TNA, WO 208/4132.

376. SRA 5114, 29 March 1944, TNA, WO 208/4133.

377. Ibid.

378. SRA 5531, 26 July 1944, TNA, WO 208/4134.

379. SRA 5456, 15 July 1944, TNA, WO 208/4134.

380. SRA 5732, 15 January 1945, TNA, WO 208/4135.

381. Jeffrey L. Ethell and Alfred Price, *Deutsche Düsenflugzeuge im Kampfeinsatz, 1944/45* (Stuttgart: Motorbuch, 1981), p. 70ff.

382. Ralf Blank, "Kriegsalltag und Luftkrieg an der 'Heimatfront,' " in *Das Deutsche Reich und der Zweite Weltkrieg,* Vol. 9/1, pp. 433–36. See also Heinz Dieter Hölsken, *Die V-Waffen: Entstehung, Propaganda, Kriegseinsatz* (Stuttgart: Deutsche Verlags-Anstalt, 1984); Ralf Schabel, *Die Illusion der Wunderwaffen: Die Rolle der Düsenflugzeuge und Flugabwehrraketen in der Rüstungspolitik des Dritten Reiches* (Munich: Oldenbourg Wissenschaftsverlag, 1994).

383. SRN 1559, 25 March 1943, TNA, WO 208/4145.

384. SRN 1622, 11 April 1943, TNA, WO 208/4145.

385. SRN 1986, 25 July 1943, TNA, WO 208/4146.

386. SRX 1532, 24 January 1943, TNA, WO 208/4162.

387. SRM 263, 27 October 1943, TNA, WO 208/4137.

388. SRX 1617, 11 March 1943, TNA, WO 208/4162.

389. SRN 2989, 3 March 1944, TNA, WO 208/4149; SRN 3379, 20 April 1944, TNA, WO 208/4151.

390. SRM 601, 25 June 1944, TNA, WO 208/4138; SRM 655, 18 July 1944, TNA, WO 208/4138.

391. SRM 263, 27 October 1943; SRM 291, 9 November 1943, TNA, WO 208/4137; SRN 2636, 4 January 1944, TNA, WO 208/4148; SRM 499, 21 March 1944, TNA, WO 208/4138; SRM 680, 26 July 1944, TNA, WO 208/4138; SRA 5199, 27 April 1944, TNA, WO 208/4133.

392. SRM 639, 8 July 1944, TNA, WO 208/4138.

393. SRM 491, 14 March 1944, TNA, WO 208/4138.

394. SRN 2851, 25 January 1944, TNA, WO 208/4149.

395. SRA 5196, 25 April 1944, TNA, WO 208/4133.

396. Hölsken, *Die V-Waffen,* p. 131ff.

397. Ibid., p. 103.

398. Ibid., p. 104ff.

399. Ibid., p. 109.

400. SRN 3922, 8 July 1944, TNA, WO 208/4153.

401. For example, Otto Elfeldt (SRGG 988, 24 August 1944, TNA, WO 208/4168) and Erwin Menny, *Tagebuchblätter aus der Gefangenschaft,* BA/MA, N 267/4.

402. SRM 655, 18 July 1944, TNA, WO 208/4138.

403. SRM 847, 30 August 1944, TNA, WO 208/4139. See also SRM 960, 10 October 1944, TNA, WO 208/4139; SRM 1077, 29 November 1944, TNA WO 208/4139; SRX 2075, 29 December 1944, TNA, WO 208/4164.

404. SRN 4130, 16 August 1944, TNA, WO 208/4155.

405. SRX 2048, 4 November 1944, TNA, WO 208/4164. See also SRN 4031, 4 August 1944, TNA, WO 208/4154. A V2 had the explosive capacity of two to three thousand bombs.

406. Lieutenant Borbonus of SS Junkerschule in Bad Tölz refers to such a speech by Hitler. SRM 914, 20 September 1944, TNA, WO 208/4139.

407. SRGG 543, 9 November 1943, TNA, WO 208/4167.

408. SRGG 596, 26 November 1943, TNA, WO 208/4167. On criticism of the V weapons, see SRM 722, 30 July 1944, TNA, WO 208/4138; SRM 1094, 21 November 1944, TNA, WO 208/4139.

409. See Kehrt, *Moderne Krieger,* pp. 291–97.

410. SRA 5512, 23 July 1944, TNA, WO 208/4134.

411. SRA 5532, 25 July 1944, TNA, WO 208/4134.

412. SRA 2058, 2 August 1941, TNA, WO 208/4125.

413. SRA 2660, 18 June 1942, TNA, WO 208/4126. Zastrau was a member of 5/KG 2 and was shot down on 23 April 1942 over Exeter. Balke, *Luftkrieg in Europa,* p. 430.

414. SRA 4862, 23 January 1944, TNA, WO 208/4132. This description refers to the German bombardment of Bari during the night of 3 December 1943. German bombs and explosions aboard the ammunition carriers *John E. Motley* and *Joseph Wheeler,* as well as the tanker ship *Aroostock,* destroyed eighteen ships with a gross tonnage of 71,566. There were more than 1,000 dead and wounded. Firefighting and rescue attempts were hindered by the fact that the U.S. freighter *John Harvey* was carrying mustard gas. http://www.wlb-stuttgart.de/seekrieg/43–12.htm (accessed 30 August 2010).

415. SRA 1557, 23 April 1941, TNA, WO 208/4123.

416. SRM 606, 27 June 1944, TNA, WO 208/4138.

417. Förster, in *Das Deutsche Reich,* Vol. 9/1, p. 469.

418. SRA 281, 4 August 1940, TNA, WO 208/4137.

419. SRA 453, 4 September 1940, TNA, WO 208/4137.

420. SRA 450, 4 September 1940, TNA, WO 208/4137.

421. SRA 549, 17 September 1940, TNA, WO 208/4138.

422. Wilhelm von Thoma diary entry, 21 January 1942, BA/MA, N 2/2.

423. SRA 2655, 18 June 1942, TNA, WO 208/4126; see also SRA 2635, 15 June 1942, TNA, WO 208/4127.

424. Förster, in *Das Deutsche Reich,* Vol. 9/1, p. 540.

425. Hans Meier-Welcker, *Aufzeichnungen eines Generalstabsoffiziers, 1919 bis 1942* (Freiburg: Rombach Druck- und Verlagshaus, 1982), p. 158 (23 August 1942).

426. SRN 129, 15 November 1940, TNA, WO 208/4141.

427. SRN 395, 8 June 1941, TNA, WO 208/4142.

428. SRN 183, 21 March 1941, TNA, WO 208/4141.

429. SRN 370, 28 May 1941, TNA, WO 208/4142.

430. SRN 127, 16 November 1940, TNA, WO 208/4141.

431. SRN 720, 25 December 1941, TNA, WO 208/4143.

432. For the results of the questionnaires filled out by German POWs November 1941–March 1943, see TNA, WO 208/4180.

433. SRN 690, 7 November 1941, TNA, WO 208/4143.

434. SRN 933, 31 March 1942, TNA, WO 208/4143. Josef Przyklenk (born 10 January 1914) was machinist aboard U-93 and was captured on 15 January 1942.

435. SRN 731, 31 December 1941, TNA, WO 208/4143. The British listed him, in contrast to the crew registry, as Karl Wedekinn.

436. SRN 969, 22 August 1942, TNA, WO 208/4143; SRN 968, 22 August 1942, TNA, WO 208/4143. U-210 was sunk on her maiden patrol.

437. Bernhard R. Kroener, "'Nun Volk steht auf . . . !' Stalingrad und der totale Krieg, 1942–1943," in *Stalingrad: Ereignis, Wirkung, Symbol,* Jurgen Förster,

ed. (Munich: Piper, 1992), pp. 151–70; Martin Humbug, *Das Gesicht des Krieges: Feldpostbriefe von Wehrmachtssoldaten aus der Sowjetunion, 1941–1944* (Opladen: Westdeutscher Verlag, 1998), p. 118ff.

438. SRA 3717, 2 March 1943, TNA, WO 208/4129.

439. SRA 3442, 28 December 1942, TNA, WO 208/4128.

440. SRA 3868, 22 March 1943, TNA, WO 208/4129.

441. SRA 4012, 18 May 1943, TNA, WO 208/4130; SRA 4222, 28 July 1943, TNA, WO 208/4130. There were opinions like this in the navy, but not in the army. See SRN 1643, 14 April 1943, TNA, WO 208/4145.

442. SRA 4791, 6 January 1944, TNA, WO 208/4132.

443. The reference is to the commander of the II/KG 2, Major Heinz Engel, who had joined the group in October 1941 and had led it since February 1943. Balke, *Luftkrieg in Europa,* p. 409.

444. SRA 5272, 16 May 1944, TNA, WO 208/4133.

445. Ibid.

446. SRA 4747, 22 December 1943, TNA, WO 208/4132.

447. SRN 2509, 27 November 1943, TNA, WO 208/4148.

448. See SRN 2521, 11 December 1943, TNA, WO 208/4148.

449. SRN 2768, 17 January 1944, TNA, WO 208/4149. Even weapons of retribution seemed to hold out little hope in this regard. SRN 3613, 8 May 1944, TNA, WO 208/4152.

450. "Erlass gegen Kritiksucht und Meckerei," 9 September 1943, cited in Salewski, *Seekriegsleitung,* p. 638ff.

451. The British forced some of the POWs in the surveillance camps to fill out standardized questionnaires. Between March 1943 and January 1944, they surveyed five groups of 35 to 71 men, 240 in total. The majority came from the German navy, a smaller percentage from the Luftwaffe. CSDIC (UK), Survey of German P/W Opinion, GRS 10, 24 February 1944, TNA, WO 208/5522.

452. Rafael A. Zagovec, "Gespräche mit der 'Volksgemeinschaft'" in *Die deutsche Kriegsgesellschaft, 1939 bis 1945—Ausbeutung, Deutungen, Ausgrenzung,* Vol. 9/2, Militärgeschichtliches Forschungsamt, ed. (Stuttgart: Deutsche Verlags-Anstalt, 2005), p. 327.

453. Jörg Echternkamp, "Im Kampf an der inneren und äußeren Front: Grundzüge der deutschen Gesellschaft im Zweiten Weltkrieg," in *Das Deutsche Reich,* Vol. 9/1, p. 47.

454. Heinz Boberach, ed., *Meldungen aus dem Reich* (Munich: Pawlak Verlag Herrsching, 1968), p. 511.

455. Michael Salewski, "Die Abwehr der Invasion als Schlüssel zum 'Endsieg'?" in *Die Wehrmacht, Mythos und Realität,* Rolf-Dieter Müller, and Hans-Erich Volkmann, eds. (Munich: Oldenbourg Wissenschaftsverlag, 1999), pp. 210–23.

456. SRM 519, 7 June 1944, TNA, WO 208/4138.

457. SRM 526, 9 June 1944, TNA, WO 208/4138.

458. SRM 547, 13 June 1944, TNA, WO 208/4138.

459. SRM 606, 27 June 1944, TNA, WO 208/4138. Kuhle was the commander of III/IR 1050 of the 77th Infantry Division, while Saldern led the dramatically weakened Grenadier Regiment 1057 of the 91st Airborne Division. Major

Bornhard, commander of the Feldersatzbataillon of the 77th Infantry Division, was captured on 18 June 1944 and was interned together with Kuhle at Wilton Park. From 1 February to 25 April 1944, Lieutenant General Walter Poppe commanded the 77th Infantry Division, in which Kuhle served. On 5 July, Poppe took over a new command. The basis for the rumors of treason is unclear.

460. SRM 610, 29 June 1944, TNA, WO 208/4138.
461. SRM 830, 24 August 1944, TNA, WO 208/4139.
462. SRM 849, 27 August 1944, TNA, WO 208/4139.
463. For a summary of current research, see Neitzel, *Abgehört*, p. 61ff.
464. SRM 639, 8 July 1944, TNA, WO 208/4138.
465. SRM 637, 7 July 1944, TNA, WO 208/4138.
466. We owe this analysis to Felix Römer in Mainz.
467. A Lieutenant Trettner, for example, asserted that eight paratrooper divisions would soon be deployed and that "there was much to be done." SRM 813, 24 August 1944, TNA, WO 208/4139.
468. SRM 796, 19 August 1944, TNA, WO 208/4138.
469. This is based on an analysis of moral questionnaires carried out by Felix Römer in Mainz. On navy men, see SRN 3815, 9 July 1944, TNA, WO 208/4153; SRN 3830, 12 June 1944, TNA, WO 208/4153; SRN 3931, 11 July 1944, TNA, WO 208/4154; SRN 4032, 3 August 1944, TNA, WO 208/4154.
470. This conclusion was reached by an American study based on interrogations of German POWs shortly after they had been taken captive. M. I. Gurfein and Morris Janowitz, "Trends in Wehrmacht Morale," *Public Opinion Quarterly* 10 (1946), p. 81.
471. NCO Brandt of the 11/NJG 3 told of a superior's address to the troops shortly before the Ardennes Offensive: "He said that if we don't regain aerial dominance soon, we will have lost the war. And the group commander said: 'The offensive in the West right now will be all-decisive. If it's halted, it will be the last offensive battle we can afford.' That's what the group commander said in public before all of his airmen, whom he had called together." SRX 2091, 11 January 1945, TNA, WO 208/4164. See also SRM 1133, 18 December 1944, TNA, WO 208/4140; SRM 1168, 8 January 1945, TNA, WO 208/4140.
472. SRX 2030, 25 October 1944, TNA, WO 208/4164.
473. Zagovec, "Gespräche mit der 'Volksgemeinschaft,' " p. 358.
474. Meldung des OB West v. 7. 2. 1945, KTB OKW, Vol. 4/2, p. 1364.
475. SRA 5829, 18 March 1945, TNA, WO 208/4135.
476. For example, General von Thoma. See Neitzel, *Abgehört*, p. 33.
477. SRM 79, 20 November 1942, TNA, WO 208/4136.
478. SRA 5835, 22 March 1945, TNA, WO 208/4135.
479. Cited in Ian Kershaw, *Hitler, 1936–1945* (Munich: Pantheon Verlag, 2002), p. 15.
480. Ibid., p. 64ff.
481. SRGG 1125, 27 January 1945, TNA, WO 208/4169.
482. W. G. Sebald, *Luftkrieg und Literatur* (Frankfurt/Main: Eichborn, 2001), p. 110.

Notes to Pages 212–219

483. Hans Mommsen, *Zur Geschichte Deutschlands im 20. Jahrhundert. Demokratie, Diktatur, Widerstand* (Munich: Deutsche Verlags-Anstalt, 2010), p. 159ff.

484. Saul K. Padover, *Lügendetektor: Vernehmungen im besiegten Deutschland, 1944/45* (Frankfurt/Main: Eichborn Verlag, 1999).

485. SRA 123, 17 June 1940, TNA, WO 208/4118.

486. SRA 200, 22 July 1940, TNA, WO 208/4118.

487. SRA 495, 10 September 1940, TNA, WO 208/4119; SRA 554, 18 September 1940, TNA, WO 208/4119; SRA 1383, 5 March 1941, TNA, WO 208/4123.

488. SRX 154, 17 November 1940, TNA, WO 208/4158.

489. SRX 228, 29 March 1941, TNA, WO 208/4158.

490. SRA 1619, 29 April 1941, TNA, WO 208/4123.

491. SRA 3807, 10 March 1943, TNA, WO 208/4129.

492. SRA. 4656, 23 November 1943, TNA, WO 208/4132.

493. The story that Hitler got so angry he literally bit a carpet was spread after journalist William Shirer wrote an article about Hitler's meeting with Neville Chamberlain on 22 September 1938. Shirer himself had only written that Hitler seemed on the verge of a nervous breakdown. But the image of Hitler as "carpet chewer" proved persistent. See Kershaw, *Hitler,* p. 169.

494. Details like "the Führer's beautiful hands" were part of his public image and were passed on by the media. See Kershaw, *Hitler,* p. 410. People who met him also tended to emphasize precisely those details that conformed to his public image.

495. SRX 1167, 15 October 1942, TNA, WO 208/4161.

496. Kershaw, *Hitler,* p. 407.

497. SRX 1167, 15 October 1942, TNA, WO 208/4161.

498. SRX 1802, 24 June 1943, TNA, WO 208/4163.

499. SRA 3430, 23 December 1942, TNA, WO 208/4128.

500. SRA 3452, 29 December 1942, TNA, WO 208/4128.

501. American sociologist Leon Festinger and colleagues illustrated their theory of cognitive dissonance with the example of an American religious sect, whose members sold all their possessions and assembled atop a mountain because they expected the end of the world and viewed themselves as the chosen ones. When the apocalypse did not happen, the sect members suffered cognitive dissonance. Festinger and his colleagues interviewed them and found that they did not doubt the correctness of their beliefs. Instead they interpreted their disappointed expectations as a further divine test of their faith. The theory proposes that people always try to square reality with their beliefs so as to minimize dissonance. This can happen in two ways. Either expectations can be made to fit the facts, or the facts can be interpreted so as to fit expectations. See Leon Festinger, Henry W. Riecken, and Stanley Schachter, *When Prophecy Fails* (Minneapolis: HarperTorchbooks, 1956).

502. SRA 4166, 7 July 1943, TNA, WO 208/4130.

503. SRA 3795, 12 March 1943, TNA, WO 208/4129.

504. SRGG 216, 12 July 1943, TNA, WO 208/4165.

505. SRA 3660, 9 February 1943, TNA, WO 208/4129.

506. SRA 3781, 7 March 1941, TNA, WO 208/4129.

507. SRM 1090, 29 November 1944, TNA, WO 208/4139.
508. SRGG 250, 20 July 1943, TNA, WO 208/4165.
509. SRA 4246, 3 August 1943, TNA, WO 208/4130.
510. SRA 3620, 1 February 1943, TNA, WO 208/4129.
511. SRA 2702, 28 June 1942, TNA, WO 208/4126.
512. SRM 477, 14 February 1944, TNA, WO 208/4138.
513. Ibid.
514. SRA 5610, 7 September 1944, TNA, WO 208/4134.
515. SRM 672, 21 July 1944, TNA, WO 208/4138.
516. SRGG 1234 (C), 20 May 1945, TNA, WO 208/4170.
517. SRGG 1176 (C), 2 May 1945, TNA, WO 208/4169.
518. SRGG 408, 9 September 1943, TNA, WO 208/4166.
519. SRM 202, 20 June 1943, TNA, WO 208/4136.
520. SRGG 220, 12 July 1943, TNA, WO 208/4165.
521. SRA 5084, 20 March 1944, TNA, WO 208/4133.
522. SRM 612, 28 June 1944, TNA, WO 208/4138.
523. SRA 5127, 3 April 1944, TNA, WO 208/4133.
524. SRM 1262, 6 May 1945, TNA, WO 208/4140.
525. Nicole Bögli, "Als kriegsgefangener Soldat in Fort Hunt" (Master's thesis, University of Bern, 2010); Stéphanie Fuchs, " 'Ich bin kein Nazi, aber Deutscher' " (Master's thesis, University of Bern, 2010).
526. This would seem to support the conclusions in Alexander and Margarete Mitscherlich's book *Die Unfähigkeit zu trauern*. Germans do in fact seem to have loved their Führer, and a thorough reevaluation of the history of the Third Reich and its crimes would have required Germans to grieve for the lost object of their affections.
527. SRM 468, 2 February 1944, TNA, WO 208/4137.
528. SRA 3963, 23 April 1943, TNA, WO 208/4130.
529. SRA 3540, 12 January 1943, TNA, WO 208/4129.
530. SRA 1008, 11 December 1940, TNA, WO 208/4122: "That is what I fail to understand. I, too, was in the Hitler Youth and fought. And it was a good idea too. No one can say anything against it. But there were things that were unnecessary like cutting off all the Jews."
531. SRA 1259, 8 February 1941, TNA, WO 208/4123: "The Jews have systematically stirred people up against Germany. In Poland too. Anyway, who are the Poles? They're at such a low level of culture. You can't compare them with Germans at all."
532. SRM 614, 1 July 1944, TNA, WO 208/4138.
533. SRN 2912, 10 February 1944, TNA, WO 208/4149.
534. SRM 1061, 27 November 1944, TNA, WO 208/4139.
535. SRA 289, 6 August 1940, TNA, WO 208/4118.
536. Alexander Hoerkens, "Kämpfer des Dritten Reiches? Die nationalsozialistische Durchdringung der Wehrmacht" (Master's thesis, University of Mainz, 2009).
537. SRA 5118, 28 March 1944, TNA, WO 208/4133.
538. SRM 45, 10 February 1942, TNA, WO 208/4136.

539. Heinrich von Kleist, *Über die allmähliche Verfertigung der Gedanken beim Sprechen* (Frankfurt/Main: Dielmann, 2010).

540. SRN 151, 7 December 1940, TNA, WO 208/4141.

541. Room Conversation, Kotschi-Graupe-Schwartze-Boscheinen, 25 February 1945, NARA, RG 164, Entry 179, Box 475.

542. SRN 1767, 8 May 1943, TNA, WO 208/4145.

543. Hoerkens, "Kämpfer des Dritten Reiches?"

544. SRN 1715, 1 May 1943, TNA, WO 208/4145.

545. SRM 832, 26 August 1944, TNA, WO 208/4139.

546. SRM 560, 15 June 1944, TNA, WO 208/4138.

547. SRM 584, 22 June 1944, TNA, WO 208/4138.

548. SRA 1742, 19 May 1941, TNA, WO 208/4145.

549. SRM 914, 20 September 1944, TNA, WO 208/4139.

550. SRN 1505, 5 March 1943, TNA, WO 208/4145.

551. SRN 1617, 12 April 1943, TNA, WO 208/4145.

552. SRCMF X 61, 1 October 1944, TNA, WO 208/5513.

553. SRCMF X 15, 27 May 1944, TNA, WO 208/5513.

554. SRN 2471, 23 November 1943, TNA, WO 208/4148.

555. SRM 523, 8 June 1944, TNA, WO 208/4138.

556. Gordon Allport, *Die Natur des Vorurteils* (Cologne: Kiepenheuer & Witsch, 1971); Norbert Elias and John L. Scotson, *Etablierte und Außenseiter* (Frankfurt/Main: Suhrkamp Verlag, 1990); Henri Taijfel, *Gruppenkonflikt und Vorurteil: Entstehung und Funktion sozialer Stereotypen* (Bern: Verlag Hans Huber, 1982).

557. For example, Aly, *Volksstaat;* Wildt, *Volksgemeinschaft.*

558. SRGG 411, 10 September 1943, TNA, WO 208/4166.

559. SRGG 452, 2 October 1943, TNA, WO 208/4166.

560. SRM 745, 4 August 1944, TNA, WO 208/4238.

561. Interrogation Report, Wilimzig–Malner, 2 August 1944, NARA, RG 165, Entry 179, Box 563. See also Wilimzig's personal file, NARA, RG 165, Entry 179, Box 563; and Felix Römer, "Alfred Andersch abgehört: Kriegsgefangene 'Anti-Nazi' im amerikanischen Vernehmungslager Fort Hunt," *VfZG* 58 (2010), p. 578.

562. Room Conversation, Mayer–Ahnelt, 5 July 1944, NARA, RG 165, Entry 179, Box 441.

563. Room Conversation, Lange–Laemmel, 27 August 1944, NARA, RG 165, Entry 179, Box 506.

564. SRM 711, 28 July 1944, TNA, WO 208/4138.

565. SRM 1215, 14 February 1945, TNA, WO 208/4140.

566. See Martin Treutlein, "Paris im August 1944," in Welzer, Neitzel, and Gudehus, eds., *"Der Führer."*

567. Thomas Kühne, *Kameradschaft: Die Soldaten des nationalsozialistischen Krieges und das 20. Jahrhundert* (Gottingen: Vandenhoeck & Ruprecht, 2006), p. 197.

568. SRN 97, 2 November 1940, TNA, WO 208/4141.

569. SRN 624, 9 August 1941, TNA, WO 208/4143.

570. "Gedanken des Oberbefehlshabers der Kriegsmarine zum Kriegsausbruch

3 September 1939," in Werner Rahn and Gerhard Schreiber, eds., *Kriegstage-buch der Seekriegsleitung, 1939–1945,* Teil A, Vol. 1 (Bonn: E. S. Mittler & Sohn, 1988), p. 16.

571. An especially impressive example of this attitude is Kriegstagebuch des "Führers der Zerstörer" aus dem Jahr 1944, BA/MA, RM 54/8.

572. On Hitler: Admiral/Führerhauptquartier GKdos 2877/44, 6 August 1944, BA-MA, RM 7/137; on Goebbels: Elke Fröhlich, ed., *Tagebücher von Joseph Goebbels: Sämtliche Fragmente,* Vols. 1–15 (28 February 1945) (London: Muenchen, 1987–98), p. 383.

573. Room Conversation, Neumann–Tschernett–Petzelmayer, 13 June 1944, NARA, RG 165, Entry 179, Box 521.

574. HDv 2, Abschnitt 9, p. 53, cited in BA/MA, RS 4/1446. We owe this reference to Peter Lieb, Sandhurst.

575. "I swear by God this sacred oath that I will show absolute obedience to the leader of the German Empire and people, *Adolf Hitler,* the supreme com-mander of the Wehrmacht, and am prepared as a courageous soldier to give my life at all times for this oath."

576. Cited in Klaus Reinhardt, *Die Wende vor Moskau: Das Scheitern der Stra-tegie Hitlers im Winter 1941/42* (Stuttgart: Deutsche Verlags-Anstalt, 1972), p. 220.

577. OKW/WFSt, Abt. L, No. 442277/41 gKdos Chefs., 26 December 1941, cited in Hürter, *Hitlers Heerführer,* p. 327, FN 243.

578. Ibid., p. 332.

579. Ibid., p. 344.

580. OKW/WFSt/Op No. 004059/42 g.K. v. 3 November 1942, BA/MA, RH 19 VIII/34, S. 171 f.

581. Karl-Günter Zelle, *Hitlers zweifelnde Elite* (Paderborn: Schoeningh Verlag, 2010), pp. 28–32.

582. KTB OKW, Vol. 3, p. 465.

583. POW officers Werner Heuer and Adolf Hempel agreed in conversation that the command to fight to the last man should not be taken literally. Room Conversation, Heuer–Hempel, 26 October 1944, NARA, RG 165, Entry 179, Box 484.

584. SRGG 844, 24 February 1944, TNA, WO 208/4168.

585. SRX 1798, 1799, 23 June 1943; SRX 1806, 24 June 1943, TNA, WO 208/4163. See also SRGG 252, 18 July 1943, TNA, WO 208/4165.

586. Fröhlich, ed., *Tagebücher von Joseph Goebbels,* 29 June 1944, p. 567.

587. See Horst Boog, Gerhard Krebs, and Detlef Vogel, eds., *Das Deutsche Reich und der Zweite Weltkrieg,* Vol. 7 (Stuttgart: Deutsche Verlags-Anstalt, 2001), p. 463, FN 42. See also Nikolaus Meier, "Warum Krieg? Die Sinndeutung des Krieges in der deutschen Militärelite, 1871–1945" (Ph.D. dissertation, Uni-versity of Zurich, 2010), pp. 297–304.

588. Boog, Krebs, and Vogel, eds. *Das Deutsche Reich,* Vol. 7, p. 469.

589. Hans-Günther Kluge to Hitler, 21 July 1944, BA-MA, RH 19 IX/8.

590. John Zimmermann, *Pflicht zum Untergang: Die deutsche Kriegführung im Westen des Reiches, 1944/45* (Paderborn: Schoeningh Verlag, 2009).

591. Ibid., esp. pp. 282–323.

592. SRX 1965, 9 July 1944, TNA, WO 208/4164

593. The situation was the same on the Eastern and Western fronts. On 30 June 1941 some two hundred men from the Army Group South were captured and killed by Russian soldiers. Korpstagesbefehl KG III, AK, 3 July 1941; BA/MA, RH 27—14/2.

594. SRM 521, 8 June 1944, TNA, WO 208/4138. Gundlach directed the combat academy of the 716th Infantry Division, which offered training for noncommissioned officers. Little is known about him, but he must have been an infantry officer with combat experience. An account of the battle from the perspective of Private Josef Häger is contained in Cornelius Ryan, *Der längste Tag: Normandie: 6. Juni 1944* (Frankfurt/Main: Heyne, 1976), pp. 190–93.

595. SRM 716, 31 July 1944, TNA, WO 208/4138.

596. SRM 622, 6 July 1944, TNA, WO 208/4138.

597. Radio Message, 27 June 1944, B. No. 1/Skl 19633/44 GKdos, BA/MA, RM 7/148.

598. SRN 3925, 10 July 1944, TNA, WO 208/4153.

599. SRM 639, 8 July 1944, TNA, WO 208/4138.

600. SRGG 1061, 24 September 1944, TNA, WO 208/4169; Welf Botho Elster, *Die Grenzen des Gehorsams: Das Leben des Generalmajors Botho Henning Elster in Briefen und Zeitzeugnissen* (Hildesheim: Olms, 2005).

601. For example, Friedrich Paulus in Stalingrad, Hans Aulock in Saint-Malo, and Bernhard Ramcke in Brest. See Sönke Neitzel, "Der Kampf um die deutschen Atlantik- und Kanalfestungen und sein Einfluß auf den alliierten Nachschub während der Befreiung Frankreichs, 1944/45," in *MGM* 55 (Munich: Oldenbourg Verlag, 1996), pp. 381–430.

602. SRN 3924, 8 July 1944, TNA, WO 208/4153.

603. SRN 3932, 11 July 1944, TNA, WO 208/4154.

604. SRGG 934, 1 July 1944, TNA, WO 208/4168.

605. Room Conversation, Bernzen-Almenröder, 11 February 1945, NARA, RG 165, Entry 179, Box 448.

606. SRN 3935, 11 July 1944, TNA, WO 208/4154.

607. Neitzel, *Abgehört,* p. 83.

608. BA/MA, N 267/4, 11 November 1944

609. SRM 160, 4 February 1943, TNA, WO 208/4136.

610. SRX 1548, 4 February 1943, TNA, WO 208/4162.

611. SRM 71, 20 November 1942, TNA, WO 208/4136.

612. Murawski, *Wehrmachtbericht,* p. 180.

613. Zagovec, "Gespräche mit der 'Volksgemeinschaft,' " in particular, p. 358.

614. GRGG 270, 9 March 1945, TNA, WO 208/4177.

615. Günter Wegmann, *Das Kriegsende zwischen Weser und Ems* (Osnabrück: Verlag Wenner, 2000), p. 102ff.; Sönke Neitzel, "Der Bedeutungswandel der Kriegsmarine im Zweiten Weltkrieg," in Rolf-Dieter Müller and Hans-Erich Volkmann, eds., *Die Wehrmacht: Mythos und Realität,* p. 263ff.

616. SRGG 1125, 27 January 1945, TNA, WO 208/4169.

617. GRGG 276, 25–27 March 1945, TNA, WO 208/4177.

618. SRM 1158, 2 January 1945, TNA, WO 208/4140.

619. Room Conversation, Neher–Glar, 19 September 1944, NARA, RG 165, Entry 179, Box 474.

620. SRGG 934, 1 July 1944, TNA, WO 208/4168.

621. SRGG 935, 2 July 1944, TNA, WO 208/4168.

622. SRM 539, 12 June 1944, TNA, WO 208/4138.

623. SRM 522, 9 June 1944, TNA, WO 208/4138.

624. SRGG 844, 24 February 1944, TNA, WO 208/4168.

625. See Room Conversation, Guetter-Tschitschko, 27 June 1944, NARA, RG 165, Entry 179, Box 477.

626. See ibid.

627. Kurt Böhme, *Die deutschen Kriegsgefangenen in sowjetischer Hand: Eine Bilanz* (Munich: Ernst & Werner GmbH, 1966), p. 49; Elke Scherstjanoi, *Wege in die Kriegsgefangenschaft: Erinnerungen und Erfahrungen deutscher Soldaten* (Berlin: Dietz, 2010) contains evidence of positive experiences from soldiers who fell into Soviet hands.

628. "Gedanken des Oberbefehlshabers der Kriegsmarine," in Rahn and Schreiber, eds., *Kriegstagebuch der Seekriegsleitung*, Teil A, Vol. 1, p. 16.

629. See Michael Salewski, *Die deutsche Seekriegsleitung*, Vol. 1 (Frankfurt/Main: Bernard & Graefe Verlag, 1970), p. 164.

630. 1. Skl No. 18142/43 g., 17 June 1943, BA/MA, RM 7/98. See also KTB Skl, Teil A, 17 August 1944, S. 417.

631. See Holger Afflerbach, " 'Mit wehender Fahne untergehen': Kapitulationsverweigerung in der deutschen Marine," *VfZG* 49 (2001), pp. 593–612.

632. Andreas Leipold, "Die Deutsche Seekriegsführung im Pazifik in den Jahren 1914 und 1915" (Ph.D. disseration, University of Bayreuth, 2010).

633. *Lagevorträge des Oberbefehlshaber der Kriegsmarine var Hitler 1939–1945* (26 March 1945), Gerhard Wagner, ed. (Munich: Lehmanns, 1972), p. 686.

634. Cited in Rolf-Dieter Müller and Gerd R. Ueberschär, *Kriegsende 1945: Die Zerstörung des Deutschen Reiches* (Frankfurt/Main: Primu Verlag, 1994), p. 175.

635. "Die Invasion": Erlebnisbericht und Betrachtungen eines T-Boot-Fahrers auf "Möwe," BA/MA, RM 8/1875; Clay Blair, *Der U-Boot-Krieg*, Vol. 2 (Munich: Bechtermuenz, 2001), p. 679.

636. Address of the Japanese ambassador, General Hiroshi Oshima, during ceremonies at the Joachimsthalsches Gymnasium, 25 November 1944, PAAA, R 61405.

637. Room Conversation, Grote–Wiljotti–Brinkmann, 12 August 1944, NARA, RG 165, Entry 179, Box 476. Wiljotti's interlocutor felt no need to expand on the fight that saw seventeen S-boats go down with their entire crews in the Baie de la Seine. In fact, there is no instance in World War II of an S-boat going down with all its crew. There were always survivors. This is a typical example of a storyteller exaggerating to make a narrative more interesting.

638. See the report of the Navy high command about tonnages, 19 October 1944, Neitzel, "Bedeutungswandel der Kriegsmarine," p. 256.

639. SRA 2589, 5 June 1942, TNA, WO 208/4126.

640. Ernst Stilla, "Die Luftwaffe im Kampf um die Luftherrschaft" (Ph.D. dis-

sertation, University of Bonn, 2005), p. 234ff.; Karl-Heinz Frieser et al., *Das Deutsche Reich und der Zweite Weltkrieg,* Vol. 8 (Stuttgart: Deutsche Verlags-Anstalt DVA, 2007), p. 859. Lieutenant Trettau of the 6/JG 27, for example, reported that, according to a command in March 1945, relatives of POWs who had been captured uninjured would be ineligible for government benefits. SRA 5840, 11 April 1945, TNA, WO 208/4135.

641. NARA, T-321, Reel 54, pp. 290–403; Günther W. Gellermann, *Moskau ruft Heeresgruppe Mitte . . . Was nicht im Wehrmachtbericht stand — Die Einsätze des geheimen Kampfgeschwaders 200 im Zweiten Weltkrieg* (Koblenz: Bernard & Graefe, 1988), pp. 42–60; Arno Rose, *Radikaler Luftkampf: Die Geschichte der deutschen Rammjäger* (Stuttgart: Motorbuch Verlag, 1979).

642. See, for example, SRA 5544, 29 July 1944, TNA, WO 208/4134.

643. SRA 4776, 4 January 1944; SRA 4813, 13 January 1944, TNA, WO 208/4132. In June 1942, a lieutenant described the command to ram enemy ships and planes as "idiocy." SRA 2589, 5 June 1942, TNA, WO 208/4126.

644. SRGG 1248, 18 May 1945, TNA, WO 208/4135.

645. KTB OB West, 21 September 1944, BA/MA, RH 19 IV/56, S. 319.

646. SRX 349, 13 June 1941, TNA, WO 208/4159.

647. SRA 1575, 26 April 1941, TNA, WO 208/4123.

648. SRX 1240, 6 November 1942, TNA, WO 208/4161.

649. Ibid.

650. SRGG 779, 20 January 1944, TNA, WO 208/4167.

651. SRX 703, 15 January 1942, TNA, WO 208/4160.

652. SRN 675, 29 October 1941, TNA, WO 208/4143.

653. SRX 1171, 16 October 1942, TNA, WO 208/4161.

654. SRA 2615, 9 June 1942, TNA, WO 208/4126.

655. SRX 1513, 20 January 1943, TNA, WO 208/4162.

656. SRA 3731, 3 March 1943, TNA, WO 208/4129.

657. SRGG 483, 14 October 1943, TNA, WO 208/4166.

658. SRM 104, 22 November 1942, TNA, WO 208/4136.

659. SRX 1819, 8 July 1943, TNA, WO 208/4163.

660. SRM 129, 26 November 1942, TNA, WO 208/4136.

661. SRGG 59, 24 May 1943, TNA, WO 208/4165.

662. SRM 129, 26 November 1942, TNA, WO 208/4136.

663. SRGG 650, 12 December 1943, TNA, WO 208/4167.

664. SRN 2021, 28 July 1943, TNA, WO 208/4146; SRN 2021, 28 July 1943, TNA, WO 208/4146.

665. SRX 1125, 24 September 1942, TNA WO 208/4161.

666. SRM 136, 29 November 1942, TNA, WO 208/4136.

667. Ibid.

668. SRX 1181, 24 October 1942, TNA, WO 208/4161.

669. "Denkschrift über Gliederung, Bewaffnung und Ausrüstung einer Fallschirm-jägerdivision sowie über die Grundsätze der Gefechtsführung im Rahmen einer Fallschirmjägerdivision," 11 September 1944, BA/MA RH 11 I/24. We owe this reference to Adrian Wettstein, Bern.

670. SRGG 16, 16 May 1943, TNA, WO 208/4165.

671. SRGG 217, 11 July 1943, TNA, WO 208/4165.

672. SRX 1839, 16 July 1943, TNA, WO 208/4163.

673. Room Conversation, Grote-Wiljotti-Brinkmann, 15 August 1944, NARA, RG 165, Entry 179, Box 563.

674. Ibid.

675. SRGG 914, 4 June 1944, TNA, WO 208/4168. On soldiers' experience of battles in Sicily and southern Italy, see BA/MA RH 11 I/27, 4 November 1943. We owe this reference to Adrian Wettstein, Bern.

676. SRX 1149, 9 October 1942, TNA, WO 208/4161.

677. SRM 22, 17 January 1942, TNA, WO 208/4136.

678. SRM 49, 24 February 1942, TNA, WO 208/4136.

679. SRGG 243, 17 July 1943, TNA, WO 208/4165.

680. SRX 1402, 19 December 1942, TNA, WO 208/4162.

681. SRM 797, 19 August 1944, TNA, WO 208/4138.

682. SRM 469, 2 February 1944, TNA, WO 208/4137.

683. SRM 863, 27 August 1944, TNA, WO 208/4139.

684. SRM 965, 16 Ocotber 1944, TNA, WO 208/4139.

685. SRM 613, 29 June 1944, TNA, WO 208/4138.

686. SRM 700, 27 July 1944, TNA WO 208/4138.

687. SRM 982, 26 October 1944, TNA, WO 208/4139.

688. SRCMF, X 113, 29 December 1944, TNA, WO 208/5516.

689. SRM 640, 10 July 1944, TNA, WO 208/4138.

690. See also SRCMF, X 110, 23 December 1944, TNA, WO 208/5516. There has been a lot of research on the topic of desertion. See especially Magnus Koch, *Fahnenfluchten: Deserteure der Wehrmacht im Zweiten Weltkrieg— Lebenswege und Entscheidungen* (Paderborn: Schoeningh Verlag, 2008); Wolfram Wette, *Das letzte Tabu: NS-Militärjustiz und "Kriegsverrat"* (Berlin: Aufbau Verlag, 2007); Benjamin Ziemann, "Fluchten aus dem Konsens zum Durchhalten: Ergebnisse, Probleme und Perspektiven der Erforschung soldatischer Verweigerungsformen in der Wehrmacht, 1939–1945," in Rolf-Dieter Müller and Hans-Erich Volkmann, eds., *Die Wehrmacht. Mythos und Realität,* pp. 589–613; Wolfram Wette, *Deserteure der Wehrmacht: Feiglinge—Opfer—Hoffnungsträger? Dokumentation eines Meinungswandels* (Essen: Klartext-Verlag, 1995); Norbert Haase and Gerhard Paul, eds., *Die anderen Soldaten: Wehrkraftzersetzung, Gehorsamsverweigerung, Fahnenflucht* (Frankfurt/Main: Fischer Taschenbuch Verlag, 1995).

691. Felix Römer, "Alfred Andersch abgehört," p. 571ff.

692. Room Conversation, Templin—Erlwein—Friedl, 16 February 1945, NARA, RG 165, Entry 178, Box 553.

693. Manfred Messerschmitt, *Die Wehrmachtjustiz, 1933–1945* (Paderborn: Schoeningh Verlag, 2005), p. 172.

694. SRM 419, 19 December 1943, TNA, WO 208/4137.

695. GRGG 182, 27–28 August 1944, TNA, WO 208/4363.

696. SRGG 1021, 2 September 1944, TNA, WO 208/4168.

697. SRM 1148, 31 December 1944, TNA, WO 208/4140.

698. SRM 536, 11 June 1944, TNA, WO 208/4138.

699. SRM 729, 29 July 1944, TNA, WO 208/4138. See SRM 225, 8 July 1943, TNA, WO 208/4136.

700. SRM 593, 25 June 1944, TNA, WO 208/4138.

701. SRX 1138, 3 October 1942, TNA, WO 208/4161.

702. SRN 823, 1 March 1942, TNA, WO 208/4143.

703. SRN 181, 21 March 1941; SRN 184, 21 March 1941; SRN 193, 22 March 1941, TNA, WO 208/4141.

704. René Schilling, "Die 'Helden der Wehrmacht'—Konstruktion und Rezeption," in Rolf-Dieter Müller and Hans-Erich Volkmann, eds., *Die Wehrmacht: Mythos und Realität*, pp. 552–56.

705. SRN 3732, 18 May 1944, TNA, WO 208/4152.

706. SRN 2606, 4 January 1944, TNA, WO 208/4148.

707. SRN 2574, 4 January 1944, TNA, WO 208/4148.

708. SRN 2636, 4 January 1944, TNA, WO 208/4148.

709. Christian Hartmann, *Halder: Generalstabschef Hitlers, 1938–1942* (Paderborn: Schoeningh, 2010), p. 331.

710. For more detail on Reichenau, see Johannes Hürter, *Hitlers Heerführer: Die deutschen Oberbefehlshaber im Krieg gegen die Sowjetunion, 1941/42* (Munich: Oldenbourg Verlag, 2006). See also Brendan Simms, "Walther von Reichenau—Der politische General," in *Die Militärelite des Dritten Reiches,* Ronald Smesler and Enrico Syring, eds. (Berlin: Ullstein, 1995), pp. 423–45. Timm Richter is also writing a dissertation on Reichenau.

711. GRGG 161, TNA, WO 208/4363

712. SRGG 83, 29 May 1943, TNA, WO 208/4165.

713. SRGG 578, 21 November 1943, TNA, WO 208/4167.

714. Neitzel, *Abgehört,* p. 446.

715. SRX 2029, 25 October 1944, TNA, WO 208/4164.

716. SRX 36, 14 February 1940, TNA, WO 208/4158.

717. SRA 224, 26 July 1940, TNA, WO 208/4118.

718. SRA 258, 1 August 1940, TNA, WO 208/4118.

719. SRM 149, 7 December 1942, TNA, WO 208/4136.

720. SRX 1955, 23 February1944, TNA, WO 208/4164. See also SRA 705, 8 October 1940, TNA, WO 208/4120.

721. Neitzel, *Einsatz der deutschen Luftwaffe,* p. 40.

722. Murawski, *Wehrmachtbericht,* p. 42.

723. Clay Blair, *Der U-Boot-Krieg,* Vol. 2 (Munich: Bechtermuenz, 1999), pp. 738, 778.

724. For example, *Wochenschau,* 21 October 1942.

725. Alberto Santoni, "The Italian Submarine Campaign," in *The Battle of the Atlantic, 1939–1945,* Stephen Howarth and Derel Law, eds. (London: Greenhill, 1994), pp. 329–32.

726. SRN 4797, 31 March 1945, TNA, WO 208/4157.

727. SRA 2996, 14 August 1942, TNA, WO 208/4127.

728. SRN 129, 15 November 1940, TNA, WO 208/4141. See also SRA 2178, 1 October 1941, TNA, WO 208/4125.

729. SRA 5777, 1 February 1945, TNA, WO 208/4135. There were many variations on the joke about Göring's fondness for decorations. See Hans-Jochen

Gamm, *Der Flüsterwitz im Dritten Reich: Mündliche Dokumente zur Lage der Deutschen während des Nationalsozialismus* (Munich: Piper, 1990), p. 165.

730. Amedeo Osti Guerrazzi, *"Noi non sappiamo odiare" L'esercito italiano tra fascismo e democrazia* (Turin: UTET Libera, 2010), p. 166.

731. SRIG 329, 17 October 1943, TNA, WO 208/4187. Ficalla was the commander of the 202nd Coastal Division and was captured on 21 July 1943 in Sicily. Salza was the chaplain of the 1st Italian Army and was captured on 1 May 1943 in Tunisia.

732. CSDIC Middle East No. 662(I), 5 January 1943, TNA, WO 208/5574.

733. SRIG 221, 11 August 1943, TNA, WO 208/4186.

734. CSDIC Middle East No. 626(I), 15 November 1942, TNA, WO 208/5574.

735. Italian soldiers were more interested in material rewards than decorations. A fighter pilot reported that he could earn 5,000 lire for every hit. CSDIC Middle East No. 488(I), 13 April 1942, TNA, WO 208/5518.

736. CSDIC Middle East No. 713(I), 23 March 1943, TNA, WO 208/5574.

737. See ISRM 49, 17 July 1943, TNA, WO 208/4188.

738. Even members of Italian elite units showed more emotion than average German soldiers. See the description of a pursuit involving depth charges by an officer of the Italian submarine MS *Glauco*. I/SRN 76, 29 July 1941, TNA, WO 208/4189.

739. I/SRN 68, 24 July 1941, TNA, WO 208/4189.

740. CSDIC Middle East No. 489(I), 14 April 1942. See also CSDIC Middle East No. 471(I), 25 March 1942, TNA, WO 208/5518.

741. CSDIC AFHQ No. 58(I), 31 August 1943, TNA, WO 208/5508.

742. Ibid.

743. I/SRN 70, 24 July 1941; I/SRN 90, 18 August 1941, TNA, WO 208/4189.

744. I/SRN 65, 20 July 1941. See I/SRN 88, TNA, WO 208/4189.

745. See I/SRN 54, 15 January 1941; I/SRN 72, 25 July 1941; I/SRN 97, 25 August 1941, TNA, WO 208/4189.

746. SRIG 138, 17 July 1943, TNA, WO 208/4186.

747. Michael E. Stevens, *Letters from the Front, 1898–1945* (Madison: State Historical Society of Wisconsin, 1992), p. 135.

748. Ulrich Straus, *The Anguish of Surrender: Japanese POW's of World War II* (Seattle: University of Washington Press, 2003), p. 48ff.

749. Hirofumi Hayashi, "Japanese Deserters and Prisoners of War in the Battle of Okinawa," in *Prisoners of War, Prisoners of Peace: Captivity: Homecoming and Memory in World War II*, Barbara Hately-Broad and Bob Moore, eds. (Oxford: Oxford University Press, 2005), p. 54. Findings in Burma are similar. See Takuma Melber, "Verhört: Alliierte Studien zu Moral und Psyche japanischer Soldaten im Zweiten Weltkrieg," in Welzer, Neitzel, and Gudehus, eds., *"Der Führer."*

750. Rüdiger Overmans, *Deutsche militärische Verluste im Zweiten Weltkrieg* (Munich: Oldenbourg Verlag, 1999), p. 215.

751. SRM 1022, 15 November 1944, TNA, WO 208/4139.

752. For the most recent research on the Waffen SS, see Martin Cüppers, *Wegbereiter der Shoah: Die Waffen-SS, der Kommandostab Reichsführer-SS und die Judenvernichtung, 1939–1945* (Darmstadt: Wissenschaftliche Buchgesell-

schaft, 2005); Carlo Gentile, *Wehrmacht, Waffen-SS und Polizei im Kampf gegen Partisanen und Zivilbevölkerung in Italien, 1943–1945* (Paderborn: Schoeningh Verlag, 2011); Lieb, *Konventioneller Krieg*; René Rohrkamp, *Weltanschaulich gefestigte Kämpfer: Die Soldaten der Waffen-SS, 1933–1945: Organisation—Personal—Sozialstruktur* (Paderborn: Schoeningh Verlag, 2010); and above all, Jean-Luc Leleu, *La Waffen-SS: Soldats politiques en Guerre* (Paris: Editions Perrin, 2007). See also Jochen Lehnhardt, "Die Waffen-SS in der NS-Propaganda" (Ph.D. dissertation, University of Mainz, 2011).

753. SRM 8, 23 July 1940, TNA, WO 208/4136.

754. Hartmann, *Wehrmacht im Ostkrieg,* pp. 106, 237.

755. KTB SS Infanterie Regiment 4 (mot.), 9 December 1941–29 April 1942.

756. Rohrkamp, *Weltanschaulich gefestigte Kämpfer.*

757. SRGG 429, 22 September 1943, TNA, WO 208/4166; see also SRM 786, 12 August 1944, TNA, WO 208/4138.

758. SRM 747, 3 August 1944, TNA, WO 208/4138; Kritik auch bei Lingner, SRM 1216, February 1945, TNA, WO 208/4140.

759. SRM 1019, 14 November 1944, TNA, WO 208/4139; SRX 2055, 9 November 1944, TNA, WO 208/4164; SRGG 1024 (C), 2 September 1944, TNA WO 208/4168.

760. SRM 786, 12 August 1944, TNA, WO 208/4138.

761. SRGG 1034 (C), 8 September 1944, TNA, WO 208/4168.

762. KTB Division Großdeutschland, Aktennotiz Ia, 6–7 January 1943, S. 2, BA/MA, RH 26—1005/10.

763. SRM 786, 12 August 1944, TNA, WO 208/4138.

764. SRGG 971, 9 August 1944, TNA, WO 208/4168. On the similarities between the Waffen SS and the "Hermann Göring" Division, see SRGG 39, 16 May 1943, TNA, WO 208/4165.

765. SRA 2877, 5 August 1942, TNA, WO 208/4168; SRX 87, 9 June 1940, TNA, WO 208/4158; SRA 2621, 11 June 1942, TNA, WO 208/4126.

766. SRA 3236, 5 October 1942, TNA, WO 208/4128.

767. SRGG 39, 22 May 1943, TNA, WO 208/4165.

768. Ibid.

769. SRGG 971, 9 August 1944, TNA, WO 208/4165.

770. Henry Dicks, *The Psychological Foundations of the Wehrmacht,* TNA, WO 241/1.

771. Cited in Karl-Günter Zelle, *Hitlers zweifelnde Elite,* p. 209.

772. Lieb, *Konventioneller Krieg,* p. 441.

773. SRM 956, 10 October 1944, TNA, WO 208/4139.

774. GRGG 262, 18–20 February 1945, p. 3, TNA, WO 208/4177.

775. SRGG, 19 February 1944, TNA, WO 208/4168. The interrogation of Kurt Meyer on 15 November 1944 makes it clear how much he hated the "Bolshevists from the steppes." SRM 1022, 15 November 1944, p. 8, TNA, WO 208/4139.

776. SRM 1211, 12 February 1945, TNA, WO 208/4140.

777. Room Conversation, Becker–Steiner, 14 February 1945, NARA, RG 165, Entry 179, Box 447.

778. Overmans, *Deutsche militärische Verluste,* pp. 257, 293–96.

779. Peter Lieb, " 'Rücksichtslos ohne Pause angreifen, dabei ritterlich bleiben': Eskalation und Ermordung von Kriegsgefangenen an der Westfront 1944," in Neitzel and Hohrath, eds., *Kriegsgreuel,* pp. 346–50. See also Antony Beevor, *D-Day—Die Schlacht in der Normandie* (Munich: C. Bertelsman Verlag, 2010).

780. Lieb, *Konventioneller Krieg,* pp. 435–48. There are numerous Allied reports in which SS men are described as "preferring to die, rather to give in." Charles P. Stacey, *The Victory Campaign: The Operations in North-West Europe, 1944–1945* (Ottawa: Queen's Printer, 1960), p. 249.

781. On the Eastern Front, SS troops inflicted heavy casualties on Soviet units without suffering disproportionate losses of their own. One example was Operation Zitadelle in summer 1943. See Roman Töppel, "Kursk—Mythen und Wirklichkeit einer Schlacht," *VfZG* 57 (2009), pp. 349–84, esp. p. 373ff.; Karl-Heinz Frieser et al., *Das Deutsche Reich,* Vol. 8, pp. 104–38.

782. SRGG 513, 29 October 1943, TNA, WO 208/4166.

783. BA/MA, RH 20—8/95, 10 August 1943.

784. "Panzergruppe Eberbach bei Alençon und beim Durchbruch aus dem Kessel von Falaise," BA-MA, RH 20/7/149. This document is based on notes Eberbach made in Trent Park in October 1944.

785. Lieb, *Konventioneller Krieg,* p. 426. Major Heimann reported about a battalion of the "Leibstandarte Adolf Hitler" fighting around Aachen in October 1944: "The Obersturmführer of the Leibstandarte—they were the remnants of Leibstandarte from Aachen—Obersturmführer Rink (?) served around the same battalion commander as I did. The battalion commander once came to me—three or four days before we surrendered—and said: 'Tonight they're taking off.' And in fact, the SS intended to flee. We then cautioned them that there was a direct order from the Führer to defend the city to the last, and that this order applied to the SS as well." SRM 982, 26 October 1944, TNA, WO 208/4139.

786. SRM 640, 10 July 1944, TNA, WO 208/4138.

787. SRM 968, 18 October 1944, TNA, WO 208/4139.

788. In April 1944, the commanding general of the XXXXVIII Armored Corps, Hermann Balck, bitterly complained about the 9th SS Tank Division, protesting that the mid-level leadership was not up to its jobs. His anger at the commander, Obergruppenführer Wilhelm Bittrich, was such that Balck petitioned for him to be relieved of command, even though he praised Bittrich's personal bravery. See Gert Fricke, *"Fester Platz" Tarnopol, 1944* (Freiburg: Rombach, 1969), pp. 107–11, 116–19. See also BA/MA, RH 19 IV/50.

789. SRA 4273, 14 August 1943, TNA, WO 208/4130. On 1 February 1943 Hitler met with Field Marshal Erich von Manstein in the headquarters of Army Group South in Zaporizhia, Ukraine, and gave the go-ahead for a counteroffensive. The SS division "Leibstandarte Adolf Hitler" was also deployed.

790. SRM 662, 19 July 1944, TNA, WO 208/4138.

791. Lieb, *Konventioneller Krieg,* p. 428.

792. Letter from Eberbach to his wife, 8 July, 11 July 1944, BA/MA, MSG 1/1010.

793. SRA 3677, 18 February 1943, TNA, WO 208/4129.

794. SRX 201, 22 March 1941, TNA, WO 208/4158.
795. SRX 201, 22 March 1941, TNA, WO 208/4158. See also SRN 1013, 1 September 1942, TNA, WO 208/4143.
796. SRA 2378, 9 December 1941, TNA, WO 208/4126.
797. On war crimes committed in France, see Lieb, *Konventioneller Krieg,* pp. 15–20; on the Totenkopf division, see Charles W. Sydnor, *Soldaten des Todes: Die 3. SS-Division "Totenkopf," 1933–1945* (Paderborn: Schoeningh Verlag, 2002), pp. 76–102; Jean-Luc Leleu, "La Division SS-Totenkopf face à la population civile du Nord de la France en mai 1940," *Revue du Nord* 83 (2001), pp. 821–40. On the murder of soldiers from French colonies, see Raffael Scheck, *Hitler's African Victims: The German Army Massacres of French Black Soldiers, 1940* (Cambridge: Cambridge University Press, 2006).
798. See SRM 892, 15 September 1944, TNA, WO 208/4139.
799. SRM 705, 28 July 1944, TNA, WO 208/4138.
800. SRM 746, 3 August 1944, TNA, WO 208/4138. Both units fought in the same division between October 1943 and January 1944.
801. SRM 746, 3 August 1944, TNA, WO 208/4138.
802. SRX 1978, 13 August 1944, TNA, WO 208/4164.
803. SRM 726, 30 July 1944, TNA, WO 208/4138.
804. SRM 1150, 30 December 1944, TNA, WO 208/4140. The anti-Semitic commentary supposedly came from the division commander, SS brigade leader Heinz Lammerding.
805. SRM 899, 15 September 1944, TNA, WO 208/4139. On plunder, see SRM 772, 1 August 1944, TNA, WO 208/4138.
806. An NCO reported that ten English POWs had been shot in his unit. SRM 741, 4 August 1944, TNA, WO 208/4138. NCO Kaun reported that a Canadian POW was killed with a pickax. The perpetrator could have been a member of the SS division "Hitler Youth" or a regular army soldier. SRM 737, 3 August 1944, TNA, WO 208/4138.
807. For a general overview, see Lieb, *Konventioneller Krieg.*
808. SRM 892, 15 September 1944, TNA, WO 208/4139.
809. SRM 855, 29 August 1944, TNA, WO 208/4139.
810. Room Conversation, Hanelt–Breitlich, 3 April 1945, NARA, RG 165, Entry 179, Box 479. The mention of tanks destroying the village makes it seem likely that this incident was part of the battle against "partisans," carried out by Waffen SS units and not by a Security Service commando.
811. GRGG 225, 18–19 November 1944, TNA, WO 208/4364.
812. See Neitzel, *Abgehört,* pp. 300–303, 572ff.
813. SRX 1799, 23 June 1943, TNA, WO 208/4162.
814. There is unfortunately only scant research on the topic of war crimes committed by the Waffen SS on the Eastern Front.
815. SRN 3929, 10 July 1944, TNA, WO 208/4153.
816. SRM 1079, 24 November 1944, TNA, WO 208/4139. On massacres of civilians in Belarus, see the statement by Rottenführer Otto Gregor. PWIS (H) LDC/762, TNA, WO 208/4295. Lieutenant Colonel Müller-Rienzburg told as a POW of how Standartenführer Kurt Meyer had bragged at a training session of how he took Charkow with only two casualties and then destroyed

the entire village, including "women, children and old people." SRGG 832, 13 February 1944, TNA, WO 208/4168.

817. SRM 648, 15 July 1944, TNA, WO 208/4138.
818. SRM 643, 13 July 1944, TNA, WO 208/4138. On the execution of POWs by the SS Division "The Reich," see SRM 764, 8 August 1944, TNA, WO 208/4138. Untersturmführer Karl-Walter Becker from 12th SS Division "Hitler Youth" recalled comrades telling him about the invasion: "In Russia, the standard operating procedure was that only the POWs who seemed most important would be transported. All others were usually murdered." TNA, WO 208/4295.
819. SRM 1205, 12 February 1945, TNA, WO 208/4140. On the crimes of the 12th SS Armored Division in Normandy, see Howard Margolian, *Conduct Unbecoming: The Story of the Murder of Canadian Prisoners of War in Normandy* (Toronto: University of Toronto Press, 1998); Lieb, *Konventioneller Krieg,* pp. 158–66.
820. SRM 753, 3 August 1944, TNA, WO 208/4138.
821. Further crimes are mentioned in SRM 706, 28 July 1944, TNA, WO 208/4138; SRM 367, 9 November 1943, TNA, WO 208/4137 (the murder of hostages in Panevo, Serbia, in April 1941).
822. Leleu, *La Waffen-SS,* pp. 233–35; 420–41; Jürgen Matthäus, Konrad Kwiet, Jürgen Förster, and Richard Breitman, eds., *Ausbildungsziel Judenmord? "Weltanschauliche Erziehung" von SS, Polizei und Waffen-SS im Rahmen der "Endlösung"* (Frankfurt/Main: Fischer Taschenbuch Verlag, 2003).
823. GRGG 262, 18–20 February 1945, TNA, WO 208/4177.
824. SRM 1214, 12 February 1945, TNA, WO 208/4140.
825. SRM 1216, 16 February 1945, TNA, WO 208/4140. The wording of Himmler's order of 20 February 1943 was nearly identical. See Matthäus et al., eds., *Ausbildungsziel Judenmord?,* p. 106.
826. Bernd Wegner, *Hitlers politische Soldaten: Die Waffen-SS, 1933–1945* (Paderborn: Schoeningh Verlag, 2009), p. 189.
827. Matthäus et al., eds., *Ausbildungsziel Judenmord?*
828. SRM 649, 16 July 1944, TNA, WO 208/4138.
829. Leleu, *La Waffen-SS,* pp. 468–70.
830. Wegner, *Hitlers politische Soldaten,* p. 48ff.; Leleu, *La Waffen-SS,* pp. 456ff., 483ff.
831. SRM 649, 16 July 1944, TNA, WO 208/4138.
832. SRM 705, 28 July 1944, TNA, WO 208/4138.
833. SRM 649, 16 July 1944, TNA, WO 208/4138.
834. Carlo Gentile, " 'Politische Soldaten': Die 16. SS-Panzer-Grenadier-Division 'Reichsführer-SS' in Italien 1944" *Quellen und Forschungen aus italienischen Archiven und Bibliotheken* 81 (2001), pp. 529–61.
835. Peter Lieb, " 'Die Ausführung der Maßnahme hielt sich anscheinend nicht im Rahmen der gegebenen Weisung': Die Suche nach Hergang, Tätern und Motiven des Massakers von Maillé am 25. August 1944," *Militärgeschichtliche Zeitschrift* 68 (2009), pp. 345–78.
836. SRM 766, 8 August 1944, TNA, WO 208/4138.
837. Leleu, *La Waffen-SS,* p. 794ff.

838. SRM 668, 21 July 1944, TNA, WO 208/4138.

839. See Matthias Weusmann, "Die Schlacht in der Normandie 1944: Wahrnehmungen und Deutungen deutscher Soldaten" (Master's thesis, University of Mainz, 2009).

840. Christian Gerlach, *Kalkulierte Morde: Die deutsche Wirtschafts- und Vernichtungspolitik in Weißrußland* (Hamburg: Hamburger Edition, 1999), pp. 609–22; Peter Lieb, "Die Judenmorde der 707: Infanterie division 1941/42," *VfZG* 50 (2002), pp. 523–58, esp. 535–44.

841. Hartmann, *Wehrmacht im Ostkrieg*, pp. 469–788; Hermann Frank, *Blutiges Edelweiss: Die 1. Gebirgsdivision im Zweiten Weltkrieg* (Berlin: Ch. Links Verlag, 2008); Peter Lieb, "Generalleutnant Harald von Hirschfeld: Eine nationalsozialistische Karriere in der Wehrmacht," in *Von Feldherrn und Gefreiten: Zur biographischen Dimension des Zweiten Weltkrieges,* Christian Hartmann, ed., (Munich: Oldenbourg, 2008), pp. 45–56.

842. See Hans-Martin Stimpel, *Die deutsche Fallschirmtruppe, 1936–1945: Innenansichten von Führung und Truppe* (Hamburg: Mittler & Sohn, 2009).

843. The British concluded that the officer POWs of the 3rd Paratrooper Division consisted almost exclusively of Nazi true believers. Corps Intelligence Summary, No. 56, 8 September 1944, TNA, WO 171/287. We owe this reference to Peter Lieb, Sandhurst.

844. SRGG 971, 9 August 1944, TNA, WO 208/4168.

845. That is the conclusion reached by a study that systematically compared the surveillance protocols of officers from the Waffen SS and paratrooper divisions. Frederik Müllers, "Des Teufels Soldaten? Denk- und Deutungsmuster von Soldaten der Waffen-SS" (Master's thesis, University of Mainz, 2011).

846. This is the conclusion reached by Tobias Seidl in his dissertation, "Führerpersönlichkeiten": Deutungen und Interpretationen deutscher Wehrmachtgeneräle in britischer Kriegsgefangenschaft (Ph.D. dissertation, University of Mainz, 2011)

847. See Richard Germann, "'Österreichische' Soldaten im deutschen Gleichschritt?" in Welzer, Neitzel, Gudehus, eds., *"Der Führer."*

848. Ulrich Herbert, *Best: Biographische Studien über Radikalismus, Weltanschauung und Vernunft, 1903–1989* (Bonn: Dietz, 1996); Michael Wildt, *Generation des Unbedingten: Das Führungskorps des Reichssicherheitshauptamtes* (Hamburg: Hamburger Edition, 2002); Isabel Heinemann, *"Rasse, Siedlung, deutsches Blut." Das Rasse- und Siedlungshauptamt der SS und die rassenpolitische Neuordnung Europas* (Göttingen: Wallstein, 2003).

849. www.collateralmurder.com.

850. David L. Anderson, "What Really Happened?" in *Facing My Lai: Beyond the Massacre,* David L. Anderson, ed. (Kansas: Self-published, 1998), p. 2.

851. Greiner, *Krieg ohne Fronten,* p. 113.

852. Ibid., p. 407.

853. *Der Spiegel,* 16/2010, p. 21.

854. Harald Potempa, *Die Perzeption des Kleinen Krieges im Spiegel der deutschen Militärpublizistik (1871 bis 1945) am Beispiel des Militärwochenblattes* (Potsdam, 2009).

855. *Der Spiegel*, 16/2010, p. 20.

856. Walter Manoschek, " 'Wo der Partisan ist, ist der Jude, wo der Jude ist, ist der Partisan': Die Wehrmacht und die Shoah," in *Täter der Shoah, Fanatische Nationalsozialisten oder ganz normale Deutsche?*, Gerhard Paul, ed. (Göttingen, 2002), pp. 167–86; Helmut Krausnick and Hans-Heinrich Wilhelm, eds., *Die Truppe des Weltanschauungskrieges: Die Einsatzgruppen der Sicherheitspolizei und des SD, 1938–1942* (Stuttgart: Deutsche Verlags-Anstalt, 1981), p. 248.

857. Alison Des Forges, *Kein Zeuge darf überleben: Der Genozid in Ruanda* (Hamburg: Hamburger Edition, 2002), p. 94.

858. Bill Adler, ed., *Letters from Vietnam* (New York: Dutton, 1967), p. 22.

859. Jonathan Shay, *Achill in Vietnam: Kampftrauma und Persönlichkeitsverlust* (Hamburg: Dutton, 1998), p. 271.

860. Philip Caputo, *A Rumor of War* (New York: Holt Paperbacks, 1977), p. 231.

861. Stevens, *Letters*, p. 110.

862. Samuel A. Stouffer et al., *The American Soldier: Adjustment During Army Life*, Studies in Social Psychology in World War II, Vol. 1, (Princeton: Princeton University Press, 1949), pp. 108–10, 149–72.

863. *Süddeutsche Zeitung Magazin* (2009), "Briefe von der Front," available at: http://sz-magazin.sueddeutsche.de/texte/anzeigen/31953, accessed on 27 August 2010.

864. The desire for revenge featured in many letters home written by Vietnam soldiers. Here is another example: "I lost quite a few buddies that day, and all I hope for now is the chance to get back at them and make them pay for it. I'm sorry for writing like this. I try not to write home about any action I've been in, but I just can't help feeling bitter and vengeful toward them." Bernard Edelman, ed., *Dear America: Letters Home from Vietnam* (New York: Pocket Books, 1985), p. 79.

865. For a summary, see Overmans, in *Das Deutsche Reich*, Vol. 9/2, pp. 799, 820.

866. See Konrad Jarausch and Klaus-Jochen Arnold, *"Das stille Sterben . . ." Feldpostbriefe von Konrad Jarausch aus Polen und Russland* (Paderborn: Schoeningh Verlag, 2008).

867. See Neitzel and Hohrath, eds., *Kriegsgreuel*, particularly Oswald Überegger, " 'Verbrannte Erde' und 'baumelnde Gehenkte': Zur europäischen Dimension militärischer Normübertretungen im Ersten Weltkrieg," pp. 241–78; Bourke, *Intimate History*, p. 182.

868. Lieb, " 'Rücksichtslos ohne Pause angreifen, dabei ritterlich bleiben' " pp. 337–52.

869. Hans-Ulrich Wehler, *Deutsche Gesellschaftsgeschichte: Vom Beginn des Ersten Weltkrieges bis zur Gründung der beiden deutschen Staaten, 1914–1949*, Vol. 4 (Munich: C. H. Beck, 2003), p. 842.

870. Gerald F. Linderman, *The World Within War: America's Combat Experience in World War II* (Cambridge: Harvard University Press, 1997), p. 111.

871. On 14 July 1943, soldiers from the 45th U.S. Infantry Division killed seventy Italian and German POWs near the Sicilian village of Biscari. This happened after an order by General George Patton in which he implicitly sanctioned

the murder of prisoners. Bourke, *Intimate History,* p. 184. Similar cases are known in the initial days after the Normandy invasion. See Lieb, *Rücksichtslos.*

872. Linderman, *The World Within War,* pp. 112–26.

873. Lieb, "Rücksichtslos," p. 349ff.

874. Welzer, *Täter,* p. 256.

875. Jens Ebert, "Zwischen Mythos und Wirklichkeit: Die Schlacht um Stalingrad in deutschsprachigen authentischen und literarischen Texten" (Ph.D. dissertation, University of Berlin, 1989), p. 38; Ute Daniel and Jürgen Reulecke, "Nachwort der deutschen Herausgeber," in *"Ich will raus aus diesem Wahnsinn": Deutsche Briefe von der Ostfront, 1941–1945: Aus sowjetischen Archiven,* Anatolij Golovanskij et al., eds. (Wuppertal: Hammer, 1991), p. 314. See also Linderman, *The World Within War,* pp. 48–55; and Alf Lüdtke, "The Appeal of Exterminating 'Others': German Workers and the Limits of Resistance," *Journal of Modern History* 64 (1992), Special Issue, pp. 66–67.

876. Edelman, *Dear America,* p. 136.

877. Rolf-Dieter Müller and Hans-Erich Volkmann, eds., *Die Wehrmacht: Mythos und Realität,* pp. 87–174.

878. Römer, " 'Seid hart und unerbittlich . . .': Gefangenenerschießungen und Gewalteskalation im deutsch-sowjetischen Krieg 1941/42," in Sönke Neitzel and Daniel Hohrath, eds., *Kriegsgreuel: Die Entgrenzung der Gewalt in kriegerischen Konflikten vom Mittelalter bis ins 20. Jahrhundert* (Paderborn: Ferdinand Schöningh, 2008), pp. 317–36.

879. On this topic, see Linderman, *The World Within War,* pp. 90ff., 169.

880. Stouffer et al., *The American Soldier,* p. 149.

881. Shils and Janowitz, "Cohesion and Disintegration."

882. See also Martin van Creveld, *Fighting Power: German and U.S. Army Performance, 1939–1945* (Westport, Conn.: Greenwood Publishing, 1982); Welzer, *Täter.*

883. Erving Goffman, *Stigma: Über Techniken der Bewältigung beschädigter Identität* (Frankfurt/Main: Suhrkamp, 1974).

884. Lifton, *Ärzte,* p. 58.

885. Greiner, *Krieg ohne Fronten,* p. 249.

886. Reese, *Mir selber,* Schmitz, ed., p. 136ff.

887. The formation of groups also occurs on a more general level in the creation of borders between combat soldiers and the rest of the world. Biehl and Keller have described this phenomenon with reference to modern-day German Bundeswehr soldiers serving abroad: "The dialectic of soldiers' latent ideology and their anti-ideological reflexes leads them to identify to a high degree with their mission and its aims. At the same time, they maintain a distanced and even negative attitude toward the media, society at large and leading politicians. Soldiers adopt an anti-elitist stance, in which they play the stylized role of people of action who get things done and upon whom the ultimate success of the mission depends. This mechanism helps them to deal with the stress and danger of their situation. In the process, the soldiers establish a black-and-white distinction between 'us on the front lines' and 'them back home.' These determine categories of belonging and respect."

Heiko Biehl and Jörg Keller, "Hohe Identifikation und nüchterner Blick," in *Auslandseinsätze der Bundeswehr: Sozialwissenschaftliche Analysen, Diagnosen und Perspektiven,* Sabine Jaberg, Heiko Biehl, Günter Mohrmann, and Maren Tomforde, eds. (Berlin: Dunker and Humboldt, 2009), pp. 121–41, pp. 134–35. Maren Tomforde has examined the creation of a special identity among Bundeswehr soldiers serving in Afghanistan. For example, their pale pink tropical uniforms serve as a sign of group membership and distinguish them from members of other contingents. This leads to the creation of allegiances beyond their Bundeswehr identity during foreign deployments. Maren Tomforder, " 'Meine rosa Uniform zeigt, dass ich dazu gehöre': Soziokulturelle Dimensionen des Bundeswehr-Einsatzes in Afghanistan," in *Afghanistan — Land ohne Hoffnung? Kriegsfolgen und Perspektiven in einem verwundeten Land,* Vol. 30 Horst Schuh and Siegfried Schwan, eds. (Brühl: Die Deutschen Bibliotek, 2007), pp. 134–59.

888. A minority of soldiers, of course, do view their mission in terms of political goals and ideology to which they remain committed. One example are the veterans of the Abraham Lincoln Brigade, a troop of U.S. volunteers for the Spanish Civil War who were motivated by strong antifascist convictions when fighting the Nazis in World War II. See Peter N. Carroll et al., eds., *The Good Fight Continues: World War II Letters from the Abraham Lincoln Brigade* (New York: NYU Press, 2006).

889. Edelman, *Dear America,* p. 216.

890. *Der Spiegel,* 16/2010, p. 23.

891. Andrew Carroll, ed., *War Letters: Extraordinary Correspondence from American Wars* (New York: Scribner, 2002), p. 474.

892. Aly, *Volksstaat.*

893. Loretana de Libero, *Tradition im Zeichen der Transformation: Zum Traditionsverständnis der Bundeswehr im frühen 21. Jahrhundert* (Paderborn: Schoeningh, 2006).

894. See Benjamin Ziemann, *Front und Heimat: Ländliche Kriegserfahrungen im südlichen Bayern 1914–1923* (Essen: Klartext, 1997).

895. Kühne, *Kameradschaft,* p. 197.

896. See Felix Römer, "Volksgemeinschaft in der Wehrmacht? Milieus, Mentalitäten und militärische Moral in den Streitkräften des NS-Staates," in Welzer, Neitzel, and Gudehus, eds., *"Der Führer."*

897. "The Story of M.I.19," not dated, p. 1, TNA WO 208/4970; cf. Francis H. Hinsley, *British Intelligence in the Second World War,* Vol. 1 (London: Cambridge University Press, 1979), p. 283.

898. "The Story of M.I.19," not dated, p. 6, TNA, WO 208/4970.

899. "The History of C.S.D.I.C. (U.K.)," not dated, p. 4, TNA WO 208/4970.

900. "Interrogation of Ps/W," 17 May 1943, NARA, RG 38, OP-16-Z, Records of the Navy Unit, Tracy, Box 16: "Centres are, at present, established as follows: In England, 3 Centres for German & Italians, In North Africa, 2 Centres for German & Italians, In East Africa, 1 Centre (dismantled) for Japs, In India, 1 Centre for Japanese, In Australia, 1 Centre (A.T.I.S.) for Japanese, In U.S.A., 2 Centres for Germans, Italians and Japanese."

901. For 3,838 German navy men, 4,826 surveillance protocols were made. The

corresponding numbers for the Luftwaffe were 3,609 and 5,795; for the army (including the Waffen SS), 2,748 and 1,254. In addition, there are 2,076 protocols that record the words of members of different military branches. Protocols concerning army men were labeled S.R. The reports S.R.M. 1–1264 take up five files (TNA, WO 208/4136–4140); those concerning Luftwaffe men (S.R.A. 1–5836), nineteen; and those concerning navy men (S.R.N. 1–4857), seventeen. The mixed protocols S.R.X 1–2141 fill seven folders (TNA, WO 208/4158–4164); and those concerning staff officers and generals SRGG 1–1350; GRGG 1–363, eleven (WO 208/4165–4170, 4178, 4363–4366).

902. Neder, *Kriegsschauplatz Mittelmeerraum*, p. 12ff.

903. See Report of the Activities of Two Agencies of the CPM Branch, MIS, G-2, WDGS, o.D. (1945), NARA, RG 165, Entry 179, Box 575.

904. On the scope and history of the files, see "Study on Peacetime Disposition of 'X' and 'Y' Files," no date, in Memorandum of the WDGS, Intelligence Division, Exploitation Branch, 14 March 1947, NARA, RG 319, Entry 81, Box 3.

905. See Römer, "Volksgemeinschaft in der Wehrmacht?".

906. See PAAA, R 41141.

907. OKW A Ausl./Abw.-Abt. Abw. III No. 4091/41 G vom 11 June 1941, BA/MA, RM 7/3137.

908. Generalstabsoffizier No. 1595/43 gKdos, 4 November 1943, BA/MA, RL 3/51. We owe this reference to Klaus Schmider, Sandhurst.

909. See SRN 4677, March 1945, TNA, WO 208/4157. On cautionary warnings not to reveal sensitive information, see extract from S. R. Draft No. 2142, TNA, WO 208/4200.

910. See SRN 185, 22 March 1941, TNA, WO 208/4141; SRN 418, 19 June 1941; SRN 462, 28 June 1941, TNA, WO 208/4142; SRN 741 10 January 1942, TNA, WO 208/4143.

911. See SRM 741, 4 August 1944, TNA, WO 208/4138.

912. There is only one verified case of POWs discovering a concealed microphone. Extract from Draft No. 2148, 5 March 1944, TNA, WO 208/4200.

913. On interrogation strategies, see Neitzel, *Abgehört*, pp. 16–18.

914. Forty-nine informants were used in British surveillance camps. They reported on 1,506 POWs. Hinsley, *British Intelligence*, Vol. 1, p. 282ff. See CSDIC (UK), p. 6, TNA, WO 208/4970.

915. See the interrogation reports on Lieutenant Max Coreth, 18 March–22 May 1944, NARA, RG 165, Entry 179, Box 458.

916. See Falko Bell, "Großbritannien und die deutschen Vergeltungswaffen: Die Bedeutung der Human Intelligence im Zweiten Weltkrieg" (Master's thesis, University of Mainz, 2009); Falko Bell, "Informationsquelle Gefangene: Die Human Intelligence Großbritannien," in Welzer, Neitzel, Gudehus, eds., *"Der Führer."*

917. Stephen Tyas, "Allied Intelligence Agencies and the Holocaust: Information Acquired from German Prisoners of War," *Holocaust and Genocide Studies*, 22 (2008), p. 16.

BIBLIOGRAPHY

Aders, Gebhard. *Geschichte der deutschen Nachtjagd, 1917–1945*. Stuttgart: Motorbuch Verlag, 1978.

Adler, Bill, ed. *Letters from Vietnam*. New York: Dutton, 1967.

Afflerbach, Holger. " 'Mit wehender Fahne untergehen': Kapitulationsverweigerung in der deutschen Marine." *VfZG* 49 (2001), pp. 593–612.

Allport, Gordon. *Die Natur des Vorurteils*. Cologne: Kiepenheuer & Witsch, 1971.

Aly, Götz. *Hitlers Volksstaat: Raub, Rassenkrieg und nationaler Sozialismus*. Frankfurt/Main: Fischer Verlag, 2005. English edition: *Hitler's Beneficiaries: Plunder, Racial War and the Nazi Welfare State*. New York: Metropolitan Books, 2007.

———, ed. *Volkes Stimme. Skepsis und Führervertrauen im Nationalsozialismus*. Frankfurt/Main: Fischer Taschenbuch Verlag, 2006.

Anderson, David L., ed. "What Really Happened?" In *Facing My Lai: Moving Beyond the Massacre*. Kansas: Self-published, 1998, pp. 1–17.

Angrick, Andrej. *Besatzungspolitik und Massenmord: Die Einsatzgruppe D in der südlichen Sowjetunion, 1941–1943*. Hamburg: Hamburger Edition HIS Verlag, 2003.

Angrick, Andrej, et al. " 'Da hätte man schon ein Tagebuch führen müssen': Das Polizeibataillon 322 und die Judenmorde im Bereich der Heeresgruppe Mitte während des Sommers und Herbstes 1941." In *Die Normalität des Verbrechens: Bilanz und Perspektiven der Forschung zu den nationalsozialistischen Gewaltverbrechen*. Helge Grabitz et al., eds. Berlin Editions Hentrich, 1994, pp. 325–85.

Anonyma. *Eine Frau in Berlin: Tagebuchaufzeichnungen vom 20. April bis 22. Juni 1945*. Frankfurt/Main: Eichborn Verlag, 2003.

Arendt, Hannah. *Eichmann in Jerusalem: Ein Bericht von der Banalität des Bösen*. Leipzig: R. Piper & Co. Verlag, 1986.

Bajohr, Frank, and Dieter Pohl. *Der Holocaust als offenes Geheimnis: Die Deutschen, die NS-Führung und die Alliierten*. Munich: C. H. Beck Verlag, 2006.

Balke, Ulf. *Der Luftkrieg in Europa: Die operativen Einsätze des Kampfgeschwaders 2 im Zweiten Weltkrieg*, Vol. 2. Bonn: Bernard & Graefe, 1990.

Bartlett, Frederic. *Remembering: A Study in Experimental and Social Psychology*. Cambridge: Cambridge University Press, 1997.

Bartusevicius, Vincas, Joachim Tauber, and Wolfram Wette, eds. *Holocaust in Litauen: Krieg, Judenmorde und Kollaboration*. Cologne: Boehlau Verlag, 2003.

Bateson, Gregory. *Ökologie des Geistes*. Frankfurt/Main: Suhrkamp, 1999.

Beck, Birgit. *Wehrmacht und sexuelle Gewalt: Sexualverbrechen vor deutschen Militärgerichten*. Paderborn: Schoeningh, 2004.

Beevor, Antony. *D-Day — Die Schlacht in der Normandie*. Munich: C. Bertelsmann Verlag, 2010.

Behrenbeck, Sabine. "Zwischen Trauer und Heroisierung: Vom Umgang mit Kriegstod und Niederlage nach 1918." In *Kriegsende 1918: Ereignis, Wirkung, Nachwirkung*. Jörg Duppler and Gerhard P. Groß, eds. Munich: Oldenbourg, 1999, pp. 315–42.

Bell, Falko. "Großbritannien und die deutschen Vergeltungswaffen: Die Bedeutung der Human Intelligence im Zweiten Weltkrieg." Master's thesis, University of Mainz, 2009.

———. "Informationsquelle Gefangene: Die Human Intelligence in Großbritannien." In *"Der Führer war wieder viel zu human, zu gefühlvoll!"* Harald Welzer, Sönke Neitzel, and Christian Gudehus, eds. Frankfurt/Main: Fischer, 2011.

Benz, Wolfgang, Hermann Graml, and Hermann Weiß, eds. *Enzyklopädie des Nationalsozialismus*. Munich: Dtv., 1998.

Beradt, Charlotte. *Das Dritte Reich des Traumes*. Frankfurt/Main: Suhrkamp, 1981.

Bergien, Rüdiger. *Die bellizistische Republik: Wehrkonsens und "Wehrhaftmachung" in Deutschland, 1918–1933*. Munich: Oldenbourg Wissenschaftsverlag, 2010.

Biehl, Heiko, and Jörg Keller. "Hohe Identifikation und nüchterner Blick." In *Auslandseinsätze der Bundeswehr: Sozialwissenschaftliche Analysen, Diagnosen und Perspektiven*. Sabine Jaberg, Heiko Biehl, Günter Mohrmann, and Maren Tomforde, eds. Sozialwissenschaftliche Schriften 47. Berlin: Dunker and Humboldt, 2009, pp. 121–41.

Birn, Ruth Bettina. *Die Höheren SS- und Polizeiführer: Himmlers Vertreter im Reich und in den besetzten Gebieten*. Düsseldorf: Droste Verlag, 1986.

Blair, Clay. *Der U-Boot-Krieg*, Vol. 2. Munich: Bechtermuenz, 2001.

Boberach, Heinz, ed. *Meldungen aus dem Reich*. Munich: Pawlak Verlag Herrsching, 1968.

Bögli, Nicole. "Als kriegsgefangener Soldat in Fort Hunt." Master's thesis, University of Bern, 2010.

Böhler, Jochen. *Auftakt zum Vernichtungskrieg: Die Wehrmacht in Polen, 1939*. Frankfurt/Main: Fischer, 2006.

Böhme, Kurt. *Die deutschen Kriegsgefangenen in sowjetischer Hand: Eine Bilanz*. Munich: Ernst & Werner, 1966.

Böhme, Manfred. *Jagdgeschwader 7: Die Chronik eines Me 262-Geschwaders*. Stuttgart: Motorbuch, 1983.

Boog, Horst, Gerhard Krebs, and Detlef Vogel, eds. *Das Deutsche Reich und der Zweite Weltkrieg*, Vol. 7. Stuttgart: Deutsche Verlags-Anstalt, 2001.

Borgert, Heinz-Ludger. "Kriegsverbrechen der Kriegsmarine." In *Kriegsverbrechen im 20. Jahrhundert*. Wolfram Wette and Gerd Ueberschär, eds. Darmstadt: Wissenschaftlicher Burgergesellschaft, 2001, pp. 310–12.

Bourke, Joanna. *An Intimate History of Killing*. London: Granta Books, 1999.

Broszat, Martin, ed. *Rudolf Höß: Kommandant in Auschwitz: Autobiographische Aufzeichnungen des Rudolf Höß*. Munich: Deutsche Verlags-Anstalt, 1989.

Browning, Christopher R. *Ganz normale Männer: Das Reserve-Polizeibataillon*

101 und die "Endlösung" in Polen. Reinbek: Rororo, 1996. English edition: *Ordinary Men: Reserve Police Battalion 101 and the Final Solution in Poland.* New York: HarperCollins, 1992.

Bruns-Wüstefeld, Alex. *Lohnende Geschäfte: Die "Entjudung" am Beispiel Göttingens.* Hanover: Fackeltraeger-Verlag, 1997.

Budraß, Lutz. *Flugzeugindustrie und Luftrüstung in Deutschland, 1918–1945.* Düsseldorf: Droste Verlag, 1998.

Caputo, Philip. *A Rumor of War.* New York: Holt Paperbacks, 1977.

Carroll, Andrew, ed. *War Letters: Extraordinary Correspondence from American Wars.* New York: Scribner, 2002.

Carroll, Peter N., et al., eds. *The Good Fight Continues: World War II Letters from the Abraham Lincoln Brigade.* New York: NYU Press, 2006.

Chickering, Roger, and Stig Förster. "Are We There Yet? World War II and the Theory of Total War." In *A World at Total War: Global Conflict and the Politics of Destruction, 1937–1945.* Roger Chickering, Stig Förster, and Bernd Greiner, eds. Cambridge: Cambridge University Press, 2005, pp. 1–18.

Christ, Michaela. *Die Dynamik des Tötens.* Frankfurt/Main: Fischer Verlag, 2011.

———. "Kriegsverbrechen." In *"Der Führer war wieder viel zu human, zu gefühlvoll!"* Harald Welzer, Sönke Neitzel, and Christian Gudehus, eds. Frankfurt/Main: Fischer, 2011.

Creveld, Martin van. *Fighting Power: German and U.S. Army Performance, 1939–1945.* Westport, Conn.: Greenwood Publishing, 1982.

Cüppers, Martin. *Wegbereiter der Shoah: Die Waffen-SS, der Kommandostab Reichsführer-SS und die Judenvernichtung, 1939–1945.* Darmstadt: Wissenschaftliche Buchgesellschaft, 2005.

Daniel, Ute, and Jürgen Reulecke. "Nachwort der deutschen Herausgeber." In *"Ich will raus aus diesem Wahnsinn": Deutsche Briefe von der Ostfront, 1941–1945: Aus sowjetischen Archiven.* Anatolij Golovanskij et al., eds. Wuppertal: Hammer, 1991.

Demeter, Karl. *Das Deutsche Offizierskorps, 1650–1945.* Frankfurt/Main: Bernard & Graefe, 1965.

Der Spiegel. "Warum sterben Kameraden?" 16/2010, p. 20ff.

Des Forges, Alison. *Kein Zeuge darf überleben: Der Genozid in Ruanda.* Hamburg: Hamburger Edition, 2002.

Diamond, Jared. *Kollaps.* Frankfurt/Main: S. Fischer Verlag, 2005.

Dörr, Manfred. *Die Träger der Nahkampfspange in Gold. Heer. Luftwaffe. Waffen-SS.* Osnabruck: Biblio Verlag, 1996.

Ebert, Jens. "Zwischen Mythos und Wirklichkeit: Die Schlacht um Stalingrad in deutschsprachigen authentischen und literarischen Texten." Ph.D. dissertation, University of Berlin, 1989.

Echternkamp, Jörg. "Im Kampf an der inneren und äußeren Front: Grundzüge der deutschen Gesellschaft im Zweiten Weltkrieg." In *Das Deutsche Reich und der Zweite Weltkrieg,* Vol. 9/1. Militärgeschichtliches Forschungsamt, ed. Munich: Deutsche Verlags-Anstalt, 2004, pp. 1–76.

Edelman, Bernard. *Dear America: Letters Home from Vietnam.* New York: Pocket Books, 1985.

Elias, Norbert. *Studien über die Deutschen*. Frankfurt/Main: Suhrkamp Verlag, 1989.

———. *Was ist Soziologie?* Munich: Juventa, 2004.

Elias, Norbert, and John L. Scotson. *Etablierte und Außenseiter*. Frankfurt/Main: Suhrkamp Verlag, 1990.

Elster, Welf Botho. *Die Grenzen des Gehorsams: Das Leben des Generalmajors Botho Henning Elster in Briefen und Zeitzeugnissen*. Hildesheim: Olms, 2005.

Ethell, Jeffrey L., and Alfred Price. *Deutsche Düsenflugzeuge im Kampfeinsatz, 1944/45*. Stuttgart: Motorbuch, 1981.

Evans, Richard J. *Das Dritte Reich*, 3 Vols. Munich: Deutsche Verlags-Anstalt, 2004, 2007, 2009.

Feltman, Brian K. "Death Before Dishonor: The Heldentod Ideal and the Dishonor of Surrender on the Western Front, 1914–1918." Lecture manuscript, 10 September 2010, University of Bern.

Festinger, Leon, Henry W. Riecken, and Stanley Schachter. *When Prophecy Fails*. Minneapolis: Harper Torchbooks, 1956.

Förster, Jürgen. "Geistige Kriegführung im Deutschland 1919 bis 1945." In *Das Deutsche Reich und der Zweite Weltkrieg*, Vol. 9/1. Militärgeschichtliches Forschungsamt, ed. Munich: Deutsche Verlags-Anstalt, 2004, pp. 469–640.

Förster, Stig, ed. *An der Schwelle zum Totalen Krieg: Die militärische Debatte um den Krieg der Zukunft, 1919–1939*. Paderborn: Schoeningh, 2002.

———. "Ein militarisiertes Land? Zur gesellschaftlichen Stellung des Militärs im Deutschen Kaiserreich." In *Das Deutsche Kaiserreich, 1890–1914*. Bernd Heidenreichand and Sönke Neitzel, eds. Paderborn: Schoeningh, 2011.

Foucault, Michel. *Überwachen und Strafen*. Frankfurt/Main: Suhrkamp Verlag, 1994.

Frank, Hermann. *Blutiges Edelweiss: Die 1. Gebirgsdivision im Zweiten Weltkrieg*. Berlin: Ch. Links Verlag, 2008.

Frei, Norbert. *1945 und wir: Das Dritte Reich im Bewußtsein der Deutschen*. Munich: C. H. Beck Verlag, 2005.

Fricke, Gert. *"Fester Platz" Tarnopol, 1944*. Freiburg: Rombach, 1969.

Friedländer, Saul. *Das Dritte Reich und die Juden. Die Jahre der Verfolgung, 1933–1945*. Munich: Deutsche Taschenbuch Verlag, 1998.

Frieser, Karl-Heinz, et al. *Das Deutsche Reich und der Zweite Weltkrieg*, Vol. 8. Stuttgart: Deutsche Verlags-Anstalt DVA, 2007.

Fröhlich, Elke, ed. *Tagebücher von Joseph Goebbels, Sämtliche Fragmente*, Vol. 1–15. London: Munich et al., 1987–1998.

Fuchs, Stéphanie. " 'Ich bin kein Nazi, aber Deutscher.' " Master's thesis, University of Bern, 2010.

Gamm, Hans-Jochen. *Der Flüsterwitz im Dritten Reich: Mündliche Dokumente zur Lage der Deutschen während des Nationalsozialismus*. Munich: Piper, 1990.

Ganglmair, Siegwald, and Regina Forstner-Karner, eds. *Der Novemberpogrom 1938: Die "Reichskristallnacht" in Wien*. Vienna: Museen der Stadt Wien, 1988.

Gellermann, Günther W. *Moskau ruft Heeresgruppe Mitte . . . Was nicht im Wehrmachtbericht stand—Die Einsätze des geheimen Kampfgeschwaders 200 im Zweiten Weltkrieg*. Koblenz: Bernard & Graefe, 1988.

Gentile, Carlo. "'Politische Soldaten': Die 16. SS-Panzer-Grenadier-Division 'Reichsführer-SS' in Italien 1944." *Quellen und Forschungen aus italienischen Archiven und Bibliotheken* 81 (2001), pp. 529–61.

——. *Wehrmacht, Waffen-SS und Polizei im Kampf gegen Partisanen und Zivilbevölkerung in Italien, 1943–1945.* Paderborn: Schoeningh, 2011.

Gerlach, Christian. *Kalkulierte Morde: Die deutsche Wirtschafts- und Vernichtungspolitik in Weißrußland.* Hamburg: Hamburger Edition, 1999.

Germann, Richard. "'Österreichische' Soldaten in Ost- und Südosteuropa, 1941–1945: Deutsche Krieger – Nationalsozialistische Verbrecher – Österreichische Opfer?" Ph.D. Dissertation, University of Vienna, 2006.

——. "'Österreichische' Soldaten im deutschen Gleichschritt?" In *"Der Führer war wieder viel zu human, zu gefühlvoll!"* Harald Welzer, Sönke Neitzel, and Christian Gudehus, eds. Frankfurt/Main: Fischer, 2011.

Goffman, Erving. *Asyle: Über die Situation psychiatrischer Patienten und anderer Insassen.* Frankfurt/Main: Suhrkamp, 1973.

——. "Rollendistanz." In *Symbolische Interaktion.* Heinz Steinert, ed. Stuttgart: Piper, 1973, pp. 260–79.

——. *Stigma: Über Techniken der Bewältigung beschädigter Identität.* Frankfurt/Main: Suhrkamp, 1974.

——. *Rahmenanalyse.* Frankfurt/Main: Suhrkamp, 1980.

Goldhagen, Daniel Jonah. *Hitlers willige Vollstrecker: Ganz gewöhnliche Deutsche und der Holocaust.* Munich: Siedler, 1996. English edition: *Hitler's Willing Executioners: Ordinary Germans and the Holocaust.* New York: Alfred A. Knopf, 1996.

Goldschmidt, Georges-Arthur. *Die Befreiung.* Zurich: Ammann Verlag, 2007.

Goltermann, Svenja. *Die Gesellschaft der Überlebenden: Deutsche Kriegsheimkehrer und ihre Gewalterfahrungen im Zweiten Weltkrieg.* Stuttgart: Dt. Verlag, 2009.

Grabitz, Helge, et al., eds. *Die Normalität des Verbrechens: Bilanz und Perspektiven der Forschung zu den nationalsozialistischen Gewaltverbrechen.* Berlin: Edition Hentrich, 1994.

Greiner, Bernd. *Krieg ohne Fronten: Die USA in Vietnam.* Hamburg: Hamburger Edition, 2007.

Groß, Raphael. *Anständig geblieben: Nationalsozialistische Moral.* Frankfurt/Main: Fischer Verlag, 2010.

Gurfein, M. I., and Morris Janowitz. "Trends in Wehrmacht Morale." *The Public Opinion Quarterly* 10 (1946), pp. 78–84.

Gutman, Israel, Eberhard Jäckel, Peter Longerich, and Julius H. Schoeps, eds. *Enzyklopädie des Holocaust: Die Verfolgung und Ermordung der europäischen Juden,* Vols. 1 and 2. Berlin: Argon Verlag, 1993.

Haase, Norbert, and Gerhard Paul, eds. *Die anderen Soldaten: Wehrkraftzersetzung, Gehorsamsverweigerung. Fahnenflucht.* Frankfurt/Main: Fischer Taschenbuch Verlag, 1995.

Haffner, Sebastian. *Geschichte eines Deutschen. Erinnerungen, 1914–1933.* Munich: Der Hoerverlag, 2002.

Hartmann, Christian. "Massensterben oder Massenvernichtung? Sowjetische

Kriegsgefangene im 'Unternehmen Barbarossa': Aus dem Tagebuch eines deutschen Lagerkommandanten." *VfZG* 49 (2001), pp. 97–158.

——. *Wehrmacht im Ostkrieg: Front und militärisches Hinterland, 1941/42.* Munich: Oldenbourg Wissenschaftsverlag, 2009.

——. *Halder: Generalstabschef Hitlers, 1938–1942.* Paderborn: Schoeningh, 2010.

Hartwig, Dieter. *Großadmiral Karl Dönitz: Legende und Wirklichkeit.* Paderborn: Schoeningh, 2010.

Haupt, Heribert van. "Der Heldenkampf der deutschen Infanterie vor Moskau." *Deutsche Allgemeine Zeitung,* Berlin afternoon edition No. 28, (16 January 1942), p. 2.

Haus der Wannsee-Konferenz, ed. *Die Wannsee-Konferenz und der Völkermord an den europäischen Juden.* Berlin: Haus der Wannsee-Konferenz, 2006.

Hayashi, Hirofumi. "Japanese Deserters and Prisoners of War in the Battle of Okinawa." In *Prisoners of War, Prisoners of Peace: Captivity, Homecoming and Memory in World War II.* Barbara Hately-Broad and Bob Moore, eds. Oxford: Oxford University Press, 2005, pp. 49–58.

Heidenreich, Bernd, and Sönke Neitzel, eds. *Das Deutsche Kaiserreich, 1890–1914.* Paderborn: Schoeningh, 2011.

Heinemann, Isabel. *"Rasse, Siedlung, deutsches Blut": Das Rasse- und Siedlungshauptamt der SS und die rassenpolitische Neuordnung Europas.* Göttingen: Wallstein, 2003.

Heinzelmann, Martin. *Göttingen im Luftkrieg.* Gottingen: Die Werkstatt, 2003.

Herbert, Ulrich. *Best: Biographische Studien über Radikalismus, Weltanschauung und Vernunft, 1903–1989.* Bonn: Dietz, 1996.

Herde, Peter. *Der Japanflug: Planungen und Verwirklichung einer Flugverbindung zwischen den Achsenmächten und Japan, 1942–1945.* Stuttgart: Steiner, 2000.

Hilberg, Raul. *Die Vernichtung der europäischen Juden,* 3 Vols. Frankfurt/Main: Fischer, 1990.

——. *Täter, Opfer, Zuschauer: Die Vernichtung der Juden, 1933–1945.* Frankfurt/Main: Fischer, 1992.

Hinsley, Francis H. *British Intelligence in the Second World War,* Vol. 1. London: Cambridge University Press, 1979.

Hoerkens, Alexander. "Kämpfer des Dritten Reiches? Die nationalsozialistische Durchdringung der Wehrmacht." Master's thesis, University of Mainz, 2009.

Hohlweck, Hubert, "Soldat und Politik." *Deutsche Allgemeine Zeitung.* Berlin edition No. 543 (13 November 1943), p. 1ff.

Hölsken, Heinz Dieter. *Die V-Waffen: Entstehung, Propaganda, Kriegseinsatz.* Stuttgart: Deutsche Verlags-Anstalt, 1984.

Hubatsch, Walter, ed. *Hitlers Weisungen für die Kriegsführung, 1939–1945: Dokumente des Oberkommandos der Wehrmacht.* Uttingen: Doerfler im Nebel-Verlag, 2000.

Hull, Isabel V. *Absolute Destruction: Military Culture and the Practices of War in Imperial Germany.* Ithaca: Cornell University Press, 2005.

Humbug, Martin. *Das Gesicht des Krieges: Feldpostbriefe von Wehrmachtssoldaten aus der Sowjetunion, 1941–1944.* Opladen: Westdeutscher Verlag, 1998.

Hunt, Morton. *Das Rätsel der Nächstenliebe.* Frankfurt/Main: Suhrkamp Taschenbuch, 1988.

Hürter, Johannes. *Wilhelm Groener: Reichswehrminister am Ende der Weimarer Republik*. Munich: Oldenbourg, 1993.

———. *Ein deutscher General an der Ostfront: Die Briefe und Tagebücher des Gotthard Heinrici, 1941/42*. Erfurt: Sutton Verlag, 2001.

———. *Hitlers Heerführer: Die deutschen Oberbefehlshaber im Krieg gegen die Sowjetunion, 1941/42*. Munich: Oldenbourg Verlag, 2006.

Internationaler Militärgerichtshof, ed. *Der Prozess gegen die Hauptkriegsverbrecher*, Vol. 29. Nuremberg: Delphin Verlag, 1948.

Jäger, Herbert. *Verbrechen unter totalitärer Herrschaft: Studien zur nationalsozialistischen Gewaltkriminalität*. Frankfurt/Main: Suhrkamp, 1982.

Jarausch, Konrad H., and Klaus-Jochen Arnold. *"Das stille Sterben . . ." Feldpostbriefe von Konrad Jarausch aus Polen und Russland*. Paderborn: Schoeningh Verlag, 2008.

Johnson, Eric, and Karl-Heinz Reuband. *What We Knew: Terror, Mass Murder and Everyday Life in Nazi Germany*. London: Basic Books, 2005.

Jung, Michael. *Sabotage unter Wasser: Die deutschen Kampfschwimmer im Zweiten Weltkrieg*. Hamburg: Verlag E. S. Mittler & Sohn GmbH, 2004.

Jünger, Ernst. *Kriegstagebuch, 1914–1918*. Helmuth Kiesel, ed. Stuttgart: Klett-Cotta, 2010.

Kaldor, Mary. *New and Old Wars: Organised Violence in a Global Era*. Cambridge: Polity Press, 2006.

Kämmerer, Jörn Axel. "Kriegsrepressalie oder Kriegsverbrechen? Zur rechtlichen Beurteilung der Massenexekutionen von Zivilisten durch die deutsche Besatzungsmacht im Zweiten Weltkrieg." *Archiv des Völkerrechts* 37 (1999), pp. 283–317.

Kehrt, Christian. *Moderne Krieger: Die Technikerfahrungen deutscher Militärpiloten, 1910–1945*. Paderborn: Schoeningh Verlag, 2010.

Keppler, Angela. *Tischgespräche*. Frankfurt/Main: Suhrkamp Verlag, 1994.

Kershaw, Ian. *Hitler, 1936–1945*. Munich: Pantheon Verlag, 2002.

Klee, Ernst. *"Euthanasie" im NS-Staat. Die Vernichtung lebensunwerten Lebens*. Frankfurt/Main: Fischer Verlag, 1985.

Klein, Peter, ed. *Die Einsatzgruppen in der besetzten Sowjetunion, 1941/42: Tätigkeits- und Lageberichte des Chefs der Sicherheitspolizei und des SD*. Berlin: Hentrich, 1997.

Kleist, Heinrich von. *Über die allmähliche Verfertigung der Gedanken beim Sprechen*. Frankfurt/Main: Dielmann, 2010.

Koch, Magnus. *Fahnenfluchten: Deserteure der Wehrmacht im Zweiten Weltkrieg— Lebenswege und Entscheidungen*. Paderborn: Schoeningh Verlag, 2008.

Kosin, Rüdiger. *Die Entwicklung der deutschen Jagdflugzeuge*. Bonn: Bernard & Graefe, 1990.

Kössler, Karl, and Günther Ott. *Die großen Dessauer: Die Geschichte einer Flugzeugfamilie*. Planegg: Aviatic-Verlag GmbH, 1993.

Kramer, Alan. *Dynamic of Destruction: Culture and Mass Killing in the First World War*. Oxford: Oxford University Press, 2007.

Krausnick, Helmut, and Hans-Heinrich Wilhelm. *Die Truppe des Weltanschauungskrieges: Die Einsatzgruppen der Sicherheitspolizei und des SD, 1938–1942*. Stuttgart: Deutsche Verlags-Anstalt, 1981.

Kroener, Bernhard R. " 'Nun Volk steht auf . . .!' Stalingrad und der totale Krieg, 1942–1943." In *Stalingrad: Ereignis, Wirkung, Symbol.* Jürgen Förster, ed. Munich: Piper, 1992, pp. 151–70.

Kühne, Thomas. *Kameradschaft: Die Soldaten des nationalsozialistischen Krieges und das 20. Jahrhundert.* Göttingen: Vandenhoeck & Ruprecht, 2006.

Kwiet, Konrad."Auftakt zum Holocaust. Ein Polizeibataillon im Osteinsatz." In *Der Nationalsozialismus: Studien zur Ideologie und Herrschaft.* Wolfgang Benz et al., eds. Frankfurt/Main: Fischer, 1995, pp. 191–208.

Lehnhardt, Jochen. "Die Waffen-SS in der NS-Propaganda." Ph.D. dissertation, University of Mainz, 2011.

Leipold, Andreas. "Die deutsche Seekriegsführung im Pazifik in den Jahren 1914 und 1915." Ph.D. dissertation, University of Bayreuth, 2010.

Leleu, Jean-Luc. "La Division SS-Totenkopf face à la population civile du Nord de la France en mai 1940." *Revue du Nord* 83 (2001), pp. 821–40.

———. *La Waffen-SS: Soldats politiques en guerre.* Paris: Editions Perrin, 2007.

Leonhard, Jörn. *Bellizismus und Nation: Kriegsdeutung und Nationsbestimmung in Europa und den Vereinigten Staaten, 1750–1914.* Munich: Oldenbourg Verlag, 2008.

Libero, Loretana de. *Tradition im Zeichen der Transformation: Zum Traditionsverständnis der Bundeswehr im frühen 21. Jahrhundert.* Paderborn: Schoeningh, 2006.

Lieb, Peter. "Die Judenmorde der 707. Infanteriedivision, 1941/42." *VfZG* 50 (2002), pp. 523–58.

———. *Konventioneller Krieg oder NS-Weltanschauungskrieg? Kriegführung und Partisanenbekämpfung in Frankreich, 1943/44.* Munich: Oldenbourg Verlag, 2007.

———. " 'Rücksichtslos ohne Pause angreifen, dabei ritterlich bleiben': Eskalation und Ermordung von Kriegsgefangenen an der Westfront 1944." In *Kriegsgreuel: Die Entgrenzung der Gewalt in kriegerischen Konflikten vom Mittelalter bis ins 20. Jahrhundert.* Sönke Neitzel and Daniel Hohrath, eds. Paderborn: Schoeningh Verlag, 2008, pp. 337–52.

———. "Generalleutnant Harald von Hirschfeld: Eine nationalsozialistische Karriere in der Wehrmacht." In *Von Feldherrn und Gefreiten: Zur biographischen Dimension des Zweiten Weltkrieges.* Christian Hartmann, ed. Munich: Oldenbourg, 2008, pp. 45–56.

———. " 'Die Ausführung der Maßnahme hielt sich anscheinend nicht im Rahmen der gegebenen Weisung': Die Suche nach Hergang, Tätern und Motiven des Massakers von Maillé am 25. August 1944." *Militärgeschichtliche Zeitschrift* 68 (2009), pp. 345–78.

Lifton, Robert J. *Ärzte im Dritten Reich.* Stuttgart: Ullstein Tb. Auflag, 1999.

Linderman, Gerald F. *The World Within War: America's Combat Experience in World War II.* Cambridge: Harvard University Press, 1997.

Longerich, Peter. *Politik der Vernichtung: Eine Gesamtdarstellung der nationalsozialistischen Judenverfolgung.* Munich: Piper Verlag, 1998.

———. *"Davon haben wir nichts gewusst!" Die Deutschen und die Judenverfolgung, 1933–1945.* Munich: Siedler, 2006.

Lüdtke, Alf. "The Appeal of Exterminating 'Others': German Workers and the Limits of Resistance." *Journal of Modern History,* Special Issue (1992), pp. 46–67.

———. "Gewalt und Alltag im 20. Jahrhundert." In *Gewalt und Terror.* Wolfgang Bergsdorf et al., eds. Weimar: Rhino-Verlag, 2003, pp. 35–52.

Maier, Klaus A., eds., et al. *Das Deutsche Reich und der Zweite Weltkrieg,* Vol. 2. Stuttgart: Deutsche Verlag, 1979.

Mallmann, Klaus-Michael, Volker Rieß, and Wolfram Pyta, eds. *Deutscher Osten, 1939–1945: Der Weltanschauungskrieg in Photos und Texten.* Darmstadt: Wissenschaftlicher Buchgesellschaft, 2003.

Manoschek, Walter. "Wo der Partisan ist, ist der Jude, wo der Jude ist, ist der Partisan": Die Wehrmacht und die Shoah. In *Täter der Shoah, Fanatische Nationalsozialisten oder ganz normale Deutsche?* Paul Gerhard, ed. Göttingen: Wallstein, 2002, pp. 167–86.

Margolian, Howard. *Conduct Unbecoming: The Story of the Murder of Canadian Prisoners of War in Normandy.* Toronto: University of Toronto Press, 1998.

Margolis, Rachel, and Jim Tobias, eds. *Die geheimen Notizen des K. Sakowicz: Dokumente zur Judenvernichtung in Ponary, 1941–1943.* Frankfurt/Main: Fischer Tb., 2005.

Matthäus, Jürgen, Konrat Kweit, Jürgen Förster, and Richard Breitman, eds. *Ausbildungsziel Judenmord? "Weltanschauliche Erziehung" von SS, Polizei und Waffen-SS im Rahmen der "Endlösung."* Frankfurt/Main: Fischer Taschenbuch Verlag, 2003.

Matthäus, Jürgen. "Operation Barbarossa and the Onset of the Holocaust." In *The Origins of the Final Solution: The Evolution of Nazi Jewish Policy, September 1939-March 1942.* Jürgen Matthäus and Christopher Browning, eds. Lincoln: University of Nebraska 2004, pp. 242–309.

Meier, Niklaus. "Warum Krieg? Die Sinndeutung des Krieges in der deutschen Militärelite 1871–1945." Ph.D. dissertation, University of Zurich, 2009.

Meier-Welcker, Hans, ed. *Offiziere im Bild von Dokumenten aus drei Jahrhunderten.* Stuttgart: Militärgeschichtlichen Vorschungsamt, 1964.

———. *Aufzeichnungen eines Generalstabsoffiziers, 1919 bis 1942.* Freiburg: Rombach Druck- und Verlagshaus, 1982.

Melber, Takuma."Verhört: Alliierte Studien zu Moral und Psyche japanischer Soldaten im Zweiten Weltkrieg." In *"Der Führer war wieder viel zu human, zu gefühlvoll!"* Harald Welzer, Sönke Neitzel, and Christian Gudehus, eds. Frankfurt/Main: Fischer, 2011.

Messerschmitt, Manfred. *Die Wehrmachtjustiz, 1933–1945.* Paderborn: Schoeningh Verlag, 2005.

Mitscherlich, Margarete, and Alexander Mitscherlich. *Die Unfähigkeit zu trauern.* Munich: Piper Verlag, 1991.

Mühlhäuser, Regina. *Eroberungen, Sexuelle Gewalttaten und intime Beziehungen deutscher Soldaten in der Sowjetunion, 1941–1945.* Hamburg: Hamburger Edition, 2010.

Müller, Rolf-Dieter, and Gerd R. Ueberschär. *Kriegsende 1945: Die Zerstörung des Deutschen Reiches.* Frankfurt/Main: Primu Verlag, 1994.

Müller, Rolf-Dieter, and Hans-Erich Volkmann, eds. *Die Wehrmacht: Mythos und Realität*. Munich: Oldenbourg Wissenschaftsverlag, 1999.

Müllers, Frederik. "Des Teufels Soldaten? Denk- und Deutungsmuster von Soldaten der Waffen-SS." Master's thesis, University of Mainz, 2011.

Münkler, Herfried. *Über den Krieg: Stationen der Kriegsgeschichte im Spiegel ihrer theoretischen Reflexion*. Weilerswist: Velbrück, 2003.

Murawski, Erich. *Der deutsche Wehrmachtbericht*. Boppard: Boldt, 1962.

Murray, Williamson, and Allan R. Millet. *A War to Be Won: Fighting the Second World War*. Cambridge: Harvard University Press, 2001.

Musil, Robert. *Die Verwirrungen des Zöglings Törleß*. Reinbek: Rohwolt, 2006.

Neder, Anette. "Kriegsschauplatz Mittelmeerraum—Wahrnehmungen und Deutungen deutscher Soldaten in britischer Kriegsgefangenschaft." Master's thesis, University of Mainz, 2010.

Neitzel, Sönke. *Der Einsatz der deutschen Luftwaffe über dem Atlantik und der Nordsee, 1939–1945*. Bonn: Bernard & Graefe, 1995.

———. "Der Kampf um die deutschen Atlantik- und Kanalfestungen und sein Einfluß auf den alliierten Nachschub während der Befreiung Frankreichs, 1944/45." *Militärgeschichtliche Mitteilungen* 55. Munich: Oldenbourg Verlag, 1996, pp. 381–430.

———. "Der Bedeutungswandel der Kriegsmarine im Zweiten Weltkrieg." In *Die Wehrmacht, Mythos und Realität*. Rolf-Dieter Müller and Hans-Erich Volkmann, eds. Munich: Oldenbourg Verlag, 1999, pp. 245–66.

———. *Abgehört: Deutsche Generäle in britischer Kriegsgefangenschaft, 1942–1945*. Berlin: List Taschenbuch, 2009.

Niethammer, Lutz, and Alexander von Plato. *"Wir kriegen jetzt andere Zeiten."* Bonn: Dietz Verlag J. H. W. Nachf, 1985.

Nurick, Lester, and Roger W. Barrett. "Legality of Guerrilla Forces Under the Laws of War." *American Journal of International Law* 40 (1946), pp. 563–83.

O'Brien, Philipps. "East Versus West in the Defeat of Nazi Germany." *Journal of Strategic Studies* 23 (2000), pp. 89–113.

Ogorreck, Ralf. *Die Einsatzgruppen und die "Genesis der Endlösung."* Berlin: Metropol, 1994.

Oltmer, Jochen, ed. *Kriegsgefangene im Europa des Ersten Weltkrieges*. Paderborn: Schoeningh, 2006.

Orlowski, Hubert, and Thomas F. Schneider, eds. *"Erschießen will ich nicht": Als Offizier und Christ im Totalen Krieg: Das Kriegstagebuch des Dr. August Töpperwien*. Düsseldorf: Schoeningh Verlag, 2006.

Osti Guerrazzi, Amedeo. *"Noi non sappiano odiare": L'esercito italiano tra fascismo e democrazia*. Turin: UTET, 2010.

———. "'Wir können nicht hassen!': Zum Selbstbild der italienischen Armee während und nach dem Krieg." In *"Der Führer war wieder viel zu human, zu gefühlvoll!"* Harald Welzer, Sönke Neitzel, and Christian Gudehus, eds. Frankfurt/Main: Fischer, 2011.

Overmans, Rüdiger. *Deutsche militärische Verluste im Zweiten Weltkrieg*. Munich: Oldenbourg Verlag, 1999.

———. "Die Kriegsgefangenenpolitik des Deutschen Reiches, 1939 bis 1945." In

Das Deutsche Reich und der Zweite Weltkrieg, Vol. 9/2. Militärgeschichtliches Forschungsamt, ed. Munich: 2005, pp. 729–875.

Padover, Saul K. *Lügendetektor: Vernehmungen im besiegten Deutschland, 1944/45.* Frankfurt/Main: Eichborn Verlag, 1999.

Paul, Gerhard. *Bilder des Krieges, Krieg der Bilder: Die Visualisierung des modernen Krieges.* Paderborn: Schoeningh Verlag, 2004.

Philipp, Marc. *Hitler ist tot, aber ich lebe noch: Zeitzeugenerinnerungen an den Nationalsozialismus.* Berlin: Bebra Verlag, 2010.

Pohl, Dieter. *Die Herrschaft der Wehrmacht: Deutsche Militärbesatzung und einheimische Bevölkerung in der Sowjetunion, 1941–1944.* Munich: Oldenbourg Verlag, 2008.

Polkinghorne, Donald E. "Narrative Psychologie und Geschichtsbewußtsein: Beziehungen und Perspektiven." In *Erzählung, Identität und historisches Bewußtsein: Die psychologische Konstruktion von Zeit und Geschichte: Erinnerung, Geschichte, Identität I.* Jürgen Straub, ed. Frankfurt/Main: Suhrkamp, 1998, pp. 12–45.

Potempa, Harald. *Die Perzeption des Kleinen Krieges im Spiegel der deutschen Militärpublizistik (1871 bis 1945) am Beispiel des Militärwochenblattes.* Potsdam, 2009.

Pressac, Jean-Claude. *Die Krematorien von Auschwitz: Die Technik des Massenmordes.* Munich: Piper, 1994.

Priller, Josef. *Geschichte eines Jagdgeschwaders: Das J.G. 26 (Schlageter) 1937–1945.* Stuttgart: Motorbuch Verlag, 1956.

Proctor, Robert N. *Racial Hygiene: Medicine Under the Nazis.* Cambridge: Harvard University Press, 1990.

Rahn, Werner, and Gerhard Schreiber, eds. *Kriegstagebuch der Seekriegsleitung, 1939–1945*, Teil A, Vol. 1. Bonn: E. S. Mittler & Sohn, 1988.

Rahn, Werner, et al. *Das Deutsche Reich und der Zweite Weltkrieg*, Vol. 6. Stuttgart: Deutsche Verlags-Anstalt, 1990.

Rass, Christoph. *"Menschenmaterial": Deutsche Soldaten an der Ostfront: Innenansichten einer Infanteriedivision, 1939–1945.* Paderborn: Schoeningh Verlag, 2003.

Reemtsma, Jan Philipp. *Vertrauen und Gewalt: Versuch über eine besondere Konstellation der Moderne.* Hamburg: Hamburger Edition, 2008.

Reese, Willy Peter. *Mir selber seltsam fremd: Die Unmenschlichkeit des Krieges: Russland, 1941–44.* Stefan Schmitz, ed. Munich: Claassen Verlag, 2003.

Reinhardt, Klaus. *Die Wende vor Moskau: Das Scheitern der Strategie Hitlers im Winter 1941/42.* Stuttgart: Deutsche Verlags-Anstalt, 1972.

Reuband, Karl-Heinz. "Das NS-Regime zwischen Akzeptanz und Ablehnung: Eine retrospektive Analyse von Bevölkerungseinstellungen im Dritten Reich auf der Basis von Umfragedaten." *Geschichte und Gesellschaft* 32 (2006), pp. 315–43.

Roberts, Adam. "Land Warfare: From Hague to Nuremberg." In *The Laws of War: Constraints on Warfare in the Western World.* Michael Howard, George J. Andresopoulos, and Mark R. Shulman, eds. New Haven: Yale University Press, 1994, pp. 116–39.

Rohrkamp, René. *"Weltanschaulich gefestigte Kämpfer": Die Soldaten der Waffen-SS, 1933–1945.* Paderborn: Schoeningh Verlag, 2010.

Römer, Felix. "Im alten Deutschland wäre ein solcher Befehl nicht möglich gewesen: Rezeption, Adaptation and Umsetzung des Kriegsgerichtsbarkeitserlasses im Ostheer, 1941/42." *VfZG* 56 (2008), pp. 53–99.

——. *Kommissarbefehl: Wehrmacht und NS-Verbrechen an der Ostfront, 1941/42.* Paderborn: Scheoningh Verlag, 2008.

——. "'Seid hart und unerbittlich …' Gefangenenerschießungen und Gewalteskalation im deutsch-sowjetischen Krieg, 1941/42." In *Kriegsgreuel: Die Entgrenzung der Gewalt in kriegerischen Konflikten vom Mittelalter bis ins 20. Jahrhundert.* Sönke Neitzel and Daniel Hohrath, eds. Paderborn: Schoeningh Verlag, 2008, pp. 317–35.

——. "Alfred Andersch abgehört: Kriegsgefangene 'Anti-Nazis' im amerikanischen Vernehmungslager Fort Hunt." *VfZG* 58 (2010), pp. 563–98.

——. "Volksgemeinschaft in der Wehrmacht? Milieus, Mentalitäten und militärische Moral in den Streitkräften des NS-Staates." In *"Der Führer war wieder viel zu human, zu gefühlvoll!"* Harald Welzer, Sönke Neitzel, and Christian Gudehus, eds. Frankfurt/Main: Fischer, 2011.

Rose, Arno. *Radikaler Luftkampf: Die Geschichte der deutschen Rammjäger.* Stuttgart: Motorbuch Verlag, 1979.

Rosenkranz, Herbert. *Reichskristallnacht: 9. November 1938 in Österreich.* Vienna: Europa Verlag, 1968.

Roskill, Stephen W. *Royal Navy: Britische Seekriegsgeschichte, 1939–1945.* Hamburg: Stalling, 1961.

Ryan, Cornelius. *Der längste Tag: Normandie: 6. Juni 1944.* Frankfurt/Main: Heyne, 1976.

Ryan, William: *Blaming the Victim.* London: Pantheon, 1972.

Salewski, Michael. *Die deutsche Seekriegsleitung,* 3 Vols. Munich: Bernard & Graefe Verlag, 1970–75.

——. "Die Abwehr der Invasion als Schlüssel zum 'Endsieg'?" In *Die Wehrmacht: Mythos und Realität.* Rolf-Dieter Müller and Hans-Erich Volkmann, eds. Munich: Oldenbourg Wissenschaftsverlag, 1999, pp. 210–23.

Sandkühler, Thomas. *"Endlösung" in Galizien.* Bonn: Dietz, 1996.

Santoni, Alberto. "The Italian Submarine Campaign." In *The Battle of the Atlantic, 1939–1945.* Stephen Howarth and Derel Law, eds. London: Greenhill, 1994, pp. 329–32.

Schabel, Ralf. *Die Illusion der Wunderwaffen: Düsenflugzeuge und Flugabwehrraketen in der Rüstungspolitik des Dritten Reiches.* Munich: Oldenbourg Wissenschaftsverlag, 1994.

Schäfer, Hans Dieter. *Das gespaltene Bewußtsein: Vom Dritten Reich bis zu den langen Fünfziger Jahren.* Göttingen: Wallstein, 2009.

Scheck, Raffael. *Hitler's African Victims: The German Army Massacres of French Black Soldiers, 1940.* Cambridge: Cambridge University Press, 2006.

Scherstjanoi, Elke. *Wege in die Kriegsgefangenschaft: Erinnerungen und Erfahrungen Deutscher Soldaten.* Berlin: Dietz, 2010.

Schilling, René. "Die 'Helden der Wehrmacht'—Konstruktion und Rezeption."

In *Die Wehrmacht, Mythos und Realität.* Rolf-Dieter Müller and Hans-Erich Volkmann, eds. Munich: Schoeningh Verlag, 1999, pp. 552–56.

———. *"Kriegshelden": Deutungsmuster heroischer Männlichkeit in Deutschland, 1813–1945.* Paderborn: Schoeningh Verlag, 2002.

Schmider, Klaus. *Partisanenkrieg in Jugoslawien, 1941–1944.* Hamburg: Mittler & Sohn, 2002.

———. "The Last of the First: Veterans of the Jagdwaffe Tell Their Story." *Journal of Military History* 73 (2009), pp. 246–50.

Schörken, Rolf. *Luftwaffenhelfer und Drittes Reich: Die Entstehung eines politischen Bewusstseins.* Stuttgart: Klett-Cotta Verlag, 1985.

Schröder, Hans Joachim. "Ich hänge hier, weil ich getürmt bin." In *Der Krieg des kleinen Mannes. Eine Militärgeschichte von unten.* Wolfram Wette, ed. Munich: Prestel, 1985, pp. 279–94.

Schüler-Springorum, Stefanie. *Krieg und Fliegen: Die Legion Condor im Spanischen Bürgerkrieg.* Paderborn: Schoeningh Verlag, 2010.

Schütz, Alfred. *Der sinnhafte Aufbau der sozialen Welt: Eine Einleitung in die verstehende Soziologie.* Frankfurt/Main: Suhrkamp, 1993.

Sebald, W. G. *Luftkrieg und Literatur.* Frankfurt/Main: Eichborn, 2001.

Seemen, Gerhard von. *Die Ritterkreuzträger, 1939–1945.* Friedberg: Podzun Verlag, 1976.

Seidl, Tobias. "Führerpersönlichkeiten": Deutungen und Interpretationen deutscher Wehrmachtgeneräle in britischer Kriegsgefangenschaft." Ph.D. dissertation, University of Mainz, 2011.

Shay, Jonathan. *Achill in Vietnam: Kampftrauma und Persönlichkeitsverlust.* Hamburg: Hamburger Edition, 1998.

Shils, Edward A., and Morris Janowitz. "Cohesion and Disintegration in the Wehrmacht in World War II." *Public Opinion Quarterly* 12 (1948), pp. 280–315.

Simms, Brendan. "Walther von Reichenau—Der politische General." In *Die Militärelite des Dritten Reiches.* Ronald Smesler and Enrico Syring, eds. Berlin: Ullstein, 1995, pp. 423–45.

Sprenger, Matthias. *Landsknechte auf dem Weg ins Dritte Reich? Zu Genese und Wandel des Freikorpsmythos.* Paderborn: Schoeningh Verlag, 2008.

Stacey, Charles P. *The Victory Campaign: The Operations in North-West Europe, 1944–1945.* Ottawa: Queen's Printer, 1960.

Stephan, Rudolf. "Das politische Gesicht des Soldaten." *Deutsche Allgemeine Zeitung,* Berlin afternoon edition No. 566, (26 November 1942), p. 2.

Stevens, Michael E. *Letters from the Front, 1898–1945.* Madison: State Historical Society of Wisconsin, 1992.

Stilla, Ernst. "Die Luftwaffe im Kampf um die Luftherrschaft." Ph.D. dissertation, University of Bonn, 2005.

Stimpel, Hans-Martin. *Die deutsche Fallschirmtruppe, 1936–1945: Innenansichten von Führung und Truppe.* Hamburg: Mittler & Sohn, 2009.

Stouffer, Samuel A., et al. *The American Soldier: Adjustment During Army Life.* Studies in Social Psychology in World War II, Vol. 1. Princeton: Princeton University Press, 1949.

Straus, Ulrich. *The Anguish of Surrender: Japanese POW's of World War II.* London: University of Washington Press, 2003.

Streim, Alfred. *Sowjetische Gefangene in Hitlers Vernichtungskrieg: Berichte und Dokumente.* Heidelberg: C. F. Müller Juristicher Verlag, 1982.

Streit, Christian. *Keine Kameraden: Die Wehrmacht und die sowjetischen Kriegsgefangenen, 1941–1945.* Stuttgart: Deutsche Verlags-Anstalt, 1980.

Süddeutsche Zeitung Magazin. *Brief aus Kundus, Briefe von der Front.* Available online at http://sz-magazin.sueddeutsche.de/texte/anzeigen/31953 (accessed 27 August 2010).

Sydnor, Charles W. *Soldaten des Todes: Die 3. SS-Division "Totenkopf," 1933–1945.* Paderborn: Schoeningh Verlag, 2002.

Taijfel, Henri. *Gruppenkonflikt und Vorurteil: Entstehung und Funktion sozialer Stereotypen.* Bern: Verlag Hans Huber, 1982.

Tomforder, Maren. "'Meine rosa Uniform zeigt, dass ich dazu gehöre': Soziokulturelle Dimensionen des Bundeswehr-Einsatzes in Afghanistan." In *Afghanistan Land ohne Hoffnung? Kriegsfolgen und Perspektiven in einem verwundeten Land.* Horst Schuh and Siegfried Schwan, eds. Beiträge zur inneren Sicherheit, Vol. 30. Brühl: Die Deutschen Bibliotek, 2007, pp. 134–59.

Töppel, Roman. "Kursk—Mythen und Wirklichkeit einer Schlacht." *VfZG* 57 (2009), pp. 349–84.

Treutlein, Martin. "Paris im August 1944." In *"Der Führer war wieder viel zu human, zu gefühlvoll!"* Harald Welzer, Sönke Neitzel, and Christian Gudehus, eds. Frankfurt/Main: Fischer, 2011.

Tyas, Stephen. "Allied Intelligence Agencies and the Holocaust: Information Acquired from German Prisoners of War." *Holocaust and Genocide Studies* 22 (2008), pp. 1–24.

Überegger, Oswald. "'Verbrannte Erde' und 'baumelnde Gehenkte': Zur europäischen Dimension militärischer Normübertretungen im Ersten Weltkrieg." In *Kriegsgreuel: Die Entgrenzung der Gewalt in kriegerischen Konflikten vom Mittelalter bis ins 20. Jahrhundert.* Sönke Neitzel and Daniel Hohrath, eds. Paderborn, Schoeningh Verlag, 2008, pp. 241–78.

Ulshöfer, Helmut Karl, ed. *Liebesbriefe an Adolf Hitler: Briefe in den Tod: Unveröffentlichte Dokumente aus der Reichskanzlei.* Frankfurt/Main: VAS, 1994.

Ungváry, Krisztián. *Die Schlacht um Budapest 1944/45: Stalingrad an der Donau.* Munich: Herbig Verlagsbuchhandlung, 1999.

Vardi, Gil-il. "Joachim von Stülpnagel's Military Thought and Planning." *War in History* 17 (2010), pp. 193–216.

Waller, James. *Becoming Evil: How Ordinary People Commit Genocide and Mass Killing.* Oxford: Oxford University Press, 2002.

Watson, Alexander. *Enduring the Great War: Combat, Morale and Collapse in the German and the British Armies, 1914–1918.* New York: Cambridge University Press, 2008.

Wegmann, Günter. *Das Kriegsende zwischen Weser und Ems.* Osnabrück: Verlag Wenner, 2000.

Wegner, Bernd. *Hitlers politische Soldaten: Die Waffen-SS, 1933–1945.* Paderborn: Schoeningh Verlag, 2009.

Wehler, Hans-Ulrich. *Deutsche Gesellschaftsgeschichte: Vom Beginn des Ersten Weltkrieges bis zur Gründung der beiden deutschen Staaten, 1914–1949,* Vol. 4. Munich: C. H. Beck, 2003.

Weick, Karl E., and Kathleen M. Sutcliffe. *Das Unerwartete managen: Wie Unternehmen aus Extremsituationen lernen.* Stuttgart: Schaeffer-Poescher, 2003.

Welzer, Harald. *Verweilen beim Grauen.* Tübingen: Edition Diskord, 1998.

———. *Das kommunikative Gedächtnis: Eine Theorie der Erinnerung.* Munich: Beck, 2002.

———. *Täter: Wie aus ganz normalen Menschen Massenmörder werden.* Frankfurt/ Main: Fischer, 2005.

———. "Die Deutschen und ihr Drittes Reich." *Aus Politik und Zeitgeschichte* 14–15 (2007), pp. 21–28.

———. *Klimakriege: Wofür im 21. Jahrhundert getötet wird.* Frankfurt/Main: Fischer, 2008.

———. "Jeder die Gestapo des anderen: Über totale Gruppen." In *Stadt der Sklaven/Slave City.* Museum Folkwang, ed. Cologne: DuMont, 2008, pp. 177– 90.

Welzer, Harald, Sabine Moller, and Karoline Tschuggnall. *"Opa war kein Nazi": Nationalsozialismus und Holocaust im Familiengedächtnis.* Frankfurt/Main: Fischer, 2002.

Welzer, Harald, Robert Montau, and Christine Plaß. *"Was wir für böse Menschen sind!" Der Nationalsozialismus im Gespräch zwischen den Generationen.* Tübingen: Edition Diskord, 1997.

Welzer, Harald, Sönke Neitzel, and Christian Gudehus, eds. *"Der Führer war wieder viel zu human, zu gefühlvoll!"* Frankfurt/Main: Fischer, 2011.

Werle, Gerhard. *Justiz-Strafrecht und deutsche Verbrechensbekämpfung im Dritten Reich.* Berlin/New York: De Gruyter, 1989.

Wette, Wolfram. *Deserteure der Wehrmacht: Feiglinge Opfer—Hoffnungsträger? Dokumentation eines Meinungswandels.* Essen: Klartext-Verlag, 1995.

———. *Retter in Uniform: Handlungsspielräume im Vernichtungskrieg der Wehrmacht.* Frankfurt/Main: Fischer Taschenbuch Verlag, 2003.

———, ed. *Stille Helden—Judenretter im Dreiländereck während des Zweiten Weltkriegs.* Freiburg: Herder, 2005.

———. *Das letzte Tabu: NS-Militärjustiz und "Kriegsverrat."* Berlin: Aufbau Verlag, 2007.

Wette, Wolfram, et al., eds. *Das Deutsche Reich und der Zweite Weltkrieg,* Vol. 1. Stuttgart: Metzler Verlag, 1991.

Wettstein, Adrian. " 'Dieser unheimliche, grausame Krieg': Die Wehrmacht im Stadtkampf, 1939–1942." Ph.D. dissertation, University of Bern, 2010.

Weusmann, Matthias. "Die Schlacht in der Normandie, 1944: Wahrnehmungen und Deutungen deutscher Soldaten." Master's thesis, University of Mainz, 2009.

Wildt, Michael. *Generation des Unbedingten: Das Führungskorps des Reichssicherheitshauptamtes.* Hamburg: Hamburger Edition, 2002.

———. *Volksgemeinschaft als Selbstermächtigung: Gewalt gegen Juden in der deutschen Provinz, 1919–1939.* Hamburg: Hamburger Edition, 2007.

Winkle, Ralph. *Der Dank des Vaterlandes: Eine Symbolgeschichte des Eisernen Kreuzes, 1914 bis 1936*. Essen: Klartext, 2007.

Wurzer, Georg. "Die Erfahrung der Extreme: Kriegsgefangene in Rußland, 1914–1918." In *Kriegsgefangene im Europa des Ersten Weltkrieges*. Jochen Oltmer, ed. Paderborn: 2006.

Zagovec, Rafael A. "Gespräche mit der 'Volksgemeinschaft.' " In *Die deutsche Kriegsgesellschaft, 1939 bis 1945 — Ausbeutung, Deutungen, Ausgrenzung*. Vol. 9/2. Bernard Chiari et al., eds. Stuttgart: Deutsche Verlags-Anstalt, 2005, pp. 289–381.

Zelle, Karl-Günter. *Hitlers zweifelnde Elite: Goebbels — Göring — Himmler — Speer*. Paderborn: Schoeningh Verlag, 2010.

Ziemann, Benjamin. *Front und Heimat: Ländliche Kriegserfahrungen im südlichen Bayern, 1914–1923*. Essen: Klartext, 1997.

———. "Fluchten aus dem Konsens zum Durchhalten: Ergebnisse, Probleme und Perspektiven der Erforschung soldatischer Verweigerungsformen in der Wehrmacht, 1939–1945." In *Die Wehrmacht: Mythos und Realität*. Rolf-Dieter Müller and Hans-Erich Volkmann, eds. Munich: Oldenbourg, 1999, pp. 589–613.

Zimmermann, John. *Pflicht zum Untergang, Kriegsende im Westen, 1944/45*. Paderborn: Schoeningh Verlag, 2009.

Index

Page numbers in *italics* refer to illustrations.

Index

SÖNKE NEITZEL AND HARALD WELZER

SOLDIERS

Sönke Neitzel is currently a professor of international history at the London School of Economics. He has previously taught modern history at the Universities of Glasgow, Saarbrücken, Bern, and Mainz.

Harald Welzer is a professor of transformation design at the University of Flensburg, teaches social psychology at the University of St. Gallen, and is head of the foundation at Futur-Zwei.

Printed in the United States
by Baker & Taylor Publisher Services